A NEW
RUSSIAN GRAMMAR

ANNA H. SEMEONOFF has also written:

A FIRST RUSSIAN READER

A KEY TO A NEW RUSSIAN GRAMMAR

A NEW
RUSSIAN GRAMMAR

IN TWO PARTS

by

ANNA H. SEMEONOFF

(*Teacher of Russian in George Watson's Boys' College, Edinburgh.
Author of " Brush Up Your Russian "*)

Part I

Lessons on Rules of Grammar and
Syntax, with Exercises

Part II

A systematic treatment of Grammar

Russian and English Vocabularies

Written in accordance with the New Orthography
and the stabilised Grammar confirmed by the
Commissariat of Education of R.S.F.S.R. 1933.

FOURTH (REVISED) EDITION

NEW YORK: E. P. DUTTON & CO. INC.

Published by
E. P. Dutton & Co., Inc.
All Rights Reserved
Printed in U. S. A.

First Published	1934
Reprinted (with corrections)	1935
Third Revised Edition	1937
Fourth Revised Edition	1941
Reprinted	1942
Reprinted	1943
Reprinted	1944
Reprinted	1945

PREFACE

This grammar, though elementary in form, is intended to be a practical manual for the reading, writing, and speaking of Russian. This is a big undertaking for a small book, and yet I hope to be able to show that Russian is not nearly so difficult as it is reputed to be.

This book is the result of my long experience in teaching Russian to foreigners, and all my explanations have been tried out in classes of various types. In this respect I should like to thank all my pupils, who have thus unconsciously co-operated in this work.

Well aware of the fact that the alphabet often frightens people off altogether, I have found it unnecessary to burden my pupils with the whole alphabet at once. In this book the letters are introduced gradually, so that whilst getting used to the new alphabet, the student acquires a certain amount of knowledge about the language.

Grammar should not be studied without reading, and this should be started as early as possible. Unfortunately, through lack of space, reading material from Russian authors could not be supplied in this book. But the material of the book has been arranged in such a way as to give the pupil an idea of the Russian construction from the very first lesson, and in the later lessons quotations from Russian originals are given as often as possible as illustrations of the rules, with or without translations, so that the student may have an idea of the living language, and not merely grammatical examples. The most characteristic feature of the Russian verb, its Aspects, is mentioned simply and shortly as early as in the second lesson, so that one may recognise the forms when one comes across them in reading.

Further, each lesson, beginning with the third, has, in addition to the usual exercises from and into Russian, an exercise consisting of simple sentences in both Russian and English, designed to help the student to use correctly, in proper Russian, the grammatical rules and words given. These exercises (marked A) also contain a certain number of idiomatic expressions founded on the rules given. In this way the student is gradually introduced to the language as a whole. In the lessons the parts of speech are introduced gradually, as required. In Part II, however, the whole Grammar is given systematically, so that the student at a very early stage can refer to it and extend his knowledge in his own way.

The principal aim of this work, as well as of my teaching in general, is to give a "feeling" for the language, an understanding of the mind of the people which created it. I have in view not just the learning of new or peculiar words and forms, but an understanding of *why* these forms are used and *how* these words are formed. For this purpose special attention has been paid to word-building. The permutation of Russian vowels and consonants plays a great part in the formation of words, and a knowledge of it helps immensely in learning the vocabulary.

As to pronunciation, the student will find amazingly few rules given, but by keeping strictly to these few rules, and in particular observing the distinction between hard and soft vowels and consonants, a fairly accurate pronunciation may be acquired.

I should like also to explain the absence of phonetic transcription, though I occasionally refer to phonetics and phonetic signs. The Russian alphabet is so perfect in its accuracy and consistency in the representation of Slavonic sounds, that it does not require any other signs. In Russian one letter never has two values, and two letters are never used to represent one sound.

The book is written consistently in the new orthography, according to the "Decree of the Introduction of the New Orthography" dated October 10th, 1918, which practically repeats a resolution of the Academy of Science of May 11th, 1917. It has also been verified with the stabilised Grammar confirmed by the Commissariat of Education of the R.S.F.S.R. in 1933. The differences between the new and the old orthography are summarised and given separately.

Though every teacher naturally prefers to use his own method in imparting knowledge, I should like to give just a few practical hints. I have found it most helpful to start teaching with writing, and not with reading, because in the written alphabet the same elements are used as in the Latin alphabet (see p. 7). The permutation of vowels and consonants which is explained in the Chapter on Pronunciation should be referred to as often as possible. References to it will be found in the lessons. Reference to the Table of Vowels should also be made very often. After Lessons XI and XI *a*, and after acquaintance has been made with the meanings of prefixes, the pupils should be invited to try to form independently the perfective aspect of verbs. All this can be done side by side with reading.

The introductory chapter may be read for its own interest as an introduction to the study of the language. But some parts of the introductory chapter, notably those on the Permutation of Vowels and Consonants, need not be studied carefully in the beginning, but only when references are made to it in the lessons. By beginning with Lesson I, and consulting the introductory sections on writing and pronunciation, the student will avoid the confusion which may occur if the material is not studied in the proper order.

Though the lessons are numbered I to XXV, there are thirty-two in all, since some are double and are marked II*a*, III*a*, etc. As each whole lesson is intended to present a complete topic, each "*a*" lesson is supplementary to the preceding lesson.

In conclusion I should like to express my thanks to all those who have helped me in the production of this book, and especially to my son, Boris Semeonoff, M.A., B.Ed.

ANNA SEMEONOFF

EDINBURGH, 1934

NOTE TO THE SECOND EDITION

No major changes have been made in the Second Edition, but the book has been thoroughly revised, and a number of typographical errors corrected.

Certain alterations have been made in the text of the Lessons and a few paragraphs added. The vocabularies to the Lessons and some exercises have been slightly adjusted and about fifty words added to the general Vocabulary.

The following advice on reading will be found useful.

The reading of simple texts should be begun as soon as the student reaches Lesson XI, or even earlier, if one is studying with a teacher. The forms of the plural and other points of grammar which are treated later can easily be looked up, for which purpose one should use the Index.

After carefully reading two or three graded readers with notes the student should be able to attempt ordinary Russian texts, including newspapers, carrying on a parallel study of the grammar. The later lessons and Part II require closer attention, and additional reading is very necessary to supplement the exercises which have been limited owing to the lack of space.

NOTE TO SECOND EDITION

Though it is most important to learn the vocabulary and grammatical forms along with the accents, the reading of accented texts should not be carried too far. Russian books (just as English ones) are not printed with accents, so that students should try as soon as possible to become independent of the marked accents.

A. H. S.

EDINBURGH
October 1935

NOTE TO THE THIRD EDITION

Thanks to the kind cooperation of my Publishers I have been able to introduce a number of additions in this edition. These include an additional reading passage, in expository style, and some sentences in exercises D. The vocabulary has been adjusted accordingly. Certain points of grammar have also been added or amplified.

Though numerous extracts from Russian authors will be found throughout the lessons, *A First Russian Reader* (Dent, 3s. 6d.), with its Notes written in accordance with this Grammar, will be found most helpful in the illustration of various points as early as Lesson VI and right through the book.

As this edition of the Grammar may be considered definitive, a Key for all exercises, both Russian and English is being published.

The Key may be obtained from the booksellers, price 5s.

A. H. S.

EDINBURGH
May 1937

NOTE TO THE FOURTH EDITION

I have made some additions to the lists of verbs governing various cases, and in a few other places explanations have been amplified.

A. H. S.

EDINBURGH
May 1941

CONTENTS

PART I. LESSONS AND EXERCISES

CONTENTS

PART II. GRAMMAR

INTRODUCTORY

The Russian language constitutes the largest branch of Slavonic languages, as it is spoken by the most numerous of the Slavonic races. It may be considered a key for the understanding of other Slavonic tongues, especially Bulgarian, Serbo-Croatian and Slovenian; Polish and Czech, however, both more influenced by Latin, have deviated further from the original Pra-Slavonic.

The Russian literary language takes its origin from the Old Bulgarian, which was akin to the language spoken by the tribes on the river Volga, and the literary tongue has never widely differed from the popular Russian speech, as is the case with some other languages. For some time, however, the Church Slavonic, which also took its origin from the Old Bulgarian, was exclusively used in Church services and in ecclesiastical books and gradually became differentiated from the language of the people. Never influenced by the spoken language and indeed less and less understood, it was preserved as New Church Slavonic, in which the Russian Scriptures were written and services held, up to the latest times. Church Slavonic elements may be found throughout the language and are seen in such words as: град, город (town); брег, берег (bank); влас, волос (hair); глава, голова (head); древо, дерево (tree); здравие, здоровье (health); etc.

An interesting point in connection with the origin of the Russian literary language is that certain changes in the new orthography seem to be in accordance with the Old Bulgarian language, e.g. the endings -аго and -яго were introduced by the New Church-Slavonic language and indeed have never been pronounced as spelt.

The spoken language, on the other hand, though of the same origin, permeated by the rich and varied language of the people, gradually became the literary language.

Traces of this popular influence can be seen as early as the eleventh century. The end of the fourteenth century, when the centre of learning was transferred from Kiev to Moscow, i.e. from south-west to north-east, marks a new phase in the development of the language. The language of the Moscow district influenced the business language used in приказы (offices).

In the eighteenth century, with Lomonosov (1711–65), the great scientist, philologist and poet, the Russian literary language again falls more into line with the spoken language. In his *Российская Грамматика* he reveals the true sources of the national language. In the first half of the nineteenth century Pushkin and Gogol, with whom modern literature begins, finally rid the literary tongue of its pedantic tendencies and identified it with the popular speech.

Following the Russian philologist Shakhmatov, one may say in summing up, that the modern literary language is in its origin Old Bulgarian, transplanted to Russia as Church Slavonic. First in the south-west, then in the north-east, it underwent a process of permeation by the spoken Russian of the people, became "Russified", and as a result became almost identical with the present spoken language of Central Russia. Thus the book language and the spoken language were finally brought together and the former stilted book language became almost obsolete.

Shakhmatov compares the history of literary Russian with that of English. The Old Slavonic occupies in Russian the same position as Latin does in English. The elements of the popular speech gradually permeated the Old Bulgarian language, just as the Anglo-Saxon elements prevailed over the Franco-Roman elements in English after the Norman Conquest. Thus in both countries the language of the people asserted itself.[1]

Speaking of the Russian language as it is presented to a foreign student, one must notice first of all that it is in many ways similar to other European languages. It belongs to the same Indo-European family, and on the whole has developed on the same lines. Being an inflected language, it resembles Latin, Greek and German from the point of view of morphology. The difficulties of the Russian alphabet, as has been explained in my Preface, are often greatly exaggerated. In spite of being different, it has many advantages. Its phonetic qualities are mentioned in the chapter on Pronunciation. It owes these qualities to the inventor, Cyril of Thessalia, who lived in the first half of the ninth century. He and his brother Methodius, born in Thessalia but believed to be of Slav origin, are known to all Slavonic races as the "Apostles of the Slavs". The alphabet, known as Cyrillic, represented every Slavonic sound in the most perfect and scientific way. Outwardly it underwent several modifications and was finally modernised by Peter the Great, but the phonetic principle has remained the same.

---

[1] А. А. Шахматов, *Очерк Современного Русского Литературного Языка.* ГИЗ. Ленинград, 1925.

The main difference between Russian and other languages lies in the way of thinking, or perhaps I should say in the philosophy of the language. The construction itself is not difficult. One can write a book in Russian almost without using a subordinate clause. There is no rigid "order of words"; there is no sequence of tenses. The Russian verb with its aspects reveals the philosophy of the language and, once it is understood, the language is not difficult. But grammar alone is not sufficient in studying the language. Reading, with the help of the grammar, should be attempted at a very early stage.

As to speaking, it all depends on the opportunities one has, and in attempting to speak, students should not be deterred by the fact that the stress or accent is not fixed in Russian; the same is true of English. Yet the accent in Russian has become quite a bugbear, and one reads in the prefaces to various grammars that unaccented texts should not be attempted until one has studied for several years, etc.

It is true that unstressed vowels in Russian lose their full value; English vowels do the same. But in Russian, spelling, as far as symbols are concerned, is quite phonetic. So if one reads a word without any stress, not accenting any syllable, but quite evenly, the pronunciation will be perfectly correct. Everyone knows that in the northern parts of every country the language has more distinct vowel sounds. So it is in Russia. In the northern districts people say говорю, хорошо, вода with quite distinct o's. And although the northern pronunciation is not considered very good, it is not wrong. Therefore if a foreigner, especially when in doubt, avoids stressing any syllable, the pronunciation will not suffer. But beware of laying wrong stress, or giving deliberate wrong values to unstressed vowels, as, for example, pronouncing я in язык as "ye".

When Russian needs the change of o into a or of e into и it is indicated by the corresponding spelling (see Permutation of Vowels and Consonants, p. 15). To acquire a fairly accurate pronunciation one should observe the distinctions between hard and soft vowels, give the vowels the Russian values as indicated and beware especially of importing into Russian the vowel sounds peculiar to English.

As to the terms "hard" and "soft" consonants and "hard" and "soft" vowels, one should bear in mind whether the spoken or written language is under discussion. For Russians, who naturally speak before writing or reading the written language, it is a case of hard and soft consonants, because vowel sounds cannot be either hard or soft. Thus:

hard т + a gives та (т is hard),
soft ть + a gives тя (т is soft).

But when the sounds come to be represented in writing, there certainly arises the difficulty of representing hard and soft consonants, and instead of a special set of consonants, soft vowels were introduced, thus:

т + a = та   т + y = ту
but ть + a = тя   *but* ть + y = тю

For a foreign student who usually begins the study of the language with a book the question of hard and soft consonants exists only so far as he sees them in combination with hard and soft vowels.

Since я, е, ё, ю are understood to be ь + a, ь + э, etc., the initial я, е, ё, ю are heard as a, э, o, y with the й placed before, as in яма (йама), ель (йэль), ёлка (йолка), юг (йуг).

But as я for the English-speaking student can be represented as "ya" in yard, е as "ye" in yet, ё as "yo" in yonder, and ю as "you" in youth, there is no difference between the initial я and the я after a consonant, and the same with other soft vowels.

One can see once more that the system of hard and soft vowels is very practical, and is the only thing to be considered. The above points have to be cleared up to combat the existing tendency to make the pronunciation more complicated than it really is.

THE RUSSIAN ALPHABET

The Russian alphabet consists of 31 letters. The alphabet, as far as every sound is represented by a separate sign, may be considered phonetic. It should be noticed that no letter serves more than one purpose, and that two letters never represent one sound.

Printed		Written		English equivalent
А	a	*A*	*a*	a in car
Б	б	*Б*	*б*	b „ bar
В	в	*B*	*в*	v „ vice
Г	г	*Г*	*г*	g „ get

THE RUSSIAN ALPHABET

Printed		Written		English equivalent
Д	д	*Д*	*д*	**d** in day
Е	е	*Е*	*е*	**ye** „ yet
	ё		*ё*	**yo** „ yonder
Ж	ж	*Ж*	*ж*	**s** „ pleasure
З	з	*З*	*з*	**z** „ zero
И	и	*И*	*и*	**ee** „ meet
	й		*й*	**y** „ boy
К	к	*К*	*к*	**k** „ Kate
Л	л	*Л*	*л*	**l** „ lamp
М	м	*М*	*м*	**m** „ might
Н	н	*Н*	*н*	**n** „ nine
О	о	*О*	*о*	**o** „ or (never *oh*)
П	п	*П*	*п*	**p** „ pipe
Р	р	*Р*	*р*	**r** „ rose
С	с	*С*	*с*	**s** „ site
Т	т	*Т*	*т*	**t** „ time
У	у	*У*	*у*	**oo** „ foot
Ф	ф	*Ф*	*ф*	**f** „ fine
Х	х	*Х*	*х*	**h** „ hard
Ц	ц	*Ц*	*ц*	**z** „ German zu, or **ts**
Ч	ч	*Ч*	*ч*	**ch** „ church
Ш	ш	*Ш*	*ш*	**sh** „ short
Щ	щ	*Щ*	*щ*	**sh** (longer) suggestion of y after it
	ы		*ы*	**i** in writ
	ъ		*ъ*	hard sign, used after a consonant to separate it from a vowel
	ь		*ь*	soft sign, used after a consonant to soften it, i.e. to produce an effect similar to that of putting y after it

Printed		Written		English equivalent
Э	э	*Э*	*э*	e in met
Ю	ю	*Ю*	*ю*	u ,, use
Я	я	*Я*	*я*	ya ,, yard

HOW TO WRITE RUSSIAN

Whereas the printed Russian alphabet was partly adapted from Greek, and still bears some likeness to it in a few letters, the written alphabet is based on the elements of the Latin written script, since there was no written Greek alphabet. Some letters, as *a, o, e*, etc., were taken over as they were, and for some the same elements were adapted with the exception of a few curves. The resulting written alphabet differs very little from the Latin *except* that some letters while the same in form serve different purposes, for example the Latin *b, n, p* are in Russian *v, p, r*.

In the beginning the writing was very ornamental, and this ornamentation obscured the likeness between the two scripts, but gradually people began to write as simply as possible.

In learning to write Russian, children practise the same "pot-hooks" as children writing Latin script. As will be seen from the examples given, very few new elements are needed for Russian writing. Therefore it is very advisable to begin studying Russian with writing rather than reading, but again, as in the case of pronunciation, care must be taken to be accurate.

The only essential point different from Latin writing is that the small letters *л, м, я*, as in (3), begin with the same curve or "hook" as the capital *M* in English, but in the Latin script this small hook never occurs in the middle of a word. This point must be carefully observed when writing words as in (9). After "o" these letters must not be joined (10).

The capital letters are mostly written in the same way as the small *except Б*. The small *i, n, m* can be used as the initials (11). Russian small "t" can be written in a simpler way as in *стал* in (12). The alternative way of writing *д*, i.e. like the English "*g*", frequently occurs, but is not advisable.

In quick writing some letters, as *m, ш, u, n*, etc., run into each other, so the stroke over *m* and under *ш* is often used (see 11).

1) г г, ии, ггг, гг, и ш, п т, р,

2) с с, зз, х, ж, о, а, зз, д д, б б, ф ф

3) /// , л л, м м // °° я я, / ι я

4) ь ь, ч ч, ъ ъ, ы ы, н н, ю ю

5) ц ц, щ щ, у у, з з Э, З, Х, Ж

6) Г Г, П П, Т Т; (7) Ч, Ш, Щ, Ц

8) В, Б Б, Ф Ф, У У, Ю Ю, Я Я, Л, М

9) мама, или, яма, лампа, фамилия

10) ломать, моя, голубка, громкий

11) Александр Пушкин. Лев Толстой.
Максим Горький. Иван Никитин.

12) "Благодаря языку человек стал человеком".
Гумбольдт.

("By Speech Man became Man".)
Humboldt.

THE NEW ORTHOGRAPHY

The following changes constitute the New Orthography introduced in 1917–18 (see Preface):

(1) The letter ѣ has been abolished, and replaced by е (the words все, в доме, лес used to be spelled with ѣ).

(2) The letter ѳ is replaced by ф (e.g. Фома, кафедра).

(3) The letter i which used to be written before a vowel is replaced by и (e.g. Россия, синий).

(4) The ъ has been abolished at the end of words, but has been kept in the middle of words as a separating sign (see p. 12). Sometimes in the latter case the apostrophe (') is used instead.

(5) The prefixes из-, воз-, вз-, раз-, роз-, низ-, без-, чрез-, через- before vowels and voiced consonants are written with з, but before unvoiced consonants, including с, are written with с (see p. 13).

(6) The genitive endings -аго and -яго of adjectives, pronouns and participles have been abolished and replaced by -ого and -его.

(7) The nominative and accusative plural endings -ые, -ие are to be uniform for all three genders, instead of -ыя, -ия, which were formerly used for feminine and neuter.

(8) The third person plural они is to be used for the feminine instead of онѣ.

(9) The form одни (plural of one) is to be used for the feminine instead of однѣ.

(10) The genitive singular of the personal pronoun она is like the accusative, i.e. её instead of ея.

PRONUNCIATION

Vowels

Russian vowels as compared with the standard vowel sounds may be represented as follows:

Standard vowel sounds	*a*	*e*	*i*	*o*	*u*	
Russian vowels	а	э	ы (ъ)	о	у	hard
	я	е	и (ь)	ё	ю	soft
			й			

In examining the above table it is to be noticed that for each standard vowel sound there are two sounds in Russian, e.g. а and я for "a", э and е for "e", etc. The vowels in the upper row of Russian vowels are called **hard** vowels, to distinguish them from the **soft** or iotated vowels, which in English may also be described as modified by prefixing *y*.[1]

The pronunciation of the "hard" and "soft" vowels may be defined by the position of the tongue and lips. For the "hard" vowels the tongue remains in the middle of the mouth and carefully avoids touching roof, cheeks or teeth. In pronouncing the upper row, from а to у, the lips are gradually drawn into a round position (for "у"). For the "soft" vowels the tongue comes forward and touches the lower teeth, while the lips do the same work as in pronouncing the "hard" vowels. Thus the difference between а and я is only in the position of the tongue. So also with э and е, у and ю, etc. This is especially important for the sounds ы and и. The sound ы has no exact equivalent in English, but it can be described as и with the tongue taken back from the lower teeth and put into the same position as for а and у.

й (short "ee") is a semi-vowel. It is used only after a vowel forming the second element of a diphthong (cf. "y" in "boy" or "may"):

ай	эй	ый	ой	уй
яй	ей	ий	ёй	юй

The hard and soft signs (ъ, ь) are also semi-vowels, but originally were vowels of the "i" kind, as they took the place of the reduced ы and и in the Old Slavonic. The infinitive ending of verbs, for example, used always to be (and in Serbian still is) -ти, e.g. читати, любити, instead of читать, любить (in songs and poetry this form is still sometimes used).

[1] Even и, although its English equivalent is "ee", is better identified with "yee" in order to make a preceding consonant really soft.

The names "hard" and "soft" signs show that they are the signs in writing of the hard and soft pronunciation of consonants.[1] Before the latest change in the orthography ъ was used at the end of words after a hard consonant, e.g. онъ, столъ. But since a consonant alone or before another consonant is always hard (*except* ч and щ which are always soft), the use of ъ after a final consonant has been abolished. The soft sign, however, which indicates the soft pronunciation, has been retained.

We see therefore that consonants in Russian may be pronounced hard or soft. In fact, it is the hard and soft consonants that are responsible for the names of the hard and soft vowels.

Before ы consonants are always hard; before и always soft, *except* ж, ш, ц; before а, э, о, у they may be either hard or soft.

As there is no separate set of soft consonants, the soft pronunciation of a consonant is shown in writing by the vowels я, е, ё, ю. For practical purposes, and in particular for foreign students, it is the hard and soft vowels that really matter, as they make all the difference to the pronunciation of consonants.

Examples for practice:

д	да	дэ	ды	до	ду
дь	дя	де	ди	дё	дю
н	на	нэ	ны	но	ну
нь	ня	не	ни	нё	ню
п	па	пэ	пы	по	пу
пь	пя	пе	пи	пё	пю
т	та	тэ	ты	то	ту
ть	тя	те	ти	тё	тю

Since ж, ш and ц are always hard, е, ё, and и after these consonants sound as э, о, and ы respectively, as in жечь, жёлтый, жизнь. And since ч and щ are always soft, hard vowels after these consonants sound soft, as in чáща, чýдо.

The most important thing in the pronunciation of Russian is to keep to this distinction between vowels (allowing for the accent), and to pronounce consonants accordingly.[2]

[1] The easiest example of hard and soft consonants, for English-speaking people, is the pronunciation of т. Followed by the hard sign ъ or by a hard vowel, as in тъ, та, то, etc., it is pronounced like the "t" in "tub". Followed by the soft sign ь or by a soft vowel, as in ть, тя, те, etc., it is pronounced like the "t" in "tube". Compare also "done" and "dew", "none" and "new", "pipe" and "pew", etc.

[2] The subject of hard and soft vowels is discussed on p. 4.

Accent

As in English, there is in Russian no invariable position for the accent or stress. There are, however, certain rules which guide the student. These rules are pointed out in the Lessons, and in Part II. Stress on accented vowels makes a great difference to the pronunciation, as only accented vowels have their full value, as given in the Vowel Table. Thus, to pronounce the word кото́рый first read it without any accent, ко-то-рый; then lay the stress on the second syllable and make the first o short (ŏ), more like a neutral vowel (phonetic ə). In the case of язы́к say я-зык; then with the stress on the ы the я becomes neutral, though slightly different from [ə]. The difference is simply that in the first case it is o that becomes neutral, and in the second я.

The length of the word has also an influence on the vowels, e.g. in кар-ти́-на. When stress is laid on the ти both a's have the sound of "a", but only just so much as is naturally required.

Although Russian vowels, when unstressed, lose their full value, it is very wrong to assign to them any other definite value. It is very wrong to say that the first o in кото́рый is like "a", or that вода́ is pronounced "vada". It has been found that the international signs of phonetics do not satisfactorily represent Russian sounds. Attempts have been made to invent new signs which grew almost into complicated formulae, but their usefulness is very limited. There is an equivalent in English to almost every Russian vowel, even ы is very near the English "i".

Coming back to the changed values of the unaccented vowels, we must also point out that this change will take place with a foreigner just as it does with a native. It is the stress on one vowel sound, and not the deliberate change of every other, that gives unstressed vowels a less definite value.

Syllables in Russian end, when possible, in a vowel, thus, по-ни-ма́ть. When two consonants or two vowels come together in a word, they are considered as belonging to different syllables, e.g. меж-ду-на-ро́д-ный, ко-о-пе-ра-ти́в, у-ю́т-ный.

Notice that prepositions consisting of a single consonant are joined in pronunciation to the first syllable of the following word, e.g.

в до́-ме, in the house; с на́-ми, with us.

When reading a word by syllables, the student should read it

slowly, dividing them in the way described, then stress the
accented syllable, without special attention to the rest. The
resulting pronunciation will be fairly accurate—as nearly so as is
possible without help from a native.

In "carrying" a word from one line to the next, keep to this
rule of dividing syllables.

The ъ and ь separating consonants from vowels. The soft sign,
ь, in addition to indicating the soft pronunciation of a consonant[1]
at the end of a word, as in день, соль, etc., is also used in the
middle of a word: *firstly*, to separate a consonant from a following
vowel, as in чья, питьё, ружьё; *secondly*, to separate a soft
consonant from a following hard one, as in письмо́.

The latter use is especially frequent in derivatives of words with
soft л in the stem, the л being followed by a hard consonant, e.g.
па́лец—па́л-ь-ца; лев—л-ь-ва́.

The hard sign, ъ, has not been abolished altogether, but its use
is now very limited. It is still used in prefixes, compound words
and foreign words, to separate a consonant from a soft vowel, e.g.
съесть, подъе́зд, трёхъя́русный, адъюта́нт. Before a hard vowel
the hard sign is not written, e.g. отучи́ть (отъ + учи́ть), сумасше́-
дший (съ + ума + сшедший), трёхэта́жный. Before и the consonant of the prefix is joined to the и, which becomes ы, e.g.
съ + искать becomes сыска́ть.

Consonants

The consonants are divided, firstly, according to the organs of
speech used in pronunciation:

(1) Labials: б, п, в, ф, м.
(2) Dentals (including sibilants): д, т, з, с, ц, ч, ж, ш, щ.
(3) Gutturals: г, к, х.
(4) Linguals: л, р.
(5) Palatals (nasal): н, (м).

Secondly, they are divided into "voiced" and "unvoiced", thus:

Voiced:	б	в	г	д	ж	з
Unvoiced:	п	ф	к х	т	ш	с

[1] ь is never used after the gutturals г, к, х.

At the end of a word and before an unvoiced consonant, a voiced consonant is often pronounced unvoiced, thus:

б becomes п, e.g. хлеб, before к: пробка.

д becomes т, e.g. сад, before к: лодка.

в becomes ф, e.g. кровь, лев, before к, с: лавка, встать.

г becomes almost к, e.g. снег, круг.

г becomes х in Бог, before к, т: лёгкий, ногти.

з becomes с, e.g. раз, before к: резко.

Before vowels and voiced consonants the prefixes из, воз, вз, раз, роз, низ, без retain the з; but before unvoiced consonants they are written with с, i.e. they become ис, вос, бес, рас, etc., e.g. нисходить, бесполезно.

But unvoiced с is pronounced as voiced з before voiced consonants, e.g.

зб instead of сб in сбегать.

зд instead of сд in сделать.

(Note: зд appears at the beginning of only three words: здесь, здание, здоровый, and their derivatives.)

зж instead of сж in сжечь, сжать.

(Note: зж never appears at the beginning of a word, although the sound is distinctly heard, as in the above examples.)

зг is written in only one word зги: "ни зги не видно" (pitch dark), but the sound appears in such words as сгореть, сгибать.

т before a voiced consonant sounds as д, e.g. отдать.

In the combinations стн, здн, стл, стк, the д and т are practically omitted in pronunciation, e.g.

грустный (грусть), sad.

поздний (опоздать), late.

постлан (постель), made (of a bed).

счастливый (счастье), happy.

стклянка (стекло), flask.

The same happens to в in the word здравствуйте (здравие, здоровье).

Double consonants are always carefully pronounced in Russian, e.g. in Анна, медленно; *except* in foreign words where the double consonants are used simply to preserve the foreign spelling, e.g. профессор, теннис, etc.

The genitive endings -ого, -его are pronounced ово, ево, but not in other words, such as много, which is not a genitive.

Certain consonants, the gutturals г, к, х, and the sibilants ж, ч, ш, щ, cannot be followed by the vowels я, ю, ы, which are accordingly replaced by а, у, и. This is of special importance in declensions and conjugations, e.g. the genitive of книга should end in -ы, but this becomes -и in order to satisfy the demands of euphony. The same applies in the case of verbs, e.g. молчáть, which cannot have the ending -ю in the 1st person singular after ч, and therefore has -у instead. Similarly, in the 3rd person plural, -ят is replaced by -ат (see table on p. 206).

After ц, я and ю are replaced by а and у, but ы remains, since euphony does not demand any alteration, e.g. цы́фра, óвцы.

o *and* ё *after* ж, ч, ш, щ, ц.

o is written after these letters only when accented, e.g. большóй. But хорóшее has the soft ending -ее, though in the feminine the ending is hard. Cf. -е in нáше, вáше.

Summarising all that has been said about the pronunciation of Russian, one comes to the conclusion that there are really very few rules required. Once the system of Russian vowels and consonants is properly understood, one has every help in the perfect system of the alphabet, in which there is a sign for every sound, and these sounds are practically all to be found in the English language. In every word one finds an indication of how to read it, not by way of abstract rules stored in the memory, but actually before the eyes, by way of soft vowels and the soft and hard signs.

Reading accented texts is very helpful for the beginner, but as Russian books (like English) are not printed with accents, one should not depend too much on them, but rather watch the accents when learning declensions and conjugations. In these a certain degree of consistency in accent will be found.

PERMUTATION OF VOWELS AND CONSONANTS

Permutation, or interchange of vowels and consonants, plays a very important part in the Russian language. It owes its existence to the fact that the elements of the everyday conversational language "of the people" has influenced the literary or written language in every stage of its development, dating back as far as the eleventh century. This permutation may therefore to a great extent be explained as a demand of euphony.

In studying the language this permutation is of the utmost importance, for not only does it help in the understanding of word-building, but also explains so-called irregularities in declensions and conjugations. In the treatment of the Parts of Speech in this book, this matter is dealt with systematically, as far as space permits.

PERMUTATION OF VOWELS

In saying that certain consonants cannot be followed by certain vowels we have approached the question of the permutation of vowels.

These permutations may be summarised as follows:

я and ю after г, к, х, ж, ч, ш, щ, ц, change into а and у; e.g. мо́лча, ви́жу.

ы after г, к, х, ж, ч, ш, щ, changes into и; e.g. ре́ки, кни́ги, лу́жи, plural of река́ (river), кни́га (book), лу́жа (pool).

о after ж, ч, ш, щ, ц, changes into е if not accented; e.g. на́ше, ва́ше, па́льцем instrumental of па́лец (finger), instead of пальцо́м.

ь, after a vowel, is replaced by й; e.g. шея (neck) should take ь in the genitive plural, but instead has шей. Cf. неде́ля неде́ль (see p. 237).

Apart from the permutation of vowels in inflections, permutation often occurs in the stem of words of the same derivation, e.g.

a *may interchange with* o:

расту́, I grow; рост, stature.
тварь, creature; твори́ть, to create.
мака́ть, to dip; обмокну́ть (perf.).

e *may interchange with* a, o, и, ь, *or be deleted*:

веду́, I lead; пова́дка, habit; води́ть, to guide; поведе́ние, conduct.
нести́, to be carrying; носи́ть, на́шивать, to carry.
беру́, I take; вы́бор, choice; брать, to take; выбира́ть, to choose.
соберу́, I shall collect; сбо́ры, preparations; собра́ние, meeting; собира́ть, to collect.
тёмный, dark; тьма́, darkness.

и *interchanges with* e:

сиде́ть, to sit; седло́, saddle; седо́к, rider.
дитя́, child; де́ти, children.
висе́ть, to hang; ве́сить, to weigh; вес, weight.

у *interchanges with* ы *and* о:

душа́, soul; дыша́ть, to breathe; вздох, sigh.
слу́шать, to listen; слы́шать, to hear.

ы *interchanges with* ов *or* ав:

рыть, to dig; ров, ditch.
плыть, to be swimming; плове́ц, swimmer; пла́вать, to swim.
слыть, to be reputed; сло́вно, as if; сла́ва, reputation.
крыть, to cover; кро́вля, roof.

-ов- *changes into* у, *or* о *is deleted*:

сове́товать, to advise; сове́тую, I advise; свет, council (old word).

-ев- *changes into* ю:

клева́ть, to peck; клюю́, I peck; клюв, beak.

-ра- *changes into* -оро-:

кра́ткий, brief; коро́ткий, short.
град, town (old word); го́род, town.
граждани́н, citizen; горожа́нин, townsman.
страна́, country; сторона́, side; страни́ца, page.

-ре- *changes into* -ере-:

пред, in front; пере́дний, front, fore.
пре́док, ancestor; впереди́, in the front (adj.).

-ла- *changes into* -оло-:

младо́й, young (old word); молодо́й, young; младе́нец, baby.
глас, voice (old word); гла́сный, public; го́лос, voice.
глава́, chapter; голова́, head; гла́вный, principal.

THE INSERTION AND DELETION OF О AND Е

о and е are inserted between two consonants at the end of the stem if these are not followed by a vowel, e.g.

тру́дный, difficult; тру́ден (predicative form).
любе́зный, kind; любе́зен, etc. (see p. 248).

After the gutturals г, к, х, -о is usually inserted, e.g.

лёгкий, easy; лёгок.

The vowels о and е occurring between two consonants at the end of a word are deleted when the latter consonant is followed by a vowel; this happens usually in declensions: e.g.

оте́ц, отца́, отцу́, etc.; день, дня, дню, etc.; кусо́к, куска́; рот, рта; сон, сна; ве́тер, ве́тра.

Some prepositions, as в, к, с, become **во, ко, со** before two consonants, e.g.

ко мне; во мне; со мной.

Cf. also **пódo, нádo**, etc. (see p. 266).

о becomes **об** before a word beginning with a vowel, e.g. об э́том; and **обо** before two consonants, e.g. обо мнé.

The prefix **воз-** or **вос-** becomes **взо-** and **из-, ис-** become **изо-** before и, which becomes **й**, e.g.

восходи́ть, взойти́, to ascend; исходи́ть, изойти́, to derive, etc.

Permutation of Consonants

Consonants as well as vowels are subject to permutation, and even to a greater extent. A knowledge of the rules of permutation of consonants will considerably facilitate the recognition of cognate words of the same root, and thus the learning of the vocabulary.

The rules are as follows:

(1) г, д, з interchange with **ж**, e.g.

друг, friend; дружба, friendship; друзья́, friends.
слугá, servant; служи́ть, to serve.
ходи́ть, to walk; хожу́, I walk.
могу́, I can; мóжет, he can; мóжно, possible.
сказáть, to say; скажи́, say.

(2) з with **ж** and **с**, e.g.

рéзать, to cut; рéжу, I cut.
мáзать, to spread, smear; мáжу; мáсло, butter.
воз, cart; вози́ть, to convey; вожу́.

(3) к, т, ц interchange with **ч, щ**, e.g.

свет, light; свечá, candle; освещéние, lighting.
рукá, hand; ручнóй (adj.).
лик, face (old word); ли́чный, personal; лицó, face.
кли́кнуть, to call; клич, call; восклицáние, exclamation.
отéц, father; отéчество, fatherland.
век, century; вéчный, eternal.

(4) д sometimes changes into **жд**, e.g.

побéда, victory; побеждáть, to be victorious.
град, town (old word); граждани́н, citizen.
роди́ться, to be born; рождéние, birth.

(5) **x** and **с** into **ш**, **т**, e.g.

слух, hearing; слу́шать, to listen; послу́шный, obedient.

проси́ть, to beg; проше́ние, petition.

носи́ть, to carry; но́ша, burden; произноше́ние, pronunciation.

дух, spirit; душа́, soul; ду́шный, stifling.

цвести́, to blossom; цвето́к, flower.

лес, forest; ле́ший, forest spirit.

(6) **ск** and **ст** into **щ**, e.g.

иска́ть, to seek; ищу́, I seek; исте́ц, plaintiff.

пуска́ть, to let go; пусти́, let go; упуще́ние, omission.

ча́сто, often; ча́ще, oftener.

чистота́, cleanliness; чи́ще, cleaner.

мстить, to take vengeance; мщу; мще́ние, vengeance.

таска́ть, to drag; утащи́ть (perfective form).

весть, tidings; ве́щий, wise.

INSERTION OF CONSONANTS

(1) If a stem ends in б, п, в, ф or м, л is inserted before ю, е and sometimes я, e.g.

люби́ть, to love; люблю́; влюблённый, lover.

топи́ть, to melt; топлю́; отопле́ние, heating.

лови́ть, to catch; ловлю́; ло́вля, catching.

дешёвый, cheap; деше́вле, cheaper.

тра́фить, to fit in; тра́флю.

корми́ть, to feed; кормлю́; кормле́ние, feeding.

(2) Insertion of the consonant **н**:

(*a*) When personal pronouns of the 3rd person are used with prepositions, **н** is prefixed, e.g.

у него́; к нему́; с ней; от них; перед ни́ми; позади́ неё.

(*b*) **н** is inserted in verbs compounded from -имать, after the prefix, e.g.

под-н-има́ть, под-н-я́ть (see p. 220).

Cf. also **н** as a suffix in adjectives (see p. 252).

The words given as examples for each kind of permutation do not exhaust all the possibilities of various combinations, but they will help the student to look for similar changes in roots when reading Russian.

PART I

LESSONS AND EXERCISES

LESSON I

Letters (16): а, е, и, о, у, в, г, д, к, л, м, н, р, с, т, ч. For the pronunciation of these letters see the alphabet and the chapter on Pronunciation.

VOCABULARY

он he
она́ she
оно́ it
они́ they
кто who
что what, that
тот that (adj.) (m.)
та that (f.)
то that (n.)
где where
тут here
там there
дом house
до́ма at home
ко́мната room
окно́ window
стена́ wall
стол table
стул chair
класс class (room)

доска́ board
кни́га book
сло́во word
ка́рта map
карти́на picture
го́род town
Москва́ Moscow
река́ river
Во́лга Volga
ло́дка boat
вода́ water
село́ village
вот here is
вон there is
в in, into
на on
да yes
нет no
не not
но but

§ 1. Russian nouns are of three genders: masculine, feminine and neuter, which are distinguished by the gender endings. The gender endings are easily remembered as soon as one knows the personal pronouns of the 3rd person singular: он, она́, оно́. Он means "he", and similarly nouns which have a consonant as their last sound, i.e. those with no ending, are of masculine gender, e.g. стол. Она́ means "she", and similarly nouns ending in -a are feminine, e.g. кни́га; and as оно́ means "it", all nouns in -o are neuter, e.g. окно́. The ending -и in они́ suggests -и as a principal ending of the plural. The gender endings are very important, as adjectives in Russian always agree with the noun in gender and number, e.g. тот стол, that table; та кни́га, that book; то окно́, that window.

§ 2. There is no article in Russian, i.e. "the table" or "a table" are both translated **стол**.

§ 3. Auxiliary verbs are hardly used in Russian. The present tense of "to be" is not used as it is in English, e.g.

He is here.   Он тут.

Where is she?   Где она?

§ 4. Где? where? In answer to this question, nouns after the prepositions **в** and **на** change their ending into -**е**, showing a state of *permanency* or *rest* (locative case). In the case of a masculine noun -**е** is *added* to the stem.

Где он?   Он в доме.   Where is he? He is in the house.

Стол в комнате.   The table is in the room.

§ 5. Вот means "here is", and **вон**, "there is", when pointing out, e.g.

Вот книга.   Here is the book!

Вон окно.   There is the window!

but   Книга тут.   The book is here.

§ 6. When "there is" denotes simple existence or presence, it is not translated in Russian, and the sentence usually begins with the word indicating place or time, e.g. Exercise B, sentence 13, На стене карта.

§ 7. "It", when it stands for a masculine or feminine noun, is translated by **он** or **она** accordingly, e.g.

Где книга?   Она на столе.

Where is the book? It is on the table.

§ 8. "And" is translated by both **и** and **а**.

И is a joining conjunction, e.g. стол тут и стул **тут**.

А is a separating conjunction, e.g. стол тут, а стул **там**.

After a negative **а** has the meaning of "but", e.g. Он не в Москве, а тут.

EXERCISES I

А. 1. Вот стол. 2. Вон окно. 3. Стул тут. 4. Кто там? Там он. 5. Что там? Там книга. 6. Она дома. 7. Они не дома, они в классе. 8. В городе он? 9. Нет, он в селе. 10. Где стол? 11. Стол в доме. 12. А дом? 13. А дом в городе. 14. Село на реке. 15. Волга река, а Москва город. 16. То село на Волге. 17. Москва на реке́ Москве́, а не на Во́лге. 18. Он тут, а она́ там. 19. Кни́га на столе́, а ка́рта на стене́. 20. В кни́ге карти́на. 21. Вода́ в реке́. 22. Ло́дка на реке́. 23. Они́ в ло́дке. 24. Та ло́дка не тут. 25. Тут го́род, а не село́.

B. 1. Where is he? 2. He is here. 3. She is there. 4. What is on the table? 5. The book is on the table. 6. Where is the house? 7. The house is in the town. 8. Where is the picture? 9. It is on the wall. 10. Is he in the house? 11. Yes, he is in the house, but he is not at home. 12. What is on the wall in the class? 13. There is a map on the wall. 14. Where are the table and the chair? 15. They are in the room. 16. And where is the room? 17. It is in the house. 18. They are in Moscow. 19. That boat is on the river. 20. She is not in town; she is in the village. 21. Here is the table. 22. There they are! 23. Here is the board. 24. What is on the board? 25. The word is on the board, but not in the book. 26. Who is in the room?

LESSON II

Letters (6): ё, б, п, з, ъ, ь. (See the alphabet and the chapter on Pronunciation.)

VOCABULARY

писа́ть to write	вчера́ yesterday
чита́ть to read	никто́ nobody
говори́ть to speak	бума́га paper
ви́деть to see	перо́ pen
смотре́ть to look	мел chalk
сиде́ть to sit	а́дрес address
рабо́тать to work	конве́рт envelope
игра́ть to play	письмо́ letter
де́лать to do, make	уро́к lesson
понима́ть to understand	газе́та newspaper
по́мнить to remember	слова́рь (m.) dictionary
по-ру́сски in Russian	орга́н organ
как how, as	скри́пка violin
так so	те́ннис tennis
когда́ when	брат brother
тогда́ then	сестра́ sister
никогда́ never	ско́ро quickly, soon
иногда́ sometimes	ме́дленно slowly
всегда́ always	всё everything, all

A NEW RUSSIAN GRAMMAR

§ 9. The soft sign after т indicates that the consonant is soft.
Before the change in the orthography a hard consonant at the end
of a word used to have a hard sign after it, as онъ, столъ, etc.,
but as the consonant alone is always hard, ъ at the end of a word
has been abolished[1]; thus nouns ending in a hard consonant now
have really no ending at all, but for convenience they are sometimes referred to in this book as ending in -(ъ).

Ть is the principal ending of the *infinitive*.

§ 10. The *past tense* is very easy in Russian, and at the same
time rather peculiar, as its endings do not change by person,
but by gender and number. One need therefore know only four
endings:

-л for the masculine,
-ла for the feminine,
-ло for the neuter,
-ли for the plural (all genders).

The past tense is formed from the infinitive by taking off the
ending -ть and adding the endings -л, -ла, -ло, -ли, e.g. писá-ть:
он писá-л, онá писá-ла, онó писá-ло, они́ писá-ли.

To begin with we shall deal with only the imperfect past tense.
Он писáл means "he wrote", "he was writing", "he used to
write", but *not* "he has written".

§ 11. The *negative* form:

Он писáл. He wrote.
Он не писáл. He did not write.

The particle не is put before the verb or before the principal word
in the negative, e.g.

Он рабóтал не в гóроде, а в селé.
He worked not in the town, but in the village.

§ 12. In Russian two (or more) negatives do not make an
affirmative; i.e. the ordinary negative form is used along with the
negative pronoun or adverb, e.g.

Он никогдá не ви́дел. He never saw.
Никтó не рабóтал. No one was working.
Ни...ни. Neither...nor.
Ни он, ни она не говори́ли по-рýсски.
Neither he nor she spoke Russian.

---

[1] For more about the hard and soft signs see p. 12.

§ 13. The *interrogative* form is usually expressed simply by reversing the verb and the pronoun, e.g.

Читáл он?   Did he read?

When a question is introduced by an interrogatory word, as где? когда? etc., the inversion need not take place, e.g.

Где он рабóтал?   Where did he work?

Another interrogative form is with the particle ли, placed after the chief word in the question or immediately after the verb, e.g. читал ли он? This form, however, is mostly used in an indirect question or statement, corresponding to the English "whether", e.g.

> Он не знал, дóма ли она[1].
> He did not know whether she was at home.
> Он не вúдел, рабóтала ли она.
> He did not see whether she was working.

Ли is always used in the negative interrogative, e.g.

Не читáл ли он?   Did he not read?

§ 14. As will be noticed, the verb "to do" is used in neither negative nor interrogative constructions, nor is it used in a reply such as "she did", "she did not"; e.g.

Did she see the picture?	Вúдела онá картúну?
She did.	Вúдела.
She did not.	Нет, не вúдела.

§ 15. The *accusative case* of masculine nouns denoting inanimate objects, and of all neuter nouns, is the same as the nominative, e.g. он вúдел дом; онá писáла письмó. Feminine nouns change -a into -y in the accusative, e.g.

Он читáл кнúгу.   He was reading a book.

§ 16. The possessive pronouns "my", "his", "our", etc., are less commonly used than in English, e.g.

He was looking at his sister.   Он смотрéл на сестрý.

§ 17. Notice the following idiomatic uses of как (how):

Как по-рýсски "paper"?	What is the Russian for "paper"?
Как они говорúли?	What language were they speaking?
Он вúдел, как онá рабóтала.	He saw her working.
Как áдрес?	What is the address?

---

[1] Note that a subordinate clause in Russian is always separated by commas from the rest of the sentence (cf. p. 64).

§ 18.
To play the violin.	Игра́ть на скри́пке (loc. case).
To play tennis.	Игра́ть в те́ннис (асс. case).
To stay at home.	Сиде́ть до́ма.
To look at.	Смотре́ть на (+асс.).
but To look at *a book*.	Смотре́ть в кни́гу.
To look at the window.	Смотре́ть в окно́.
To speak Russian.	Говори́ть по-ру́сски (an adverb of manner).

EXERCISES II

A. 1. Он писа́л письмо́. 2. Она́ чита́ла кни́гу.
3. Они́ говори́ли по-ру́сски. 4. Кто рабо́тал в до́ме?
5. Что он де́лал вчера́? 6. Он сиде́л до́ма и рабо́тал.
7. В до́ме никто́ не говори́л по-ру́сски. 8. Понима́л он,
когда́ она́ говори́ла по-ру́сски? 9. Он не всегда́ пони-
ма́л, когда́ она́ говори́ла ско́ро. 10. Брат чита́л
ме́дленно. 11. Она́ смотре́ла на карти́ну. 12. Сестра́
смотре́ла в кни́гу. 13. Что она́ ви́дела в кни́ге?
14. Она́ ви́дела карти́ну. 15. Ви́дел он, кто игра́л в
те́ннис? 16. Кто игра́л вчера́ на орга́не? 17. Брат
игра́л на орга́не, а сестра́ на скри́пке. 18. Где они́
игра́ли? 19. Они́ игра́ли до́ма. 20. Когда́ он чита́л
по-ру́сски, он всегда́ смотре́л в слова́рь. 21. Он по́мнил
всё, что ви́дел. 22. Она́ понима́ла не всё, что чита́ла.
23. Ви́дел он Ленингра́д? 24. Нет, не ви́дел, но он
ви́дел Ки́ев. 25. Ки́ев на Днепре́. 26. Она́ сиде́ла в
ко́мнате и смотре́ла в окно́. 27. Что она́ ви́дела там?
28. Она́ ви́дела, как брат и сестра́ игра́ли в те́ннис.

B. 1. He wrote. 2. They read (past). 3. She was speaking.
4. He played. 5. What was she doing? 6. Did they understand? 7. He saw. 8. She saw. 9. They were working. 10. Did
they remember? 11. She was sitting. 12. She was not playing.
13. What was he playing? 14. Was she not playing? 15. They
never wrote Russian. 16. Nobody spoke. 17. Nobody saw.
18. He never worked. 19. Did he not see? 20. She was not
looking. 21. Where is the paper? 22. Here is the book, and the
paper is on the table.

C. 1. Who was reading the lesson? 2. The brother was writing the address on the envelope. 3. They were working at home. 4. He always read Russian. 5. Nobody spoke Russian there. 6. He never looked at (his) sister when he spoke. 7. Where were they sitting? 8. Were they not talking? 9. Yes, they were talking. 10. What language did they speak? 11. They spoke Russian, and spoke quickly. 12. What was she doing at home yesterday? 13. She was working. 14. Did he see her working? 15. Who was playing the violin here? 16. Nobody played the organ yesterday. 17. They always played tennis. 18. Did she see them play? 19. No, she did not. 20. Where is the dictionary? 21. He saw the dictionary on the table. 22. She was looking at the book. 23. Did she see a picture in the book? 24. What is the Russian for "pen"? 25. Leningrad is on the river Neva (Нева). 26. And where is Kharkov (Харьков)? 27. Kharkov is not on a river, but Kiev is on the Dnieper.

LESSON IIa

знать to know	ученик pupil
сказать to say	учебник text-book
учить to teach, learn	магазин shop
учитель teacher	здесь here
пока whilst	очень very

§ 19. Although the imperfect past tense is mostly used in the first ten lessons, the perfect past, which is exactly the same in form and offers no difficulty, should not be left out of consideration. There are no compound past tenses in Russian, and there is only one perfect past tense, formed from the perfect infinitive. As the auxiliary verb "to have" is not used in Russian, the English perfect infinitive "to have done" is rendered mostly by the addition of prefixes, of which the commonest is по-. The idea of the perfective "aspect", i.e. of perfect tenses in general, is dealt with later (Lesson XI), and in the Grammar (p. 203). At this stage it is enough to know that "to have written", for example, is написать; "to have read", прочитать; "to have looked", посмотреть; etc. The past tense of these verbs is formed in the usual way, e.g.

Написал он?	Has he written?
Прочитала она книгу?	Has she finished (reading) the book?

§ 20. **Сказа́л** is the past tense of **сказа́ть**, and means "said", "has said", or "had said". It must be distinguished from **говори́л** which means "was saying" as well as "was speaking". **Говори́ть** (to speak) means "to be saying" when used transitively.

§ 21. **и...и...** both...and..., e.g.

И он и она говори́ли по-русски.
Both he and she spoke Russian.

(Cf. use of **ни...ни...**, § 12.)

И may mean "also", and is attached to the significant word in the sentence, e.g.

И учитель не знал.
The teacher did not know either (*also* did not know).

§ 22. Many nouns are formed from an infinitive by taking off -ть, and adding -тель, e.g. писа́ть, писа́тель (author); чита́ть, чита́тель (reader); учить, учи́тель (teacher).

Exercises II a

A. 1. Он ви́дел тот магази́н, где она́ рабо́тала. 2. В кла́ссе никто́ не знал, что Днепр река́. 3. Киев на Днепре́. 4. Учи́тель и учени́к говори́ли по-ру́сски. 5. Никто́ не понима́л что они говори́ли. 6. Они говори́ли так ско́ро, что никто́ не понима́л. 7. Учи́тель смотре́л, как учени́к писа́л на доске́. 8. Он писа́л о́чень ме́дленно. 9. Он не знал что писа́ть. 10. Кто вчера́ игра́л здесь на скри́пке? 11. Вчера́ никто́ не игра́л ни на скри́пке, ни на орга́не. 12. Кто сказа́л, что они игра́ли здесь? 13. Учи́тель не знал, что учени́к говори́л по-ру́сски. 14. Она не зна́ла как по-ру́сски violin. 15. Пока́ сестра́ учи́ла уро́к, брат писа́л письмо́. 16. Когда́ он написа́л письмо́, он чита́л по-ру́сски. 17. Они никогда́ не рабо́тали ни до́ма, ни в магази́не. 18. Он не знал как написа́ть а́дрес по-ру́сски. 19. Прочита́л он кни́гу? 20. Нет, но сестра́ ви́дела, как он читал. 21. Написа́ли они что сказал учи́тель? 22. Он не знал, написа́ли ли они.   23. Не ви́дела ли она уче́бник на столе́?

B. 1. Did she see the picture on the wall? 2. She did. 3. Who was playing the organ yesterday? 4. Yesterday nobody played either the organ or the violin. 5. Where were they playing tennis? 6. They were not playing tennis. 7. They stayed at home and worked. 8. Here is the shop where they worked. 9. He looked at the shop. 10. They did not understand what she was saying. 11. She spoke very quickly. 12. What did she say? 13. She said that nobody understood what she was saying. 14. They did not know what to write. 15. The teacher was writing on the board. 16. They did not see what he was writing. 17. What is the Russian for "field"? 18. Sometimes they spoke Russian in the class. 19. Nobody spoke Russian yesterday. 20. The teacher saw him writing a letter in the class. 21. He did not know whether she spoke Russian. 22. Did she not see the paper?

LESSON III

Letters (5): я, э, ы, й, ю.

§ 23. TABLE OF RUSSIAN VOWELS.

Standard vowel sounds	*a*	*e*	*i*	*o*	*u*	
Russian vowels	а	э	ы (ъ)	о	у	hard
	я	е	и (ь)	ё (е)	ю	soft
			й			

This table of vowels is very important, as it helps not only with pronunciation, but also with declensions and various endings all through the language. For details concerning the vowels and their pronunciation see chapter on Pronunciation (p. 9).

VOCABULARY

быть to be	по́ле field
стоя́ть to stand	мо́ре sea
обе́дать to dine	ла́мпа lamp
обе́д dinner	день (m.) day
рука́ hand, arm	неде́ля week
нога́ foot, leg	год year
до́ктор doctor	час hour
апте́ка chemist's (shop)	мой, моя́, моё my, mine

твой, твоя, твоё thy, thine
этот, эта, это this
весь, вся, всё all, whole
утро morning
вечер evening
добрый вечер Good evening
до-свидания Au revoir
один one
два two
три three

четыре four
раз once, (one) time
первый first
последний last
новый new
старый old
по-английски in English
после after (gen.)
до till, up to, before (gen.)
у at (gen.)

§ 24. In addition to the principal gender endings, -(ъ), -a, -o, there are others which follow logically on an examination of the table of Russian vowels. From this table we derive that since -a is the ending of the feminine, -я, being the modified sound of a, is also a sign of the feminine. Similarly, neuter nouns end in -ё and -e (e being the unaccented ё), as well as in -o.

As to the masculine, we have already seen that masculine nouns end in a hard consonant, with no flexible ending; they may accordingly also end in a soft consonant, i.e. one with a soft sign after it, and in -й, which also has no sound of its own and is a semi-vowel. Thus the three endings of the masculine, -(ъ), -ь, -й, are to be found in the vertical column under "*i*"; ы and и, being the signs of the plural, do not come into gender endings.

§ 25. The only ending common to two genders is -ь, as this is also an ending of feminine nouns. It is even true that there are more feminine nouns ending in -ь than masculine. Abstract nouns in -ь, for example, are feminine. Nouns in -ь, which are not very numerous, must therefore be learned with their gender.

§ 26. The *complete table* of *gender endings*:

Masculine: (ъ), ь, й стол, день, чай (tea).

Feminine: a, я, ь комната, няня (nurse), ночь (night).

Neuter: o, ё, e окно, питьё (drink), море.

§ 27. On further examining the table, we understand that if мой is "my" in the masculine, the feminine and neuter forms of this word are моя, моё, all three ending in soft vowels. Similarly "this" is этот, эта, это (all three endings hard), and "all" *or* "whole" is весь, вся, всё.

§ 28. Since feminine nouns in -а change -а into -у in the accusative, nouns in -я correspondingly change -я into -ю, i.e. a hard ending always changes into a hard, and a soft into a soft ending, e.g.

ня́н-я	ня́н-ю
мо-я́	мо-ю́
вс-я	вс-ю

§ 29. Similarly in the *genitive*, masculine and neuter nouns with hard endings take -а; those with soft endings take -я, e.g.

стол, стола́	день, дня́	чай, ча́я
окно́, окна́	питьё, питья́	мо́ре, мо́ря

Note that the *accusative* of masculine nouns denoting animate beings is like the *genitive*, e.g.

Я ви́дел учи́теля.   I saw the teacher.

§ 30. The *genitive* of *feminine* nouns in -а ends in -ы and that of nouns in -я and -ь in -и. If, however, the stem ends in г, к, х, the ending is -и instead of -ы (see p. 15), e.g.

ко́мнат-а	ня́н-я	ноч-ь
ко́мнат-ы	ня́н-и	но́ч-и

but кни́г-а, кни́г-и.

§ 31. Looking at the table of vowels it is also easy to remember the adjectival endings.

Russian adjectives always end in two vowels, and these vowels are of the same kind as the gender endings, i.e.

-ый for masculine, но́вый.[1]
-ая for feminine,   но́вая.
-ое for neuter,   но́вое.

If one of these vowels is hard, the ending (i.e. an ending beginning with a hard vowel) is considered *hard*. (Two hard vowels never occur together.) But if both vowels are soft, the ending is considered *soft*, e.g. после́дн-ий (last), после́дн-яя, после́дн-ее.

§ 32. Э́тот, э́та, э́то (this), when used as an adjective, agrees with the noun, but э́то, when it means "this is", is a pronoun, and remains unchanged, e.g.

Э́тот стол мой.   This table is mine.
Э́то мой стол.   This is my table.

---

[1] Although not itself a gender ending, ы appears in the masculine since it is the hard equivalent of й.

§ 33. "The whole day", meaning "during the day", is **весь день** (accusative); similarly: **весь год**, the whole year; **всю неделю**, during the whole week.

Всё also means "everything".

Все, the plural of "whole", also means "everybody", and the verb in Russian is in the plural, e.g.

Все говорили по-русски.   Everybody spoke Russian.
Все так делали.   Everybody did so.

§ 34. The *past* tense of **быть**, "to be", with the personal pronouns:

	Singular	Plural
1st person	я был	мы были
2nd „	ты был	вы были
3rd „	он был	они были
	она была	(I was, have been, had
	оно было	been.)

§ 35. *Negative* form (observe the accents):

я, ты, он не́ был   мы⎫
        она не была́   вы⎬ не́ были
        оно не́ было   они⎭

For the interrogative form see § 13.

Exercises III

A. 1. Мой брат.   2. Моя сестра.   3. Моё перо.
4. Этот дом.   5. Эта комната.   6. Это окно.   7. Весь день.   8. Вся книга.   9. Всё утро.   10. Новый город.
11. Новая картина.   12. Последнее слово.   13. Последний урок.   14. Последняя неделя.   15. День недели.
16. После обеда.   17. Книга брата.   18. Комната сестры.   19. Говорить по-английски.   20. Писать по-русски.   21. Там все играли в теннис.   22. Всё было моё.   23. Это не моя книга.

B. 1. Вчера мы все были дома.   2. Мы сидели в комнате.   3. На столе стояла лампа.   4. Все работали.
5. Мама писала письмо.   6. Сестра читала книгу брата.
7. Брат играл на органе.   8. Никто не говорил.   9. Что

вы де́лали вчера́? 10. Мы весь день рабо́тали. 11. Где вы бы́ли вчера́? 12. Я был до́ма, а брат был в по́ле. 13. Бы́ли вы в Москве́? 14. Нет, я никогда́ не́ был в Москве́. 15. Моя́ сестра́ никогда́ не была́ на Во́лге. 16. Вот но́вая кни́га бра́та. 17. Не ви́дели ли вы бра́та? 18. Да, я ви́дел как он рабо́тал в по́ле. 19. Когда́ вы бы́ли в по́ле? 20. Вчера́ по́сле обе́да. 21. Что э́то? Э́то стол. 22. А э́то? Э́то кни́га.

C. 1. My house. 2. Thy picture. 3. My window. 4. The whole year. 5. The whole week. 6. He read everything. 7. Everything is on the table. 8. The new year. 9. An old picture. 10. The last letter. 11. The sister's room. 12. Good evening. 13. This town. 14. This sea. 15. The whole book. 16. She was not here. 17. Was she there? 18. The first lesson. 19. Before dinner. 20. At the window. 21. Everybody is here. 22. Everybody played. 23. Here is my hand.

D. 1. Yesterday we were reading and writing Russian. 2. Nobody spoke English. 3. Everybody spoke Russian. 4. What were they doing in town? 5. They were having dinner. 6. The brother and sister played tennis. 7. He never worked in the field. 8. Have you been on the Volga? 9. I have never been on the sea. 10. She has never seen the Volga. 11. Were you at home yesterday? 12. Who was standing in the room? Nobody. 13. She was reading the last lesson. 14. Did you see my book on the table? 15. Here is my new book. 16. Yesterday we dined in town. 17. He always dined at home. 18. What is the English for this word? 19. There is my book. 20. This book is mine. 21. This is (my) brother's dictionary.

LESSON IIIa

§ 36. The numeral **оди́н** (one) changes by gender, and is declined as an adjective (see p. 245): оди́н, одна́, одно́.

Два has a special form, **две**, for the feminine only. Other numerals do not change by gender.

After два, **три**, **четы́ре**, the genitive singular is used, e.g. две ко́мнаты, три до́ма, четы́ре сло́ва.

§ 37. Per day, "— a day", **в день** (acc.), per week, "— a week"
в неде́лю (acc.), e.g. два ра́за в день, twice a day.

§ 38. Although the present tense of **быть** is not normally used
in Russian, the 3rd person, singular and plural, **есть** (is) and **суть**
(are) exist. The latter is very seldom used. **Есть** is used with the
meaning of "there is", "there are", when "is" and "are" are
slightly emphatic (cf. French *il y a*), e.g.

В ко́мнате есть окно́.   There is a window in the room.
В ко́мнате есть о́кна.   There are windows in the room.

§ 39. **Есть** is also used instead of the verb "to have" in a
construction similar to the Latin, but with the genitive case
(instead of the dative) and the preposition **у** (at), e.g.

The genitive and accusative of **я, мы, вы,** are **меня́, нас, вас.**

Есть у вас перо́?   Have you a pen? (*lit.* Is a pen at you?)

If **есть** is used in the question it must also be used in the answer:

Да, у меня́ **есть** перо́.   Yes, I have a pen.
but   What have you in your hand?   Что у вас в руке́?
I have a pen in my hand.   У меня́ перо́ в руке́.

Here **есть** must not be used, since "what" is the principal word in
the question.

§ 40. In the past tense, to express "had" in the same construction, the verb **быть** must be used, e.g.

У меня́ был мел в руке́.   I had chalk in my hand.
У меня́ была́ кни́га.   I had a book.
У меня́ бы́ло перо́.   I had a pen.

У меня́, у нас, etc., may also be used instead of the possessive
pronouns, e.g. У меня́ в ко́мнате есть стол may be translated
by either "I have a table in my room" or "There is a table in my
room".

§ 41. Negative forms of the same construction:

У меня **нет** ме́ла.   I have no chalk.
У меня **не́ было** ме́ла.   I had no chalk.
У меня **не́ было** сестры́.   I had no sister.
У меня **не́ было** ни пера́, ни ме́ла.
I had neither pen nor chalk.

Нет, from the Slavonic **несть** (не + есть), means "is not".

After **нет, не было**, and the *negative in general*, the genitive is used, e.g. я знал уро́к, я не знал уро́ка.

§ 42. Notice the idiomatic construction of:

Меня́ не́ было до́ма. I was not at home.

Меня́ нет до́ма. I am not at home.

Я не до́ма, он не до́ма implies that I am *or* he is somewhere else, to be mentioned presently.

Exercises III *a*

A. 1. Есть у вас сестра́? Have you a sister?
2. Нет, у меня́ никогда́ не́ было сестры́. No, I never had a sister.
3. Это всё? Is that all?
4. Это не всё. That is not all.[1]
5. Не я пе́рвый, не я после́дний. I am neither first nor last.
6. В пе́рвый раз. For the first time.
7. До ве́чера. Till the evening.
8. Час но́чи (gen.). One o'clock in the morning.
9. Три часа́ дня (gen.). Three o'clock in the afternoon.
10. Что бы́ло, то бы́ло. What has been, has been.
11. Да бы́ло ли это? But did this happen?
12. Не́ были ли вы там? Were you not there?
13. А бы́ли вы там? And were you there?
14. Нет ли у вас? Have you not?
15. Мы ско́ро пообе́дали. We soon finished dinner.
16. Быть как до́ма. To make oneself at home.
17. Я тут как до́ма. I feel at home here.
18. У нас в до́ме. In our house.
19. Они обе́дали у нас. They dined with us.
20. Я был в апте́ке. I was at the chemist's.
21. Оди́н раз, когда́ я был там. Once, when I was there.
22. Он написа́л письмо́ по-ру́сски. He wrote the letter in Russian.
23. Я прочита́л эту кни́гу до обе́да. I finished this book before dinner.
24. Он рабо́тал два часа́. He was working for two hours.

B. 1. Есть у вас в ко́мнате стол? 2. Да, у меня́ есть стол и четы́ре сту́ла. 3. Где они обе́дали вчера́? 4. Они вчера́ обе́дали у нас. 5. Мы обе́дали в два часа́. 6. Что

---

[1] Note that это (this) is often used where English has "that".

вы де́лали всю неде́лю? 7. Мы рабо́тали в по́ле.
8. Сестра́ никогда́ не была́ на мо́ре. 9. У меня́ две
сестры́ и два бра́та. 10. А у вас? 11. Что у меня́ в
руке́? 12. У вас кни́га, а у меня́ перо́. 13. Она́ всегда́
обе́дала у нас раз в неде́лю. 14. Есть у вас брат?
15. Нет, у меня́ никогда́ не́ было ни бра́та, ни сестры́.
16. В ко́мнате не́ было сту́ла. 17. На столе́ бы́ли ла́мпа,
перо́ и бума́га. 18. Он чита́л по-ру́сски два часа́ в день.
19. Вот мой слова́рь. 20. Вчера́ у вас не́ было словаря́.
21. В кла́ссе нет ме́ла. 22. Что она́ сказа́ла? 23. Она́
сказа́ла: до свида́ния.

C. 1. There was a picture on the wall. 2. Did you see this
book? 3. Where did you see the doctor's sister? 4. I have never
seen the doctor's sister. 5. He was working the whole week.
6. After dinner I worked for two hours. 7. We have a lesson
three times a week. 8. Did you see this picture when you were
in Moscow? 9. Here is my old house. 10. Have you no pen?
11. No, I have no pen, but my brother has. 12. What is this on
the table? 13. This is not my book. 14. What were you doing
before (up till) dinner? 15. I wrote two letters before dinner.
16. Where did you see the doctor? 17. He was once at the
chemist's when I was working there. 18. There is a new chemist
in our town (see § 40). 19. Who said that I was not at home
yesterday? 20. And were you? 21. Yes, I was at home the
whole day. 22. This is all.

LESSON IV

Letters (3): ж, ш, х.

VOCABULARY

ходи́ть to go, to walk	шко́ла school
е́здить to go (not on foot)	ла́вка bench, little shop
гуля́ть to take a walk	изба́ hut
благодари́ть to thank	журна́л magazine
банк bank	каранда́ш pencil
парк park	пого́да weather
конто́ра office	хоро́ший good
теа́тр theatre	хорошо́ well, all right
рестора́н restaurant	плохо́й bad

плохо badly
русский, -ая Russian, a Russian
английский English
милый dear, "nice"
молодой, -ая, -ое young
англичанин Englishman
англичанка Englishwoman
господин gentleman, Mr
госпожа mistress, Mrs
дама lady
его[1] his, its, him; it (acc.)
её her, hers
их their, theirs, them

наш, наша, наше (see p. 14) our
ваш, ваша, ваше your
ничто, ничего[1] (gen.) nothing
только only
уже already
теперь now
давно long ago
долго a long time
сегодня[1] to-day
куда whither, where
никуда nowhere (motion)
туда thither, there
спасибо thank you
пожалуйста please

PRESENT TENSE.

§ 43. There are two conjugations in Russian, which differ only in the present tense:

	1st conjugation	2nd conjugation
	чита-ть	говор-ить
я	чита-ю	говор-ю
ты	чита-ешь	говор-ишь
он	чита-ет	говор-ит
она	„	„
оно	„	
мы	чита-ем	говор-им
вы	чита-ете	говор-ите
они	чита-ют	говор-ят

As a rule verbs of the 1st conjugation form their present tense from the infinitive by taking off the ending -ть, in which case the stem ends in a vowel. But sometimes the three last letters are taken from the infinitive, in which case the stem usually ends in a consonant. In such cases the consonant is often changed according to the demands of euphony, e.g. писать:

я пиш-у	мы пиш-ем
ты пиш-ешь	вы пиш-ете
он пиш-ет	они пиш-ут

(See chapter on Pronunciation, p. 15, and Part II, p. 207.)

Verbs of the 2nd conjugation always form their present tense

[1] Note that -го in the genitive of adjectives and pronouns is pronounced -во; сего is the gen. of сей (this).

by taking off the three last letters from the infinitive. The stem of these verbs thus usually ends in a consonant. Verbs in -дить and -деть change д into ж in the *1st person* singular *only*, e.g. ходить (see p. 17):

я хож-у́	мы хо́д-им
ты хо́д-ишь	вы хо́д-ите
он хо́д-ит	они хо́д-ят

ездить: я е́зжу, ты е́здишь, etc
видеть: я ви́жу, ты ви́дишь, etc.
сиде́ть: я сижу́, ты сиди́шь, etc.

§ 44. Verbs in -ать and -ять are 1st conjugation, *except* стоя́ть. (For further exceptions see p. 206.)

Monosyllabic verbs, with very few exceptions, are also 1st conjugation.

All verbs in -ить, *except* monosyllabic verbs, are 2nd conjugation. Also most verbs in -еть, as ви́деть, сиде́ть.

§ 45. The *imperative* is formed from the 2nd person singular of the present tense by changing the endings -ешь or -ишь into -й, -йте when the stem ends in a vowel, e.g.

чита́-й !	сто-й !
чита́-йте !	сто́-йте !

or into -и, -ите when the stem ends in a consonant, e.g.

говор-и́ ! говор-и́те !

§ 46. Здра́вствуйте, "how do you do", is the imperative of the verb здра́вствовать, "to keep well". The singular is здра́вствуй (see p. 16). Спаси́бо (thank you) contains the imperative of спасти́ (to save); *lit.* "God (Бог) save you" (cf. English "Good-bye").

§ 47. Куда́, "whither", "where"

In answer to the question "куда́?" to express *motion*, the accusative is used after the prepositions в and на, whereas to the question "где?" to express *state of rest*, the locative is used after the same prepositions (see § 4), e.g.

я ходи́л вчера в го́род, *or* в шко́лу (acc.).
я был вчера́ в го́роде, *or* в шко́ле (loc.).

§ 48. If the action is still going on, the present tense is used instead of the English perfect, e.g.

I have been here two hours.   Я здесь два часа́.

§ 49. **Его, её, их,** used as possessive pronouns, do not change when used before nouns of different genders, nor do they change by case, e.g.

егó брат	his brother
егó сестрá	his sister
у егó сестры́	at his sister's

§ 50. **Ничтó** (nothing) is usually used in its genitive case, **ничегó,** e.g.

На столé **ничегó** нет.   There is nothing on the table.

The reason is that "nothing" is usually used with another negative. But note these exceptions:

Ничтó не вéчно.   Nothing lasts for ever (eternal).

Ничто мне не мѝло.   Nothing pleases me (dear to me).

§ 51. When adjectives have a stem ending in a guttural, **г, к, х,** the endings seem to be mixed, hard and soft, but this is due to the rules of euphony (see p. 14), e.g. рýсский, рýсская, рýсское. If the stem ends in a sibilant, **ж, ч, ш, щ,** the endings, for the same reason, are **-ий, -ая, -ее,** e.g. хорóший, хорóшая, хорóшее. If an adjective has the accent on the ending, this ending in the masculine is **-óй,** e.g. молодóй, молодáя, молодóе.

§ 52. Feminine adjectives in **-ая** have their accusative in **-ую;** those in **-яя** have their accusative in **-юю,** e.g. рýсская, acc. рýсскую; послéдняя, acc. послéднюю.

§ 53. Adverbs are formed from adjectives by taking off **-ый** or **-ой** and adding **-о:**

хорóший	good	хорошó	well
плохóй	bad	плóхо	badly
скóрый	quick	скóро	quickly

§ 54. The impersonal expression "people say", "it is said", is rendered by **говоря́т,** e.g.

Говоря́т, что вас нé было дóма вчера.   They say that you were not at home yesterday.

The 3rd person plural of other verbs is used in the same way.

EXERCISES IV

A. 1. Что вы дéлали вчерá? What did you do yesterday?
2. Мы ходѝли в гóрод. We went to town.
3. Что вы дéлали весь день? Ничегó. What have you been doing all day? Nothing.

4. Вы давнó здесь? Have you been long here?
5. Нет, только час. No, only an hour.
6. Как дóлго вы гуля́ли вчерá? How long were you walking yesterday?
7. Что за погóда! (nom.). What weather!
8. Что это за гóрод? What sort of town is this?
9. На стенé ничегó нé было. There was nothing on the wall.
10. Он ничегó не сказáл. He said nothing.
11. Не ходи́те туда! Don't go there! — Хорошó. All right.
12. Я не знаю, хóдит ли он в театр. I don't know whether he goes to the theatre.
13. Говоря́т, что он никогда нé был в теáтре. They say he has never been to the theatre.
14. Не знаю, дóма ли она. I don't know whether she is at home.
15. Как хорошó она читает! How well she reads!
16. Хорошо говорит он по-рýсски? Does he speak Russian well?
17. Он никогда не говорит "пожáлуйста". He never says "please."
18. Он был там в пéрвый раз. He was there for the first time.
19. Я это в послéдний раз говорю́. I am saying it for the last time.
20. Егó нé было дóма. He was not at home.
21. Кто это играет на скри́пке? Who is that playing the violin?
22. Ездить на лóдке. To go in a boat.
23. Это очень ми́ло. This is very nice.
24. Она очень ми́лая. She is very nice.
25. Хорошо, что вы все ужé тут. It is nice that you are all here already.

B. 1. Он читáет по-рýсски. 2. Я ужé говорю́ по-англи́йски. 3. Мы гуля́ем в пóле. 4. Она хóдит в шкóлу. 5. Вы рабóтаете в контóре. 6. Стол стои́т в кóмнате. 7. Пóмните вы э́то слóво? 8. Я ви́дел его в словарé, но не пóмню его. 9. Что дéлает теперь вáша сестрá? 10. Она пи́шет письмо. 11. Кто этот молодóй господи́н? 12. Это наш учитель, он не рýсский, он англичáнин. 13. Ви́дели вы мою́ сестрý? 14. Я ви́дел её вчерá в теáтре. 15. Они никогдá не хóдят в театр. 16. Знáете вы э́ту англичáнку? 17. Нет, я ви́жу её в пе́рвый раз. 18. Вы всегда́ обе́даете в рестора́не? 19. Нет, то́лько иногда́. 20. Сего́дня хоро́шая пого́да, а вчера́ была́ плоха́я. 21. Говоря́т здесь по-ру́сски? 22. Нет, здесь никто́ не говори́т ни по-русски, ни по-англи́йски. 23. Чита́йте пожа́луйста ме́дленно! 24. Говори́те всегда́ по-ру́сски! 25. Не игра́й так ско́ро! 26. Куда́ вы ходи́ли вчера́? 27. Мы ходи́ли в теа́тр. 28. Где вы бы́ли сего́дня до обе́да? 29. Я был в шко́ле. 30. Понима́ете вы что я говорю́? 31. Я понима́ю всё, когда́ вы говори́те ме́дленно. 32. Не говори́те так ско́ро! 33. В избе́ сидя́т на ла́вке. 34. В го́роде магази́н, а в селе́ ла́вка. 35. Вы давно́ говори́те по-ру́сски? 36. Нет, то́лько оди́н год. 37. До́лго вы бы́ли в го́роде? Весь день. 38. Вчера́ мы ходи́ли гуля́ть в парк. 39. Они́ всегда́ гуля́ют в па́рке. 40. Я ви́жу их там два ра́за в неде́лю. 41. Вот ваш каранда́ш. 42. Спаси́бо. 43. Я всегда́ говорю́ "спаси́бо", а моя́ сестра́ говори́т "благодарю́ вас".

C. 1. My brother is in town now. 2. Where did he go yesterday? 3. He went to the office. 4. What are you doing here? 5. I am reading a newspaper. 6. Here is your magazine; read slowly, please. 7. Don't speak English in the class. 8. What do you see on the wall? 9. I am sitting at the table and I am writing a letter. 10. He does not know anything. 11. Mrs N. never goes to the theatre. 12. Do you know this English shop? 13. I never go to this shop. 14. What is the teacher saying? 15. He says that we write Russian well. 16. Where did you go on the boat to-day? 17. We went to a village on the Volga. 18. He has been doing nothing the whole day. 19. Please don't go anywhere to-day. 20. I do not understand when you read so quickly. 21. I do not know whether she goes to the bank. 22. I know him and her very well. I know them. 23. They speak Russian very badly. 24. I always thank him. 25. Does your brother speak Russian well? (Put "well" first, see A 16.) 26. Do you see this picture? This is a Russian picture. 27. Have you been here long? 28. No, only three weeks. 29. How do you do?

LESSON V

Letters (3): ц, щ, ф.

VOCABULARY

давáть to give	**мáсло** butter
отвечáть, на (+ acc.) to answer, reply to (a question)	**молокó** milk
	чай tea
отвечáть, за (+ acc.) to be responsible for	**кóфе** coffee
	винó wine
отвéт answer	**тарéлка** plate
любúть to love, like	**чáшка** cup
жить to live	**стакáн** glass
кусáть (кусáю) to bite	**нож** knife
кýшать to eat	**вúлка** fork
есть to eat	**лóжка** spoon
пить to drink	**салфéтка** serviette
зáвтракать to breakfast, lunch	**фунт** pound
ýжинать to sup, have supper	**кусóк** piece
зáвтрак breakfast, lunch	**отéц** father
ýжин supper	**сын** son
хлеб bread	**холóдный** cold
мáсо meat	**тёплый** warm
рýба fish	**горячий** hot
суп soup	**горéть** (2nd conj.) to burn (intr.)
щи (pl.) cabbage soup	
соль (f.) salt	**жáркий** hot (intangible)
сáхар sugar	**жáрить** to roast, fry

DECLENSION AND CASES.

§ 55. As Russian is an inflected language, its nouns change their endings according to their meaning in a sentence. This changing of the endings is called declension. It is not difficult to learn the endings when one has grasped the table of vowels, since hard endings always change into hard, and soft into soft (see §§ 27, 28).

There are *six cases* in Russian:

1. Nominative (case of the subject), e.g.   стол   брáт[1]
2. Genitive or possessive (transl. of the)   стол-á   брáт-а
3. Dative (transl. to the)   стол-ý   брáт-у
4. Accusative or objective (direct object)   стол   брáт-а[2]

[1] Masculine nouns terminating in a consonant have really no ending in the nominative (see p. 10); the endings of other cases are added to the stem.

[2] N.B. Like the genitive (see § 29).

5. Instrumental (transl. by the)   стол-о́м   бра́т-ом
6. Prepositional (i.e. the case which is never
   used without a preposition)   о стол-е́   о бра́т-е

The prepositional case may also be called the locative, because it mostly indicates *place* in answer to the question "where?" (see § 4). **О** means "about" (concerning); in some cases **об** (*or* **обо**) is used to facilitate pronunciation.

§ 56. Masculine and neuter nouns are declined alike, therefore **окно́** and all nouns in -о are declined like **стол**, changing the ending -о into -а, -у, etc. Masculine and neuter nouns with soft endings, i.e. nouns in -ь, -й, -ё, -е are declined like **стол**, except that the endings are soft (see table of vowels); e.g. **чай** changes -й into -я instead of -а in the genitive; into -ю instead of -у in the dative, and into -ем instead of -ом in the instrumental. The -е in the prepositional remains unchanged, being already soft. (For declension of all these words see tables, p. 236.)

§ 57. The *genitive case.* Apart from its proper meaning of "possession", the genitive case in Russian has its particular uses. Its use after the negative and certain numerals has already been pointed out in Lesson III*a* (see §§ 36, 41). The genitive is also used in a partitive sense, corresponding to the English "some", e.g.

Да́йте хле́ба.   Give me some bread.
Проси́ть воды́.   To ask for some water.

In such expressions some masculine nouns signifying mostly divisible matter take the endings -у and -ю instead of -а and -я, e.g.

ча́шка ча́ю   a cup of tea
кусо́к са́хару   a lump of sugar (see p. 238)

§ 58. The genitive is also used after certain prepositions, the commonest of which are **до, у, по́сле** (see Lesson III) and

без without   **из** out, from (a place)
для for (the sake of)   **от** from (a person) *or* farther from
(For others see p. 265.)

§ 59. **Оте́ц, кусо́к, день** lose the -о- or -е- in declension, thus:
Gen.   отца́, куска́, дня.
Dat.   отцу́, куску́, дню.
Instr.   отцо́м, куско́м, днём.
Prep.   об отце́, о куске́, о дне (see p. 238).

§ 60. The *dative case* should always be associated with the verb

дать (to give).[1] This will help in the use of this case after other
verbs, e.g. отвечáть (to answer) requires the dative in Russian
(to give an answer). For further examples see p. 269. With such
verbs the dative case is used alone, i.e. without a preposition, as
there is no *motion towards*, e.g. Я пишý письмó (acc.), брáту (dat.),
but when *motion towards* is indicated, the preposition к (to) must
be used as well, e.g.

   Я всегдá хожý к брáту. I always go to my brother's.

Only three prepositions govern the dative. К is the principal one
(see p. 265).

§ 61. The use of the accusative as the direct object is the same
as in any other language. For the use of the accusative with the
prepositions в and на see § 47, and with other prepositions, p. 266.

§ 62. The *instrumental case* is used without a preposition when
a noun or pronoun is used in the sense of an *instrument* or *agent*, e.g.

   Я пишý перóм. I write with a pen (i.e. by means of a pen);

but it requires the preposition с (with) when "with" means *along
with*, e.g.

   Я гулял с брáтом. I was walking with my brother.

The instrumental case is the *adverbial* case in Russian, i.e. a noun
is used in the instrumental case to form an adverbial expression, e.g.

     ýтром in the morning
     лéтом in summer
     днём during the day (see p. 262)

§ 63. The use of the *prepositional case* as a locative has been
pointed out in § 4. For other prepositions governing this case see
p. 266.

§ 64. *Verbs*.

пить: Present: я пью, ты пьёшь,[2] он пьёт, мы пьём, вы пьёте,
   они пьют.

   Imperative: пей, пéйте.

(For other verbs like пить see p. 207.)

жить: Present: живý, живёшь, живёт, etc.

любить: Present: люблю, любишь, любит, etc. (p. 209).

давáть: Present: даю, даёшь, даёт, etc.

   Imperative: дай, дáйте.

but in the negative: не давáй, не давáйте.

---

[1] As in Latin, the name of this case, дáтельный, is derived from the word
дать. Дать is the perfect infinitive of давáть and means "to have given".

[2] When e in the ending is accented it becomes ё (yo).

EXERCISES V

A. 1. Не кушайте мяса без соли.   Do not eat meat without salt.
2. Не давайте брату чаю.   Do not give your (or my) brother tea.
3. Дайте мне (dat.) пожалуйста хлеба.'   Please give me some bread.
4. Этот суп из рыбы.   This is fish soup.
5. Он пьёт чай из стакана.   He drinks tea out of a glass.
6. Он не пьёт вина.   He does not drink wine.
7. Я очень люблю кофе.   I am very fond of coffee.
8. Её все любят за её доброту (acc., see p. 266).   Everyone likes her for her kindness.
9. Посмотрите в окно!   Look at the window!
10. Она смотрела из окна.   She was looking out of the window.
11. Эта книга для сестры.   This book is for the sister.
12. Они живут у отца.   They live with their father (i.e. at his house).
13. Она живёт с братом.   She lives with her brother (i.e. not necessarily at his house).
14. Мы ходили к брату.   We went to our brother's.
15. Они были у брата.   They were at their brother's.
16. Что вы даёте отцу?   What are you giving your father?
17. Вы не отвечаете на вопрос.   You are not answering the question.
18. Вы не на вопрос отвечаете.   Your answer is wrong.
19. Никто за это не отвечает.   No one is responsible for this.
20. Летом все ходят без пальто.   In summer no one wears a coat.
21. Сегодня вечером.   This evening, to-night.
22. Сегодня утром.   This morning.
23. Вчера вечером.   Yesterday evening, last night.
24. На моё письмо не было ответа.   There was no reply to my letter.

B. 1. Обед на столе.   2. Кусок хлеба.   3. Стакан молока.   4. Фунт масла.   5. Тарелка супу (gen.).
6. Окно дома.   7. Он отвечает брату.   8. Мы ездили в село.   9. Они ездят из города в город.   10. После урока они ходили гулять.   11. Кто сидит у окна?   12. Я пишу пером.   13. Он гуляет с братом.   14. Чай без молока.
15. Три часа утра.   16. Она кушает мясо без хлеба.
17. У нас нет масла.   18. Дайте хлеба.   19. В комнате

один стол и два сту́ла. 20. Этот стака́н для вина́.
21. Эта ча́шка для ко́фе. 22. Сын е́здит к отцу́ в Ло́н-
дон. 23. Здесь все говоря́т о пого́де. 24. Что вы пьёте
ве́чером? 25. Лю́бите вы горя́чее молоко́? 26. Я
никогда́ не пью молока́. 27. На столе́ нет хле́ба.
28. Да́йте, пожа́луйста, салфе́тку. 29. Вот его стака́н.
30. Брат очень лю́бит жа́реную (fried) ры́бу.

C. *Decline:* хлеб, мя́со, чай, по́ле, питьё, геро́й (hero), отец,
учи́тель, день.

D. 1. The father's son. 2. The brother's book. 3. To ask for
bread. 4. A piece of meat. 5. Two lumps of sugar. 6. A cup
of tea. 7. A pound of fish. 8. After dinner. 9. At the brother's.
10. He goes to his father's. 11. From London. 12. From
father. 13. We go from village to village. 14. Eat, please.
15. He eats bread without butter. 16. I drink milk in the
morning. 17. Where do you go in the evening? 18. In the
morning I stay at home. 19. What do you do during the day?
20. He never eats meat. 21. He does not like meat. 22. He is
eating cold soup. 23. They all take wine. 24. When do you have
supper? 25. We have dinner in the evening; we never have
supper. 26. We have a cold supper to-day. 27. He was at (his)
sister's, but he did not see you. 28. They had supper in our
house. 29. I had no breakfast to-day. 30. Where is my big
spoon? 31. Give (me) a plate of soup, please. 32. Here is your
serviette.

LESSON V*a*

хоте́ть to want	ка́ша porridge
пи́ща food	фру́кты (pl.) fruit
вку́сный tasty, good	о́вощи (pl.) vegetables
скажи́! скажи́те! say, tell (im-	ещё still, more
perative)	ещё не not yet

§ 65. The dative of я, мы, вы is мне, нам, вам:

Мне хо́лодно.   I am cold.
Мне тепло́.   I am warm.

Хо́лодно and тепло́ are by form like adverbs, but in these expressions are neuter predicative adjectival forms, i.e. adjectives with
the abbreviated endings (see p. 248). Мне хо́лодно literally means
"it is cold to me", hence the neuter ending -о. Observe, however,

that "it" is never used in such expressions, the sentence usually
beginning with the word indicating place or time, e.g.

Здесь хóлодно.	It is cold here.
В кóмнате теплó.	It is warm in the room.

§ 66. The commonest prepositions which govern the instrumental case are:

над	over	за	behind
под	under	пéред	in front of

all four showing position, e.g. над столóм, под стýлом, etc.

За with the instrumental case also means "for" (after), e.g.

Он всегдá хóдит за хлéбом.　　He always goes to fetch the bread

Note also the *following*:

	at table	за столóм
	at dinner	за обéдом
but	at dinner time	в обéд (acc.)
	for dinner	на обéд (acc.)

e.g. что у нас сегóдня на обéд?　what have we for dinner to-day?

bread and butter	хлеб с мáслом
to speak to	говорúть с (instr.)

but **он говорúл мне** means "he was saying to me".

§ 67. "To take tea", "to have tea" is rendered by **пить чай.**
Similarly "to take meat", by **кýшать** *or* **есть мя́со.**

§ 68. The verb **есть** (to eat) is more regularly used in conversation than **кýшать,** which is mostly used in the second person,
whereas in the 1st person **есть** must be used, e.g.

я не ем мя́са.　　I don't eat meat.

This verb is one of the very few irregular verbs:

Present:	я ем	мы едúм
	ты ешь	вы едúте
	он ест	они едя́т

Past: ел, éла, éли

Imperative: ешь, éшьте

§ 69. Another irregular verb (though only in the present) is
хотéть (to want).

Present tense

Sing. (1st conj.)	Plur. (2nd conj.)
я хочý	мы хотúм
ты хóчешь	вы хотúте
он хóчет	они хотя́т

Observe the changed stem in the singular (see p. 207).

Exercises V*a*

A. 1. Он говори́л с учи́телем.   He spoke to the teacher.
 2. Скажи́те мне!   Tell me!
 3. Не говори́те мне!   Don't tell me!
 4. Мне никто́ не говори́л.   Nobody told me.
 5. Что мне де́лать?   What am I to do?   (Infin. with dative.)
 6. Он не говори́л мне, что не́ был там.   He did not tell me he was not there.
 7. Он сказал, что вас не́ было до́ма.   He said that you were not at home.
 8. Мне о́чень жа́рко.   I am very hot.
 9. В ко́мнате хо́лодно.   It is cold in the room.
 10. Вчера́ тут бы́ло тепло́.   It was warm here yesterday.
 11. Сего́дня не так хо́лодно.   It is not so cold to-day.
 12. Что у нас сего́дня на у́жин?   What have we for supper to-night?
 13. Кто хо́дит за бра́том в шко́лу?   Who brings your brother from school?
 14. Я пью то́лько одну́ ча́шку ча́ю.   I take only one cup of tea.
 15. Дава́ть "на чай".   To give a tip.
 16. Этот нож мой, а тот для вас.   This knife is mine, and that one is for you.
 17. Благодарю́ за ва́шу хлеб-соль.   I thank you for your hospitality.
 18. Быть, как ры́ба в воде́.   To be in one's element.
 19. Быть без куска́ хле́ба.   To be without a crust of bread (i.e. very poor).
 20. Он ещё не обе́дал.   He has not dined yet.
 21. Хоти́те ещё?   Do you want some more?
 22. Щи да ка́ша—пи́ща на́ша. (Погово́рка.)   Cabbage soup and porridge is our fare.
 23. Я пью чай без са́хара.   I don't take sugar in tea.
 24. Я хочу́ есть.   I am hungry.
 25. Он хо́чет ку́шать.   He is hungry.
 26. Мы о́чень хоти́м пить.   We are very thirsty.
 27. Как вку́сно!   How good it tastes!

B. 1. Вот стол.   2. Мы сиди́м за столо́м.   3. Мы обе́даем.   4. На столе́ хлеб, ма́сло, мя́со и ры́ба.   5. За обе́дом мы еди́м суп, мя́со, ры́бу, о́вощи и фру́кты.

6. Отец пьёт за обедом вино.   7. Что вы пьёте утром? 8. Я пью кофе, а отец любит пить чай.   9. Он пьёт чай с сахаром и с молоком.   10. У нас в доме никто не ест мяса утром.   11. За завтраком мы едим рыбу.   12. Что у нас на ужин сегодня?   13. Дайте мне пожалуйста хлеба.   14. Когда мы живём в городе, мы всегда обедаем вечером.   15. Утром они кушали хлеб с маслом и пили кофе.   16. Я ем мясо только два раза в неделю. 17. Сегодня очень тепло.   18. Мы не любим есть рыбу, когда так тепло.   19. В три часа она всегда пьёт чашку чаю.   20. Холодно вам здесь?   21. Нет, мне не холодно. 22. Вчера здесь было очень жарко.   23. Мой брат живёт в школе.   24. У нас в школе хорошая пища. 25. Дайте мне воды, пожалуйста, я очень хочу пить. 26. Вы очень хотите кушать.   27. Вот фрукты и хлеб с маслом, а молока у нас нет.

C. 1. I love.   2. You give (sing.).   3. He lives.   4. They live. 5. We eat.   6. You eat.   7. They drink.   8. She was having breakfast.   9. You had no supper.   10. Who answers?   11. He is responsible for this.   12. She is thirsty.   13. Are you hungry? 14. Are you cold?   15. I am warm.   16. Eat, please.   17. Tell me, please. 18. Don't tell us. 19. What do you want? 20. I don't want anything.   21. Who wants?   22. They want to have supper.

D. 1. She always takes a cup of tea at four o'clock in the morning.   2. At lunch she takes fish, but she never takes meat. 3. At dinner the father takes wine, but the son has only milk. 4. Yesterday after dinner we went to the theatre.   5. It was very hot there.   6. We had tea in town to-day.   7. Do you take sugar in your tea?   8. We never take tea after dinner. 9. Here is your knife and fork; eat, please! 10. Would you like some more?   11. I have not yet finished (съел) what I have on my plate.   12. This glass is for milk, and that one is for wine. 13. Do you like cabbage soup?   14. He drinks tea out of a glass. 15. Don't drink water at dinner.   16. Please give me a plate of soup and a piece of bread.   17. In the evening she likes to take warm milk.   18. It is very cold in the room.   19. It is warm here now, but yesterday it was very cold.   20. She does not like to

give tips.   21. Who told you that the lamp does not burn?
22. Father told me that he saw you in the theatre.   23. Don't
drink cold water when you are hot.   24. At dinner they always
spoke Russian.   25. What do you want to eat to-day?   26. I do
not want to eat anything; I am only thirsty.

LESSON VI

слушать to listen
слышать to hear
петь to sing
пение singing (noun)
песня song
чтение reading (noun)
уметь to know how, be able
ум mind
умный clever
объяснять to explain
ясный clear
сад garden
дерево tree
деревня village
пол floor
потолок ceiling
угол corner, angle
весна, весной spring, in spring
лето, летом summer, in summer
осень (f.), осенью autumn, in autumn
зима, зимой winter, in winter
земля earth, land

экскурсия excursion
карман pocket
дверь (f.) door
ключ key, clue
дед, дедушка grandfather
бабушка grandmother
дядя uncle
тётя aunt
девушка, девица young girl
девочка little girl
мальчик boy
маленький small, little
хорошенький pretty
красивый beautiful
красный red (fig. beautiful)
ученица pupil (f.)
учительница teacher (f.)
тетрадь (f.) copy-book
птица bird
гнездо nest
Россия Russia
Англия England
Шотландия Scotland
Франция France

§ 70. Declension of *feminine* nouns.

	Hard		Soft			
Nom.	комнат-а		ня́н-я		ноч-ь	ли́ни-я (line)
Gen.	,, ы		,, и		,, и	,, и
Dat.	,, е		,, е		,, и	,, и
Acc.	,, у		,, ю		,, ь	,, ю
Instr.	,, ой (ою)[1]		,, ей (ею)		,, ью	,, ей (ею)
Prep.	о ,, е	о ,, е	о ,, и	о ,, и

[1] The endings -ой, -ою; and -ей, -ею are interchangeable.

In the declension of feminine nouns it should be observed that the endings of **ня́ня** are similar to those of **ко́мната**, only the former are soft, i.e. **-и** occurs instead of **-ы**, **-ю** instead of **-у**, and **-ей** instead of **-ой**. The **-е** of the dative and prepositional remains unchanged.

In the declension of nouns in **-ь** the endings are all soft and vary little. The same applies to nouns in **-я** with a preceding **и**.

§ 71. The prepositional case of feminine nouns in **-ь** and **-ия** and also of neuter nouns in **-ие**, which are very few (see tables), has the ending **-и** instead of **-е**. This must be especially noted in the names of countries, e.g.

в Росси́и	in Russia
в А́нглии	in England
в Шотла́ндии	in Scotland
во Фра́нции	in France, etc. (see p. 236)

§ 72. The prepositional case of certain masculine nouns (mostly monosyllabic) is in **-у́** (always accented) instead of **-е**, after the prepositions **в** and **на**, e.g. в саду́, на полу́, на углу́ (at the corner), в углу́ (in the corner). In **у́гол** (and **потоло́к**) the **-о-** is lost in declension (see § 59).

§ 73. The verb **уме́ть** (to be able, know how, 1st conjugation) means "to be able *mentally*" (cf. French *savoir*). Note the logical connection between the words **ум** (mind), **у́мный** (clever), and **уме́ть** (to know how). Groups of related words such as this are very important in Russian word-building, and will be pointed out when space permits; **я́сный** and **объясня́ть** provide another example.

§ 74. Adjectives are often formed from nouns by the endings **-ый**, **-ий**, or **ой**, joined to the stem by the suffix **-н-**, as **у́м-н-ый**, **зи́м-н-ий** (see Grammar, p. 253).

§ 75. **Слу́шать** (to listen) is 1st conjugation; *but* **слы́шать** (to hear) is 2nd conjugation, therefore the present tense is **слы́шу**, **слы́шишь**, etc. **Петь** has the present tense **пою́**, **поёшь**, etc.

§ 76. The verb **учи́ть** means both "to teach" and "to learn". **Учи́ть** (to teach) requires the dative case of the subject taught, e.g.

Я учу́ сестру́ (acc.) чте́нию и письму́.

I am teaching my sister reading and writing.

(чте́ние, reading; письмо́, writing *as well as* letter.)

§ 77. **Дéдушка** (grandfather) is masculine, although it ends in -a. It is declined as a feminine noun, but adjectives qualifying it have masculine endings, e.g. дóбрый дéдушка. Another such word is **дáдя** (uncle). (For others see p. 233.)

§ 78. Nouns used in a diminutive sense are formed by various suffixes, and mostly keep their gender endings. Thus, masculine diminutive nouns end in -ик, -ок, these endings being added to the stem, e.g. дóм-ик, сын-óк.

Feminine diminutives end in -ка or -ица, e.g.

> сумá (bag), dim. сýмка.
> рукá (hand), dim. рýчка.
> ногá (foot), dim. нóжка.
> сестрá, dim. сестрúца.

The ending -ка replaces -a, but in words like **рукá, ногá**, the г and к of the stem change into ж and ч respectively, according to the rules of the permutation of consonants (see p. 17).

Neuter diminutives end mostly in -ышко, e.g.

> перó (feather), пёрышко.
> гнездó (nest), гнёздышко.
> сóлнце (sun), сóлнышко.

More about diminutives will be found in the Grammar, p. 234.

Russian adjectives can also be used in a diminutive sense; the ending is -енький, which takes the place of the endings -ый, -ой, -ий, e.g.

> хорóший, dim. хорóшенький.
> ýмный, dim. ýмненький.

Мáленький (small) exists only in the diminutive form.

EXERCISES VI

A. 1. Кто эта дéвочка? Это моя́ сестрá.   Who is this little girl? She is my sister.
2. Онá пéрвая ученúца в клáссе.   She is the best pupil in the class.
3. Она ýмница.   She is a good girl.
4. Ваш брат ýмница (see p. 233).   Your brother is very gifted.
5. Он очень ýмненький мáльчик.   He is a very clever little boy.
6. Крáсная дéвица.   A beautiful girl.

7. Кра́сное со́лнышко. Radiant sun (affectionately).
8. Со́лнышко, со́лнышко, вы́глянь в око́шечко! "Dear little sun, look out of your window." (Children's rhyme.)
9. Тепе́рь всё я́сно. Everything is clear now.
10. Э́то я́сно. This is clear.
11. Я́сный день. A fine (clear) day.
12. На не́бе я́сно. The sky is clear.
13. Говори́те, я вас слу́шаю. Speak, I am listening.
14. Слу́шать ле́кцию. To attend a lecture.
15. Слу́шатели. The audience.
16. Слу́шатель. One of the audience, a student.
17. Слу́шай! Послу́шай! Послу́шайте! Listen!
18. Как краси́во поёт э́та пти́чка! How prettily this little bird sings!
19. Я люблю́ слу́шать, когда́ она́ поёт. I like to listen to her singing.
20. Я слы́шал её весно́й. I heard her sing in spring.
21. Слы́шали вы Шаля́пина? Have you heard Chaliapine?
22. Я учу́ пе́нию (dat.). I teach singing.
23. Он не уме́ет петь. He cannot sing.
24. Я уме́ю чита́ть по-ру́сски. I can read Russian.
25. Мы с сестро́й бы́ли в теа́тре. My sister and I were at the theatre.
26. Где ключ от ко́мнаты? Он в двери́. Where is the key of the room? It is in the door.
27. Да́йте мне кни́гу для чте́ния. Give me a book to read.

B. 1. Есть у вас ба́бушка? 2. У меня́ нет ни ба́бушки, ни де́душки. 3. Э́та молода́я де́вушка[1] его́ сестра́. 4. Э́тот ма́ленький ма́льчик пе́рвый учени́к в шко́ле. 5. Я хожу́ к тёте два ра́за в неде́лю. 6. Бы́ли вы в Росси́и? 7. Нет, я никогда́ не́ был в Росси́и. 8. Когда́ ваш дя́дя е́здил в Росси́ю? 9. Он е́здил туда́ ле́том с экску́рсией. 10. Что вы де́лаете ле́том? 11. Ле́том мы рабо́таем в саду́ и в по́ле. 12. Уме́ете вы чита́ть по-ру́сски? 13. Я уме́ю чита́ть и писа́ть, но не говори́ть. 14. У нас в шко́ле но́вая учи́тельница пе́ния. 15. Она́ о́чень хорошо́

[1] The adjectives молодо́й, ста́рый are never used with the words де́вочка, ма́льчик.

поёт. 16. Слу́шаете вы, когда учи́тельница объясня́ет урок? 17. Да, я всегда́ слу́шаю. 18. У вас очень хо́ро́шенькая сестра́. 19. Она́ очень у́мненькая де́вочка. 20. Учи́тельница говори́т, что э́та учени́ца тепе́рь очень хорошо́ чита́ет. 21. Ва́ша учи́тельница ру́сская? 22. Да, она́ из Москвы́. 23. Слы́шали вы, как поёт эта ма́ленькая пти́чка? 24. Мы слушали её весно́й в саду́; у неё (§ 95) там на де́реве гнездо́. 25. В углу ко́мнаты стои́т ма́ленький сто́лик. 26. Не ви́дели ли вы ключа́ от са́да? 27. Не в две́ри ли он? 28. Я ви́дел его́ утром на полу́ у две́ри. 29. Бы́ли вы во Фра́нции? 30. Да, я е́здила во Фра́нцию два ра́за.

C. 1. You are explaining. 2. We are listening. 3. Listen, please! 4. She was not listening. 5. They sang. 6. He does not hear. 7. I did not hear. 8. Do you hear? 9. We hear nothing. 10. He is singing. 11. They sing. 12. Can you read? 13. She cannot write. 14. A kind uncle. 15. My old grandfather. 16. In the garden. 17. In the corner. 18. At the corner. 19. In Scotland. 20. In England. 21. Our clever uncle. 22. His little sister.

D. 1. Who is this old lady? 2. She is my aunt. 3. Can she speak Russian? 4. Has she been in Russia? 5. Yes, she went there in autumn with an excursion. 6. When did you go to France? 7. I have never been in France. 8. What do you do in the evening in winter? 9. I stay at home and read. 10. Can you read Russian? 11. Yes, but I always read with a dictionary. 12. Is your teacher Russian? 13. No, she is English, but she speaks Russian very well. 14. Your little sister is the best pupil in the class. 15. She is a very clever little girl. 16. And she is very pretty. 17. We have a big garden. 18. We like to sit in the garden in spring. 19. Do you hear the little bird sing? 20. It sings very beautifully. 21. Did you see its little nest in the garden? 22. There are two little birds in the nest. 23. They sing the whole summer. 24. Where is the key of (from) the house? 25. It is not in the door. 26. It is in my pocket. 27. Do you know this Russian song? 28. No, I have never heard it. 29. Everyone sings it in Russia. 30. This is a very pretty song.

LESSON VII

Verbs of "going" and "carrying", etc., are dealt with in this
lesson, but are not listed separately in the vocabulary.

по́езд train
по́ездом (instr.) by train
пое́здка trip
трамва́й tram-car
трамва́ем (instr.) by tram
носи́льщик porter
чемода́н trunk
экипа́ж carriage
автомоби́ль (m.) motor-car
пальто́ coat
костю́м costume, suit
шля́па hat
ша́пка cap
пла́тье dress
кало́ши goloshes
зо́нтик umbrella
дождь (m.) rain

снег snow
библиоте́ка library
му́зыка music
домо́й home (homewards)
нигде́ nowhere
сюда́ hither
отсю́да hence
отту́да thence
отку́да whence
ча́сто often
ре́дко seldom
за́втра to-morrow
ка́ждый every, each
большо́й (-а́я, -о́е) big
зи́мний winter (adj.)
ле́тний summer (adj.)
носи́ть to wear
и́ли or

VERBS "TO GO".

§ 79. As has already been mentioned, there is only one present
tense in Russian. Thus я чита́ю means both "I read" and "I am
reading". There is no progressive form in Russian. But all verbs
which indicate an action of "going" have two forms, or rather
there are two verbs: one means *to go*, and the other *to be going*.
The former simply *describe* an action, while the latter imply that
the action is performed with a definite *purpose*. A distinction is
also made between *going on foot* and any other way, i.e. by vehicle,
boat, train, etc.; these verbs will be clearly seen and understood
from the following tables.

$$\text{on foot} \left\{ \begin{matrix} \text{ходи́ть} \\ \text{идти́} \end{matrix} \right. \underbrace{ \qquad\qquad\qquad } \left. \begin{matrix} \text{е́здить} \\ \text{е́хать} \end{matrix} \right\} \text{not on foot}$$

to go

to be going

§ 80. A similar table can be made for the verbs which literally mean *to carry* or *to convey*, if not actually walking. In English, however, these verbs are usually rendered by "to take".

to carry

when on foot $\left\{ \begin{array}{ll} носи́ть & вози́ть \\ нести́ & везти́ \end{array} \right\}$ when not on foot

to be carrying

§ 81. The verb води́ть (to lead) has also a corresponding verb вести́ (to be leading). In English these verbs can be translated by "to conduct", or again by "to take".

To take a person by train is the same as to take things by train, therefore to express both these meanings the same verbs, вози́ть and везти́, are used.

Since the understanding and proper use of these verbs is very important they are introduced thus early and are often referred to.

§ 82. For the present tense of ходи́ть and е́здить see Lesson IV. The present tense of носи́ть, вози́ть, води́ть is similar to that of ходи́ть (see Permutation of Consonants, p. 17), e.g.

> ношу́, но́сишь, etc.
> вожу́, во́зишь, etc.
> вожу́, во́дишь, etc.

The present tense of :

> идти́ : иду́, идёшь, идёт, идём, идёте, иду́т.
> е́хать : е́ду, е́дешь, е́дет, е́дем, е́дете, е́дут.
> нести́ : несу́, несёшь, несёт, etc.
> везти́ : везу́, везёшь, etc.
> вести́ : веду́, ведёшь, etc.

§ 83. The past tense of the verbs which correspond to the progressive form (*except* е́хать) is irregular :

> идти́   Past tense: шёл, шла, шло, шли.
> нести́   нёс, несла́, несло́, несли́.
> везти́   вёз, везла́, везло́, везли́.
> вести́   вёл, вела́, вело́, вели́.

All verbs in -сть and -сти have a past tense of this type (see p. 208).

§ 84. Носи́ть (to wear), not being a "going" verb, has no other form, i.e. it also means *to be wearing*, e.g.

Она́ всегда́ но́сит э́то платье.   She always wears this dress.

To express actual *wearing*, other expressions are used, e.g.

> На ней (see p. 256) бы́ло бе́лое пла́тье.
> She was wearing a white dress (*lit.* on her was).

or   Она́ была́ в костю́ме.
> She was wearing a costume.

Similarly **ходи́ть** when it means "to walk" also means *to be walking*, e.g.

Он хо́дит по ко́мнате.   He is walking up and down the room.

§ 85. The verb **идти́** means *to be actually on the way*, e.g.

> Ви́дели вы меня́, когда́ я шёл в шко́лу?

In the present tense it may be used instead of the near future, just as in English, e.g.

> Я иду́ сего́дня ве́чером в теа́тр.
> I am going to the theatre to-night.

So also with **е́хать**:

> Я е́ду в Росси́ю ле́том.
> I am going to Russia in summer.

Идти is also used in the sense of *to be coming*, e.g.

Поезд идёт! The train is coming!   Иду́! I am coming!

and, idiomatically, of *to suit*, e.g.

Это пла́тье мне не идёт.   This dress does not suit me.

Similarly **нести́, везти́, вести́**, may be used in the sense of *to be bringing*.

Exercises VII

A. 1. Мы с бра́том.   My brother and I.
    2. Вы с сестро́й.   You and your sister.
    3. Иди́ домо́й!   Go home!
    4. Не ходи́те в дом!   Don't go into the house!
    5. Не иди́ так ско́ро!   Don't go so quickly!
    6. Иди́те сюда́!   Come here (hither).
    7. Кто это идёт?   Who is this coming?
    8. Я иду́ домо́й.   I am going home.
    9. Ча́сто вы хо́дите в теа́тр?   Do you often go to the theatre?
  10. Нет, но я иду́ сего́дня ве́чером. No, but I am going this evening.
  11. Куда́ вы ходи́ли вчера́?⎫ Where were you (did you go)
  12. Где вы бы́ли вчера́?   ⎭ yesterday?
  13. Как ско́ро идёт наш по́езд!   How quickly our train is going!
  14. Я иду́ к до́ктору.   I am going to see the doctor.

15. Куда́ вы шли, когда́ я ви́дела вас? Where were you going when I saw you?
16. Я иду́ отсю́да домо́й. From here I am going home.
17. По́езд идёт отту́да. The train comes from there.
18. Мы е́здим в го́род по́ездом. We go to town by train.
19. Куда́ вы е́дете и что везёте? Where are you going and what are you taking? (Spoken, e.g., in a train.)
20. Вези́те меня́ домо́й. Take me home.
21. Веди́те меня́; я ничего́ не ви́жу. Lead me, I cannot see.
22. Она́ ведёт де́вочку за́ руку. She is leading the little girl by the hand.
23. Что он везёт в го́род? What is he taking to town?
24. Носи́льщик несёт чемода́н. The porter is carrying the trunk.
25. Он никогда́ не хо́дит без зо́нтика. He never goes without an umbrella.
26. Когда́ идёт дождь, он но́сит кало́ши. When it rains he wears goloshes.
27. Вчера́ шёл снег. It was snowing yesterday.

B. 1. Куда́ вы идёте? 2. Я иду́ в шко́лу. 3. Куда́ она́ ходи́ла вчера́ по́сле обе́да? 4. Она́ ходи́ла гуля́ть в по́ле. 5. Ча́сто вы е́здите в Ло́ндон? 6. Оте́ц е́здит ка́ждый год, а мы с сестро́й о́чень ре́дко. 7. Брат е́здил в Ло́ндон весно́й, когда́ там пел Шаля́пин. 8. Он и тётю вози́л; она́ о́чень лю́бит му́зыку и пе́ние. 9. Я ви́дел вас, когда́ вы шли в библиоте́ку. 10. Куда́ вы ведёте ва́шу ма́ленькую сестру́? 11. О́сенью мы всегда́ е́здим в Шотла́ндию. 12. Когда́ я е́ду в по́езде, я люблю́ смотре́ть в окно́. 13. Я ви́дела её из окна́ трамва́я. 14. Она́ е́хала в автомоби́ле и везла́ большо́й чемода́н. 15. Что он несёт в руке́? 16. Вчера́ весь день шёл дождь. 17. Они́ всю зи́му сиде́ли до́ма; никуда́ не ходи́ли и не е́здили. 18. В А́нглии о́чень ре́дко идёт снег. 19. Но дождь идёт иногда́ ка́ждый день. 20. О́сенью никто́ не хо́дит без зо́нтика. 21. Не ви́дели ли вы носи́льщика? 22. Вот он идёт и несёт ва́ши два чемода́на. 23. Куда́ идёт э́тот по́езд? 24. Э́тот по́езд в

Глазго.   25. Он носит этот костюм только зимой.
26. Сегодня после чая я иду в школу, а оттуда в театр.

C. 1. He goes to school in the morning.   2. She is not going
to town to-day.   3. Where are you going?   4. What is he carrying?
5. We are going to the theatre by tram to-day.   6. Are you going
by tram or in a car?   7. Where are you going in winter?   8. I always
go to London in winter.   9. I am taking this letter to (my) sister.
10. The doctor is taking my sister to London.   11. We went to
Russia in summer.   12. Who is that going with the little girl?
13. It is our teacher; she is taking the little girl to school.   14. My
sister goes alone (одна); she is big now.   15. Did you see our house
when you were going to the office?   16. I did not go to the office
to-day.   17. Yesterday I was alone in the office.   18. I do
not like to go by tram.   19. What do you wear when you go
to the theatre?   20. In winter he wears a cap, and in summer a
hat.   21. This is her summer hat.   22. What do you carry in
(your) pocket?   23. There is the porter; he is taking the trunk
into the house.   24. She never goes without a coat.   25. This is
his winter coat.   26. Do you often go to London?   27. Yes, I go
there every year.

LESSON VIIa

летать to fly
аэроплан aeroplane
вокзал station (building)
станция station
улица street
фабрика factory
завод mill
базар bazaar

рынок market
двор yard, court
почта post, post-office
почтальон postman
прямо straight (adv.)
близко near
далеко far ⎫ all with
недалеко not far ⎭ от + gen.

§ 86. Different renderings of English *to* and *at*.

"To", meaning "into", is в with the accusative, e.g. я иду в
школу.

"To", meaning "towards", is к with the dative, e.g. я иду к
окну.

§ 87. "At", meaning "in", is translated by в, e.g.

I was at the theatre; at school.   Я был в театре; в школе.

But with certain words на is used in Russian instead of в. These words usually *stand for* a place rather than actually being *the name* of a place, e.g. на уро́ке, на конце́рте (at a concert), на ле́кции (at a lecture). Also, на у́лице, на по́чте, на ста́нции, на заво́де, на фа́брике, на ры́нке.

The same preposition is used with the accusative case to express *motion*, e.g. Я иду́ на уро́к, на по́чту, на рабо́ту (to my work).

§ 88. With the same nouns the preposition **с** (off) is used instead of **из** (from), and requires the same case as **из**, i.e. the genitive, e.g.

She is coming from the lesson.

Она́ идёт с уро́ка, с по́чты, с фа́брики, с у́лицы, etc.

§ 89. **Лета́ть** (to fly) and **лете́ть** (to be flying) are used in exactly the same way as **ходи́ть** and **идти́**.

For other verbs of this type, i.e. "going" verbs, see Grammar, p. 224.

Лете́ть is 2nd conjugation, therefore the stem **лет-** in the present tense changes т into ч and has -у in the 1st person singular (see p. 17), я лечу́, ты лети́шь, etc.

Exercises VIIa

A. 1. Мы живём недалеко́ от ста́нции. We live not far from the station.
2. Далеко́ от вас до по́чты? Is it far from your house to the post-office?
3. Он идёт со ста́нции. He is coming from the station.
4. Мы идём на ры́нок. We are going to market.
5. Я несу́ письмо́ на по́чту. I am taking a letter to the post.
6. Он вози́л о́вощи на ры́нок. He used to take vegetables to market.
7. Я иду́ за мя́сом. I am going to buy meat.
8. Мы идём пря́мо домо́й. We are going straight home.
9. На у́лице хо́лодно. It is cold outside.
10. На дворе́ дождь и снег. It is raining and snowing (outside).
11. Идти́ со двора́. To go out.
12. Лета́ли вы на аэропла́не? Have you been up in an aeroplane?
13. Мы е́дем на мо́ре. We are going to the sea-side.
14. Эта доро́га ведёт на ста́нцию. This road leads to the station.
15. Вам далеко́ идти́? Have you far to go?
16. Я пря́мо с вокза́ла. I have come straight from the station.
17. Это его́ ста́рый чемода́н. This is an old trunk of his.

В. 1. Когда вы хо́дите на уро́к, утром или ве́чером? 2. Я всегда́ хожу́ утром, но сего́дня иду́ ве́чером. 3. Ча́сто хо́дит ва́ша сестра́ в теа́тр? 4. Мы все очень ре́дко хо́дим в теа́тр. 5. Лю́бите вы е́здить в автомоби́ле? 6. Мы вчера́ е́здили в го́род на ло́дке. 7. Что э́то он несёт в руке́? 8. Он всегда́ но́сит зо́нтик. 9. Сего́дня весь день идёт дождь, а у меня́ нет зо́нтика. 10. Он везёт бра́та в Ло́ндон к до́ктору. 11. Он е́дет в автомоби́ле, а не по́ездом. 12. Я не люблю́ е́здить в по́езде ле́том. 13. Носи́льщик несёт чемода́н на ста́нцию. 14. Не вози́те сестру́ сего́дня в теа́тр. 15. Он вёз ры́бу на база́р. 16. Когда́ я шла в конто́ру, я ви́дела но́вый магази́н. 17. Зимо́й он но́сит тёплый костю́м. 18. Она́ всегда́ носи́ла ле́том бе́лое пла́тье. 19. Почтальо́н несёт моё письмо́ на по́чту. 20. Тепе́рь они́ на мо́ре; они́ е́дут в Росси́ю. 21. Куда́ лети́т эта пти́ца? 22. Тепе́рь осень, она́ лети́т туда́, где всегда́ тепло́. 23. Ле́том мы лета́ли на аэропла́не. 24. Я ви́дел вас на у́лице сего́дня; куда́ вы шли? 25. Я шла на ры́нок за ры́бой. 26. В Росси́и зимо́й ча́сто идёт снег.

C. 1. Father goes to school in the evening. 2. We never go to London in winter. 3. I do not like to go to the theatre during the day. 4. We are going to the theatre in a car. 5. Are you taking this book to the library? 6. He always goes without a coat. 7. I am going to the market this morning. 8. We always take fruit and vegetables to the market. 9. Did you see fruit at the market to-day? 10. No, only vegetables were there to-day. 11. He was going to the factory when I was going to the office. 12. His sister was standing in front of the post-office and was speaking to the postman. 13. I saw her when I was taking a letter to the post. 14. This street leads to the station. 15. They live very near the mill. 16. The market is not far from the post-office. 17. We go there every day. 18. Both his brother and his sister are working in the factory. 19. The little boy is leading (his) grandfather to the post-office. 20. There is a letter for him at the post-office. 21. What does she wear when she goes to the market? 22. She wears an old hat and (old) coat. 23. Where are you taking your sister in summer? 24. We are taking her to the sea-side.

LESSON VIII

держа́ть to hold, keep	тако́й of that kind, such
лежа́ть to lie	кото́рый which
принадлежа́ть to belong	второ́й second
спать to sleep	тре́тий third
посте́ль (f.) bed	четвёртый fourth
пье́са play (theatre)	пять, пя́тый five, fifth
сце́на stage (theatre)	шесть, шесто́й six, sixth
ме́сяц month	семь, седьмо́й seven, seventh
луна́ moon	во́семь, восьмо́й eight, eighth
число́ date	де́вять, девя́тый nine, ninth
пра́вда truth	де́сять, деся́тый ten, tenth
поправля́ть to correct	оди́ннадцать, -атый eleven,
пра́вильный correct	eleventh
пра́вый right	двена́дцать, -атый twelve,
ле́вый left	twelfth
бе́дный poor	че́тверть (f.) quarter
бога́тый rich	полови́на half
си́ний blue	полчаса́ half an hour
како́й of what kind, what	мину́та minute

Дни неде́ли (days of the week). Monday is considered the first day:

понеде́льник, вто́рник, среда́, четве́рг, пя́тница, суббо́та, воскресе́нье.

Ме́сяцы го́да (months of the year):

янва́рь, февра́ль, март, апре́ль, май, ию́нь, ию́ль, а́вгуст, сентя́брь, октя́брь, ноя́брь, дека́брь.

The names of days and months are written with a small letter. All names of months are masculine.

DECLENSION OF ADJECTIVES.

§ 90. *Declension of adjectives in the masculine and neuter*, and of the *personal pronoun* он.

An adjective agrees with the noun which it qualifies in gender, number and case. Just as masculine and neuter nouns are declined alike, so with adjectives, in all cases except the nominative. The ending -ый is considered hard because the first vowel is hard. The endings of the other cases therefore also begin with a hard vowel, which changes into a corresponding soft vowel in words having the soft ending -ий (both vowels soft). It must further be noticed that the declension of the pronoun **он** repeats itself in the soft endings of the adjectives in -**ий**; the declension of **он** is therefore placed alongside. (See the table of declension of adjectives and pronouns in the Grammar, p. 244, and compare the endings.)

	Hard	Soft	
Nom.	нóв-ый (ое)	сúн-ий (ее)	он (онó)
Gen.	,, ого	,, его	егó
Dat.	,, ому	,, ему	емý
Acc.	Like nom. *or* gen.		егó
Instr.	,, ым	,, им	им
Prep.	о ,, ом	о ,, ем	о нём

Note that the accusative of masculine adjectives is like the genitive when it qualifies the names of animate beings (cf. § 29).

§ 91. Adjectives with the stem ending in a guttural г, к, х, as **русский**, are declined like **новый**, *except* in the instrumental case, which is **рýсским** (see p. 246). Adjectives with the stem in a sibilant, ж, ч, ш, щ, as **горячий**, are declined like **синий**. Adjectives in -**ой**, as **молодóй** and **большóй**, are declined like **новый**, *except* that the endings are accented, e.g. молодóго, молодóму, etc. The instr. of большóй is большúм (see p. 14).

§ 92. *Declension of adjectives in the feminine,* and of the *personal pronoun* **онá.**

	Hard	Soft	
Nom.	нóв-ая	сúн-яя	онá
Gen.	,, ой	,, ей	её
Dat.	,, ой	,, ей	ей
Acc.	,, ую	,, юю	её
Instr.	,, ой (ою)[1]	,, ей (ею)	ей (éю)
Prep.	о ,, ой	о ,, ей	о ней

As in the masculine, the feminine ending -**ая** is considered hard, and -**яя** soft. The declension of **онá** may be compared with the soft endings of **синяя**. The only differences are in the genitive and accusative.

§ 93. **Рýсская** and other adjectives with the stem ending in a guttural are declined like **новая**. **Горя́чая** and others with the

---

[1] The endings -**ой**, -**ою** (and -**ей**, -**ею**) in the instrumental are interchangeable, as in the case of nouns (see p. 236). An adjective and noun coming together should both have the same ending, e.g. доброй сестрóй *or* доброю сестрою.

stem ending in a sibilant are declined like **синяя**, *except* in the accusative, which is **горячую** (see p. 14).

§ 94. Мой, твой, наш, ваш are declined in all genders like **синий, -яя, -ее**. The stems are **мо-, тво-, наш-, ваш-**. The accusative feminine ends in **-ю** or **-у**.

§ 95. When a personal pronoun is preceded by a preposition **н-** is affixed to it, as in **о нём, о ней**. This rule applies to all prepositions, cf.

с **ним**	with him	с **ней**	with her
у **него**	he has	у **неё**	she has
к **нему**	to him	к **ней**	to her

§ 96. Ordinal numerals are adjectives, and are declined according to their endings. **Третий** is declined like **лисий** (see p. 247). For the remaining numerals see Lesson XX and the Grammar (p. 257).

§ 97. Expressions of *time*:

Час. One o'clock.

Два часа. Two o'clock.

Половина третьего. Half past two (i.e. half of the third).

Четверть четвёртого. Quarter past three (i.e. a quarter of the fourth).

Пять часов. Five o'clock.

Без четверти шесть
Три четверти шестого $\Big\}$ Quarter to six.

Десять минут седьмого. Ten minutes past six.

Без двадцати пяти восемь. Twenty-five minutes to eight.

Без четверти в девять. At a quarter to nine.

Половина десятого. At half past nine (*or* 9.30).

Одиннадцатый час. After ten o'clock.

Ровно двенадцать. Exactly twelve o'clock.

Note that after the numerals **пять, шесть**, etc., the genitive plural is used. The genitive plural of **час** is **часов**; of **минута, минут**.

§ 98. The relative pronoun **который** (which) is used instead of **кто** (who) when the antecedent is a noun; but if the antecedent is a pronoun, **кто** is used,[1] e.g.

	Мальчик, который говорил.	The boy who spoke.
but	Тот, кто говорил.	He who was saying.

[1] Subordinate clauses. introduced by **который** or **кто** are preceded by a comma, cf. pp. 159, 160, 212.

Что may be used as a relative pronoun meaning "that", "who" or "which", e.g.

Всё, что лежит здесь, моё. Everything that is lying here is mine.

§ 99. The verbs держáть, лежáть, принадлежáть, спать are 2nd conjugation.

Present tense:

> держý, дéржишь, etc.
> лежý, лежúшь, etc.
> сплю, спишь, etc. (see p. 18).

EXERCISES VIII

A. 1. В котóром часý вы обéдаете? At what time do you dine?
2. В час. At one o'clock.
3. Котóрый тепéрь час? Мои часы стоят. What time is it now? My watch has stopped.
4. Семь часóв. Seven o'clock.
5. Какóе сегóдня числó? What is the date?
6. Пятое февраля. The 5th of February.
7. В какóй день у вас рýсский урóк? What day do you have your Russian lesson?
8. В понедéльник, в срéду, и в пятницу. On Monday, Wednesday, and Friday.
9. Котóрого числá вы éдете в Москвý? Пятого мáрта. On what date are you going to Moscow? On the 5th of March.
10. Сегóдня пéрвое мáя. To-day is the first of May.
11. Какóй сегóдня день? Суббóта. What day is it? Saturday.
12. Какáя хорóшая погóда! What fine weather!
13. У неё в кóмнате нет столá. She has no table in her room.
14. Кто эта дáма, что сидúт у окнá? Who is that lady sitting at the window?
15. Éздить зá город.[1] To go out of town.
16. Мы жúли зá городом.[1] We used to live out of town.
17. Я здесь живý ужé вторóй год. This is my second year here.
18. Мы идём в кино (indecl.). We are going to the cinema.
19. Прáвда ли это? Is that true?
20. Его часы всегдá идýт прáвильно. His watch is always right.
21. Кто он такóй? Who is he?
22. Что такóе? What is it?
23. Что это такóе? What is this?

[1] See § 318 for expressions with accent on a preposition.

B. 1. У меня́ на столе́ лежи́т но́вая ру́сская кни́га.
2. Чита́ли вы после́днюю пье́су Шоу? 3. Нет, но я
ви́дела её на сце́не (on the stage). 4. В понеде́льник
всегда́ даю́т но́вую пье́су. 5. Вто́рник второ́й день
неде́ли, а среда́ тре́тий. 6. Кто э́тот ста́рый господи́н,
что говори́т с на́шим учи́телем? 7. Э́то его́ оте́ц. 8. У
него́ очень бога́тый де́душка. 9. Большо́й но́вый дом на
ва́шей у́лице принадлежи́т ему́. 10. Ско́лько (§ 109) часо́в
в день вы спи́те? 11. Я сплю во́семь часо́в и во́семь
часо́в рабо́таю. 12. Что вы де́лаете, когда́ вы не рабо́-
таете? 13. Я гуля́ю, чита́ю, до́ма и́ли в библио́теке, и
иногда́ хожу́ в кино́. 14. В како́й день вы хо́дите в
библио́теку? 15. В како́й руке́ вы де́ржите перо́, когда́
вы пи́шете? 16. Как ви́дите, я пишу́ ле́вой руко́й.
17. Я не уме́ю писа́ть пра́вой. 18. В суббо́ту она́ всё
утро игра́ла с ма́леньким бра́том. 19. В воскресе́нье,
когда́ хоро́шая пого́да, мы всегда́ е́здим за́ город.
20. Како́е пла́тье она́ но́сит тепе́рь ка́ждый день?
21. Вчера́ я ви́дел её в но́вом си́нем пла́тье. 22. Мы
е́дем в Ло́ндон в сентябре́. 23. Кака́я была́ пого́да,
когда́ вы бы́ли там в после́дний раз? 24. Ка́ждый день
шёл дождь. 25. Пра́вда э́то, что он уже́ втору́ю неде́лю
лежи́т в посте́ли? 26. Пра́вда. 27. Вчера́ я попра-
вля́ла тетра́ди до оди́ннадцати (gen.) часо́в. 28. Таку́ю
большу́ю рабо́ту вы мне да́ли.

C. *Translate and decline:* Russian teacher. Russian book.
Russian word. Hot day. Hot stove (печь f.). Golden pen. Kind
boy. Poor girl. Big field. Our old house. Old lady. Old tree.
Blue pencil. My blue hat. Blue sea. Small window. Your big
room.

D. 1. What was the weather like yesterday? 2. It was raining
yesterday, but it is clear to-day. 3. On the second of January
we are going to London. 4. When we go to London we go to the
theatre every day. 5. She reads Russian three hours a day.
6. Where were you in April? 7. What do you keep in the little

room? 8. We keep fruit and vegetables there. 9. Who lives in his big house? 10. His rich grandmother. 11. At what time do you dine when you live in town? 12. We always dine at seven o'clock, and on Sunday at one. 13. Where are you going on Friday night? 14. My sister and I are going to the pictures. 15. You have never been in our new theatre. 16. I always have two or three pencils lying on the table, but I do not like writing with a blue pencil. 17. What are you doing this morning? 18. I am going for a walk (идти гулять) with my old uncle. 19. When are you taking your little brother to the doctor? 20. I do not know a good doctor here. 21. On what day do you have your lesson? 22. I have a lesson every day. 23. In hot weather he likes to lie under a tree. 24. The rich often do not understand the poor (use sing.). 25. What is the date to-day? 26. Yesterday was the eighth, and to-day is the ninth of January. 27. What does she wear in winter? 28. When I saw her last (time) she had a black dress on. 29. Everybody in town is speaking about a new play which is being given on Monday. 30. This is a Russian play.

LESSON IX

продавать to sell
покупать to buy
вставать to get up
стоить to cost, be worth
желать (+gen.) to wish
желание wish
мне надо I need
должен, должна, -но, -ны must, has or have to
должно быть it must be
покупатель customer, buyer
купец merchant
продавец salesman
покупка purchase, parcel
цена price
копейка copeck
рубль (m.) rouble
платок, -тка handkerchief
нужный necessary

больше bigger, more
великий great
дорогой, дорого expensive, dear
недорогой, -ого inexpensive
дешёвый, дёшево cheap
рано early
поздно late
слишком too (much)
лишний superfluous, extra
тоже ⎫
также ⎭ too, also
почему why
потому что because
поэтому therefore
сколько how much, many
много much, many
мало little, few
немного a little

PREDICATIVE ADJECTIVES.

§ 100. The *predicative* form of adjectives, used when an adjective helps to form a predicate as a complement, has the same endings as nouns, e.g.

The house is old.	Дом стар.
The book is old.	Книга старá.
The pen is old.	Перо старó.

This form is also called the *abbreviated* form.

§ 101. When the stem of an adjective ends in two consonants, as холóдный, -e- or -o- is inserted between these two consonants in the abbreviated form of the *masculine*, e.g. хóлоден, *but* холоднá, хóлодно.

§ 102. Adverbs formed from adjectives of quality have the same ending as the neuter abbreviated form, e.g. хóлодно means "coldly" (adv.); and also "is cold", in the expressions здесь хóлодно, мне хóлодно, etc. (see p. 262).

§ 103. The adjectives большóй and мáленький are not used predicatively, but instead the adjectives велúкий (great) and мáлый are used, e.g.

This house is too big.	Этот дом слúшком велúк.
This hat is too small for me.	Эта шляпа мне малá.

Хорóш, хорошá means (*is*) *beautiful, fine, good,* etc., e.g.

Как хорошá она былá вчерá!
How beautiful she looked yesterday!

§ 104. The predicative form of какóй is какóв, -овá, -овó, -овы́ (derived from the rare form каковóй), e.g.

А каковá погóда? Погóда не плохá.
And what is the weather like? Not bad.

§ 105. The abbreviated form may almost always be replaced by the full form, e.g.

This house is old *or* an old one.
Этот дом старый ("one" is understood).

More about the abbreviated forms will be found in the Grammar, p. 248.

§ 106. Нýжно is the abbreviated form of the adjective нýжный or нýж-д-ный (needful, necessary), from the word нуждá (need, want) (see the formation of adjectives from nouns, p. 253).

Мне нужно, "I need" or "it is necessary to me", e.g.

Мне нужно идти.   I have to go.

Надо has the same meaning:

Мне надо *or* нужно много читать.   I need to read a great deal.

But when "I need" is followed by an object, the following construction is used:

I need a table.   Мне (dat.) нужен стол (nom.).

I do not need them.   Мне они не нужны.

The predicative adjective thus agrees with the true subject of the Russian construction.

§ 107. **Я должен, она должна, мы должны,** etc., may also mean "I owe", "she owes", "we owe", etc., e.g.

Я должен вам (dat.).   I owe you.

Она должна мне.   She owes me.

The past tense is:

Я был должен.   I owed.

but   Я должен был.   I *had to.*

Долг means "debt" as well as "duty" (see p. 17).

§ 108. The declension of **кто** and **что** must be specially noted, though the endings are on the whole similar to the usual adjectival endings, except as regards the instrumental. This is also true in the case of **этот** (see p. 256).

			Masc. and neut.	Fem.
Nom.	кто	что	этот, это	эта
Gen.	кого	чего	этого	этой
Dat.	кому	чему	этому	этой
Acc.	кого	что	as nom. or gen.	эту
Instr.	кем	чем	этим	этой
Prep.	о ком	о чём	об этом	об этой

Тот, то is declined like **этот,** except in the instrumental, which is **тем** (cf. **кем**); **та** throughout like **эта**; **весь, вся** (see p. 245).

§ 109. After **много, мало,** and **сколько** the genitive singular is used when these words mean "much", "little" and "how much", and the genitive plural when the meaning is "many", "few" and "how many", e.g.

много хлеба   much bread

мало часов   few hours

сколько раз (gen. pl.)?   how many times?

Бо́льше is the comparative of both большо́й and мно́го. Comparatives are treated in Lesson XV.

§ 110. The particle же means "also" and is often used for emphasis, e.g.

желаю вам того́ же   I wish you the same
тепе́рь же   immediately
сего́дня же   this very day

§ 111. The verbs продава́ть and встава́ть are conjugated like дава́ть, deleting -ва- in the present tense: продаю́, продаёшь; встаю́, встаёшь, etc.

EXERCISES IX

A. 1. Ско́лько это сто́ит? Два рубля́. How much does this cost? Two roubles.

2. Почему́ так дёшево? Why so cheap?

3. Это сли́шком до́рого. This is too dear.

4. Это ничего́ не сто́ит. It costs nothing.

5. Не сто́ит благода́рности. Don't mention it.

6. Не сто́ит с ним говори́ть. It is not worth while speaking to him.

7. Сто́ит! It is worth it!

8. У меня́ нет ни копе́йки. I haven't a halfpenny.

9. Я до́лжен был идти́. I had to go.

10. Я был до́лжен ему́ три рубля́. I owed him three roubles.

11. Ско́лько я вам до́лжен? How much do I owe you?

12. Вы не должны́ э́того говори́ть. You must not say that.

13. Этот дом должно́ быть сто́ит до́рого. This house must cost a great deal.

14. Его́ должно́ быть нет до́ма. He must be out.

15. У него́ всё до́рого. Everything he has is expensive.

16. Он говори́т, что это его́ долг. He says it is his duty.

17. У меня́ нет долго́в (gen. pl.). I have no debts.

18. Что вам на́до? What do you want?

19. Мне ничего́ не на́до. I need nothing.

20. Так ему́ и на́до. It serves him right.

21. Вам нужна́ эта газе́та? Do you require this newspaper?

22. Мне бо́льше не на́до. I don't need any more.

23. Я бо́льше не хочу́. I don't want any more.

24. Он бо́льше не хо́дит в шко́лу. He no longer goes to school.

25. Желаю вам до́брой но́чи (gen.). I wish you good-night.

26. И вам того́ же.   I wish you the same.
27. Споко́йной но́чи! (gen.).   Good-night!
28. Ра́но или по́здно.   Sooner or later.
29. Какова́ была́ у вас зима́ во Фра́нции?   What sort of winter did you have in France?
30. Она́ така́я ми́лая!   She is such a dear!
31. Он не зна́ет цены́ э́той кни́ги (gen.).   He does not know the price of this book.
32. Никто́ не знает цены́ э́той кни́ге (dat.).   No one knows *the value* of this book.

B. 1. Мне ну́жен ру́сский уче́бник.   2. Я иду́ в кни́жный магази́н.   3. Я покупа́ю кни́гу, каку́ю мне на́до, потому́ что она́ сто́ит недо́рого.   4. А ско́лько она́ сто́ит? Четы́ре рубля́.   5. Он бо́льше не хо́дит в теа́тр, потому́ что он до́лжен мно́го рабо́тать тепе́рь.   6. Уже́ по́здно, мне на́до идти́.   7. Почему́ вы должны́ идти́ так ра́но?   8. Потому́ что я живу́ с сестро́й, и она́ дома одна́ (alone).   9. Что продаю́т в этом магази́не?   10. Всё, что жела́ете; вчера́ я ви́дела там очень ре́дкую карти́ну.   11. Эта карти́на сли́шком дорога́.   12. Она́ та́кже сли́шком велика́ для мое́й ко́мнаты.   13. Ско́лько сто́ит ру́сский рубль тепе́рь?   14. Когда́ мы е́здили в Росси́ю, нам дава́ли шесть рубле́й за фунт.   15. Это о́чень ма́ло.   16. Но там мы покупа́ли очень мно́го на фунт (with a pound).   17. Копе́йка сто́ит очень немно́го.   18. Эта ко́мната сли́шком мала́.   19. В ней очень жа́рко ве́чером.   20. Когда́ мне нужна́ но́вая шля́па, я всегда́ хожу́ покупа́ть с сестро́й.   21. Я не люблю́ покупа́ть ничего́ сли́шком дешёвого.   22. В како́м карма́не вы де́ржите плато́к? 23. Всегда́ в пра́вом карма́не пальто́. 24. Тепе́рь должно́ быть по́здно.   25. Мой долг сказа́ть вам это.   26. Я зна́ю, что вы должны́ рано встава́ть.   27. У меня́ нет жела́ния никуда́ идти́.   28. У вас есть всё, что вам на́до.

C. 1. I get up.   2. She used to get up.   3. We are getting up.

4. Do you need them? 5. What do you wish? 6. I must.
7. She must. 8. We had to. 9. You must not. 10. What do
you sell? 11. I need a book. 12. You need a pen. 13. She
does not need them. 14. He is too big. 15. She is too small.
16. Much bread. 17. Little sugar. 18. A little salt. 19. How
many hours? 20. Why do you not sell? 21. Because I don't
want (to). 22. Does he not buy? 23. Do you not need this?
24. I need nothing. 25. He owes me. 26. We owe him.

D. 1. Do you need this book? 2. Yes, I want to read it to-
night. 3. She must read Russian every day, because she reads
badly. 4. This hat must cost a great deal. 5. This coat is too
big for her. 6. I don't need this dress, it is too old. 7. Why
don't you buy anything at this merchant's? 8. I no longer go to
his shop, because everything he has is very dear. 9. I have only
one wish now; I want to speak Russian well. 10. It is not worth
writing to her; she does not remember me. 11. About what were
you speaking at the lesson? 12. Is it expensive to live in Russia
now? 13. Everybody says that it is very expensive. 14. I do
not know whether it is true. 15. How much do I owe you?
16. You owe me nothing. 17. It must be late, I have to go.
18. Don't go, it is not late yet. 19. Here is your parcel. 20. Carry
it carefully! (осторо́жно). 21. With whom are you going?
22. This merchant is a very good salesman. 23. He always tells
me that I am an old customer of his. (See Ex. VII a, A 17.)
24. I wish you good-night. 25. Thank you; I wish you the same.

LESSON X

боле́ть to be ill, ache
больно́й ill (adj.), patient (noun)
я бо́лен, -льна́ I am ill
больни́ца hospital
здоро́вье health
здоро́вый well, healthy
я здоро́в, -а I am well
я нездоро́в, -а I am unwell
здоро́ваться с (+ instr.) to greet
мыть (мо́ю, мо́ешь) to wash
мы́ться to wash oneself
умыва́ться to wash the face

мы́ло soap
одева́ть to dress
надева́ть to put on
одева́ться to dress oneself
переодева́ться to change one's
  clothes
пла́кать to weep, cry
голова́ head
язы́к tongue, language
нра́виться to please
смея́ться (над + instr.) to laugh
  (at)

учи́ться to study

изуча́ть to study (trans.)

встреча́ть to meet

встреча́ться to meet one another

проща́ть to forgive

проща́ться to take leave, say good-bye

проща́й, -те good-bye

бледне́ть to turn pale

бле́дный pale

красне́ть to blush, grow red

чёрный black

лу́чше better

совсе́м altogether, quite

отчего́ for what reason? why?

оттого́ что for the reason, because of

§ 112. The declension of personal pronouns of the 3rd person has already been given together with that of adjectives (see Lesson VIII). The declension of the 1st and 2nd persons, and of the reflexive pronoun себя́ (oneself), follows:

	Singular		Plural		
Nom.	я	ты	мы	вы	(none)
Gen.	меня́	тебя́	нас	вас	себя́
Dat.	мне	тебе́	нам	вам	себе́
Acc.	меня́	тебя́	нас	вас	себя́
Instr.	мно́ю (о́й)	тобо́ю (о́й)	на́ми	ва́ми	собо́ю (о́й)
Prep.	обо мне	о тебе́	о нас	о вас	о себе́

§ 113. The reflexive pronoun себя́ has no nominative, as it is never a subject. It is used of all persons, singular and plural.

REFLEXIVE VERBS.

§ 114. Reflexive verbs in Russian have the ending -ся after the usual endings -ть, -ти, -чь of the infinitive, e.g.

> мы́ться   to wash oneself
>
> одева́ться   to dress

This -ся is really a short form of the reflexive pronoun себя́ (oneself) which is used for all persons. Thus

> мыть + себя = мыться
>
> одевать + себя = одеваться

In exceptional cases себя́ may be found used separately, e.g.

> Он одевает себя.   He pays for his own clothes.

Present tense of одева́ться

я одева́юсь	мы одева́емся
ты одева́ешься	вы одева́етесь
он одева́ется	они одева́ются

Past tense

одева́лся, одева́лась, одева́лись

Note that after a vowel -ся is further shortened to -сь. (The soft sign must not be omitted.)

§ 115. Not all verbs in -ся are reflexive verbs. Such verbs as здоро́ваться, встреча́ться (to meet one another) are called reciprocal verbs (cf. French *se rencontrer*, and see Grammar, p. 229). These, and all verbs in -ся, are conjugated like одева́ться.

§ 116. The verb встреча́ть is used in the same way as any other transitive verb, e.g.

Я встреча́ю его́.   I meet him.

But встреча́ться, здоро́ваться and проща́ться require the preposition с with the instrumental case, e.g.

Мы встреча́емся с ним.   He and I meet.

Я здоро́ваюсь с ней.   I say "how-do-you-do" to her.

Они́ до́лго проща́лись с ва́ми.

They took a long time to say good-bye to you.

§ 117. A common verb in -ся is нра́виться (to please); present: нра́в-л-юсь, нра́вишься, etc. (see p. 209). Its use in the following construction must be specially noted.

Эта карти́на мне нра́вится.   I like this picture.

Эти карти́ны мне нра́вятся.   I like these pictures.

The object in English becomes the subject in Russian, and the English subject is put in the dative. This construction is mostly used in the 3rd person, singular and plural. Я нра́влюсь им means "I please them" *or* "They like me" (see p. 18).

§ 118. The difference between я люблю́ and мне нра́вится is the same as between "I love" and "I like". Мне нра́вится is usually used when the object is discussed for the first time, e.g.

Эта карти́на мне нра́вится.   I like this picture; it appeals to me.

But я люблю́ эту карти́ну can be used if the picture is widely known or if one is accustomed to it.

§ 119. Verbs in -еть, like красне́ть, formed from adjectives, are 1st conjugation (see p. 207). Беле́ть means "to seem white", черне́ть, "to appear black", etc.

The verb **болѣ́ть** may be either 1st or 2nd conjugation, and has different meanings accordingly. **Я болѣ́ю, ты болѣ́ешь**, etc., means "I am ailing", e.g.

> Я ча́сто болѣ́ю.   I am often ill.

When **болѣ́ть** is 2nd conjugation, it is used only in the 3rd person and means "aches", e.g.

> У меня́ голова́ боли́т.   I have a headache.

§ 120. The present tense of **смѣя́ться** is **смѣю́сь, смѣёшься**, etc., **-я-** being deleted to avoid the occurrence of three vowels in succession.

Пла́кать has the present tense: пла́чу, пла́чешь, etc. (see p. 207).

Изуча́ть must have a direct object, e.g.

> Что он изуча́ет?   What is he studying?

Учи́ться also means "to go to school" (see Exercise A).

§ 121. **То...то...** means "now...now...", e.g.

Она то пла́чет, то смѣётся.   Now she cries, now she laughs.

Exercises X

A. 1. Отчего́ она́ така́я блѣ́дная? Она́ поблѣднѣ́ла от бо́ли
   (боль, f.). Why is she so pale? She has grown pale from pain.
   2. Она́ ча́сто краснѣ́ет. She often blushes.
   3. Что у вас боли́т? What ails you?
   4. Я была́ нездоро́ва. I was unwell.
   5. Она́ ча́сто болѣ́ет. She is often ill.
   6. У меня́ боли́т зу́бы (teeth). I have toothache.
   7. У меня́ боли́т нога́. My foot is sore.
   8. Как ва́ше здоро́вье? How are you?
   9. Спаси́бо, хорошо́. Very well, thank you.
  10. Вам лу́чше сего́дня? Are you better to-day?
  11. Я не совсѣ́м здоро́ва. I am not quite well.
  12. Здоро́вались вы с отцо́м? Have you said "good morning"
   to your father?
  13. Я не проща́юсь с ва́ми. I am not saying good-bye (to you).
  14. Я не люблю́ с ним встрѣча́ться. I do not like meeting him.
  15. Как вам нра́вится э́та кни́га? How do you like this book?
  16. Как вам нра́вятся э́ти карти́ны? How do you like these
   pictures?
  17. Мнѣ ничего́ не нра́вится. I don't like anything.

18. Мне они очень нравятся.   I like them very much.
19. Они ему очень не нравятся.   He dislikes them very much.
20. Вы нравитесь моей тёте.   My aunt likes you.
21. Я нравлюсь вашей тёте.   Your aunt likes me.
22. Они то плачут, то смеются.   Now they weep, now they laugh.
23. Чему смеётесь? Над собой смеётесь! (Гоголь.)   What are you laughing at? You are laughing at yourself!
24. Не смейтесь надо мной!   Do not laugh at me!
25. Он учится в хорошей школе.   He is at a good school.
26. Где учится ваш брат?   What school does your brother attend?
27. Сегодня не учиться!   No school to-day!
28. Он очень долго одевается.   He takes very long to dress.
29. Она всегда переодевается после работы.   She always changes after her work.
30. Он лежит в больнице.   He is in hospital.
31. Сидеть в тюрьме (nom. тюрьма).   To be in prison (cf. Eng. "lie").

B. 1. Как здоровье вашего отца?   2. Спасибо, очень хорошо.   3. Почему вы не были вчера на уроке?   4. Я был болен и должен был сидеть дома.   5. Знаете вы больницу, где лежит его тётя?   6. Да, это очень хорошая больница.   7. Я знаю доктора в этой больнице.   8. Он нездоров и должен идти домой.   9. Он любит умываться холодной водой.   10. Вы должны мыть руки горячей водой с мылом.   11. Они не умывались сегодня, потому что в доме не было воды.   12. Каждое утро она должна одевать сестру.   13. Моя маленькая сестра очень долго одевается.   14. Почему вы не надеваете вашего нового платья?   15. Я не люблю его.   16. Нравится вам мой новый костюм?   17. Мне больше нравился ваш старый.   18. Почему плачет эта маленькая девочка?   19. Она не хочет со мной прощаться.   20. А здоровалась она с вами сегодня?   21. Нет, она никогда не здоровается и не прощается.   22. Она то бледнеет, то краснеет: она должно быть нездорова.   23. Нет, сегодня ей лучше.

24. Часто вы встречаете моего дядю? **25.** Мы с ним встречались в клубе (club) каждый четверг. **26.** Теперь я его нигде больше не встречаю.

C. 1. I have a headache. 2. She is ill. 3. He was ill. 4. They were ill. 5. I am better. 6. Are you better? 7. I am washing myself. 8. Did you wash yourself? 9. They are dressing. 10. What are you putting on? 11. I put on a coat. 12. She was dressing. 13. She is crying. 14. They were crying. 15. I never cry. 16. Do you like this? 17. I like this book. 18. He likes them. 19. Good-bye. 20. I greet you. 21. They greet me. 22. She is blushing. 23. She turns pale. 24. I study. 25. They study. 26. He studied. 27. I am not laughing. 28. They laughed. 29. I am saying good-bye to you.

D. 1. I like this book very much. 2. I am very fond of this book. 3. They are very fond of fruit. 4. She does not like this fruit. 5. Why do you not like her? 6. How are you to-day? 7. I am quite well, thank you. 8. I was ill the whole week. 9. I had a headache every day. 10. Are you better now? 11. Much better, thanks. 12. I never meet your uncle; where is he now? 13. He is in the hospital; he is very ill. 14. I have a sore arm. 15. I never put on this coat; it is too small. 16. Why do you take so long to dress yourself? 17. I like to dress slowly. 18. Do you often meet our teacher? 19. I used to meet him every Friday in the theatre. 20. I never spoke to him; we only said how-do-you-do. 21. What school did you go to? 22. I have not been to school. 23. We had a governess (гувернантка); my sister and I had lessons at home. 24. We studied English with her. 25. The little girl was crying. 26. She did not want to have her face washed in the morning. 27. Now she is laughing at herself. 28. I am not saying good-bye to you. 29. Did he see you putting on (your) coat? 30. I must go now, Good-bye!

LESSON XI

In the list overleaf verbs which have been used in previous lessons are given with their perfect infinitive (i.e. together with their perfective aspect).

Verbs which have their perfect infinitive formed by the addition of the prefix по-:

Imperfective aspect		*Perfective aspect*
говори́ть	to speak	поговори́ть
смотре́ть	to look	посмотре́ть
спать	to sleep	поспа́ть

similarly:

слу́шать to listen to
сиде́ть to sit
стоя́ть to stand
лежа́ть to lie
ходи́ть to walk, go
идти́ (perf. пойти́) to be going
е́здить to go (not on foot)
е́хать to be going (not on foot)
лета́ть to fly
лете́ть to be flying
носи́ть to carry
нести́ to be carrying
вози́ть to convey
везти́ to be conveying
води́ть to lead

вести́ to be leading
гуля́ть to go for a walk
рабо́тать to work
держа́ть to hold
жела́ть to wish
благодари́ть to thank
здоро́ваться to greet
нра́виться to please
люби́ть to love
за́втракать to breakfast
обе́дать to dine
у́жинать to sup
красне́ть to blush
бледне́ть to turn pale
черне́ть to seem black

With prefixes other than по-, and otherwise:

писа́ть	to write	написать
чита́ть	to read	прочитать
ви́деть	to see	увидеть
слы́шать	to hear	услышать
знать	to know	узнать
уме́ть	to be able	суметь
игра́ть	to play	поиграть, сыграть[1]
де́лать	to do, make	сделать
куса́ть	to bite	откуси́ть, укуси́ть
ку́шать	to eat	по-, скушать
есть	to eat	по-, съесть
пить	to drink	по-, вы́пить
пе́ть	to sing	по-, спеть
горе́ть	to burn	по-, сгореть
жа́рить	to roast, fry	зажарить

[1] с (ъ) + игра́ть; ъ + и makes the sound ы (see p. 12).

учи́ть	to teach	научить
учи́ть	to learn	вы́учить
изуча́ть	to study (trans.)	изучи́ть
учи́ться	to study	на-, вы́учиться
боле́ть	to ache, be ill	заболеть
смея́ться	to laugh	засмеяться
пла́кать	to weep	заплакать
хоте́ть	to want	захотеть
дава́ть	to give	дать
продава́ть	to sell	прода́ть
встава́ть	to get up	встать
одева́ть(ся)	to dress	оде́ть(ся)
надева́ть	to put on	наде́ть
покупа́ть	to buy	купи́ть
по́мнить	to remember	запомнить
понима́ть	to understand	поня́ть
мыть	to wash	вы́мыть
умыва́ться	to have a wash	умы́ться
объясня́ть	to explain	объясни́ть
отвеча́ть	to answer	отве́тить
встреча́ть	to meet (trans.)	встре́тить
встреча́ться	to meet (intrans.)	встре́титься
проща́ть	to forgive	прости́ть
проща́ться	to take leave	прости́ться
жить	to live	по-, прожить
принадлежа́ть	to belong	have no perfective
сто́ить	to cost	

FUTURE TENSE.

§ 122. The *future tense* in Russian has no endings of its own, but has the same endings as the present tense.

Future tense of бы́ть (to be):

я бу́ду	мы бу́дем
ты бу́дешь	вы бу́дете
он бу́дет	они бу́дут

§ 123. The future tense of *other* verbs is the only compound tense in Russian, i.e. is formed with the auxiliary verb бы́ть, e.g.

Future tense of чита́ть

я бу́ду чита́ть, ты бу́дешь чита́ть, etc.

чита́ть is not changed (see Grammar, p. 204).

The translation of я буду читать is "I shall read"; but the translation of я буду is "I shall be", therefore я буду читать implies "be", and can be rendered by "I shall be reading". In this example the imperfective or "lasting" nature of the action is clearly seen, while at the same time it suggests the need of another future tense. In English the future perfect, e.g. "I shall have read", is seldom used, though it exists and is used when emphasis is required. In Russian the future perfect is very much used, just as much as the past perfect, according to the meaning desired.

ASPECTS.

§ 124. As has already been mentioned in Lesson II *a*, the idea of perfect tenses is expressed in Russian by *aspects* (виды). We also saw that a different aspect meant a different infinitive, from which the past perfect tense is formed.

In speaking of any action, i.e. of a verb, Russian grammars usually state that a verb changes its forms according to person and number, time and *aspect* (also gender in the past tense).

The aspects are different forms of one and the same verb, differentiating between the DURATION *and the* COMPLETION *of an action.*

There are two aspects: the *imperfective* which expresses an action in its *duration* without indicating its beginning or its end, and the *perfective* which expresses an action in its *completion* in either the past or the future, with its beginning and its end; or, at least, the beginning must be complete, e.g.

Я писа́л.   I was writing (imperfective).
Я написа́л.   I have *or* had written (perfective).
Я пошёл.   I went, i.e. I have set off (perfective showing the beginning of the action completed).

The perfective aspect has no present tense, as in the present time any action or state is incomplete, and in a "lasting" state.

§ 125. When it is said that a verb changes its forms by aspects, it means that the speaker has to consider whether the action he is speaking about has been completed or is going to be completed, or whether the verb is being used merely to describe the action in present, past or future. There are only these three tenses in Russian, used according to the time meant. One has only to bear in mind the difference between the imperfect, i.e. incomplete, and the perfect, i.e. complete.[1]

§ 126. In Russian, as in Latin, the verb *to have* is not used as an auxiliary verb, so that Russian perfect tenses are never compound. Whereas in English the perfect tenses are formed from the perfect or past infinitive, as "I have read" from "to have read", or "I had written" from "to have written", in Russian they are formed from the infinitive of the perfective aspect of these verbs, which corresponds to the perfect or past infinitive in English. This distinction between the present and the past infinitive is really what is known as aspects of the verb, so far as *conjugation* is concerned. E.g.

The infinitive of the *imperfective*   The infinitive of the *perfective*

читáть	to read	прочитáть	to have read
писáть	to write	написáть	to have written

§ 127. The word вид means "view" or "appearance", which suggests the *point of view* from which the verb is used by the speaker. The meaning "appearance" may be said also to account for the difference in *appearance* of the perfect infinitive, which is due either to the addition of a prefix or to a change in suffix. Since the perfect infinitive is in a sense a separate verb, it is often referred to simply as a perfective verb.

The formation of the perfective aspect is fully discussed in the Grammar (pp. 215–223). In the following lessons, groups of verbs will be taken separately and illustrated by examples.

§ 128. From the list given on pp. 78, 79 it will be seen that most verbs form their perfective aspect with the prefix по-, some with other prefixes, and some by a change in the suffix, i.e. the part before the ending. The verbs with the prefix по- may be compared with the English forms "to have a talk" (поговорить), "to take a walk" (погулять), "to have a look" (посмотреть), etc. More about the prefix по- will be found in the Grammar, p. 215.

§ 129. In the case of perfect infinitives formed with prefixes, the conjugation in the perfective aspect is the same as in the imperfective, with, of course, the addition of the prefix, thus:

---

[1] The idiomatic use of tenses is dealt with later in Lesson XXV.

Imperfective aspect	*Perfective aspect*
читáть, to read	прочитáть, to have read

Present

| я читáю, I am reading, I read | none |

Past

| я читáл, I was reading, I read | я прочитáл, I have, had read |

Future

| я бýду читáть, I shall read | я прочитáю, I shall have read |

§ 130. It must be specially noted that the future tense in the perfective aspect is *never compound*. One can never use **я бýду** with the perfect infinitive. The future perfect is by form the same as the present of the imperfective aspect, but formed from the perfect infinitive, according to the same rules with regard to conjugation, permutation of consonants, etc. One could even say that in form the perfective aspect has no future tense, but that its present (the present perfect) serves as a future. For the full table of conjugation see Grammar, pp. 204, 205.

§ 131. Whereas in English the perfect or past infinitive is very seldom used, the infinitive of the perfective aspect, i.e. the perfect infinitive, is used in just the same way as the present infinitive or the infinitive of the imperfective aspect. One has only to consider again whether the action expressed in the infinitive is *lasting* or *complete*, e.g. я хочý купи́ть эту кни́гу.

The imperfect **покупáть**[1] would mean "go on buying", and one cannot go on buying any definite number of books:

Он хотéл написáть мне.   He wanted to write to me.

(Meaning "to have let me know in writing" and not just "to write to me".)

§ 132. It must be specially noted that the perfect tenses in Russian are not always a translation of the English perfect tenses. The explanation of this lies in the particular rules which govern the use of the English tenses, e.g.

Have you read this book?
Did you read this book yesterday?   } Читáли вы эту
Had you read it before you knew English? }   кни́гу?

---

[1] The verb покупáть, with the prefix по- although an imperfective, appears to be an exception, купи́ть being its perfective form. See Grammar, p. 218.

In all these sentences the imperfect past tense is used in Russian; *but*

Have you finished this book?	Прочитáли вы эту книгу?
When did you finish this book?	Когда вы прочитáли...?
I had finished reading.	Я прочитáл.

Again in all cases the same tense is used in Russian, but this time the perfect past. From these examples it can again be seen that the only difference made is that between incomplete and complete actions, without considering whether the time is mentioned or not.

§ 133. After **когдá** (when), **éсли** (if), and other conjunctions introducing adverbial clauses of *time*, the future tense (both perfect and imperfect) is used, if the time referred to is the future, e.g.

Я буду вам чáсто писáть, когда бýду жить в Москвé.
I shall write to you often when I live in Moscow.
Если погóда бýдет хорóшая, я пойдý гулять.
If the weather is good I shall go for a walk.

EXERCISES XI

A. 1. Вчерá я писал весь день.   Yesterday I was writing the whole day.
2. Читáли вы газéту сегóдня?   Have you read the paper to-day?
3. Написáли вы?   Have you written it?
4. Я прочитáл эту кнúгу в одúн день.   I read this book in one day.
5. Она бýдет вам чáсто писáть.   She will write to you often.
6. Она напúшет вам егó áдрес.   She will write down his address for you.
7. Обéдали вы сегóдня?   Have you had dinner?
8. Когда я пообéдаю, я пойдý гулять.   When I have had dinner I shall go for a walk.
9. В котóром часý вы бýдете обéдать?   At what time will you dine?
10. Мы хорошó пообéдали.   We have had a good dinner.
11. Почемý вы не кýшали мя́са?   Why did you not take any meat?
12. Почемý вы не скýшали э́того кускá?   Why have you not eaten this piece?
13. Мы немнóго посидéли и пошлú домóй.   We sat for a while and then went home.

14. Мы сегодня не будем говорить по-английски. To-day we shall speak no English.
15. Я буду у вас завтра и мы поговорим. I shall come to see you to-morrow and we shall have a talk.
16. Что вы сделали? What have you done?
17. Мы ничего не делали сегодня. We have done nothing to-day.
18. Я хочу вымыть руки. I want to wash my hands.
19. Мне надо купить новое перо. I need to buy a new pen.
20. Завтра урока не будет. There will be no lesson to-morrow.
21. Я видела как вы покупали эту шляпу. I saw you buying this hat.
22. Я поблагодарил его. I thanked him.
23. Хотите и вы поехать в Лондон? Would you like to go to London too?
24. Я тоже поеду. I shall go too.
25. Я хочу пойти в театр сегодня. I want to go to the theatre to-day.
26. Хотите я прочитаю вам её письмо? Would you like me to read you her letter?
27. Он изучал русский язык в России. He studied Russian in Russia.
28. Она покраснела. She blushed.

B. 1. Почему вы не выучили урока? 2. Потому что вы мне не дали книги. 3. Вчера у меня был ваш брат, и мы очень хорошо поговорили. 4. Вы говорили по-русски? 5. Нет, я думал, что он не будет меня понимать. 6. Он говорит, что понял всё, о чём вы говорили в классе. 7. Теперь я поработаю час или два, а вечером буду читать. 8. А что вы будете делать потом? 9. Потом я пойду купить вечернюю (see § 74) газету. 10. Сегодня за завтраком я выпила две чашки чаю. 11. Я встретил вашу сестру в библиотеке сегодня. 12. Говорили вы с ней? 13. Нет, она пошла в другую комнату, где читают газеты. 14. В котором часу вы встали сегодня? 15. Я всегда встаю очень рано, а сегодня встал в девять часов. 16. Я позавтракал и пошёл гулять. 17. Где вы будете жить летом? 18. Мы

проживём месяц в Лóндоне, а потом поéдем в Москвý.
19. Где вы купи́ли вáшу траммáтику?   20. Я купила
её у (from) ученикá, котóрому она тепéрь не нужнá.
21. Кто вас научи́л читáть по-рýсски?   22. Мой брат,
котóрый дóлго жил в Росси́и.   23. Что вы надéнете в
воскресéнье, когда пойдёте к бáбушке?   24. Как вам
понрáвилась нóвая пьéса?   25. Мне она óчень понрáвилась, когдá я ви́дела её в Лóндоне.   26. Здесь она вам
не понрáвится.   27. Тепéрь я попрощáюсь и пойдý.

C. 1. I was reading. 2. He has read this word well. 3. Have
you written? 4. We shall write now. 5. I shall write this word
on the board. 6. I have sat for a little. 7. I shall be at home.
8. I shall not be at home (see § 42). 9. Will you be in the class?
10. They will have to. 11. He will be ill. 12. I shall not have
a headache. 13. They will sit. 14. He set off. 15. I shall not
have supper. 16. I have had breakfast. 17. We shall have a
talk. 18. What language will you speak? 19. We shall speak
Russian. 20. Who told you this?

D. 1. Where did you buy this book? 2. I bought it in the
shop where I buy paper and envelopes. 3. Will you be reading it
to-night? 4. Yes, I must finish it to-night. 5. Please give it
to me when you have finished it. 6. Have you written to your
sister? 7. Yes, I wrote to her this morning. 8. She used to
write to me often when she lived in Russia. 9. At what time
did you get up to-day? 10. I always get up early, but to-day
I got up at nine o'clock. 11. What did you do after breakfast?
12. I wanted to go to the library, but it was too cold. 13. I read
at home all morning. 14. What will you do to-morrow night?
15. We shall go to the theatre after dinner. 16. Would you like
to come with us? 17. What time will you have breakfast to-
morrow? 18. When I have had breakfast I shall go with you.
19. He finished breakfast and went to school. 20. She grew pale
when I told her this. 21. I shall not have dinner at home to-day.
22. With whom will you have dinner on Wednesday? 23. What
did you talk about at dinner? 24. Everybody was talking about
Russia. 25. Last night our teacher came to see us, and we had
a good talk. 26. We had a very good walk this morning.

LESSON XIa

ду́мать (perf. по-)[1] to think
открыва́ть, откры́ть to open
откры́тый open
закрыва́ть, закры́ть to close
закры́тый closed
звони́ть (perf. по-) to ring
звоно́к bell
начина́ть, нача́ть to begin
нача́ло beginning
снача́ла at first
сейча́с presently

конча́ть, ко́нчить to end, finish
  (see p. 218)
коне́ц (gen. конца́) end
ме́сто place, room
прика́зчик assistant
сда́ча change (money)
расска́зывать, рассказа́ть to
  narrate
разгова́ривать (no perf.) to
  converse
разгово́р conversation

§ 134. There is no "sequence of tenses" in Russian, i.e. the past
tense need not be followed by the past tense in a subordinate
clause as is the case in English, e.g.

> I did not know that you were here.
> Я не знал, что вы здесь (*lit.* "you are here").

But вы бы́ли здесь would mean "you were here (e.g. yesterday)"
or "you had been here". (There is no pluperfect in Russian.) The
same applies in the case of the future:

> He said that he would go.   Он сказа́л, что он пойдёт.
> He says that he will go.   Он говори́т, что он пойдёт.

In both cases the future пойдёт is used.

§ 135. In the case of verbs like написа́ть, прочита́ть, вы́пить,
the difference in prefixes is accounted for by the nature of the
action expressed in each particular verb. Prefixes are usually
prepositions, and preserve the meaning of these prepositions.
Bearing this in mind one can understand why a certain prefix
occurs in a certain perfect infinitive. E.g. *writing* suggests writing
on something, hence написа́ть, to have written (на, *on*[2]). "To have
read" means to have gone *through* a certain number of words (or
lines, pages, etc.), hence прочита́ть, to have read (про, *through*).
The prefix вы-, not itself a preposition, means *out*, as can be seen
in the verbs вы́пить, вы́мыть, вы́учить. (N.B. вы- in perfective verbs is always accented, see Grammar, p. 225.) These verbs,
as well as many others, can also be used with the prefix по-, but

---

[1] After this lesson verbs are given in both aspects, together with the
perfect future, when necessary. Verbs having their perfective formed with
по- or other prefixes are not printed in full in the perfective.

[2] The prefix на- has also the force of "doing a lot" or "piling up".

with a limited meaning (see p. 215). In each case the respective prefix completes the required perfective meaning. The prefix с- (with) in сдѣлать, for example, may be compared with the English "to have done with". It gives the same idea of completeness in the verbs сыгра́ть, ску́шать, etc. This prefix is very frequently used in the formation of the perfective aspect.

§ 136. Жить has two perfectives: пожи́ть, which simply means "to have lived"; and прожи́ть, which is used to express the idea of *completeness*, mentioning the exact length of time lived. Пожи́ть has its own imperfective пожива́ть, meaning "to get on", e.g.

Как вы поживаете?   How are you?

§ 137. When a verb in the imperfective aspect already has a prefix, as объясня́ть, изуча́ть, понима́ть, the perfective aspect is formed by a change in the suffix, which often leads to a change of conjugation, as объясни́ть, изучи́ть (both 2nd conjugation).

Note that a verb of the 1st conjugation becomes 2nd; never vice versa.

The future of объясни́ть is объясню́, объясни́шь, etc., i.e. is formed from the infinitive in the same way as a present tense (see § 130). Other verbs which change conjugation in this way will be found in the Grammar, p. 218 (Group A).

Понима́ть, perfective поня́ть, has the future perfect пойму́, поймёшь, etc. This verb belongs to Group D in the Grammar (p. 220).

Поправля́ть, perfective попра́вить; future perfective попра́влю, попра́вишь. All verbs in -влять have -вить in the perfective, see Grammar, p. 219 (Group C), and p. 18.

Встреча́ть, проща́ть become in the perfective встре́тить, прости́ть; i.e. 2nd conjugation but with a change in the consonants of the stem. Other verbs of this kind are in Group B (p. 219).

§ 138. The perfective of дава́ть is дать, the future of which is irregular:

я дам	мы дади́м
ты дашь	вы дади́те
он даст	они даду́т

This is similar to the present of есть (to eat) except in the 3rd person plural (see § 68). These are the only two verbs of this kind, in which can be seen the influence of the Old Slavonic present tense. The suffix -ва-, however, is often deleted in the perfective aspect; this suffix is in general a sign of the imperfective (see Grammar, p. 217). **Встать, закрыть, одеть** are other examples of the deleted -ва-. The future of **встать** is **встану, встанешь**; of **закрыть**: **закрою, закроешь**; of **одеть**: **одену, оденешь**.

Начать, perfective of **начинать**, has the suffix -ин- deleted. Future: **начну, начнёшь**, etc.

§ 139. **Открытый** and **закрытый** are past passive participles, which in Russian are used as verbal adjectives. The passive voice of the verb in its proper form is very little used (see Lesson XXI), and is often represented by reflexive forms in -ся, e.g.

открываться	to be open
закрываться	to be closed
называться	to be called, named (used with the instrumental case when in the sense of *definition*)

Cf. also

начинаться	to begin (intrans. "to be begun")
кончаться	to end (intrans. "to be ended")

§ 140. Some verbs are very seldom used in the perfective aspect, e.g. **видеть, слышать, знать**, the perfectives of which are **у-видеть, услышать, узнать**, e.g.

Я **видел** её очень давно (imperf.).   I had seen her long ago.

In Russian the imperfective past is used because the action of seeing is one which cannot be described, in this case, as having a beginning and an end. *But*:

Я **увидел** её, когда вы её мне указали.
I saw her when you pointed her out to me.

The perfective past is here used because the beginning of seeing is identified with the time of pointing. **Увидеть** may be translated as "to catch sight of", **услышать** as "to catch the sound of", **узнать** as "to have learned". **Узнать** also means "to have recognised"—the perfective of **узнавать** (to recognise) (see Grammar, p. 217).

§ 141. The prefix за- often indicates the *commencement* of an action, as in **захотеть** (to conceive a desire), **замолчать** (to become silent), **заплакать** (to burst into tears), **засмеяться** (to burst out laughing). But sometimes it means *conclusion* as in **зажарить** (to have roasted).

§ 142. The verb **сказать** (future **скажу, скажешь**), although it has its own imperfective aspect, **сказывать**, may be considered as the perfective of **говорить**, which in all tenses (not only in the

present) may mean "to say", or rather "to be saying", as well
as "to speak". The verb **сказывать** has the meaning of *telling a
tale*; hence **сказка** (fairy tale). E.g. Стáну скáзывать я скáзки
(Лермонтов) (I shall tell you fairy tales). **Расскáзывать, рас-
сказáть** means *to relate*; cf. **расскáз** (a story). **Разговáривать** (to
converse) has no perfective.

Note that under the influence of the accent о after в becomes а.

§ 143. **Показáть** (future **покажý, покáжешь**), the perfective of
покáзывать, is at the same time the perfective of **казáть**, which
itself has the meaning "to show", but is seldom found. The verb
казáть with other prefixes has various meanings. The idea of
"showing", however, is common to all of them.

The imperfective of each of these verbs has the suffix **-ыва-**
(see p. 216), e.g.

заказывать (у + gen.), заказáть	to order from
приказывать, приказáть	to give orders
наказывать, наказáть	to punish, instruct
указывать, указáть	to point out
отказывать(-ся), отказáть(-ся)	to deny, refuse

Many nouns are formed from these verbs, e.g.

укáз, прикáз	order, decree, command
закáз	order (e.g. in a restaurant)
наказáние	punishment

Exercises XI *a*

A. 1. Я не знал, что вы здесь.   I did not know you were here.
2. Он говорил мне, что вы бы́ли в Ло́ндоне.   He was telling me
   that you had been in London.
3. Мне сказáли, что вас нет до́ма.   I was told that you were
   not at home.
4. Он сказáл, что сдáчи не даст.   He said he would not give
   change.
5. Я ско́ро ко́нчу.   I shall soon finish.
6. Мы начнём ходи́ть в шко́лу в октябре́.   We shall begin school
   in October.
7. Он давно́ ко́нчил шко́лу.   He left school a long time ago.
8. Уче́ние начинáется в сентябре́.   School starts in September.
9. Спаси́бо, что вы мне показáли.   Thank you for showing me.
10. Отдавáть приказáния.   To give orders.
11. Он заказáл себе́ пальто́.   He ordered a coat for himself.

12. Ему отказа́ли от ме́ста.   He was discharged (dismissed).
13. Он отказа́лся от ме́ста.   He gave up his post.
14. Он себе́ во всём (prep.) отка́зывает.   He denies himself everything.
15. Пальто́ бу́дет сто́ить недо́рого.   The coat will not cost much.
16. Что вам сто́ит.   It costs you no effort.
17. Что ей сто́ит показа́ть ещё две-три шля́пы.   It is surely not difficult for her to show two or three more hats.
18. Сейча́с откро́ю.   I shall open presently.
19. Я хочу́ купи́ть ещё одну́ кни́гу.   I want to buy one more book.
20. Я пойду́ за поку́пками.   I shall go out shopping.
21. Никого́ не бу́дет до́ма.   No one will be at home.
22. Услы́шите вы звоно́к?   Will you hear the bell?
23. Там уви́дим.   We shall see.
24. Как вы пожива́ете? Спаси́бо, о́чень хорошо́.   How are you? Very well, thank you.
25. Я уже́ два го́да живу́ здесь.   I have lived here two years already.
26. С нача́ла до конца́.   From beginning to end.
27. Мы ещё не написа́ли.   We have not written yet.

В. 1. Мы встре́тились в пе́рвый раз на уро́ке ру́сского языка́.   2. Е́сли вы бу́дете ходи́ть по э́той у́лице, вы всегда́ бу́дете встреча́ть его́.   3. Если она́ пойдёт по́лем, она́ никого́ не встре́тит.   4. Никто́ не пока́жет ей куда́ идти́.   5. Нра́вилось вам жить в Москве́?   6. Снача́ла нам не нра́вилось, а пото́м о́чень понра́вилось.   7. Сего́дня в на́шем го́роде откры́лся но́вый теа́тр.   8. Здесь хо́лодно, я закро́ю окно́.   9. Ле́том библиоте́ка бу́дет закрыва́ться ра́но.   10. Зимо́й её закрыва́ли в де́вять часо́в.   11. В кото́ром часу́ начина́ете вы рабо́тать?   12. Я начина́ю всегда́ в во́семь, но сего́дня я на́чал по́здно.   13. Ле́том я не бу́ду начина́ть так ра́но.   14. Я заказа́л себе́ пальто́ в ва́шем магази́не.   15. Прика́зчик показа́л мне два или три костю́ма.   16. Она́ ещё не ко́нчила шко́лы.   17. Когда́ я ко́нчу шко́лу, я пое́ду в Росси́ю и проживу́ там всю зи́му.   18. Где вы бу́дете жить?   19. Я бу́ду жить с бра́том; он уже́ два го́да

живёт в Москве́.   20. Моего́ бра́та наказа́ли сего́дня в
шко́ле.   21. Он сказа́л, что бо́льше не пойдёт в э́ту
шко́лу.   22. Когда́ уро́к ко́нчится, я скажу́ вам кото́рый
час.   23. По́сле уро́ка мы пойдём пить ко́фе.   24. Я
поведу́ вас в но́вую кофе́йню (café), кото́рая то́лько что
откры́лась.   25. Я не откажу́сь вы́пить ча́шку кофе.
26. Но сего́дня я закажу́ ко́фе.   27. Хорошо́, там уви́дим.

C. 1. I met him yesterday.   2. I shall finish presently.   3. He
gives orders.   4. He gave an order.   5. She has ordered a coat.
6. He used to show her (dat.).   7. We open the door.   8. You
closed the window.   9. He told me a story.   10. Now I shall
begin.   11. You will never finish.   12. I rang the bell.   13. You
will ring a long time.   14. The bell does not ring.   15. They were
talking.   16. We shall finish presently.   17. They have not finished
yet.   18. I got up.   19. We used to get up.   20. We shall get
up to-morrow.

D. 1. I used to meet him at the library.   2. We shall meet
to-morrow in the club.   3. How did you like the new picture?
4. I saw it yesterday for the first time and liked it very much.
5. How much change did he give you yesterday?   6. At first
he did not want to give me change.   7. Have you finished reading
your new book?   8. I have not finished it yet.   9. When I finish
it I shall give it to your sister.   10. I did not know that the
lesson had already begun.   11. I could not hear what he was
saying to you.   12. When did you see my uncle?   13. I saw him
yesterday; he was speaking to our teacher.   14. She has never
seen my uncle.   15. And I thought that she did not recognise
him when we met her.   16. Do you know why the theatre is
closed?   17. No, but I shall find out when I go out shopping.
18. Why did you shut the window?   19. Because I was cold.
20. Who will open the door for me if nobody is at home?   21. I shall
be at home the whole evening, and I shall hear the bell.   22. It is
too warm here; you must open the window.   23. I have not read
this book to the end (дочита́ть, to read to the end); I did not like it.
24. I shall tell you the time when I finish writing.   25. I want to
buy a new hat; I shall go to the shop after dinner.   26. The assistant
will show me three or four hats.   27. If they do not cost too much,
I shall buy two.   28. We spoke Russian the whole evening.   29. She
refused to answer the question.

LESSON XII

проси́ть, по- to beg
спра́шивать, спроси́ть to ask
посыла́ть, посла́ть (пошлю́, пошлёшь) to send away
присыла́ть, присла́ть (as above) to send here
счита́ть, сосчита́ть to count
повторя́ть, повтори́ть to repeat
плати́ть, за- to pay
молча́ть, за- to be silent, to become silent (2nd conj.)
про́сьба request
счёт account
доро́га road, way
откры́тка post-card
вопро́с question
задава́ть вопро́с to ask a question

труд work, labour
тру́дный difficult
лёгкий easy, light (weight)
тяжёлый heavy
любе́зный kind
друг friend
друго́й other
на друго́й день next day
вдруг suddenly
подру́га chum, friend (f.)
това́рищ comrade
портно́й tailor
городово́й policeman
столо́вая dining-room
пере́дняя (entrance) hall
спа́льная, спа́льня bedroom
напра́сно in vain
че́рез in (after) (+acc.)

THE IMPERATIVE.

§ 144. The imperative of **быть** is

будь !   be ! (sing.)   бу́дьте !   be ! (plur.)
пусть он бу́дет ! let him be !   пусть они́ бу́дут ! let them be !

As the verb "to be" is not used in the present tense, the imperative (**будь, -те**) is formed from the future, by adding the endings to the stem of the 2nd person singular.

Notice the expression:

будь так добр, добра́; бу́дьте так добры́, be so kind.

Добр, добра́, добры́ are the abbreviated forms of **до́брый**.

Observe that although **добр** has a stem ending in two consonants, -e- is not inserted between the б and p, for the reason that б and p together are considered euphonic (see p. 249). *But* **будь любе́зен, бу́дьте любе́зны** (also "be so kind") from **любе́зный**.

Пусть is derived from **пусти́**, the imperative of the verb **пусти́ть** (to let go).

§ 145. In addition to the endings -й, -йте and -и, -ите the imperative may end in -ь, -ьте, as can be seen in **будь**. These endings can be added only to stems ending in a consonant, and only when the stem of the infinitive is *accented*, e.g.

не плачь, не плачьте.   Don't cry, do not weep,

from пла́кать: пла́чу, пла́чешь; *but* заплати́, заплати́те from заплати́ть, the perfective of плати́ть (плачу́, пла́тишь, etc.), since the stem of the infinitive is not accented.

§ 146. The perfect imperative is formed from the future. It is very characteristic of Russian that not only does the perfect imperative exist, but that it is very much used. The form itself may be compared with the English "have it done", "have it finished", which in English, however, is used only in cases of special emphasis.

Прочита́й (or прочти́) means *lit.* "have it read"; напиши́ means "have it written", but this is exactly what is meant when one says "Write your name", etc. Чита́й and пиши́, on the other hand, mean "go on reading", and "go on writing".

§ 147. It must be specially noted that the *negative imperative* is practically always imperfective, e.g.

Не говори́те!   Don't speak!
Не ходи́те!   Don't go!

Не забу́дь (don't forget) is one of the few exceptions.

§ 148. Дава́й, дава́йте is used as a kind of auxiliary in certain imperative expressions, as

Дава́йте чита́ть.   Let us read.
Дава́йте говори́ть по-ру́сски. Let us speak Russian.

§ 149. The normal "let us", as the 1st person plural imperative, is expressed by the perfect future, e.g.

Тепе́рь почита́ем.   Now let us read.
Пое́дем.   Let us go.

The form пое́демте is also used.

§ 150. Some verbs are not used in the imperative, as принадле-жа́ть (to belong), хоте́ть (to want). Certain existing imperatives are seldom found; e.g. едь, е́дьте (from е́хать) is usually replaced by поезжа́й, -те (go! start going!). The verb поезжа́ть itself is no longer used.

§ 151. The infinitive is sometimes used in the sense of an imperative in order to express emphasis or compulsion, e.g.

Молча́ть!   Be silent!
Не разгова́ривать!   No talking!

§ 152. Care must be taken in using the verbs **просить** and **спросить**. **Просить** (to beg) has the perfective **попросить**, which may be compared with "to have a request (to make)". **Спросить**, i.e. **просить** with a different prefix, really means "to have asked something" (a question or a thing), and has its imperfective in **спрашивать** (to ask), e.g.

Я хочу вас **попросить** сделать это.
I want to ask you to do this.

but   Я хотел вас **спросить** который час.
I wanted to ask you what time it was.

or   **Спросите** у него карандаш.
Ask him for a pencil.

but   **Попросите** у него карандаш.
Ask him to give you a pencil.

Note that the preposition **у**, with the genitive, is used with this verb, as also with **покупать** (to buy from), and **заказывать** (to order from).

§ 153. **Прочесть** is another form of **прочитать**; past: **прочёл**, **прочла**, etc.; future: **прочту**, **прочтёшь**, etc.

Счесть is another form of **сосчитать**; past: **счёл**, **сочла**, etc.; future: **сочту**, **сочтёшь**, etc. **Считаться** (with the instrumental) means "to be considered".

§ 154. Nouns like **портной**, **городовой** have adjectival endings, and are declined like adjectives. Such nouns are fairly frequent in Russian, e.g.

столовая   dining-room
передняя   hall (entrance)

§ 155. **Друг** and **товарищ**, although masculine nouns, are often applied to women, i.e. are of common gender, e.g.

Она мой старый друг.   She is an old friend of mine.
Она хороший товарищ.   She is a good comrade.

Exercises XII

A. 1. Будьте любезны дать мне ⎫
   2. Будьте любезны дайте мне ⎬ Be so kind as to give me.
   3. Не давайте им ничего.   Give them nothing.
   4. Не говорите мне этого.   Don't tell me such a thing.

5. Скажи́те пожа́луйста ско́лько вы заплати́ли за кни́гу. Please tell me how much you paid for this book (acc.).

6. Спроси́те его и он вам ска́жет.   Ask him and he will tell you.

7. Попроси́те его объясни́ть.   Ask him to explain.

8. Учи́тель англи́йского языка́ задаёт очень мно́го.   The English master gives out a great deal of work.

9. Како́й уро́к он за́дал на за́втра?   What lesson did he set for to-morrow?

10. Заплати́ть по счёту.   To pay an account.

11. Спроси́те доро́гу у городово́го.   Ask a policeman the way.

12. Быть и́ли не быть—вот вопро́с.   To be or not to be? That is the question.

13. У меня́ к вам про́сьба.   I have a request to make of you.

14. Я хочу́ вас попроси́ть.   I want to ask you.

15. Попроси́те его в столо́вую.   Ask him into the dining-room.

16. Поезжа́йте трамва́ем.   Take a tram-car.

17. Пойди́(те) (or поди́те) сюда́.   Come here.

18. Пойди́те в другу́ю ко́мнату.   Go into the next room.

19. Что вы де́лали на друго́й день?   What did you do next day?

20. В друго́й раз.   Some other time.

21. Она́ моя́ подру́га по шко́ле.   She is a school friend of mine.

22. Он мой шко́льный това́рищ.   He is a school-mate of mine.

23. Её счита́ют мое́й подру́гой.   She is considered my friend.

24. У меня́ то́лько оди́н друг.   I have only one friend.

25. Вдруг пошёл дождь.   Suddenly it began to rain.

26. Ру́сский язы́к счита́ется тру́дным.   The Russian language is considered difficult.

27. Без труда́ ничего́ не даётся.   Nothing is accomplished (*lit.* is given) without work.

28. Мы проживём здесь до конца́ го́да.   We shall live here till the end of the year.

29. Мне с ва́ми не по доро́ге.   You and I go different ways.

30. Все замолча́ли, а пото́м все вдруг заговори́ли.   Everybody became silent, then suddenly all began to talk.

31. Помолчи́те немно́го.   Be silent for a little.

32. Не забу́дьте заплати́ть за меня́ (acc.).   Don't forget to pay for me.

B. 1. Бу́дьте добры́, скажи́те, как проче́сть это сло́во.

2. Прочти́те ме́дленно и вы уви́дите, что это не так тру́дно.   3. Он не отве́тил на вопро́с, но не хоте́л

сказа́ть, что не по́нял вас.   4. Поду́майте немно́го и
тогда́ отвеча́йте.   5. Если вы не зна́ете, спроси́те
учи́теля и он вам объясни́т.   6. Ко́нчите э́тот уро́к и
тогда́ мы начнём но́вый расска́з.   7. Это о́чень хоро́шая
ска́зка, она́ очень понра́вилась мое́й ма́ленькой сестре́.
8. Пожа́луйста напиши́те ему́, что за́втра уро́ка не
бу́дет.   9. Не говори́те ва́шему ма́ленькому бра́ту, что
вы идёте в теа́тр ; он то́же захо́чет пойти́, а пье́са не для
него́.   10. Не спра́шивайте ка́ждое сло́во, посмотри́те
в слова́рь.   11. Не начина́йте но́вого уро́ка без меня́, я
вам объясню́ его́.   12. Поезжа́йте ле́том во Фра́нцию,
вам там понра́вится.   13. Вы за́дали мне очень тру́дный
вопро́с.   14. На него́ не легко́ отве́тить.   15. Повтори́те
ещё раз, я не слы́шал что вы сказа́ли.   16. Не ду́майте,
что ру́сский язы́к очень тру́ден.   17. Не плати́те сего́дня,
вы запла́тите в друго́й раз.   18. Попроси́те его посиде́ть
в столо́вой.   19. Не тяжело́ вам нести́ тако́й большо́й
слова́рь?   20. Ваш друг тепе́рь в Росси́и : пошли́те ему
откры́тку.   21. Попроси́те его присла́ть вам ру́сскую
газе́ту.   22. Сосчита́йте пожа́луйста, ско́лько я вам
до́лжен за кни́ги (plur.).   23. Вот счёт ; всего́ де́сять
ши́ллингов.   24. Сыгра́йте это ; я хочу послу́шать, как
вы игра́ете.   25. Если вам не откро́ют—позвони́те ещё
раз.   26. Не плачь, дитя́ (child), не плачь напра́сно.
(Ле́рмонтов.)   27. Я вам дам э́ту кни́гу через неде́лю,
когда́ мы все прочтём её.   28. Закажи́те себе́ пальто́ у
на́шего портно́го.   29. Не разгова́ривайте так до́лго в
пере́дней.   30. Пойдёмте в столо́вую.

C. 1. Be so kind (sing.).   2. Be so kind (plur.).   3. Ask him.
4. Don't ask me.   5. Give me. . . .   6. Don't give her. . . .   7. Come
here.   8. Send away to him.   9. Send me. . . .   10. Repeat.
11. Don't repeat.   12. Call him here.   13. Don't cry.   14. Don't
laugh.   15. Count.   16. Don't count.   17. He will repeat once.
18. Don't forget.   19. Do this for me, please.   20. Write this

word. 21. Read this word. 22. Tell me where she is. 23. Answer my question. 24. Think a little. 25. Be silent.

D. 1. Please answer my question. 2. It is not a difficult question, just think a little. 3. Don't go to town by tram-car, take the train. 4. Read this story; it is about life in Russia. 5. When you are finished with it, give it to my sister. 6. Why did you not send me a p.c.? 7. Because I had no post-card at home. 8. Ask her whether she will be at home to-morrow night. 9. Ask him what time it is. 10. Don't ask me about Moscow; I have not been there for a long time. 11. Don't give coffee to such a small girl; give her some milk. 12. She does not like milk; she always asks for tea or coffee. 13. Why do you ask me? —you know how to say this in Russian. 14. I want to ask you to do this for me. 15. Put on your warm coat, it is cold now. 16. I want to know how many lessons we have had. 17. Count them. 18. Play this sonata; I am very fond of it. 19. Please read a little; I want to hear you read. 20. Don't wear this dress; it does not suit you. 21. They were at the theatre on Monday, and next day they were not at the lesson. 22. Please explain this to us. 23. I shall explain this lesson next time. 24. Send me a post-card when you live in Leningrad. 25. Don't forget to ask me about this to-morrow. 26. Go to London in a week, and I shall go with you. 27. Ask them into the dining-room.

LESSON XIII

приходи́ть, прийти́, приезжа́ть, прие́хать } to come

уходи́ть, уйти́, уезжа́ть, уе́хать } to go away

находи́ть, найти́ to find

находи́ться (no perf. in this meaning) to be situated

ждать, подожда́ть to wait for

приноси́ть, принести́, привози́ть, привезти́, приводи́ть, привести́ } to bring

ировожа́ть, проводи́ть to see off

прихо́д, прие́зд arrival

отхо́д, отъе́зд departure

вход entrance, entry[1]

въезд entry (action)

подъе́зд gate, entrance

вы́ход exit

зал hall

биле́т ticket

се́вер, -ный north

[1] The use of вход and въезд may be seen in the expression Вход (or въезд) воспреща́ется, "No admittance".

юг, ю́жный south
восто́к, -чный east
за́пад, -ный west
ве́тер wind
дуть (по-) to blow
Эдинбу́рг Edinburgh
Пари́ж Paris

мужчи́на man
муж husband
жена́ wife
же́нщина woman
надо́лго for a long time
навсегда́ for ever
то́лько что just

§ 156. The perfective aspect of the "going" verbs ходи́ть, идти́, носи́ть, etc., is formed by the prefix по-. It must be particularly noted, however, that the perfect infinitive of the verbs meaning *to go* is seldom used. Походи́ть and пое́здить merely mean "to have done a little walking or riding", e.g.

Я люблю походи́ть в саду́ по́сле обе́да.

I like to have a stroll in the garden after dinner.

Still more limited are the meanings of поноси́ть, повози́ть, поводи́ть.

When the perfective forms of these verbs are required, the perfective aspect of the verbs meaning *to be going* must be used, i.e. пойти́, понести́, повезти́, повести́. The same applies to all "going" verbs. Note the spelling of пойти́. After prefixes the verb идти́ is usually written -йти, though the spelling пойдти́, придти́ is also found.

§ 157. *Verbs "to go" with prefixes.* In the case of "going" verbs which exist in the two forms *to go* and *to be going*, the addition of prefixes to the verb meaning *to go* does not make it a perfective verb, but alters its meaning, e.g.

приходи́ть means "to come"
уходи́ть   „   "to go away"
выходи́ть   „   "to leave", etc.

The perfective of these verbs is formed by adding the same prefix to the verb meaning *to be going*, thus прийти́ is the perfective of приходи́ть, уйти́ of уходи́ть, etc.

The same applies to all other "going" verbs, e.g. прилета́ть (to come flying), perfective прилете́ть; приноси́ть (to bring) perfective принести́.

§ 158. In the case of verbs meaning *to go* (*not on foot*) the prefix is added not to е́здить but to the verb езжа́ть, which is hardly ever used without a prefix. To form the perfective, the prefix is added to the verb е́хать, corresponding to идти́. Thus: to come, to arrive: **приезжа́ть, прие́хать**; to go away: **уезжа́ть, уе́хать**; to leave: **выезжа́ть, вы́ехать**.

All the "going" verbs with prefixes are not given in this lesson. They will be found in the Grammar, p. 225, and in the Vocabulary.

Note the verb **пройти́сь** (to take a stroll), which is used mostly as a perfective verb, though there is an imperfective, **проха́живаться**, e.g.

Я пойду́ пройти́сь.   I shall go for a stroll.

§ 159. The meanings of the various prefixes is best learned in conjunction with verbs, and this holds particularly in the case of **ходи́ть** and its compounds.[1]

The meaning of the prefixes **на-, по-, вы-, с-, за-, про-** has already been given (Lesson XI a). Other prefixes are as follows:

(1) **В-** keeps the meaning *in*, e.g. входи́ть (to enter).

(2) **Воз- (вос- or вз-)** has the meaning of *up*, e.g. восходи́ть (to rise); возда́ть (to reward).

(3) **До-** is used of an action *carried to its end*, or *up to a certain point*, e.g. доходи́ть (to reach); дописа́ть (to finish off (writing)).

(4) **Из- (ис-)** means "out" and has the same meaning as **вы-**, but is used mostly in a figurative sense, e.g. исходи́ть (to be derived).

(5) **Об- (о-)** means "about" and has also the meaning of *avoiding*, e.g. обходи́ть (to avoid).

(6) **От-** means "further from", e.g. отходи́ть (to depart).

(7) **Пере-** means *across*, or *change from one state into another*, e.g. переводи́ть (to translate), переходи́ть (to cross), переста́ть (to stop).

(8) **Пре-** has a meaning similar to that of **пере-** and must not be confused with **при-**, e.g. преда́ть (to betray), *but* прида́ть (to assign).

(9) **При-** as a preposition means *in the presence of*, and as a prefix suggests *approach, adding* or *joining*, e.g. приходи́ть (to come), принести́ (to bring), привяза́ть (to tie to).

(10) **Под-** means "under", and suggests *close approach*, e.g. подходи́ть (to approach), поднима́ть (to lift).

(11) **Раз- (рас-)** has the meaning of *distribution*, e.g. разби́ть (to smash), расходи́ться (to disperse).

[1] It will be seen from the Vocabulary of this lesson that many nouns are formed from these verbs with prefixes.

(12) **С-** means "off" and suggests the meaning *down*, e.g. сходи́ть (to descend).

(13) **У-** gives the meaning of *away*, e.g. унести́ (to take away).

§ 160. **Находи́ться**... means "to be situated", "to be found" (cf. French *se trouver*). It has no perfective aspect with this meaning, but **найти́сь** can be used idiomatically in:

Он не нашёлся ничего́ сказа́ть.   He was at a loss to say.

У меня́ не нашло́сь ни копе́йки.   I hadn't a halfpenny.

§ 161. **Ждать** (to wait): present **жду, ждёшь,** etc.; perfective **подожда́ть.** This verb requires the genitive when it has the meaning "to wait for a thing", e.g. я жду письма́, по́езда, etc.

But when it means "to wait for a *particular* thing" it is followed by the accusative, e.g. я жду сестру́. The accusative is also used when the meaning is "to have been waiting for some time", e.g.

Я жду уже́ неде́лю.   I have been waiting for a week already.

§ 162. There are three verbs *to bring* in Russian: (*a*) **приноси́ть** (to bring a thing carrying it), (*b*) **привози́ть** (to bring a thing or person in a conveyance), and (*c*) **приводи́ть** (to bring a person).

(*a*) Я принёс кни́гу.   I have brought the book.

(*b*) Я привёз её из Ло́ндона.   I brought it *or* her from London.

(*c*) Я привёл сестру́.   I have brought my sister.

§ 163. **Прийди́те** *or* **приди́те** (perfective) is the usual imperative. **Приходи́те** (imperfective) rather implies *invitation*. (See Ex. A.)

§ 164. The English "for" used to express *future duration of time* is translated in Russian by **на** with the accusative, e.g.

Он уе́хал на неде́лю.   He has gone away for a week.

Я ухожу́ на мину́тку.   I am going away for a moment.

The adverbs **навсегда́** (for ever) and **надо́лго** (for a long time) may be compared with this construction.

But simple *length of time* (and also *distance*) is expressed by the accusative *without* a preposition, e.g.

Он жил там неде́лю.   He lived there a week.

Он прое́хал версту́.   He travelled one verst.

Exercises XIII

A. 1. Приходи́те к нам сего́дня ве́чером.   Come to see us to-night.

2. Приходи́те к нам за́втра пить чай.   Come to tea with us to-morrow.

3. Не уходи́те так ра́но. Don't go away so early.
4. Отойди́те от окна́. Go away from the window.
5. Подожди́те меня́. Wait for me.
6. Она придёт ве́чером. She will come in the evening.
7. Как пройти́ к вокза́лу? How do I get to the station?
8. Вы́ход на друго́м конце́. The exit is at the other end.
9. Окно́ выхо́дит на юг. THe window faces the south.
10. Он подошёл ко мне. He approached me.
11. Вот она идёт. Here she comes.
12. Она прихо́дит ра́но. She comes early.
13. Приходи́те меня́ провожа́ть. Come and see me off.
14. Я не люблю́ никуда́ заезжа́ть по доро́ге в Ло́ндон. I don't like to call anywhere on my way to London.
15. Я вы́ехал из Ло́ндона. I left London.
16. Надо́лго вы уезжа́ете? Are you going away for long?
17. Я уезжа́ю навсегда́. I am going away for good.
18. Он приезжа́ет сего́дня. He arrives to-day.
19. Когда́ вы уезжа́ете? When do you leave?
20. Перед отъ́ездом. Before departure; before going away.
21. Я ухожу́ не надо́лго. I shall not be long.
22. Я жду по́езда о́коло ча́са. I have been waiting for a train about an hour.
23. Я бу́ду вас ждать о́коло (*or* у) подъ́езда. I shall wait for you beside the entrance.
24. Чего́ вы ждёте? What are you waiting for?
25. Подожди́те, я пойду́ с ва́ми. Wait a moment, I shall come with you.
26. Я зайду́ за вами. I shall call for you.
27. Пойдёмте со мной! Хоти́те пойти со мной? } Will you come with me?
28. Приведи́те с собо́й това́рища. Bring your friend with you.
29. Из две́ри ду́ет. There is a draught through the door.
30. По́сле обе́да он лю́бит пойти пройти́сь *or* прогуля́ться. He likes to go for a stroll after dinner.
31. Пройди́тесь по ко́мнате (dat.); я посмотрю́ как вы хо́дите. Walk across the room; I want to see how you walk.

В. 1. В кото́ром часу́ вы прихо́дите на уро́к? 2. Мы прихо́дим в семь часо́в, а ухо́дим в де́вять. 3. Почему́ вы не пришли́ на уро́к вчера́? 4. Я уезжа́ла к сестре́ и прие́хала то́лько сего́дня у́тром. 5. Тогда́ приходи́те за́втра в шесть часо́в. 6. Почему́ вы должны́ уйти́ так ра́но сего́дня? 7. Потому́ что за́втра у́тром я иду́ встре-ча́ть това́рища. 8. По́езд из Ло́ндона прихо́дит в семь часо́в утра́. 9. Я до́лжен быть на вокза́ле до прихо́да по́езда. 10. Когда́ уезжа́ет муж ва́шей сестры́? 11. Он не уезжа́ет до среды́. 12. Когда́ вы уезжа́ете на юг? 13. Мы вы́едем пя́того января́ и проживём там до конца́ ма́рта. 14. Я не знал, что вы уезжа́ете так надо́лго. 15. Зайди́те к нам пе́ред отъе́здом во Фра́нцию. 16. Когда ве́тер ду́ет с за́пада, всегда́ идёт дождь. 17. Ло́ндон нахо́дится на ю́ге Англии, а Эдинбу́рг на восто́ке Шотла́ндии. 18. Кто эта молода́я же́нщина, с кото́рой вы то́лько что разгова́ривали у вхо́да в теа́тр? 19. Это жена́ бра́та; почему́ вы не подошли́ к нам? 20. Нашли́ вы доро́гу домо́й? 21. Нет, я до́лжен был спроси́ть у городово́го. 22. Муж подру́ги уе́хал во Фра́нцию на́ год, и она́ тепе́рь бу́дет жить со мной. 23. Что он привезёт ей из Пари́жа? 24. Не забу́дьте принести́ грамма́тику за́втра. 25. За́втра я приведу́ с собо́й сестру́ на уро́к. 26. Она́ то́же хо́чет изуча́ть ру́сский язы́к. 27. Она́ зашла́ за мной и мы пошли́ пройти́сь по го́роду. 28. Тепе́рь мне на́до идти́, меня́ бу́дут ждать до́ма.

C. 1. He came home. 2. She always comes. 3. We are going away. 4. They left at 3 o'clock. 5. Come to see us. 6. I shall l ave. 7. Bring the book. 8. He brought it from France. Ə. What do you bring from London? 10. Bring your sister. 11. I always bring a pencil. 12. Don't go. 13. She is leaving the room. 14. She left the room. 15. He found the ticket. 16. I shall not find. 17. What did you find? 18. Who has come? 19. They have not come. 20. He is waiting. 21. What are we waiting for? 22. They will wait long.

D. 1. When did you come from London? 2. I came last night at ten o'clock. 3. I left London at two in the afternoon. 4. Will you come to the lesson every day? 5. No, only three times a

week. 6. Bring with you paper and a pen or a pencil. 7. What
will you bring me from Russia? 8. When father went to Russia,
he brought me a Russian samovar. 9. This morning my brother's
friend arrived. 10. He went to the station to meet him. 11. He
waited about an hour for the train. 12. Who is that old man
who is standing at the gate? 13. He is my friend's father; he is
going East to-morrow. 14. Have you lived in the East? 15. No,
but I shall go there in winter. 16. It is cold to-day, because the
wind is from the North. 17. It is cold in my room also, because
the window faces the East. 18. Did you find the key?—I saw it
under the chair. 19. Where shall I find a policeman if I want to
ask the way to the station? 20. Come to dinner with us to-
morrow. 21. Call for me when you go to the lesson. 22. I shall
come to see you before going away. 23. Are you and your brother
going away for long? 24. No, only for a month. 25. How dark
it is here; where is the exit? 26. It is at the other end of the
hall; I will show you. 27. Thank you; let us go now.

LESSON XIIIa

запи́сывать, записа́ть to note, write down

подпи́сывать, подписа́ть to sign

подпи́сываться, подписа́ться to sign one's name

выпи́сывать, вы́писать to write out, "take in" (a newspaper)

перепи́сывать, переписа́ть to copy, transcribe

перепи́сываться (c + instr.) (no perf.) to correspond

переводи́ть, перевести́ to translate

переезжа́ть, перее́хать to re-move (intrans.)

произноси́ть, произнести́ to pronounce

кури́ть (по-) to smoke

заку́ривать, закури́ть to light (a cigarette)

позволя́ть, позво́лить to allow

позво́льте! allow me, may I? please!

налива́ть, нали́ть to pour out, fill

пролива́ть, проли́ть to spill

мочь, смочь to be able

помога́ть, помо́чь to help

по́мощь (f.) help

помо́щник assistant

мо́жет быть perhaps

таба́к tobacco

тру́бка (труба́) pipe (chimney)

папиро́са cigarette

бу́ква letter

кварти́ра flat, lodgings

печь (noun f.) stove

тёмный, темно́ dark

по́дпись (f.) signature

подпи́счик subscriber

запи́ска note

записна́я кни́жка notebook

перево́д translation

произноше́ние pronunciation

§ 165. It has already been pointed out (in § 137) that while the perfective aspect is mainly formed by the addition of prefixes, not all verbs with prefixes are perfective. Examples have been given of verbs with two perfectives, one with по- and one with some other prefix. In the case of **писáть**, for example, the prefix по- is insufficient for the expression of the perfective: **пописáть** means "to have done some writing"; **написáть** "to have written". By the addition of other prefixes the meaning is further changed; e.g. **подписáть** is a perfective verb meaning "to have signed". The verb "to sign", i.e. the imperfective of **подписáть** is **подпи́сывать**. Thus, a verb with the prefix под- may be an imperfective verb.

§ 166. Such imperfective verbs with prefixes may usually be recognised by the presence of the suffix -ыва-, -ива- (sometimes -ина-) (see Grammar, p. 217). Once this method of formation of both aspects is properly understood, the student is enabled in many cases to form the aspects for himself. Thus, it is not impossible to deduce that the verb **наливáть** is the imperfective form of a verb **налúть**.

§ 167. The verb **мочь** (to be able *physically*) must be distinguished from the verb **умéть** which means "to be able *mentally*" or "to know how" (see § 73).

Present tense of **мочь**

я могý	мы мóжем
ты мóжешь	вы мóжете
он мóжет	они мóгут

All verbs in -чь have similar changes of consonant in the present tense. For the present tense of **печь**, see p. 208. Note the past tenses of these verbs: **мог, моглá**, etc., **пёк, пеклá**, etc. The imperative of verbs in -чь is formed from the stem of the 1st pers. sing. of the present tense, e.g. **пекú, -úте**.

Exercises XIIIa

A. 1. Выпи́сывать журнáл *or* Подписáться на газéту.   To take in (subscribe to) a magazine or paper.
2. Он подписáлся карандашóм.   He signed in pencil.
3. Вот моя пóдпись.   Here is my signature.
4. Письмó без пóдписи.   An anonymous letter.
5. Мы все подпи́шемся на "Извéстия" (acc. pl.).   We shall all subscribe to *Izvestia*.

6. Мы перепи́сываемся ⎫ We correspond.
   Мы в перепи́ске   ⎭

7. Запиши́те меня́ на за́втра. Put my name down for to-morrow.

8. Чита́ть в перево́де. To read in translation.

9. Чита́ть в оригина́ле. To read in the original.

10. Како́го ру́сского поэ́та вы зна́ете? What Russian poet do you know?

11. Переезжа́ть на но́вую кварти́ру. To move to new quarters.

12. Нале́йте мне ча́шку ча́ю. Pour me out a cup of tea.

13. Смотри́те не проле́йте[1] молоко́. Watch you don't spill the milk.

14. Не мо́жет быть ! Impossible !

15. Ско́рая по́мощь. First aid.   Помоги́те ! Help !

16. Каре́та ско́рой по́мощи. Ambulance.

17. Я, мо́жет быть, ско́ро пое́ду в Росси́ю. I shall perhaps soon go to Russia.

18. Он мо́жет прийти́ ещё. He may come yet.

19. Позво́льте закури́ть. May I smoke? (Allow me to smoke.)

20. Он закури́л папиро́су. He lit a cigarette.

B. 1. Я запи́сываю всё, что объясня́ет учи́тель. 2. Запиши́те мой а́дрес.   3. Есть у вас записна́я кни́жка?   4. У него́ всегда́ записна́я кни́жка в карма́не. 5. Чита́ли вы Турге́нева?   6. Да, но то́лько в перево́де. 7. Ско́ро вы бу́дете чита́ть его́ по-ру́сски.   8. Кто перевёл Шекспи́ра на ру́сский язы́к?   9. Ру́сский поэ́т Ба́льмонт о́чень хорошо́ перевёл Ше́лли.   10. Да́йте мне ваш перево́д, я его́ вам перепишу́.   11. Мой това́рищ тепе́рь в Москве́.   12. Мы перепи́сываемся о́чень ча́сто. 13. Слу́шайте, когда́ э́тот учени́к говори́т по-ру́сски. 14. У него́ о́чень хоро́шее произноше́ние.   15. Когда́ вы переезжа́ете в го́род?   16. Зимо́й мы перее́дем жить в Ло́ндон.   17. Здесь о́чень темно́; я не могу́ чита́ть. 18. Это о́чень тру́дное сло́во; она́ не смо́жет прочесть его́.   19. Кто помо́г вам написа́ть это письмо́ по-ру́сски? 20. Мне никто́ не помога́л, я давно́ уме́ю писа́ть по-

[1] The negative imperative is often *perfective* after the imperative смотри́, -́те (look).

русски. 21. Найдёте вы доро́гу без мое́й по́мощи?
22. Я, может быть, не смогу́ прийти на уро́к за́втра.
23. Да́йте мне знать, пожа́луйста. 24. Хорошо́, я вам
пришлю́ запи́ску. 25. Мы выпи́сываем два журна́ла и
три газе́ты. 26. Ему́ не позволя́ют кури́ть; он был
до́лго бо́лен зимо́й. 27. Позво́льте мне не перепи́сывать
э́того перево́да. 28. Мой отец ку́рит то́лько о́чень
дорого́й таба́к.

C. 1. I copy. 2. We correspond. 3. He has copied. 4. She
is translating. 5. You will translate. 6. Write it down. 7. Copy
this. 8. Sign your name. 9. I have signed. 10. He is helping
his father. 11. You were helping. 12. I shall help you. 13. Help!
14. He never helps. 15. Have you translated? 16. I shall help
you to translate. 17. You pronounce well. 18. Pour out, please.
19. She pours out. 20. He spilt the milk. 21. You do not
smoke. 22. She lit a cigarette. 23. I shall not copy this.

D. 1. Give me your address, and I shall write to you every
week. 2. Let me know when you can come. 3. We shall all sign
this letter. 4. Copy this translation once more. 5. With whom
do you correspond in Moscow? 6. My friend has lived there
three years, and he often writes to me. 7. How do you pronounce
this long word? 8. Read every letter slowly and you will read
it very easily. 9. Russian pronunciation is not very difficult.
10. Who brought you this hat from Paris? 11. My brother's
wife went to France in spring and brought me two hats. 12. When
did they move to new quarters? 13. Their old flat was too small,
and they moved to a new house in May. 14. Can you read this
book in one day? 15. What paper do you take? 16. I do not
take any paper; I go to the library to read. 17. This paper has
many subscribers. 18. Help me to translate this letter. 19. When
did you get it? 20. Who will help you when I go away? 21. Without your help I shall not be able to read it. 22. Who signs the
papers in your office? 23. When I am not there my assistant
signs them. 24. This is a very good translation of Pushkin.
25. I want to write to Moscow for this book. 26. I cannot buy
it here. 27. I did not know that he was (is) allowed to get
(выпи́сывать) a newspaper from Russia. 28. Please sign this
letter; I want to post (отосла́ть) it to-night. 29. I think you
will have to copy this letter.

LESSON XIV

The following nouns are used in the plural:

но́вости (gen. -е́й) news
де́ньги (gen. де́нег) money
са́ни (gen. -е́й) sledge
коньки́ (sing. -конёк; gen. pl. -ко́в) skates

черни́ла (gen. -л) ink
очки́ (gen. -о́в) spectacles
часы́ (gen. -о́в) watch, clock (час hour)
су́тки (gen. -ок) 24 hours

интересова́ть, за- to interest
интересова́ться, за- to be interested in
рекомендова́ть to recommend
сове́товать, по- to advise
бесе́довать, по- to chat
звать, по- to call

ра́доваться, по-, об- to rejoice, be glad
называ́ть, назва́ть to name
знако́мить, по- to introduce, make acquainted
ката́ться, по- to go for a ride or drive (see § 175)

свет light, world
све́тлый light
сове́т council
Сове́тский Soviet (adj.)
сою́з union
респу́блика republic
фами́лия surname
назва́ние name, title
знако́мый acquaintance (noun), familiar (adj.)

челове́к (pl. лю́ди) man
спи́чка match
бесе́да chat
я рад, -а, -ы I am glad, etc.
не́сколько several
обыкнове́нно usually
интере́сный interesting
дли́нный long
рекоменда́ция, introduction, commendation

THE PLURAL OF NOUNS AND ADJECTIVES: ALL GENDERS.

§ 168. As early as Lesson I it was pointed out that и, the ending of они́, and ы, the corresponding hard vowel, might be considered the sign of the plural. Nouns ending in -и, and -ы, e.g. о́вощи, фру́кты, have already been given, as being used mostly in the plural.

The nominative plural of masculine and feminine nouns having hard endings, e.g. стол, ко́мната, ends in -ы; that of masculine nouns in -ь and -й and of feminine nouns in -я and -ь end in -и. The plural ending of neuter nouns, however, is -а or -я, e.g. окно́, plural о́кна; мо́ре, plural моря́ (cf. the neuter plural endings in both Latin and Greek). The same letters ы and и occur in the plural endings of adjectives in all three genders, but are followed

by -e, since adjectival endings in the nominative always contain
two vowels; thus **но́вые** is the plural of **но́вый, -ая, -ое** (hard);
си́ние that of **си́ний, -яя, -ее** (soft).

§ 169. Declension of adjectives and nouns in the *plural* and
of **они́**:

	Hard				Soft			
Nom.		но́в-ые		стол-ы́		си́н-ие	мор-я́	они́
Gen.	,,	ых	,,	о́в	,,	их	,, ей́[1]	их
Dat.	,,	ым	,,	а́м	,,	им	,, я́м	им
Acc.[2]			As nom. or gen.				,, я́	их
Instr.	,,	ыми	,,	а́ми	,,	ими	,, я́ми	и́ми
Prep.	о ,,	ых	,,	а́х	,,	их	,, я́х	о них

Note that in the plural adjectives are declined alike in all three
genders.

As in the case of declension in the singular, the declension of
они́ is reproduced in the soft endings of **си́ние**. It will be noticed
that apart from the change of the -ы- of **но́вые** into the -и- of
си́ние the endings are the same. Similarly, in the dative, instrumental and prepositional of nouns, the -а- of the hard endings
becomes -я- in the soft endings.

All nouns with the singular ending in -а or -о are declined in
the plural like **столы́**, and those ending in -ь (both genders), -й,
-я, -е like **моря́** (except that the nominative masculine and feminine
ends in -и).

§ 170. The endings of the *genitive plural* must, however, be
studied separately. They will be found in the Grammar, p. 237.

Nouns with hard endings (i.e. a hard consonant, -а, and -о) have
the genitive plural in -ов or no ending at all. Those with soft
endings (i.e. -ь, -й, -я, -е, -ия, -ие) have the genitive plural in
-ь, -ев, -ей, ... and a very few in -й.

§ 171. Some masculine nouns take -а (or -я) in the plural, e.g.
дом, plural **дома́**. Also **го́род, по́езд, бе́рег** (bank, shore), **лес**
(wood, forest), **луг** (meadow), **ве́чер, го́лос** (voice) and **учи́тель**,
plural **учителя́**.

N.B. *Accent*: this ending -а or -я is always accented.

Other exceptions of this kind are noted in the Grammar, p. 240.

---

[1] See § 170.
[2] See § 29, which applies in the plural to nouns and adjectives of all genders.

Some masculine and neuter nouns end in the plural in -ья; such are:

брат: бра́тья, бра́тьев, etc.

друг: друзья́, друзе́й, друзья́м, etc.

сын: сыновья́, сынове́й, сыновья́м, etc.

де́рево (tree): дере́вья, дере́вьев, etc.

перо́: пе́рья, пе́рьев, etc.

Note that **друг** and **сын** have the genitive plural in -ей without ь, but in the dative retain ь. For other nouns of this kind see Grammar, p. 240.

§ 172. Feminine nouns in -a preceded by two consonants insert -e-, -ё-, or -o- between these consonants in the genitive plural, e.g.

де́вочка	Gen. pl.	де́вочек
сестра́	,,	сестёр
ви́лка	,,	ви́лок
таре́лка	,,	таре́лок
спи́чка	,,	спи́чек
кни́жка	,,	кни́жек

For other nouns of this kind see Grammar, p. 239.

§ 173. **Са́ни** (sledge) (genitive **сане́й**) is used only in the plural, like **но́жницы** (scissors).

Лю́ди (people) has no singular of its own. It is used as the plural of **челове́к** (man, human being), *except* when used with numbers, e.g. пять челове́к,[1] не́сколько челове́к, *but* мно́го люде́й.

Лю́ди is declined like **ко́сти** (instrumental людьми́). See Grammar, p. 236.

For other nouns used only in the plural see Grammar, p. 242.

§ 174. Although after the numerals **два, три, четы́ре** nouns are used in the genitive singular (see § 36) this rule does not apply to adjectives. Adjectives after numerals in the nominative and accusative case (*except* **оди́н**) are used in the genitive plural, e.g.

два больши́х окна́

две но́вых шля́пы

§ 175. The verb **ката́ться** has no exact equivalent in English, but is a verb frequently used in Russian, and must therefore be

---

[1] Челове́к is one of a number of nouns which have the genitive plural like the nominative singular, cf. раз. (See Grammar, p. 239.)

carefully noted. The verb **катáть** means literally *to roll*, i.e. to move anything that can roll. It is one of the "going" verbs and therefore exists in two forms, the second being **катúть** (to be rolling), e.g.

Мáльчик катáет мяч.   The boy rolls the ball.

Катáться as a reflexive verb means literally "to roll oneself", and can be used in this meaning, e.g.

Он катáется пó полу (dat.).   He rolls on the floor.
Он кáтится с горы́.   He is rolling downhill.

But the normal use of **катáться** is to express motion for the mere sake of the pleasure it gives, e.g.

	катáться на лóдке	to go boating
(*but*	éздить на лóдке	to travel by boat, etc.)
	катáться в автомобúле	to go motoring
	катáться на (в) саня́х	to sledge
	катáться на конькáх	to skate, etc.

(cf. French *se promener*).

The perfective of **катáться**, as of all "going" verbs, is formed with **по-: покатáться**.

§ 176. Verbs in **-овать** and **-евать** change **-ова-** and **-ева-** into **-у-** and **-ю-** respectively before the endings of the present tense, e.g. **совéтовать** (to advise), **совéт-у-ю**, **совéт-у-ешь**, etc. (see p. 16).

Except: **сомневáться** (to doubt); present, **сомневáюсь, сомне вáешься**, and **здорóваться** (**здорóваюсь**).

§ 177. In the expression **рад, рáда** may be seen a relic of an obsolete system of compound tenses. The auxiliary verb survives in the past and future (**я был, бýду рад**), but is omitted in the present (**я рад**). These forms, as well as the verb **рáдоваться**, are followed by the dative, e.g.

Чемý вы рáды *or* рáдуетесь?   What makes you glad?

§ 178. **Звать** (to call) (perf. **позвáть**) has the present **зовý, зовёшь**, etc. **Назвáть** (to have named) has its own imperfective, **называ́ть**.

§ 179. When the complement of a verb, especially of **быть**, forms an adverbial expression, the instrumental case is used, e.g.

Он служúл просты́м солдáтом.   He served as a private.

See § 153. A list of verbs taking this construction is given in Part II, p. 271.

Exercises XIV

A. 1. Позвóльте вас пезнакóмить.   Allow me to introduce you.
  2. Позвóльте с вáми познакóмиться.   Allow me to introduce myself.
  3. Я знакóм с ним.   I am acquainted with him.
  4. Мы знакóмы.   We are acquainted.
  5. Мне это слóво незнакóмо.   This word is unfamiliar to me.
  6. Кто этот незнакóмец?   Who is this stranger?
  7. Познакóмьте меня с вáшим брáтом (instr.).   Introduce me to your brother.
  8. Я óчень рад с вáми познакóмиться.   I am very glad to make your acquaintance.
  9. Как называéтся эта шкóла?   What is the name of this school?
 10. У меня мнóго знакóмых в гóроде.   I know many people in (the) town.
 11. Как вас зовýт?   What is your name?
 12. Меня зовýт. . . .   My name is. . . .
 13. Как вáша фамилия?   What is your surname?
 14. Как фамилия вáших знакóмых?   What is your friends' surname?
 15. Что нóвого?   What's the news?
 16. Я расскажý вам все нóвости.   I shall tell you all the news.
 17. Жить на свéте интерéсно.   It is interesting to live in the world.
 18. Не без дóбрых душ на свéте.   (Некрáсов.)
     Свет не без дóбрых людéй.
     The world is not without kind people (souls).
 19. Котóрый час на вáших часáх?   What do you make the time?
 20. У меня часы не идýт.   My watch has stopped (*lit.* does not go).
 21. Вот почемý.   That's why.
 22. Нет ли у вас спичек?   Have you no matches?
 23. Шкóла для дéвочек.   A girls' school.
 24. Éсли вы пойдёте со мной.   If you come with me.
 25. Я совсéм не знáю.   I have no idea (I do not know at all).
 26. Я хорошó понимáю.   I quite understand.
 27. По суббóтам.   On Saturdays.
 28. Её сестрá звалáсь Татьяной.   (Пýшкин.)   Her sister was called Tatiana.

29. "И поля́ цвету́т, и леса́ шумя́т,
   И лежа́т в земле́ гру́ды зо́лота,
   И во все́х конца́х све́та бе́лого
   Про тебя́ идёт сла́ва гро́мкая."   (Ники́тин.)

"And your fields bloom, and your forests murmur, and masses
of gold lie hidden in your earth, and your fame is loudly
proclaimed in every corner of the wide world." (The poet is
referring to Russia.)

B. 1. По каки́м дня́м вы приезжа́ете в город? 2. По
вто́рникам и по четверга́м. 3. Лю́бите вы ката́ться на
конька́х? 4. Да, очень люблю́, но ката́юсь очень ре́дко.
5. Когда мы жи́ли в Москве́, мы часто ката́лись и на
конька́х, и на саня́х. 6. В каки́х города́х бы́ли вы, когда
вы е́здили в Росси́ю? 7. Мы бы́ли в Ленингра́де, в
Москве и во всех больши́х города́х по Волге. 8. Каких
русских писа́телей рекомендова́л вам учи́тель? 9. Он
всегда́ сове́тует читать Толсто́го. 10. Приходи́те
сегодня ве́чером,—мы побесе́дуем и о други́х писа́телях.
11. Меня очень заинтересова́ла эта кни́га. 12. О ней
были очень хоро́шие реце́нзии (reviews) во всех жур-
на́лах. 13. Эту книгу мо́жно получи́ть во всех библио́-
теках. 14. Росси́ю теперь называ́ют Сою́зом Сове́тов
(instr.) или : Советский Сою́з (nom.). 15. Теперь часто
говоря́т: "я уезжа́ю в Сою́з". 16. В Советском Сою́зе
семь респу́блик. 17. Росси́я одна из них. 18. Все
семь называ́ются Сою́зом Советских Социалисти́ческих
Респу́блик. 19. Это очень дли́нное назва́ние, поэ́тому
обыкнове́нно пи́шут С.С.С.Р. 20. Я очень хочу́ пое́хать
в Россию, но у меня нет де́нег. 21. Если вы хоти́те жить
в Москве, вы мо́жете дава́ть там уро́ки англи́йского
языка́. 22. У вас мно́го русских знако́мых, поэтому вам
так легко́ говори́ть по-русски. 23. Кто этот молодо́й
челове́к? 24. Это мой брат, позво́льте вас познако́мить.
25. Нет ли у вас чёрных черни́л, я не люблю́ писа́ть
си́ними. 26. А я совсем не могу́ писать, я забы́ла дома

ـчкй.   27. Да, здесь не очень светлó, без очкóв писать
грýдно.   28. Я рассказáл вам все нóвости.   29. Сегóдня
ﬀ нас былá óчень интерéсная бесéда.

C. Translate Exercises VIII C in the plural and decline.

D. 1. There are many good shops in our town.   2. She always
wears big hats.   3. Do you like buying books?   4. I want to
ُuy several Russian books, but I have no money.   5. Have you
ـeen the new houses in our street?   6. Yes, I saw them, but I have
ءever been in these houses.   7. My brother was saying that they
ـave (в них) very nice big rooms.   8. How many windows are there
n your sister's room?   9. It has three big windows: all three
ـook out into the garden.   10. Do you know many people in
ـondon?   11. Yes, I know many people there; that is why I like
ـoing there.   12. I go out to skate on Saturdays.   13. If you
ـave no skates, I shall give you mine.   14. Thank you, you are
very kind.   15. Allow me to introduce you to my father.   16. He
will tell you about his trips to Russia.   17. He has been there
ـeveral times.   18. What is this young man's surname?   19. Old
people like to give advice to the young.   20. I have written down
the names of all the pupils.   21. How many new pupils are there
n the class?   22. Six new pupils will come to-morrow.   23. What
ـs the time? There is no clock in the room.   24. My watch goes
very well.   25. What is the name of the shop where you bought it?
ـ6. I am always glad to see you.   27. What is the news in the
papers?   28. I shall tell you all the news after dinner.   29. She
always wanted to be a teacher.   30. I quite understand why he is
considered an authority (авторитéтом) on (в) this question.

LESSON XV

хорóший, good	лýчше	лýчший, сáмый лýчший
длѝнный, long	длиннéе	длиннéйший
корóткий, short	корóче	кратчáйший
богáтый, rich	богáче	богатéйший
бéдный, poor	беднéе	беднéйший
нóвый, new	новéе	новéйший
блѝзкий, near	блѝже	ближáйший
дорогóй, dear	дорóже	дражáйший
широ́кий, wide	шѝре	широчáйший
мéлкий, small, fine	мéльче	мельчáйший

крупный, big, coarse	крупнее	крупнейший
малый, little	меньше	малейший, slightest
низкий, low	ниже	нижайший
высокий, tall	выше	высший, высочайший
поздний, late	позднее	позднейший
строгий, severe	строже	строжайший
тонкий, thin	тоньше	тончайший
чистый, clean	чище	чистейший
дальний, distant	дальше	дальнейший

The above are some of the adjectives which possess a superlative in -ейший or -айший. Many of these superlatives have a special meaning (see Exercises XV a).

акцент accent
мир world, peace
рояль (masc.) grand piano
кланяться, поклониться to bow, greet
поклон bow, greeting

осторожный, -но careful, -ly
дешёвый, дешевле cheap, cheaper
громкий, громче loud, louder
редко, реже seldom, less often
часто, чаще often, oftener

THE COMPARISON OF ADJECTIVES.

§ 180. There are three degrees of comparison in Russian: *positive*, *comparative* and *superlative*, e.g. новый (new), новее or более новый (newer), новейший or самый новый (newest).

§ 181. The comparative degree is formed from the positive by changing the ending -ый or -ой into -ее (or -ей). This form can be used only predicatively (i.e. like the abbreviated form of adjectives), and is therefore not declined, e.g.

Этот дом красивее.   This house is prettier.

§ 182. When the object of comparison is mentioned, the comparative is followed *either* by the genitive, e.g.

Он умнее брата.   He is cleverer than his brother.

or by чем (than) with the nominative, e.g.

Наш дом красивее, чем ваш.   Our house is prettier than yours.
Нежели means the same as чем, and can be used instead. The comparative can also stand alone, as in the example in § 181 above.

§ 183. When the comparative is followed by его, её, их, used without a noun, the conjunction чем or нежели *must* be used, to avoid ambiguity, e.g. наш дом краси́вее чем их; наш дом краси́вее их would mean "prettier than they are".

§ 184. The comparative can also be formed by adding **бо́лее** (more) or **ме́нее** (less) to the positive, e.g. бо́лее краси́вый, ме́нее изве́стный (less known). This form is used when the comparative is used as an attribute, e.g.

Я хочу́ жить в бо́лее тёплом кли́мате.

As the simple comparative is not declined, this form *must* be used in the oblique cases, as in the example above.

§ 185. Some adjectives in the comparative form end in -**ший**, as **бо́льший** (greater), **ме́ньший** (smaller), and can be used attributively, though sometimes in the sense of a superlative, e.g.

> Вот лу́чшее ма́сло.   Here is better butter.
> Он с вы́сшим образова́нием.
> He has a higher (or University) education.

§ 186. A number of adjectives have their comparative ending in -**e**. Most of these have the stem ending in a guttural, therefore before the ending -e the usual change of consonant must be observed (see p. 17), e.g.

> высо́кий   comparative **вы́ше**
> дорого́й   „   **доро́же**

A complete list of these adjectives is given in the Grammar, p. 250.

§ 187. The comparative degree of adverbs (i.e. of those formed from adjectives of quality) is the same as that of the corresponding adjectives. Thus **бли́же**, **вы́ше**, etc., may be used either as adjectives or as adverbs. Most of these comparatives end in -e.

§ 188. The comparative **скоре́й** is used to express "quickly!" *lit.* "more quickly (than you are doing)". Cf. **Осторо́жнее**, "Be careful", "Carefully".

N.B. *Accent.* In connection with the comparative degree a rule concerning accent must be noted. Comparatives in -e have the accent on the second last syllable. Those in -ee or -ей, if of not more than two syllables, have the accent on the ending.

§ 189. The superlative degree is also formed in two ways:

(1) By adding **са́мый** (very *or* the most) to the positive, and sometimes to the comparative, e.g.

> са́мый краси́вый   the most beautiful
> са́мый лу́чший   the very best

(2) By adding the endings **-ейший**, **-ейшая**, **-ейшее** alway
accented) to the stem, e.g.

милейший	dearest
новейший	newest, latest

If the stem ends in a sibilant or a guttural, **-айший**, **-ая**, **-ее** (also
accented) are used, e.g.

широкий	superlative	широчайший
глубокий (deep)	,,	глубочайший
великий	,,	величайший

(See p. 252.)

§ 190. Of the two forms the first is the simpler and the more
widely used. Many adjectives do not have the second form, which,
however, is commonly used when no object of comparison is
mentioned, e.g.

Это новейшее изобретение.   This is the latest invention.

The superlative is used only attributively.

§ 191. The comparative followed by **всего** and **всех** has a superlative implication, e.g.

> Я больше всего люблю музыку.
>
> I like music more than anything else (*lit.* most of all).
>
> Он любит музыку больше всех.
>
> He likes music more than anyone else (does).

§ 192. The forms **по-лучше**, **по-дороже**, etc., mean "a little
better", "a little dearer". This use of **по-** may be compared with
its use in the formation of the perfect aspect (to do *some* reading,
etc.).

§ 193. Adjectives, as well as nouns, may be used in a diminutive
or augmentative sense. The word **маленький** is itself an example
of a diminutive adjective, as **-еньк-** and **-оньк-** are the suffixes
which form diminutive adjectives.

While **хороший** means *good*, **хорошенький** means *pretty*, usually
applied to little things, or to girls. Observe the special form of the
superlative: **прехорошенький**. See Grammar, p. 252.

§ 194. **Мелкий** and **крупный** are used of objects which admit,
as it were, of being *graded in size*. The best simple English equi-
valents are *fine* and *coarse*, but the exact translation is easily

•btained from the context. "Small" and "big" are often suffi-
ient.

У неё мелкие зубы.	She has small teeth.
Наша курица несёт крупные яйца.	Our hen lays big eggs.
Ж. Крупные деньги.	Bank-notes of high value.
Мелочь (noun f.); мелкие деньги.	Small money, change.

Exercises XV

A. 1. Мне читать легче, чем вам. It is easier for me to read than for you.

2. Мне легче читать, чем писать. I read more easily than I write.

3. У меня отец старше вашего. My father is older than yours.

4. Мой брат моложе вас. My brother is younger than you.

5. Она покупает более дешёвое масло. She buys cheaper butter.

6. Она покупает масло дешевле, чем вы. She pays less for butter than you do.

7. Я больше не буду. I'll never do it again.

8. Она больше не ходит туда. She no longer goes there.

9. Я лучше пойду домой. I had better go home.

10. Мне лучше сегодня. I feel better to-day.

11. Вам лучше всего начать сначала. The best thing for you to do is to start from the beginning.

12. Она больше всех читает по-русски. She reads Russian more than anyone else.

13. Она больше всего читает по-русски. She reads Russian more than any other language.

14. Тем не менее. Nevertheless.

15. Будьте осторожнее ! Be careful !

16. Иди скорей ! Come quickly !

17. Почему вы не сказали этого раньше? Why did you not say this before?

18. Приходите по-раньше. Come a little earlier.

19. По-реже. Not so often.

20. Это мой самый близкий друг. This is my best friend.

21. Кратчайший путь. The shortest way.

22. Ближайшая станция. The nearest station.

23. Новейший журнал. The latest magazine.

24. Беднейшее население. The poorest people (population).

25. Дражайший брат ! Dearest brother !

26. Нижайший поклон. Kindest regards (lit. a very low bow).

27. Строжа́йший вы́говор. The strictest censure.

28. Тонча́йшая рабо́та. The finest work.

29. Чисте́йший вздор. Sheerest nonsense (rubbish).

30. В дальне́йшем бу́дущем. In the very distant future.

31. Мельча́йший по́черк. The finest handwriting.

32. Крупне́йший сканда́л. The grossest scandal.

33. Дости́г я вы́сшей вла́сти. (Пушкин.) "I have attained the highest power."

34. У вас преми́ленькая до́чка. You have a very sweet little daughter.

35. Он вам кла́няется. He sends you his greetings.

36. Покло́н от бра́та. Greetings from my (your) brother.

B. 1. У них дом нове́е на́шего.   2. Они́ живу́т в бо́лее но́вом до́ме. 3. На́ша у́лица длинне́е ва́шей. 4. Моя́ ко́мната ме́ньше, чем его́. 5. Мы живём бли́же от шко́лы, чем вы. 6. Я пришёл в шко́лу ра́ньше други́х ученико́в. 7. Её шля́па краси́вее и ле́гче мое́й. 8. Ва́шей ма́ленькой сестре́ ле́гче чита́ть по-ру́сски, чем вам. 9. Её сёстры у́чатся в бо́лее дорого́й шко́ле. 10. У неё нет мла́дших сестёр. 11. Вот са́мый краси́вый дом в го́роде. 12. У него́ умне́йшая жена́. 13. Кто са́мый лу́чший учени́к в э́том кла́ссе? 14. Вот э́тот са́мый ма́ленький ма́льчик, он моло́же всех. 15. В э́том году́ (this year) у нас в шко́ле бо́льше ученико́в. 16. Чита́йте по-гро́мче, пожа́луйста. 17. У него́ го́лос гро́мче, чем у неё. 18. Ру́сский язы́к не трудне́е англи́йского. 19. Ле́гче вам тепе́рь говори́ть по-ру́сски? 20. Да, я зна́ю бо́льше слов тепе́рь. 21. Мы получа́ем все нове́йшие журна́лы. 22. Э́та газе́та выхо́дит ре́же тепе́рь. 23. Э́то высоча́йшая гора́ в ми́ре. 24. Иди́те скоре́е пожа́луйста, я не могу́ бо́льше ждать. 25. Поклони́тесь от меня́ сестре́. 26. Он присла́л всем ни́зкий покло́н.

C. Give the comparative of: ми́лый, дорого́й, дешёвый, высо́кий, ни́зкий, све́тлый, тёмный, хоро́ший, плохо́й, холо́дный, горя́чий, бли́зко, далеко́, ско́рый, ме́дленный, ча́сто, ре́дко, ра́но, по́здно, гро́мкий, ти́хий, мно́го, ма́ло, дли́нный, коро́ткий.

D. 1. His coat is shorter than mine. 2. This book is newer than yours. 3. I have bought the dearest book. 4. Which is the nearest station? 5. Which is the best library in town? 6. This room is longer than ours. 7. Have you heard the latest news? 8. I was told that you can get the latest papers in this shop. 9. Who is taller—you or I? 10. You are taller than I am. 11. It is easier for you to speak Russian because you have lived in Russia. 12. Who will show me the shortest way? 13. Fish is dearer than meat now. 14. Hats are cheaper in this shop. 15. You read better than his sister. 16. She plays the violin better than the piano. 17. They come to the lesson before anyone else. 18. Why did you not come sooner? 19. I find it easier to write now. 20. It was more difficult before. 21. She reads better than anyone else. 22. She has not the slightest accent. 23. They do not go to the theatre any more. 24. He likes the theatre more than anything else. 25. He reads Russian more than anybody else in the class. 26. Come to see us a little oftener. 27. Come quickly! 28. This is the nearest way to the station.

LESSON XVI

страна́ country
сторона́ side } see p. 16

страни́ца page

ино́й other

иностра́нец, -нца foreigner

иностра́нный foreign

стра́нный strange

за-грани́цей abroad

свобо́да freedom

свобо́дный free

свобо́дно freely, fluently

освобожда́ть, освободи́ть to liberate

освобожда́ться to be free(d)

во́ля liberty

выпуска́ть на во́лю to set free

дово́льный, -лен content, pleased

дово́льно enough, rather

удово́льствие pleasure

дово́льство plenty

возмо́жность (f.) opportunity, possibility

мо́жно it is possible, allowed, one may

нельзя́ it is impossible, one cannot

каза́ться (по-) to seem

ка́жется it seems

светáет it dawns

смерка́ется dusk falls

проводи́ть вре́мя to spend time

шить (с-) to sew (see p. 207)

конце́рт concert

ва́нна bath

ва́нная bathroom

и́мя name

вре́мя time

зна́мя standard, flag
де́ло affair, business

толпа́ crowd
про́тив (gen.) against

на про́шлой неде́ле last week
на э́той неде́ле this week
на бу́дущей неде́ле next week
в про́шлом году́ or ме́сяце last year or month
в э́том году́ this year

в бу́дущем году́ next year
в про́шлую сре́ду last Wednesday
в э́ту суббо́ту this Saturday
в бу́дущий четве́рг next Thursday

§ 195. The construction used to express the verb "to have" has already been explained in Lesson IIIa.

In the future tense the same construction is used, e.g.

За́втра у меня́ бу́дет уро́к. To-morrow I shall have a lesson
У него́ не бу́дет уро́ка. He will not have a lesson.
У нас бу́дут го́сти сего́дня. We shall have visitors to-day.

§ 196. Име́ть, *to have*, is mostly used with the meaning of *to possess*, and is, therefore, used in any "official" statement of fact. Such a statement as "Man has two eyes and two ears" may be rendered in two ways:

У челове́ка два гла́за и два у́ха,
or   Челове́к име́ет два гла́за и два у́ха.

But име́ть cannot be used in the examples in § 195 above.

Име́ть is 1st conjugation: име́ю, име́ешь, etc. It has no perfective in its direct meaning, because "to have had" would mean to a Russian "to have no longer". The perfective возъиме́ть (*or* возыме́ть) means to conceive a wish, hope, etc. There are certain other verbs which have no perfective aspect, owing to the nature of the action expressed (see p. 222).

§ 197. Although -я is a feminine gender ending, nouns in -мя are neuter. There are, however, only ten such nouns and they have a special form of declension (see p. 237).

	Singular	Plural
Nom.	и́мя	им-ен-а́
Gen.	и́м-ен-и	им-ён
Dat.	и́м-ен-и	им-ен-а́м
Acc.	и́мя	им-ен-а́
Instr.	и́м-ен-ем	им-ен-а́ми
Prep.	об и́м-ен-и	об им-ен-а́х

Like и́мя are declined вре́мя (вре́м-ен-и, etc.), зна́мя and others, see p. 233.

§ **198.** **Сам,** the emphatic personal pronoun *self,* is the same for all persons. Note the declension:

	Masculine and neuter	Feminine	Plural (all genders)
Nom.	сáм, самó	самá	сáми
Gen.	сам-огó	сам-óй	сам-úх
Dat.	сам-омý	сам-óй	сам-úм
Acc.	сам-огó	сам-оё	сам-úх
Instr.	сам-úм	сам-óй (óю)	сам-úми
Prep.	о сам-óм	о сам-óй	о сам-úх

§ **199.** The "reflexive" possessive pronoun **свой** means *one's own* (cf. Latin *suus*). It may be used of all persons, and always refers to the subject, e.g.

Я забыл **свой** очки.	I have forgotten my spectacles.
Принесли **вы свою** книгу?	Have you brought your book?
Она пишет **своим** пером.	She is writing with her own pen.
Они любят **своего** отца.	They love their father.

It must be noted that **свой** used as an adjective never qualifies the subject, e.g.

> Он говорит, что **его** (*not* свой) брат уéхал.
> He says that his brother has gone.

except in a few sayings, as

Своя рубáшка блúже к тéлу. Blood is thicker than water (*lit.* One's own shirt is closer to one's body).
Вы у нас свой человéк. You are one of us.

Used in the 3rd person singular, masculine and neuter, it helps to avoid ambiguity, e.g.

> Он любит своего отца i.e. his own father.
> Он любит его отца i.e. someone else's father.

IMPERSONAL VERBS.

§ **200.** *Impersonal verbs,* i.e. verbs used only in the 3rd person singular, are not very numerous in Russian, e.g. **смеркáется, светáет.** Another is **имéться** but it is used only idiomatically, e.g.

> у нас имéется we have

Хотéться ("to feel like", to have a desire) is a typical impersonal verb. It is frequently used in all tenses (but not in the imperative).

Its perfective is **захотéться** (to conceive a desire). The English subject is expressed in the dative. Its tenses are:

	Imperf.	*Perf.*
Present	мне хóчется	—
Past	мне хотéлось	мне захотéлось
Future	мне бýдет хотéться	мне захóчется
Conditional	мне хотéлось бы	мне захотéлось бы

Other impersonal verbs, such as **мне вéрится** (I believe), **мне не спится** (I cannot sleep), and various impersonal expressions, will be found in the Grammar, p. 232.

§ 201. **Мóжно** and **нельзя́** are also impersonal expressions, meaning "it is allowed" and "it is not allowed", thus **нельзя́** is the negative of **мóжно**; they are used with the dative or by themselves, e.g.

Мóжно войти́? May I come in?   *Reply* Мóжно. You may. Нельзя́. You may not.

Емý нельзя́ кури́ть.   He is not allowed to smoke.

The English "cannot help" is rendered by **не могý не** or **нельзя́ не**, e.g.

Я не могý не рáдоваться.   I cannot help rejoicing.

Нельзя́ не интересовáться.   One cannot but be interested.

§ 202. The word **дéло** covers anything one *does* (**дéлать**); it also means *matter, affair,* etc., e.g.

ходи́ть *or* идти́ по дéлу	to go on business
иметь дéло к (dat.)	to have business with
thus, у меня к вам дéло.	
мéжду дéлом	at odd times (i.e. between times of business)

Как идут его делá?   How are his affairs progressing?

Дело идёт о том, что...   The point in question is that...

Other examples are given in the Exercise XVI A.

§ 203. **За-грани́цей** is an adverbial expression formed with **за...** and the instrumental to denote a state of *rest*.

За-грани́цу (**за** and accusative) denotes *motion*, e.g.

жить за-грани́цей   to live abroad
ехать за-грани́цу   to go abroad

§ 204. **Проводи́ть время**, "to spend time", has as its perfective **провести́**, *but* **провожáть**, "to see off" or "accompany", has the perfective **проводить**.

Exercises XVI

A. 1. Ско́лько вре́мени вы тут?   How long have you been here?

2. Я не име́ю вре́мени ⎞
   У меня́ нет вре́мени ⎰ I have no time.

3. Име́ете вы возмо́жность? ⎞
   Есть у вас возмо́жность? ⎰ Have you the opportunity?

4. Что вы име́ете про́тив?   What have you against it?

5. Про́тив э́того ничего́ нельзя́ сказа́ть.   Nothing can be said against it.

6. Я бу́ду вас звать по и́мени.   I shall call you by your first name.

7. У меня́ нет ни мину́ты свобо́дной.   I have not a free moment.

8. Всему́ своё вре́мя.   Everything in its proper time.

9. У меня́ мно́го де́ла.   I am very busy.

10. У него́ сли́шком мно́го де́ла.   He has too much to do.

11. Э́то не его́ де́ло.   It is not his business; no business of his.

12. Како́е мне де́ло?   What do I care?

13. Я иду́ по де́лу.   I am going on business.

14. Как дела́?   How are you getting on?

15. Моё де́ло сторона́.   I wash my hands of it; it does **not** concern me.

16. Жить на чужо́й стороне́.   To live in a foreign land.

17. В са́мом де́ле?   Indeed?

18. В чём де́ло?   What is the matter?

19. Име́ю честь.   I have the honour.

20. Име́ть удово́льствие.   To have the pleasure.

21. Он всем дово́лен (instr.).   He is pleased with everything.

22. С удово́льствием!   With pleasure!

23. Дово́льно, не бу́дем бо́льше об э́том говори́ть.   Enough: we will not discuss this any further.

24. Здесь дово́льно хо́лодно.   It is rather cold here.

25. С ним нельзя́ бы́ло не согласи́ться.   One could not but agree with him.

26. Мы поговори́ли на свобо́де.   We had a quiet chat (unhindered).

27. Когда́ вы бу́дете свобо́дны (or освободи́тесь) сего́дня?   When will you be free to-day?

28. Его́ освободи́ли.   He was set free.

29. Ка́жется уже́ по́здно.   It must (seems to) be late already.

30. Как вам ка́жется?   How does it appear to you?

31. Мне захоте́лось.   I felt a desire.

32. Мне ничего не хочется. I feel I don't want anything.

33. Богатому не спится: богатый вора (gen.) бойтся. A rich man cannot sleep, for he fears thieves.

34. Позвонить по телефону. To ring up on the telephone.

35. Мы здесь все свои. We are all friends here.

B. 1. Будет у вас время перевести эту страницу? 2. На прошлой неделе у меня не было ни одного свободного дня. 3. Сделайте это для меня, когда у вас будет время. 4. У меня слишком много дела на будущей неделе. 5. У него нет возможности поехать за-границу. 6. Скоро у нас будет телефон. 7. Я всегда хотел иметь в доме телефон. 8. В этой квартире не имеется ванны. 9. У моих знакомых свой дом в Лондоне. 10. Они уже давно живут в своём доме. 11. Я никогда не была в их новом доме. 12. Он не может работать в своей комнате. 13. Я могу писать только своим пером. 14. Его шляпа мне слишком мала. 15. Он говорит, что продаёт свой дом. 16. Он сам сказал мне это. 17. Она сама сшила это платье. 18. Мои сёстры делают всё в доме сами. 19. Дайте это письмо ему самому. 20. Ему не хочется идти в театр сегодня. 21. Ей кажется, что он недоволен своей работой. 22. Все довольны его работой. 23. Сегодня мне вдруг захотелось послушать пение. 24. Я позвонила своей подруге и мы поехали на концерт. 25. Мы очень хорошо провели вечер. 26. После концерта подруга проводила меня домой. 27. Она, кажется, была очень довольна концертом. 28. Я с удовольствием думаю, что на будущей неделе приезжает драма. 29. Они теперь свободно говорят по-русски. 30. Видели вы сегодня процессию (procession) с красными знамёнами? 31. Уже смеркалось, когда мы приехали домой. (Толстой.) 32. Светает, товарищ, работать давай. (Омулевский.)

C. 1. It seems to him. 2.. I seemed to you. 3. We are going abroad. 4. I am very pleased. 5. We shall be pleased. 6. She is displeased. 7. He was freed. 8. They were freed. 9. This week I am free. 10. He is going away this year. 11. Last year. 12. Last Sunday. 13. Next Saturday. 14. This Monday. 15. We have. 16. You have not. 17. You will not have. 18. Have you not? 19. Had she not? 20. We had nothing. 21. We feel like. 22. They feel like. 23. Who will see me home? 24. He accompanies her. 25. I have spent two hours.

D. 1. I shall have no time next week. 2. I have too much to do. 3. Next week he is going to London on business. 4. After that he will be free the whole month. 5. Last week I had the pleasure of meeting your father. 6. We met several times abroad. 7. In what countries abroad have you been? 8. Do you like foreigners? 9. With what are you displeased? 10. My sister is very pleased that she is going abroad next year. 11. How long did you live abroad? 12. We have not been abroad for a long time. 13. Dusk was already falling, and I had to go home. 14. My father does not like to spend evenings alone. 15. It seems to me that during the day he has too much to do. 16. He always sits in his room. 17. It is not very warm in his room. 18. Have you an opportunity of working in the library? 19. There are very few foreign books in our libraries. 20. He is rather an old man. 21. He has several names. 22. They have a house on the other side of the street. 23. He has lived in this house all his life. 24. Are you free to-night? 25. I feel like going to the theatre; will you come with me? 26. With pleasure. 27. I am going on business; will you accompany me? 28. When I was going to my work, I saw a big crowd; they were carrying a red flag. 29. I am finishing the last page of the book (which) you gave me. 30. May I come next week?—No, you may not. 31. I cannot help being glad that our friends will be here to-morrow. 32. One cannot help agreeing (согласи́ться) that this is only just. 33. Ring me up if you are free to-morrow. 34. May I bring all my books with me when I come to live with you? 35. Of course you may, there is a big bookcase in your room. 36. There is enough room in it for all your books. 37. I cannot believe that the time has passed so quickly. 38. He himself put his name in the book.

LESSON XVII

класть, положи́ть to put "ly-ing"

ста́вить, по- to put "standing"

сажа́ть, посади́ть to put "sitting"

ложи́ться, лечь to lie down

станови́ться, стать to stand up

сади́ться, сесть to sit down

мать mother

дочь daughter

дитя́ (n., pl. де́ти) child

де́тский children's

зверь (m.) wild animal

ди́кий wild

живо́тное animal

дома́шний domestic

волк wolf

медве́дь (m.) bear

лиса́, лиси́ца fox

ло́шадь (f.) horse

коро́ва cow

ко́шка cat

мех fur

ого́нь (m. gen. огня́) fire

шкаф (loc. в—у́) cupboard

ска́терть (f.) tablecloth

накрыва́ть на стол, накры́ть to lay (set) the table

посте́ль (f.) bed, bedding

крова́ть (f.) bedstead

дива́н couch, sofa

па́лка stick

коле́но (pl. коле́ни) knee

це́рковь (f.) church

путь (m.) way

ше́ствие procession

путеше́ствие journey

путеше́ствовать to travel

ряд row

ря́дом (adv.) close by;—с+instr. beside

поря́док order

беспоря́док disorder

поря́дочный honest, respectable, considerable, decent

поря́дочно considerably, rather

служи́ть (по-) to serve

служи́тель servitor

слу́жба service, work

слуга́ (m.) servant

служа́нка maid-servant

коне́чно certainly, of course

§ 205. In Russian, adjectives which denote not only *quality* but *relation* to some person, animal, thing, or even material, are known broadly as *relative adjectives*.[1]

Apart from adjectives denoting material, nationality, etc., as золото́й, ру́сский, two groups of these adjectives should be distinguished:

(a) Those which indicate possession on the part of a person, e.g. се́стрин, -ина, -ино, -ины (sister's).

They are declined partly like nouns and partly like adjectives.

[1] These adjectives should not be confused with the relative pronoun кото́рый.

(*b*) Those referring to an animal, or to a species in general, e.g. во́лчий, во́лчья, во́лчье.

For the declension of both types of relative adjectives see Grammar, pp. 247, 248.

VERBS "TO PUT".

§ 206. A very important and interesting group of verbs is the group with the meaning *to put*, a verb so widely used in English. When using this verb in Russian one must bear in mind the *position* the action of "putting" imparts, i.e. one must think of the three verbs лежа́ть, стоя́ть, сиде́ть:

(1) **Лежа́ть** means *to lie*; *to put in a lying position* is **класть**, perfective **положи́ть**.

To lie down, i.e. *to put* oneself *in a lying position*, is **ложи́ться**, perfective **лечь**.

(2) **Стоя́ть** means *to stand*; *to put in a standing position* is **ста́вить**, perfective **поста́вить**.

To stand up, i.e. *to put* oneself *standing*, **станови́ться**, perfective **стать**.

Instead of these verbs, however, the verbs **встава́ть** and **встать** are often used.

(3) **Сиде́ть** means *to sit*; *to put sitting* is **сажа́ть**, or **сади́ть** (mostly "to plant"), perfective **посади́ть**.

To sit down or *to put* oneself *sitting* is **сади́ться**, perfective **сесть**.

§ 207. It must be particularly noted that the reflexive verbs **ложи́ться**, **станови́ться** and **сади́ться** (cf. French *se coucher* and *s'asseoir*) are not reflexive in the perfective aspect. These three verbs are the only ones of their kind, and this peculiarity may help to prevent confusion between **лежа́ть** (по-), *to lie*, which indicates state of *rest* or *permanency*, and requires a preposition with the locative (or instrumental) case, and **ложи́ться**, *to lie down*, which indicates *motion*, and requires a preposition with the accusative.

The same applies to the verbs **стоя́ть** and **станови́ться**; **сиде́ть** and **сади́ться**.

§ 208. The verb **становиться** is often used in a figurative sense, meaning *to become*, with the perfective **стать**, whereas **встать** is mostly used as the perfective of **становиться**, *to stand up*, as well as of **вставать**, *to rise* (cf. French *se lever*).

§ 209. The verb **класть** has the present: **кладу́, кладёшь**, etc.

(see p. 208). **Положить** and **ложиться, сидеть** and **посадить** are 2nd conjugation and therefore quite regular.

Лечь (future: **лягу, ляжешь,** 3rd plural **лягут**) is like **мочь** (see p. 208).

The imperative of **лечь** is **ляг, лягте**; the only one of its kind, i.e. with a hard consonant instead of **-ь** or **-и.**

Сесть: future **сяду, сядешь,** etc.

For past tenses see Grammar, pp. 226, 227.

§ 210. The verb **стать** is used as an auxiliary verb in the future tense, e.g.

Я не стану этого есть.   I shall not eat this.

With the meaning "to start" it always requires another verb as a complement, e.g.

Он стал рассказывать.   He began to relate.

Не стал has the meaning *stopped.*

§ 211. Мать and **дочь** are modern forms of the older **матерь** and **дочерь** with the suffix -**ер**-, which reappears in declension. **Дитя** in the singular is less frequently used than the other word for "child", **ребёнок** (see p. 241); but in the plural **дети** is mostly used.

For the declension of all these words, as well as of **путь** and **церковь,** see Grammar, p. 237.

§ 212. Чей (whose) is a special pronoun, used as an adjective (see p. 244). The genitive of **кто** is used only after prepositions, and is never used in the sense of *whose,* but the genitive of **который** may be so used, especially as a relative pronoun, e.g.

Ученик, отец которого был сегодня в школе, уезжает.

The pupil whose father was in school to-day is leaving.

Чей changes by gender and number, and is used in all cases; its declension is like that of **лисий** or **третий.**

Singular

	Masculine and neuter	Feminine	Plural
Nom.	чей, чьё	чья	чьи
Gen.	чьего	чьей	чьих
Dat.	чьему	чьей	чьим
Acc.	Like nom. or gen.	чью	Like nom. or gen.
Instr.	чьим	чьей (ею)	чьими
Prep.	о чьём	о чьей	о чьих

Exercises XVII

A. 1. Пора ложи́ться спать. It is time to go to bed.

2. Я до́лжен лечь ра́но сего́дня. I must go to bed early to-night.

3. Когда́ вы легли́? When did you go to bed?

4. Мы до́лго не ложи́лись спать. We did not go to bed till late.

5. Не клади́те ничего́ в э́тот я́щик (acc.). Do not put anything in this box.

6. Положи́те газе́ту на стол. Put the newspaper on the table.

7. Поста́вьте ваш стул сюда́. Put your chair here.

8. Не станови́тесь так бли́зко к огню́. Do not stand so near the fire.

9. Стань сюда́! Stand here!

10. Встань, просни́сь, не лени́сь,
    На себя́ погляди́:
    Что ты был, и что стал,
    И что есть у тебя́. (Кольцо́в.)
    Get up, wake up; don't be lazy; look at yourself—what you used to be, what has become of you, and what you have.

11. Посади́те де́вочку к себе́ на коле́ни. Take the little girl on your knee.

12. Ся́ду я за стол, да поду́маю,
    Как на све́те жить одино́кому. (Кольцов.)
    I shall sit down at the table and think how I am to live in the world all alone.

13. Ста́вить в приме́р. To set as an example.

14. Бы́ло так те́сно, что ни стать, ни сесть. The place was so crowded that one could neither sit, nor stand.

15. Сади́тесь пожа́луйста. Sit down, please.

16. Ся́дьте, е́сли не хоти́те стоя́ть. Sit down if you do not wish to stand.

17. Они́ не ста́ли (переста́ли) сажа́ть старика́ за стол. They stopped giving the old man a seat at table.

18. Мне ста́ло жа́рко. I began to feel hot.

19. Сухи́м путём. Overland (*lit.* by a dry way).

20. Во́лчий аппети́т. A wolf-like appetite.

21. С волка́ми жить—по во́лчьи выть. When in Rome, do as the Romans do (*lit.* Live with the wolves—howl with the wolves).

22. Посади́те их ря́дом. Seat them side by side.

23. Она́ живёт ря́дом со мной. She lives next door to me.

24. У вас всё в тако́м отли́чном поря́дке. Everything you have is in such beautiful order.

25. В доме цари́л беспоря́док. Disorder reigned in the house.

26. Чей это дом ря́дом с ва́шим? Whose house is this next yours?

27. Где он слу́жит? Where does he work?

28. Он не хо́дит тепе́рь на слу́жбу. He does not go to his work now.

29. Когда́ вы пришли́ со слу́жбы? (see § 88). When did you come back from your work?

30. С чьи́ми детьми́ игра́ет ваша до́чка? With whose children does your daughter play?

31. Что ста́ло с вашим бра́том? What has become of your brother?

32. Волко́в боя́ться, в лес не ходи́ть. (Посло́вица.) He who fears wolves, must not go into the wood.

B. 1. У́тренние газе́ты всегда́ лежа́т в столо́вой. 2. Кто кладёт их туда́? 3. Сего́дня служа́нка положи́ла газеты в се́стрину ко́мнату. 4. Когда́ вы ложи́тесь спать? 5. Обыкнове́нно дово́льно рано, но вчера мы все легли́ очень по́здно. 6. В чьей ко́мнате стоит тепе́рь роя́ль? 7. Кто поста́вил его туда́? 8. Он всегда́ ста́вит свою́ па́лку в угол. 9. Поста́вьте свой стул к столу́ и ся́дьте ря́дом со мной. 10. Не ложи́тесь на этот дива́н. 11. Ло́шадь и коро́ва дома́шние живо́тные, а волк и медве́дь ди́кие зве́ри. 12. Я люблю́ путеше́ствовать мо́рем, но не сухи́м путём. 13. Лисий мех доро́же во́лчьего. 14. О́сенью дни стано́вятся коро́че. 15. Коро́че станови́лся день. (Пу́шкин.) 16. Все замолча́ли и в комнате ста́ло ти́хо, как в це́ркви. 17. Они́ вошли́ и се́ли в ряд. 18. Не сади́тесь на этот стул. 19. Что вы посади́ли в саду́? 20. Не сажа́йте детей так бли́зко к огню́. 21. У его ма́тери мно́го дете́й. 22. У неё четы́ре до́чери и три сы́на. 23. Посади́те бра́та ря́дом с сестро́й. 24. Отец э́того молодо́го челове́ка слу́жит в ба́нке. 25. Каки́м путём вы е́здили в Росси́ю? 26. Мы е́здили мо́рем, че́рез Ки́льский кана́л. 27. Её ма́ленькая до́чка

хо́дит в Де́тский Сад.   28. Она́ не лю́бит ходи́ть одна́,
потому́ что бои́тся соба́к (gen.).   29. Чьи́м перо́м вы
пи́шете? Я пишу́ бра́тниным перо́м, у меня́ нет своего́.
30. Ру́сские де́ти лю́бят ска́зки про (about, +acc.) во́лка,
медве́дя и про хи́трую (sly) лису́.   31. Служа́нка накры́ла
на стол: она́ положи́ла ло́жки, ножи́ и ви́лки, но не
поста́вила таре́лок.   32. Автомоби́ль подъе́хал, и мы
пошли́ сади́ться.   33. Я ду́мал о челове́ке, в чьих рука́х
находи́лась моя́ судьба́ (fate). (Пу́шкин.).

C. 1. I am putting my hand on the table.   2. You have put
your chair at the table.   3. Put the little girl on the high chair.
4. I have planted vegetables.   5. Put your hat on the table.
6. Sit down.   7. Stand up.   8. He lay down.   9. She sat down.
10. We shall sit down.   11. You will lie down.   12. You lay
down.   13. What did you plant in the garden?   14. I am going
to bed.   15. They have gone to bed.   16. You will go to bed.
17. Don't go to bed.   18. Don't sit (down) on this chair.   19. Lie
down!   20. Don't put your stick here.   21. Don't put your book
on mine.   22. Don't plant vegetables this year.   23. She lays
the table.   24. You laid the table.   25. I have put the cup on
the table.   26. She put the plate in the cupboard.

D. 1. Little children go to bed at six o'clock.   2. When they
lived at the sea-side, they did not go to bed so early.   3. Who put
this chair at the fire?   4. I shall sit beside you, because I have
not brought my book.   5. May I put my books here?   6. Certainly,
always put everything you do not need there.   7. The maid is
laying the table; she is putting down plates, but she has forgotten
to put down forks.   8. Where am I to put my umbrella?   9. Put
it in the hall.   10. If I put it there, I shall forget it.   11. If you
feel cold, sit (down) nearer the fire.   12. Our cat always sits in
front of the fire.   13. It is getting dark early now; summer is
over (passed).   14. When we travelled in the North, we went to
bed late, because it was light during the whole night.   15. We
have brought a beautiful fox fur with us.   16. Where does your
uncle work now?   17. He works in the office, and he goes to his
work before anyone else in the house.   18. In whose office does
he work?   19. The office belongs to an English firm (фи́рма), and
he has worked there for ten years already.   20. They have excellent

order in their office. 21. But he comes from his work late at night. 22. What has become of your friend who went to Russia? 23. He is still there, but next year he will come home for the summer. 24. Does he like living there? 25. He sent a very interesting letter last week. 26. He writes that they killed a bear. 27. He will bring home a bearskin coat (шуба).

LESSON XVIII

внутри́ inside	вдвоём two together
позади́ behind, at the back	быть за́мужем to be married (of a woman)
пото́м then, next	
опя́ть again	выходи́ть, вы́йти за́муж to marry (of a woman)
сно́ва anew	
сперва́ at first, first	жени́ться to marry (of a man). See p. 223
наконе́ц at last, finally	
тому́ наза́д ago	ме́бель (f.) furniture
ина́че otherwise	отста́вка retirement
непреме́нно without fail	го́рький bitter
вероя́тно probably	кре́пкий firm, fast, sound
наприме́р for example	ду́шный, -но stuffy, stifling
постоя́нно continually	о́бщий general, common (to)
сгоряча́ in a passion, in haste	о́бщество society, community

откла́дывать	отложи́ть	to put aside, postpone
предлага́ть	предложи́ть	to offer
доставля́ть	доста́вить	to deliver
заставля́ть	заста́вить	to compel, "make", force
представля́ть	предста́вить	to introduce, present
оставля́ть	оста́вить	to leave
реша́ть	реши́ть	to decide
старе́ть	по-	to grow old
меня́ть	переменя́ть	to change (cf. непреме́нно)
переду́мывать	переду́мать	to change one's mind

ADVERBS.

§ 213. Russian adverbs are divided into the same classes as in English, i.e. into adverbs of *place*, *time*, *manner*, etc. (see Grammar, p. 261).

It must be noted, however, that Russian is more exact than English in using the adverbs "whither", "hither" and "thither".

Thus, the adverbs где (where) and куда (whither) must not be confused, e.g.

Куда вы идёте?   Where (whither) are you going?

Где вы идёте? would sound ridiculous, as the enquirer can see for himself *where* (i.e. in what place) the other person is going (i.e. walking). One must distinguish similarly between там (there) and туда (thither), здесь (here) and сюда (hither).

§ 214. Apart from simple adverbs such as где, здесь, тогда, теперь, etc., Russian adverbs may be formed from other parts of speech, following the general rules concerning cases, etc. (see below). Adverbs formed from *nouns* include:

вверх	вверху	up
наверх	наверху	upstairs
вниз	внизу	down, downstairs
вперёд	впереди	forward, in front of
назад	назади	back, at the back
наружу	снаружи	outside
всторону	всторонé	aside, at the side, etc.
набок	набоку	sideways

Наверху (upstairs) (*lit.* on the top) is formed from the preposition на and the noun верх (top), in the locative case, to indicate *state of rest* (see § 72), e.g.

жить наверху   to live upstairs

But "to go upstairs" is ходить (*or* идти) наверх, i.e. на with the accusative to indicate *motion*. Similarly внизу (downstairs, state of rest) is formed from в and низ in the locative case; вниз (down(stairs)), from в with the accusative, to indicate *motion*. The use of the instrumental case of nouns in adverbial expressions has often been mentioned already (see § 62).

§ 215. The adverb of manner вместе, *together*, is formed according to the same rule as those in the preceding paragraph. It literally means "in the same place" (locative). It should not be confused with the preposition вместо (formed from в with the accusative), *instead of*, *lit.* "in the place of". (Вместо requires the genitive.)

§ 216. Adverbs formed from *pronouns* follow the same rules, e.g.

совсем (со + instr. of всё)	altogether
зачем (за + instr. of что)	why, what for
затем (за + instr. of то)	because

почему́ (по + dat. of что)	why
потому́ что (по + dat. of то)	because
пото́м (по + prep. of то)	then
оттого́ (от + gen. of то)	because of that

§ 217. Adverbs formed from *adjectives of quality* have already been used and explained (see § 102). But there are also some adverbs formed from adjectives by means of prepositions, e.g.

сно́ва	anew	наве́рно	probably
сперва́	at first	напра́во	on the right
вообще́	in general	нале́во	on the left

§ 218. Adverbs are formed from *relative adjectives* by the prefix по-, changing the adjectival ending -ий into -и, e.g.

по-ру́сски, in Russian; по-де́тски, in a child's way (see p. 262).

Note in particular adverbs formed with the prefix по- and the dative of possessive pronouns or adjectives (see p. 262), e.g.

по-но́вому	in the new way
по-мо́ему	in my opinion

§ 219. Adverbs formed from *verbs* appear either in the form of gerunds, e.g. мо́лча (in silence), хотя́ (although), несмотря́ на (in spite of), or in an imperative form, e.g. аво́сь (perhaps), небо́сь (never fear), бу́дто (as if: будь + то), почти́ (almost).

§ 220. *Verbs "to put" with prefixes.* The verb -ложи́ть is not used alone, and with prefixes other than по- has various meanings, as:

вы́ложить	to put out
вложи́ть	to put in
отложи́ть	to postpone
наложи́ть	to fill
уложи́ть	to pack away

Their compound imperfectives are formed with the same prefixes and the verb -кла́д-ыв-ать (from класть), as: выкла́дывать, откла́дывать (see p. 227).

§ 221. The verb ста́вить with prefixes has compound imperfectives ending in -вля́ть (see p. 228), as:

вставля́ть, вста́вить	to put in
выставля́ть, вы́ставить	to put out
отставля́ть, отста́вить	to put aside

§ 222. The compound imperfectives of **садить** with prefixes are represented by **саживать**, with the same prefixes, as:

высаживать, высадить	to set down (from a vehicle)
пересаживать, пересадить	to transplant, help over

§ 223. Many of these verbs can be used as reflexive verbs, as **укладываться** (to pack), **пересаживаться** (to change places), **представляться** (to introduce oneself).

Exercises XVIII

A. 1. Это совсем другое дело. This is quite a different matter.

2. Тише едешь, дальше будешь. More hurry less speed.

3. Сколько горьких слёз украдкой
   Я в ту ночь пролью. (Лермонтов.)
   How many bitter tears shall I shed in secret that night.

4. Уж постоим мы головою за родину свою. (Лермонтов.) We will give up our lives (*lit.* heads) for our fatherland.

5. Однажды, в студёную зимнюю пору,
   Я из лесу вышел. Был сильный мороз.... (Некрасов.)
   Once, during the cold winter time, I came out of a wood. There was a severe frost.

6. Ещё ребёнком лишилась она матери. While yet a child she lost her mother.

7. Откуда ветер—оттуда счастье. (Пословица.) Whence the wind blows, thence comes happiness.

8. Пойдём, куда глаза глядят. (Пушкин.) Let us go where our eyes look (cf. follow one's nose).

9. Сперва шёл сильный дождь, потом ветер разогнал тучи, и наконец погода прояснилась. At first heavy rain fell, then a breeze dispersed the clouds, and finally the weather cleared.

10. По-нашему говорила рыбка. (Пушкин.) The little fish spoke as we do.

11. Казаки ехали молча. The Cossacks rode in silence.

12. Она выходит замуж. She is getting married.

13. Она замужем. She is married.

14. Он женится (на + prep.). He is getting married.

15. Он женат (на + prep.). He is married.

16. Он женился. He got married.

17. На ком он женат? To whom is he married?

18. Зачем вам решать немедленно? Why should you decide immediately?

19. За после́дний год. During the past year.
20. Ведь я то́же был там. You know I was also there.
21. Поезд без переса́дки. A through train.
22. Я ехал с двумя́ (see p. 259) переса́дками. I had to change twice during my journey.
23. Откла́дывать в до́лгий ящик. To put off till doomsday.
24. Там чудеса́; там ле́ший бро́дит. (Пу́шкин.) Wonders are there; there a wood spirit lurks.
25. Позво́льте вам предста́вить мою́ сестру́. May I introduce my sister.
26. Мы ви́делись два го́да тому́ наза́д. We saw each other two years ago.

B. 1. Не откла́дывай до за́втра, что мо́жешь сде́лать сего́дня. 2. Я хочу́ отложи́ть свой отъе́зд на неде́лю (see § 164). 3. На бе́рег больши́ми шага́ми он сме́ло и пря́мо идёт. (Ле́рмонтов.) 4. Наконе́ц тот же возо́к, кото́рый привёз меня́, отвёз нас опя́ть на кварти́ру. (Акса́ков.) 5. Тепе́рь на́добно рассказа́ть, куда́ привезли́ меня́. (Аксаков.) 6. Не бу́дем ничего́ реша́ть сгоряча́. 7. Иди́те пря́мо, потом напра́во, и вы вы́йдете к вокза́лу. 8. Он хо́чет де́лать всё по-сво́ему. 9. Мы жи́ли снача́ла наверху́, а потом перее́хали вниз. 10. Не огля́дывайтесь наза́д, смотри́те всегда́ вперёд. 11. Дом каза́лся лу́чше снару́жи, чем он был внутри́. 12. То́лько мно́го поздне́е мы по́няли, почему́ это было так, а не ина́че. 13. Что заста́вило его оста́вить всё и уехать? 14. Вы совсе́м не старе́ете. 15. Ведь я вам говори́ла об э́том ра́ньше, не правда ли? 16. Мой оте́ц очень постаре́л за после́дние два го́да. 17. Моему́ бра́ту предложи́ли очень интере́сную рабо́ту. 18. Он вероя́тно не мо́жет реши́ть какой дать отве́т. 19. Он вы́шел в отста́вку и живёт тепе́рь в дере́вне. 20. Я никогда́ не хожу́ за поку́пками; нам всё доставля́ют на́ дом. 21. Мне сказа́ли в библиоте́ке, что для меня́ бу́дут откла́дывать все нови́нки (new books). 22. Отста́вьте свой стул от две́ри; отту́да ду́ет. 23. Вчера́ у нас в до́ме переста́вили всю ме́бель; я совсем не узна́ла своей комнаты. 24. Я люблю ездить ночным поездом; он без пересадки. 25. Я не знал, что вы опять переменили квартиру. 26. Оставьте мне свой адрес, и я вам напишу непременно. 27. Хоть спать было душно, спал я крепко. (Лермонтов.) 28. Все были очень довольны, когда услышали, что она вышла замуж за вашего брата. 29. Как давно она замужем? 30. На ком жениться мне? (Грибоедов.)

C. 1. I always sit in the front. 2. Go forward. 3. I live upstairs. 4. We are going down. 5. Don't go upstairs. 6. The boat was lying sideways. 7. He postpones nothing. 8. She put this aside. 9. She packed her books. 10. They are packing. 11. To begin anew. 12. They began anew. 13. I am putting together my papers. 14. Put your books together. 15. He is putting them together. 16. She puts the letter in. 17. I have not put it in. 18. I have put in a new nib (pen). 19. She is putting in a new nib. 20. She is getting married. 21. She has got married. 22. She is married. 23. He married three years ago. 24. She has been married for five years (pres.).

D. 1. Put aside this hat for me, please; I shall call in half an hour. 2. May I postpone my lesson till to-morrow? 3. Come next week without fail. 4. Who delivers the paper to you? 5. I buy a paper myself when I go to the office. 6. The teacher made me copy everything again (anew). 7. First we had dinner, then went to the theatre, and finally to a café. 8. Our new theatre is very beautiful, both outside and inside. 9. During the last three years my brother and my sister got married. 10. To whom is she married? (за + instr.). 11. When did she get married? (acc.). 12. Whom did he marry? (на + prep.). 13. To whom is he married? 14. He does everything his own way. 15. In my opinion you must decide yourself. 16. I want to change my book to-night, otherwise it will be too late. 17. Introduce me to your elder brother. 18. What have you decided to do? 19. I shall go upstairs and shall read there till dinner time. 20. I shall wait for you downstairs in the dining-room. 21. It is very stuffy here, let us go outside (наружу). 22. Come here and tell me what made you change your mind. 23. Offer him some bread and butter first. 24. He will probably come with us to the concert. 25. Who left all these books on the table?

LESSON XVIII*a*

уставáть to get tired

доставáть to reach, procure, get

заставáть to find in, at

отставáть to lag behind

переставáть to cease, stop

оставáться to remain, stay

расставáться (c + instr.) to part

усáживаться to take one's seat

заседáть to sit (of a committee)

заседáние sitting, meeting

останáвливаться to stop (intr.)

недоставáть to lack

недостáток lack, want

наканýне on the eve

трéтьего дня the day before yesterday

пóсле-зáвтра the day after to-morrow

на-дня́х the other day *or* one of these days

бросáть(ся), брóсить(ся) to throw (*refl.* to rush)

угождáть, угоди́ть (dat.) to please, strive to please

негóдный good for nothing

бывáть to be usually, exist (see § 228)

бывáлый experienced

почти́ almost

всётаки all the same, yet

так как as (because)

как раз just as

зарáз at once, together

заоднó unanimously, at the same time

круг circle

кругóм round (as prep. + gen.)

ми́мо (gen.) past, by

друг дрýга one another

зáдний back (adj.)

вещь (f.) thing

вóзле (gen.) beside

§ 224. The verb стать may also be used with prefixes, which change the meaning, e.g.

отстáть	to lag behind
устáть	to get tired
перестáть	to cease, etc.

These verbs are very commonly used. The corresponding imperfectives are отста-ва-ть (pres. отстаю), etc. (See above.)

§ 225. Я устáл (past perfective) means "I *am* tired" as well as "I *was* (i.e. became) tired". The adjective *tired* is устáлый (cf. Grammar, p. 210).

§ 226. The verbs сесть and лечь are less frequently used with prefixes, but a few of these should be noted, e.g.

присесть	to sit down for a moment
прилечь	to lie down for a moment

The imperfectives are присáживаться, приклáдываться. (See Grammar, p. 228.)

§ 227. The verbs **остановить** and **остановиться** (to stop) are derived from **становить**; the imperfective is **останавливать(ся)**.

§ 228. The verb **бывать** is sometimes considered as the imperfective of **быть**, with the meaning "to be *usually*", "to happen", "to exist". In this sense it has no future, but only present and past tenses: **бываю; бывал**, e.g.

> Я бываю дома только по средам.
> I am (usually) at home only on Wednesdays.
> Люди бывают разные.
> People are of all sorts (*lit.* "various").

In the negative, an impersonal construction (3rd person singular) is generally used, e.g.

> Теперь таких людей не бывает.
> Such people do not now exist.

But **бывать** may also have the meaning "to frequent" (but intrans.), "to go to visit", and in this sense has all three tenses (future, **буду бывать**), and a perfective in **по-**, e.g.

> Теперь я буду бывать у вас часто.
> Now I shall be able to visit you often.

§ 229. **Всё** as an adverb means "always", "still", "continually", e.g.

> А он всё не кончает.   And he is still at it.
> Они всё разговаривают.   They keep on talking.

Всё ещё can be used with the same meaning.

§ 230. **Накануне**, *on the eve*, an adverb of time, is formed from **на** and the locative of **канун** (the eve). It also means "the day before", and is not confined to the eve of important events.

§ 231. **Сейчас, тотчас, сию минуту**, all mean "presently" or "directly"; **сейчас же**, "immediately".

Сей, an old variant of **этот** (**сия** f., **сие** n., **сии** pl.) is now used only in compounds and phrases such as these; cf. **сегодня**; **до сих пор**, up till now.

§ 232. Adverbs, as well as adjectives, can be used in a diminutive form, e.g.

> хорошенько   nicely
> тихонько   quietly

§ 233. **Так** is used in various idiomatic expressions, e.g.

та́к себе	"so-so"
то́лько так	with no particular meaning
так-так	Well, well!
не так	not correct(ly)

Others are given in Exercise A of this lesson.

§ 234. **Ра́зве** and **неуже́ли** are both used for emphasis, and may be translated "Is it possible that...?" When used to render the English "surely", they must be followed by **не**, e.g.

Surely you know.	Разве вы не знаете?
Can that be so?	Неужели это так?

§ 235. In the expression **друг дру́га** (one another), only the second word is declined, as:

друг другу (dat.)	to one another
друг с другом (instr.)	one with another

Exercises XVIII*a*

A. 1. Я присе́л в ожида́нии. (Турге́нев.) Whilst waiting I sat down.

2. Когда вас можно заста́ть дома? When can one find you in?

3. Я застал его за рабо́той (instr.). I found him at work.

4. Все усе́лись за стол. They all sat down at the table.

5. У меня оста́лось то́лько пять рубле́й. I had only five roubles left.

6. Мне оста́лось (past) прочесть две страни́цы. I *have* still two pages to read.

7. Они почти́ не гово́рят друг с дру́гом. They hardly speak to each other.

8. У них всегда́ недоста́ток в деньга́х. They are always short of money.

9. Мне недостаёт двух ши́ллингов. I am two shillings short.

10. Чего вам недостаёт? What do you lack? (i.e. You have everything).

11. У вас и так всего́ мно́го. You have quite enough as it is.

12. Это один из его недоста́тков. This is one of his failings.

13. Они все были заодно́. They were unanimous.

14. Я проходи́л по у́лице...меня остановил ни́щий. (Турге́нев.) I was passing along the street when a beggar stopped me.

15. А нищий всё ждал.... (Тургенев.) And still the beggar waited.

16. А волки всё близятся. (Печерский.) And the wolves are getting ever nearer.

17. Это никуда не годится. This is worth nothing.

18. Что вам угодно? What do you wish?

19. На него трудно угодить. It is difficult to please him.

20. Кто бывал в моём положении, тот меня поймёт. (Лермонтов.) Anyone who has been in my position will understand me.

21. И вдруг его как не бывало. And suddenly he disappeared (*lit.* as if he had never been).

22. Этого с ним никогда не бывало. This never happened to him.

23. Он человек бывалый. He is a man of the world.

24. Я побываю у вас на-днях. I shall visit you one of these days.

25. Как вам это нравится? Так себе. How do you like this? Just so-so.

26. Я только так это говорю. I am just saying this without any special meaning.

27. Он это только так сказал. He didn't mean it.

28. Вы не так меня поняли. You have not understood me rightly.

29. Не так ли? Is that not so?

30. Так и быть. Be it so.

31. Козла бойся спереди, коня сзади, а злого человека со всех сторон. (Поговорка.) Beware of a goat from in front, of a horse from behind, but of a wicked man from every side.

B. 1. Неужели вы не узнали меня, когда я стоял возле вас у театра? 2. Разве можно забывать старых знакомых? 3. Накануне отъезда я ходил прощаться со всеми знакомыми. 4. Сейчас же сложите всё это вместе и уложите в один ящик. 5. Он плохо спит, потому что мало бывает на открытом воздухе. 6. Они нигде не бывают, поэтому их всегда можно застать дома. 7. Если вы так устали, вы должны прилечь. 8. Я никогда так не уставала, когда мы жили в деревне. 9. Сегодня отец дома; обыкновенно он каждый вечер бывает на заседаниях. 10. Я очень рада, что у нас заседания бывают

не о́чень ча́сто. 11. Вы э́то то́лько так говори́те, а са́ми
скуча́ете, когда́ их нет. 12. Я ви́жу, вы всё ещё чита́ете
э́ту кни́гу; ско́лько страни́ц вам оста́лось проче́сть?
13. Она́ отдаёт всё, что зараба́тывает, и себе́ оставля́ет
то́лько на ме́лкие расхо́ды. 14. Останови́тесь, я хочу́
зайти́ на по́чту; вероя́тно и вам на́до ма́рок. 15. Я о́чень
люблю́ остана́вливаться пе́ред о́кнами магази́нов, э́то
мой недоста́ток. 16. Где мо́жно доста́ть тако́й мате́рии?
Мне недостаёт полъя́рда. 17. Пока́ вы бу́дете уса́живаться
в автомоби́ль, я схожу́ наве́рх за перча́тками. 18. Зара́з
(заодно́) принеси́те и мой, пожа́луйста. 19. Не оста-
ва́йтесь там сли́шком до́лго, ина́че мы должны́ бу́дем
уе́хать без вас. 20. Они́ почти́ совсе́м переста́ли быва́ть
у нас, не зна́ю почему́. 21. Мы тепе́рь никогда́ не
быва́ем друг у дру́га. 22. Мы расста́лись друзья́ми.
23. Я бро́сился пре́жде всех и усе́лся на за́днем ме́сте.
(Л. Толсто́й.)

24. Я е́ду день, я е́ду два,
И всё поля́, круго́м поля́.

(Ма́йков.)

C. 1. I often get tired. 2. We are tired. 3. I used to get tired.
4. You never get tired. 5. I have procured. 6. We have got.
7. He will get. 8. She could not get. 9. He stopped. 10. Stop!
11. I remain. 12. He cannot remain. 13. You will stay. 14. We
shall part. 15. They have parted. 16. I am short of. 17. She
stops. 18. We do not stop. 19. They have stopped. 20. He
threw. 21. He threw himself. 22. Don't rush. 23. They please.
24. He is throwing. 25. She will throw.

D. 1. Where can I get this book? 2. You can get it in any
bookshop. 3. I went to see your sister yesterday, but did not
find her in. 4. One can (мо́жно) find her in only late in the evening.
5. The rain stopped, and we went for a walk. 6. If you stay a
little longer I shall go with you. 7. Tell me if you are tired and
we shall take (go in) a tram. 8. I had meetings every night last
week, but I am free this week. 9. There are usually no meetings
in summer. 10. Are you often at school in the evening? 11. Last

year I used to be (there) on Tuesdays and Thursdays, but this
year every day. 12. There are no such things now (do not exist).
13. He said that this pencil was no use and threw it away
(вы́бросить).   14. Don't bring more books; you read quite a lot
as it is. 15. You will wait if you don't find me in, will you not
(is that not so)? 16. I shall come to see you often in summer,
but not now. 17. You must write to your mother one of these
days. 18. How much money have you left? 19. I am short of
only two or three shillings. 20. When I have paid (fut.) for the
tickets, I shall have ten roubles left. 21. It seems to me that she
has no faults. 22. Where were you the day before yesterday?—
your windows were dark (in windows it was dark) when I was
passing by. 23. The day after to-morrow my father and brother
are going to the East. 24. They were packing the whole day
yesterday; they have so many things. 25. We shall all go to see
them off. 26. You must not forget each other.

LESSON XIX

не́кий a certain
не́который a certain, some
никако́й of no kind
не́сколько several, some
брать (pres. беру́, берёшь; perf. взять; fut. возьму́, -ёшь) to take
выбира́ть, вы́брать to choose
вы́бор choice
собира́ть, собра́ть to collect, gather
собира́ться, -бра́ться to get ready, gather (intrans.)
собра́нье collection, gathering
чу́вствовать (по-) to feel
чу́вство feeling
чутьё scent, feeling (for)
чу́ткий responsive, sensitive
чуть-чуть a very little
случа́ться, случи́ться to happen

слу́чай chance, accident
случа́йно by chance
па́мять (f.) memory
грусть (f.) sorrow, grief
гру́стный sad
жа́лкий piteous
жале́ть (по-) to pity, grudge
мне жаль I pity, am sorry for
к сожале́нию unfortunately
родно́й own, related
све́жий fresh
стихи́ verses
стихотворе́ние poem
по́лный full, complete
по́лон, -на́ (gen.) full of
наполня́ть, -по́лнить to fill
исполня́ть to execute, fulfil
о́браз form, shape, image
каки́м о́бразом? how?
таки́м о́бразом thus, so

§ 236. *Compound pronouns.* Among "compound" pronouns
must be noted particularly the indefinite pronouns **не́кто** (some

one, i.e. a certain person), не́что (something), кто́-то (some one, i.e. "some one or other"), что́-то (something), кто-нибу́дь (anyone), что-нибу́дь or что-ли́бо (anything); and also the negative pronouns никто́, ничто́, не́кого, не́чего.

§ 237. Не́кто and не́что are rarely used, and then only in the nominative case. The meaning is *positive*: "a certain person *or* thing" similar to that of кто́-то and что́-то by which they are replaced in the other cases.

Не́кого, не́чего (gen.), не́кому, не́чему (dat.), не́кем, не́чем (instr.), on the other hand, are *negative* in meaning (see examples below), and are written as one word. Note, however, that in the prepositional case, and when used with prepositions in general, the preposition comes *between* не and the pronoun, e.g. не́ о ком, не́ с чем. N.B. *Accent*: не́ in these expressions is always accented.

These forms are used only in a particular construction, given in § 239, below.

§ 238. The negative pronouns никто́ and ничто́ are declined like кто and что (see p. 244). When these pronouns are used with a preposition, the preposition is placed between ни and кто or что, e.g. ни о ком, ни с кем, etc.

§ 239. The following peculiarly idiomatic construction is very commonly used:

> Я ни от кого́ не жду́ пи́сем.
>
> I am not expecting a letter from anybody.
>
> Мне не́ от кого ждать писем.
>
> I have nobody from whom to expect a letter.

The same construction is applied to all cases, further examples being given in Exercise A of this lesson.

§ 240. -то and -нибу́дь added to the pronouns кто and что impart very different meanings, which may in general be compared with the English *some* and *any*, e.g.

Кто-то пришёл.	Somebody has come.
Кто-нибу́дь мо́жет прийти́.	Somebody (i.e. anybody) may come.
Он с ке́м-то разгова́ривает.	He is speaking to somebody.
Поговори́те с кем-нибу́дь.	Talk to somebody (i.e. to anybody).

It may be seen from the above examples that -то conveys a meaning of *definiteness*, -нибу́дь that of *indefiniteness* (ни + будь = whatever it may be).

§ 241. The pronouns **нéкий, нéкоторый, ничéй** (nobody's),
никакóй are declined like adjectives, according to their endings.
Ничéй is declined like **чей** (see p. 247).

§ 242. **Кой-ктó** (a few; some one), **кое-чтó** (something) are
declined like **кто** and **что** (**кой-** and **кое-** do not change).

Кой-какóй is declined like an adjective.

§ 243. **-то** and **-нибудь** may also be added to the adverbs
когда, куда, где, откýда, как, скóлько (and to **какóй**); the meaning
imparted is the same as in the case of pronouns, e.g.

Я когдá-то вѝдел вас.	I did see you once (sometime).
Когдá-нибудь я вам скажý.	I shall tell you some day.
Отéц кудá-то ушёл.	Father has gone somewhere.
Пойдёмте кудá-нибудь сегóдня.	Let's go somewhere to-day.

§ 244. Compounds formed from the negative adverbs **не** and
ни, added to other adverbs, are written as one word, and are used
in the same way as negative pronouns, e.g.

Я никудá не хожý.	I don't go anywhere.
Мне нéкуда ходѝть.	I have nowhere to go.
Он никогдá не читáет.	He never reads.
Ему нéкогда читáть.	He has no time for reading.

§ 245. **Нéкогда** also means "once upon a time", i.e. has a
positive meaning (cf. **нéкто** and **нéчто**):

Жил нéкогда мáльчик,
Был рóстом он с пáльчик. (Children's rhyme.)
Once there lived a little boy, the height of one's finger.

(**Пáльчик,** diminutive of **пáлец** (finger).)

§ 246. Certain adverbs are compounded only with **-то,** with the
meaning of definiteness, e.g. **тепéрь-то, тáк-то, наконéц-то**; e.g.

Тепéрь-то я вѝжу.   I see it *now.*

§ 247. Among other compound adverbs should be noted:

éле-éле	scarcely, narrowly
чуть-чýть	a tiny bit
мáло-по-мáлу	little by little
давнѝм-давнó	long, long ago
вряд-ли	hardly, scarcely, it is doubtful

§ 248. The adverb **не,** with other parts of speech, is written as one word, when the resultant word has a positive meaning (see p. 265), e.g.

недорогóй   inexpensive
нездорóвый   ill
непрáвда   untruth

It is written separately, however, when a negative meaning is desired, e.g.

Это не прáвда, а ложь.   This is not true but a lie.

§ 249. The adverb **ни** compounded with other parts of speech has already been pointed out. The use of **ни** instead of **не** for *emphasis* must, however, be noticed, e.g.

Я не рáз вам говорил.   I have told you more than once.
Я ни рáзу не говорил.   I have not *once* mentioned.

and especially for emphasis on the *verb*, e.g.

Когда я ни прийдý, его нет дóма.
When I do come, he is not at home.

§ 250. **Мнóгое**, "many things", is declined as an adjective, and is used in the neuter form *only*, e.g.

Мне мнóгое в ней не нрáвится.
There are many things in her I do not like.

Мнóгие means "many people" or "many of" (partitive) and is used instead of **мнóго**, when the latter is required in an oblique case, e.g.

Мы говорили о мнóгих книгах.   We spoke about many books.
Мнóгие так говорят.   Many people say so.
Мнóгие из этих книг.   Many of these books.

§ 251. **Скóлько** and **нéсколько** (many) are declined like plural words (see p. 246). The verb may be singular or plural.

§ 252. The English "I am going to do something" may be rendered in Russian by the verb **собирáться**, one of the compound imperfectives derived from the verb **брать** with prefixes, e.g.

Я собирáюсь купить себé дом.
I am going to buy myself a house.

Брать has the perfective **взять**, which, with its own imperfective **взимáть**, belongs to a group of verbs in -**имать** and -**ять** (Group D in the Grammar, p. 220). All verbs in this group have the meaning "to take", and are treated in Lesson XXII. Verbs formed from брать with prefixes also have the meaning of "to take", and more directly than do those in -имáть and -ять, e.g.

собрать	to gather
убрáть	to take away
вы́брать	to take out, choose

The imperfective of these verbs is соб-и-рáть, выб-и-рáть, etc. (see Grammar, p. 218).

§ 253. The verb случáться (to happen), in expressions such as "it happened to me", requires с with the instrumental case, e.g.

Это случи́лось со мной (cf. I met with an accident).

Разлучáть (trans.) and разлучáться (intr. с+instr.) mean "to separate", "to part". The noun is разлýка (separation). All these words are derived from луч (ray) (see p. 17).

§ 254. Note the important construction with чуть не which in English has a *positive* meaning, "almost". It is always used with the perfective (see Exercise A).

EXERCISES XIX

A. 1. Благодарю́ вас.—Нé за что.   Thank you.—Don't mention it.
2. Как ни в чём не быва́ло.   Quite unconcerned.
3. А всё ни от кого похва́л себé не слы́шит.   (Крыло́в.)
   And all the while he hears praise from no one.
4. У нас нет ни в чём недоста́тка.   We lack nothing.
5. Вы здесь, коне́чно, по каки́м-нибудь дела́м.   (Пу́шкин.)
   You are here, of course, on business of some sort.
6. Что-то слы́шится родно́е
   В до́лгих пе́снях ямщика́.   (Пу́шкин.)
   I hear something home-like (akin) in the long songs of the driver.
7. Это что-то небыва́лое.   This is something unheard of.
8. Ны́нче но́чью кто-то до́лго пел (ны́нче = сего́дня).   (Бу́нин.)
   To-night some one was singing for a long time.
9. Как хорошо́! Но жаль кого-то
   И гру́стно Осени весь день.   (Бу́нин.)
   How beautiful! But Autumn, as if feeling pity for some one, is sad all day.
10. Скажи́те мне что-нибудь.   Tell me something.
11. Я хочу́ вам что-то сказа́ть.   I want to tell you something.

12. Я никаки́м о́бразом не смогу́ э́того сде́лать. I shall not be able to do this in any way.

13. Ну, не́когда ни пить, ни есть,
    Ни да́же ду́ху (gen.) переве́сть. (Крыло́в.)
    Well, there is no time to eat or drink, nor even to draw breath.

14. Быва́ли слу́чаи, когда́.... There were occasions when....

15. Он ма́ло где быва́ет. There are few places where he goes.

16. Как вы себя́ чу́вствуете? Так себе́, нева́жно. How do you feel? Just so-so, not too well.

17. В лесу́ чуть-чуть светле́ло. (Турге́нев.) It was growing a little lighter in the wood.

18. Она́ чуть не сказа́ла. She almost (nearly) said.

19. Они́ на́ши о́бщие знако́мые. They are common acquaintances of ours.

20. Я собира́юсь бо́льше чита́ть. I am going to read more.

21. Куда́ вы собрали́сь? Where are you off to? (have got ready to go?).

22. Я купи́л себе́ по́лное собра́ние сочине́ний Толсто́го. I have bought myself a complete edition (collection) of the works of Tolstoi.

23. А вы, друзья́, как ни сади́тесь,
    Всё в музыка́нты не годи́тесь. (Крыло́в.)
    And you, my friends, whatever way you sit, won't make musicians.

24. Там не́когда гуля́л и я,
    Но вре́ден се́вер для меня́. (Пу́шкин.)
    I too used to walk there at one time. But the north is bad for me.

25. Кото́рый Ча́цкий тут?—
    Изве́стная фами́лия...
    —С каки́м-то Ча́цким я когда́-то был знако́м.
    Вы слы́шали о нём? (Грибое́дов.)
    Which is Chatsky (here)?—It is a well-known name. I used to know a Chatsky once. Have you heard of him?

26. Ва́ше лицо́ мне знако́мо. Your face is familiar to me.

27. Он е́ле хо́дит. He can barely walk.

28. Они́ е́ле-е́ле спасли́сь. They had a narrow escape.

29. Она́ чуть жива́. She scarcely lives.

30. Полна́ наро́да за́ла. (Пу́шкин.) The room (reception room) is full of people.

31. Он напо́лнил стака́ны вино́м. He filled the glasses with wine.

B. 1. В не́котором ца́рстве, в не́котором госуда́рстве
жил-был дед. 2. На ле́то мы ушли́ в лес и три ме́сяца
ни о ком и ни о чём не слыха́ли. 3. В лесу темь (darkness), ничего́ не ви́дно, позва́ть не́кого, не́ за что спря́-
таться, не́чем укры́ться, не́кому про беду́ рассказа́ть.
4. Где-то, когда́-то, давно́-давно́ тому наза́д, я прочёл
одно́ стихотворе́ние. Оно ско́ро позабы́лось мно́ю...но
пе́рвый стих оста́лся у меня́ в па́мяти: "Как хоро́ш,
как свеж бы́ли ро́зы...". (Турге́нев.) 5. Мы все учи́лись
по-немно́гу, чему́-нибу́дь и как-нибу́дь. (Пу́шкин.)
6. Вы это поймёте, когда́ проживёте здесь не́сколько
лет. (Пу́шкин.) 7. Она о́чень чу́ткий челове́к: сра́зу
поймёт, если на́до помо́чь. 8. Он один ру́сский здесь,
ему́ не́ с кем сло́ва сказа́ть по-ру́сски. 9. Встреча́етесь
вы с кем-нибу́дь из ру́сских? 10. Мы вообще́ ни с кем
не встреча́емся, так как ре́дко когда хо́дим куда́-нибу́дь.
11. Мне кто́-то говори́л, что вы ча́сто быва́ете у на́ших
о́бщих знако́мых. 12. Они́ жи́ли ра́ньше где́-то о́коло
вокза́ла. 13. Быва́ли слу́чаи, когда кто-нибу́дь выду́-
мывал что-нибу́дь но́вое: каку́ю-нибу́дь но́вую игру́,
наприме́р. 14. Отец и мать е́здили куда́-то по свои́м
дела́м. (Акса́ков.) 15. Мы заста́ли его́ как раз в то
вре́мя, когда́ он кому́-то объясня́л, где мы живём.
16. Он ни о ко́м и ни о чём не хоте́л слы́шать. 17. При-
ходи́те сего́дня ве́чером: мне на́до вам кое-что́ показа́ть.
18. Он собира́ется принести́ мне чью-то кни́гу. 19. Что
вы собира́етесь де́лать, когда вы ко́нчите шко́лу? 20. Я
собира́юсь пое́хать куда́-нибу́дь за-грани́цу. 21. Я
случа́йно узна́ла, что моя́ подру́га живёт где́-то загра-
ни́цей. 22. Ма́ло-по-ма́лу все в кла́ссе начина́ют гово-
ри́ть по-ру́сски. 23. Она чуть не запла́кала, когда я
рассказала ей что с вами случилось.

C. 1. I take. 2. I collect. 3. We have gathered. 4. They
will gather. 5. We feel. 6. They have felt. 7. Have you chosen?

8. They never choose.   9. I shall not feel.   10. I am going to.
11. He was going to.   12. They got ready.   13. You are getting
ready.   14. You have not chosen.   15. What have you taken?
16. Take this book.   17. Don't take the dictionary.   18. Choose
something.   19. Don't take anything.   20. He has chosen something.   21. Take pity.   22. He does not take pity.   23. Do not
grudge.   24. He grudges nothing.   25. We all gathered.

D. 1. What are you going to do in summer?   2. My brother
and I are going somewhere abroad, but we do not yet know
where.   3. Some time I shall tell (relate) you about our trip to
Russia.   4. Did you meet anyone you know there?   5. There
were several English people with us, but I did not know any of
them before.   6. Tell me something about yourself; you have had
such an interesting life.   7. There is nothing to tell you (about):
I have lived at home all my life.   8. We must not go anywhere;
somebody may come in the evening.   9. They have nowhere to
go; they do not know anybody in town.   10. Sometimes she has
no one to speak to.   11. I have seen you somewhere; your face is
very familiar (to me).   12. And I have heard about *you* from
somebody; I have heard many good things about you.   13. Many
people don't like to talk about music.   14. Last night we spoke
about many things.   15. No doctor can help him if he does not
go out in the fresh air.   16. Unfortunately something has happened
in their house and nobody is allowed (нельзя + dat.) to go in.
17. It is very sad, because we were going to spend the evening
together.   18. My sister is not at home; she is at some meeting
or other.   19. We nearly[1] went without you.   20. I have brought
many pretty things from Paris.   21. Choose something for yourself
and for your sister.   22. For many people it is difficult to choose
for themselves (dat.).   23. I shall bring this book with me and
shall choose something for reading (чтéние) in class.   24. We have
collected many newspapers and magazines, and shall send them
to some hospitals.   25. I am sorry for those who have to live in
town in summer.   26. It seems to me that she is displeased with
something: she does not want to speak to anybody.   27. It is a
pity we have nobody to speak Russian to.

---

[1] Use чуть не + perf. See Ex. B, 23; also § 340.

LESSON XX

11 одиннадцать	16 шестнадцать	30 тридцать
12 двенадцать	17 семнадцать	40 сорок
13 тринадцать	18 восемнадцать	50 пятьдесят
14 четырнадцать	19 девятнадцать	90 девяносто
15 пятнадцать	20 двадцать	100 сто

половина half
полфунта half a pound
треть (f.) third
четверть (f.) quarter
восьмая (часть) eighth
часть (f.) part
полночь midnight
полдень noon
по полуночи a.m.
по полудни p.m.
полгода half a year
век century, lifetime
столетие century
цифра *or* цыфра cipher, figure
пара pair
десяток ten (collective)
дюжина dozen
рост stature

высота height
ширина breadth
глубина depth
длина length
площадь (f.) area, square
скорость (f.) speed
миля mile
марка stamp
война war
мир peace
перемирие armistice, truce
праздник holiday
праздновать to celebrate
воображать, вообразить to imagine
воображение imagination
резать, по- to cut, отрезать to cut off

Туз, двойка, тройка, четвёрка, пятёрка, шестёрка, семёрка, восьмёрка, девятка, десятка. The ace, two, three, etc. (cards).

NUMERALS.

§ 255. Numerals are declined in Russian, but only in the cardinal and ordinal forms. Один, два, оба and полтора change by gender: один, одна, одно; два, две (f.); оба, обе (f.); полтора, полторы (f.). For their declension see Grammar, p. 259. The ordinal numerals are by form like adjectives, and are declined like adjectives, e.g. первый, второй.

The numerals up to twelve, both cardinal and ordinal, have been given in Lessons IIIa and VIII. A complete list of cardinal and ordinal numerals will be found in the Grammar, pp. 257, 258.

§ 256. Cardinal numerals over ten and under twenty, i.e. the "teens", are formed by adding на- and -дцать (old form of

десять) to the numerals one to nine. Thus **одиннадцать** is really **один-на-дцать** (one over ten), and is therefore written with two **н**'s. **Двенадцать** is formed from the feminine form of "two" (**две**). Notice that in **четырнадцать** the -е of **четыре** is left out, and in **пятнадцать**, etc., the -ь of **пять**, etc.

§ 257. **Двадцать, тридцать** are formed without **на**, i.e. *lit.* "two ten(s)"; three ten(s)".

Сорок (forty) is not a Slavonic word. The Slavonic form **четыредесят** is no longer used.

§ 258. **Пятьдесят, шестьдесят**, etc., are formed in the same way as **двадцать**, but, in accordance with the general rule, **десят** (plural of **дцать**) is used after **пять**, etc.

Note that the -ь of **пять** is here retained.

Пятьдесят, etc., are declined in both parts, as also **пятьсот, шестьсот**, etc. For the declension of all numerals see Grammar, p. 259.

§ 259. The rule that the genitive singular is used after **два, три, четыре** (see Lesson III*a*) applies only to nouns. Adjectives are used in the genitive plural after *all* numerals (§ 174), e.g.

два новых стола	two new tables
две русских девочки	two Russian girls

§ 260. The ordinal numeral **третий, -ья, -ье** is declined like the relative adjective **лисий** (see p. 247).

§ 261. To express the *date*—day, month, and year—in Russian, the following construction is used:

He was born on the 7th of March 1910.

Он родился седьмого марта, тысяча девятьсот десятого года.

The ordinal numeral is used for the day, as in English, but in the genitive case. In the numerals denoting the year, the ordinal numeral is used only for the last number, and in the genitive case. But after the preposition **в** the prepositional case is used, e.g.

It was in 1917.

Это было в тысяча девятьсот семнадцатом году.

§ 262. In compound cardinal numerals, as 532 (**пятьсот тридцать два**), all parts are declined, whereas in the ordinal form only the last number is ordinal, and only this last part is declined, e.g. **пятьсот тридцать второй**.

§ 263. The preposition **по** is used with numerals to express the idea of *distribution*, as there are no special distributive numerals in Russian. With **два, три, четыре**, it requires the accusative case, e.g.

> Он дал мальчикам по два яблока.
> He gave the boys two apples each.

But with other numerals **по** requires the dative, e.g.

> по пяти (dat.) яблок   five apples each

In this construction **сто** after **по** appears as **сту**, e.g.

> по сту рублей   100 roubles each.

§ 264. "Once" is often expressed by the noun **раз** which may in this construction be considered an adverb. In "twice", "three times", "four times", **раз** is used in the genitive, e.g. **два раза**, etc. (see § 36). After **пять**, etc., the genitive plural, which is also **раз**, is used (see Grammar, p. 260).

§ 265. The words **однажды, дважды, трижды** have their origin in Old Bulgarian. They are seldom used, *except* **однажды**, when in the sense of "once upon a time".

§ 266. The collective forms **двое, трое, четверо, оба** are mostly used with nouns which have no singular, as **двое ножниц** (two pairs of scissors), **трое саней** (three sledges), **двое суток** (twice 24 hours), etc. This form can be used for numbers up to ten (see Grammar, p. 258, where their declension will also be found). They are used in idiomatic expressions, as:

> Нас семеро.   We are seven.
> У неё трое детей.   She has three children.

Тройка is also used for the Russian team of three horses.

§ 267. **Половина** and **четверть** are declined like nouns. In the expressions **три четверти** (three-quarters), **пять четвертей** (five-fourths), **две пятых** (two-fifths), **семь восьмых** (seven-eighths), etc., the rule concerning the cases of nouns and adjectives after numerals applies (see p. 260).

Пятых and **восьмых** are adjectives; "parts" being understood (see § 259).

Some expressions of time will be found in Exercise A of this lesson.

§ 268. *Idioms.* **Пропасть** (f. precipice, bottomless pit) means *a great quantity, multitude, lot,* e.g.

У него пропасть денег.　　He has an abundance of money.

Тьма (darkness) also means *an enormous quantity, beyond counting* (see Exercise A).

§ 269. **Лет** (genitive plural of **лето**) is used after numerals over five instead of **годов**; *but* **двадцать два года.**

To express "about", "approximately", the numeral is placed *after* the word **лет** or **года**, e.g.

Ей двадцать лет.　　She is twenty years old.
Ей лет двадцать.　　She is *about* twenty.

Exercises XX

A. 1. Сколько времени на ваших часах?　What is the time by your watch?

2. Двенадцатый час, пора спать !　After eleven, time to go to bed !

3. Вам (dat.) пора спать.　It is time for you to go to bed.　Пора вставать !　It is time to get up !

4. У нас все часы отстают на пять (acc.) минут.　All our clocks are five minutes slow.

5. У него часы всегда позади.　His watch is always slow.

6. Мои часы идут вперёд (*or* спешат).　My watch is going fast.

7. В двенадцать часов по ночам. (Жуковский.)　Every night at twelve o'clock.

8. Поезд отходит без четверти в восемь.　The train leaves at 7.45.

9. Сели ужинать в пятом часу утра. (Пушкин.)　They sat down to supper after four o'clock in the morning.

10. "Тройка, семёрка и туз", необыкновенно скоро бормочет Герман. (Пушкин.)　"The three, the seven, and the ace", mutters Hermann, with unusual promptitude.

11. Эх, тройка, птица-тройка, кто тебя выдумал? (Гоголь.)　Oh, troika, bird-like troika, who invented you?

12. Миллионы вас; нас тьмы, и тьмы, и тьмы. (Блок.)　You are millions, but we are countless.

13. Сколько вам лет?　How old are you?

14. Мне (dat.) пятнадцать лет.　I am fifteen years old.

15. Мне ещё нет пятнадцати лет.　I am not yet fifteen.

16. Ему тридцать два года.　He is thirty-two years old.

17. У неё дочь семнáдцати лет. She has a daughter of seventeen years of age.

18. Вчерá ему испóлнилось двенáдцать лет. Yesterday was his twelfth birthday.

19. Девятнáдцати лет пóсле смéрти отцá
    Я остáлся один сиротóю. (Никúтин.)
    At nineteen years of age, at the death of my father, I was left alone, an orphan.

20. У нее пять человéк детéй: мал, малá, мéньше. She has five tiny children, each smaller than the last.

21. "Всех скóлько вас"—ей мóлвил я.
    "И брáтьев, и сестёр?"—"Всегó нас семь."
    "Sisters and brothers—(I said to her). How many may you be?"—"Seven in all." (Wordsworth.)

22. Отцý идёт сéмьдесят пéрвый год (восьмóй десáток). My father is in his seventy-first year (eighth decade).

23. Сороковы́е гóды, шестидесáтые и семидесáтые гóды. The "forties", the "sixties" and the "seventies".

24. Пятилéтка or пятилéтний план. Five-year plan.

25. Век живú: век учúсь. Live and learn (lit. Live for a century; learn for a century).

26. Два с половúной часá. Two hours and a half.

27. День да ночь—сýтки прочь. Day and night—twenty-four hours gone !

28. Какóго числá ваше рождéнье (день рождéнья)? When (what date) is your birthday?

29. Жизнь прожúть—не пóле перейтú. To live one's life is not so easy as to cross a field.

30. Он вдвóе стáрше меня́. He is twice as old as I am.

31. В одну минýту. In a minute.

32. Какóй глубины́ и ширины́ э́та рекá? What is the depth and the breadth of this river?

33. Какóй высоты́ э́та горá? What is the height of this mountain?

34. Какóго он рóста? How tall is he?

35. Он рóстом невелúк. He is not tall.

B. 1. Кáждый шкóльник в Áнглии и Шотлáндии знáет ты́сяча шестьсóт трéтий год. 2. Послéдняя Европéйская войнá продолжáлась бóлее четырёх лет. 3. Перемúрие бы́ло заключенó одúннадцатого ноября́, ты́сяча девятьсóт

восемнáдцатого гóда.   4. Францýзская Револю́ция (Revolution) былá в тысяча семьсóт вóсемьдесят девя́том годý, а рýсская в тысяча девятьсóт семнáдцатом годý.
5. В прóшлом годý в С.С.С.Р. прáздновали шестнáдцати-лéтнюю годовщи́ну Револю́ции.   6. Седьмóе ноября́ прáзднуется там кáждый год.   7. Плóщадь С.С.С.Р. со-ставля́ет (constitutes) однý шестýю всегó земнóго шáра.
8. В тысяча девятьсóт три́дцать вторóм годý испóлнилось сто лет со дня смéрти Вáльтер Скóтта.   9. Вóлга—сáмая дли́нная рекá в Еврóпе.   10. Она длинóй в две тысячи четыреста миль, а ширинóй в нéкоторых местáх бóлее двух миль.   11. Эльбрýс—сáмая высóкая горá на Кав-кáзе (Caucasus).   12. Она в восемнáдцать тысяч, пятьсóт фýтов (feet) высотóй.   13. Пóезд шёл со скóростью шести́десяти (gen.) миль в час.   14. В Вели́ком Океáне (Pacific Ocean) есть местá бóльше семи миль глуби́ны.
15. Аэроплáн поднялся́ на высотý в дéсять миль.
16. Дáйте мне две мáрки по пятнáдцати копéек и две дю́жины пяти́копéечных.   17. Отрéжьте мне полторá мéтра (metres) э́той матéрии.   18. Это сукнó по двенáдцати рублéй метр.   19. Нам всем дáли по десяти́ копéек.
20. Идýт две мáтери, две дóчери, да бáбушка с внýчкой, а всех их трóе. Как это?   21. Вообрази́те себé человéка лет сорокá пяти́, высóкого, худóго, с дли́нным нóсом и сéрыми глáзками. (Тургéнев.)   22. Я óчень не люблю́ имéть дело с ци́фрами, поэ́тому и в шкóле я никогдá не знал годóв вóйн.   23. У нас в шкóле есть учени́к, у котóрого óчень хорóшая пáмять на ци́фры, но он знáет одни́ тóлько ци́фры и бóльше ничегó.

C. 1. 8 hours.   2. 24 hours.   3. 22 years.   4. Fifty years.
5. Three pairs of scissors.   6. Two sledges.   7. Twentieth of March.
8. The year one thousand nine hundred and thirty-four.   9. One hundred and twenty-six years.   10. In the year eighteen hundred.
11. She is fifteen.   12. Six new pupils.   13. 22 new pupils.
14. He is about sixteen.   15. Three dozen or thirty-six.   16. Two

hundred and fifty-nine pages. 17. Six hundred and twenty-five people. 18. Eight each. 19. Two each. 20. We were four. 21. Half a pound. 22. Quarter of a pound. 23. Two and a half pounds. 24. Five-eighths of a book.

D. 1. I got up at quarter to eight, and at half past eight I was already at school. 2. The lessons usually finish at three, but to-day we finished at ten minutes to three. 3. We have lunch at mid-day. 4. It is already after eight; the children must go to bed. 5. Yesterday was my little sister's tenth birthday; we always celebrate her birthday. 6. How old is your little brother? 7. He is not three yet; he will be three next month. 8. My aunt has a son of twenty and a daughter of eighteen. 9. At (after) their father's death they were six and four years of age. 10. There are four of us: two brothers and two sisters. 11. I am twice as old as this little girl. 12. We talked last night for two hours and a half. 13. How tall is your uncle? It seems to me that he is taller than all of you. 14. It is thought that Shakespeare (Шекспир) was born on the 23rd of April 1564. 15. We live in the twentieth century (use век). 16. There are fifty-two weeks in a year. 17. Our train is going at forty miles an hour (see B 13). 18. The Great European War began in August 1914. 19. If you are going to the Post Office, buy me a dozen five-copeck stamps. 20. In Russia apples are sold by tens (instr. pl.) and not by the pound (instr. pl.). 21. We shall live here another half-year, and then shall go to France. 22. When you go there, bring me three pairs of gloves and two dozen handkerchiefs. 23. Nobody knows what may happen in two or three years. 24. But you are not going to live there all that time? 25. Perhaps I shall stay there longer than I intend. 26. There is going to be an exhibition of pictures there, perhaps you will see it. 27. I don't like seeing hundreds of pictures at once. 28. Do you know how late it is?—it is half past eleven, almost midnight. 29. The greatest Russian poet Pushkin died at the age of 37. 30. He was born in 1799 and died in the beginning of 1837. 31. Three years ago we all went to Russia. 32. In 1936 more than 30,000 tourists (турист) visited the Soviet Union. 33. The population of the U.S.S.R. grows very quickly; in 1937 it reached (attained) over 170 millions. 34. What is the height of the highest mountain in Scotland?

LESSON XXI

следующий following
прохо́жий passer-by
прое́зжий passer-by (not on foot)
проше́дший, про́шлый past, last
бы́вший former, who (which) was
бу́дущее (noun) future
ни́щий beggar
люби́мый favourite
лю́бящий loving
пре́данный devoted
уважа́емый esteemed
уважа́ть to esteem, respect
могу́чий powerful
неви́данный not seen before
зря́чий seeing (opp. "blind")
слепо́й blind
бри́тый shaven
брить(ся), по- to shave (oneself)
ра́неный wounded
учёный learned, sage
уча́щиеся (pl.) scholars

настоя́щий real
окружённый surrounded
куря́щий smoker
и́збранный choice, chosen
ока́занный shown, rendered
заслужённый well-merited
рабо́чий (noun) worker
безрабо́тный unemployed
висе́ть, по- to hang (intr.)
ве́шать, пове́сить to hang (tr.)
вися́чий hanging
просыпа́ть, -спа́ть to oversleep
просыпа́ться, просну́ться to awake (intr.)
засыпа́ть, засну́ть to fall asleep
сон (gen. сна) sleep, dream
ви́деть во сне to dream about
мне сни́тся, сни́лось I dream(ed)
возвраща́ть(ся) to return; возврати́ть(ся) or верну́ть(ся) (perf.)
буди́ть, разбуди́ть (see § 43) to waken (trans.), rouse
буди́льник alarm-clock

PARTICIPLES.

§ 270. Russian *participles*, both active and passive, are *verbal adjectives*. Examples of passive participles with an adjectival force have already been seen, in откры́тый, закры́тый (see § 139). Active participles also have adjectival endings, and are declined as adjectives. They cannot, however, be used predicatively. Participles may be present or past. The verb быть alone has a future participle (бу́дущий), which is now used only as an adjective: "future".

§ 271. The *present active participle* is formed from the 3rd person plural of the present tense, by taking off -т, and adding -щий (m.), -щая (f.), -щее (n.), and -щие (pl.). Thus:

они живу́т gives живу́щий, -щая, etc.: "(one) who is living".

они стоят gives стоя́щий, -щая, -щее, etc.: "(that) which is standing".

§ 272. The *past active participle* is formed from the infinitive, imperfective or perfective, by taking off the ending -ть, and adding -вший, -вшая, -вшее, -вшие, e.g. написа́ть: написа́вший, -вшая, etc.: "(one) who had written".

Certain verbs, e.g. везти́, нести́, have the endings -ший, -шая, -шее (see Grammar, p. 212).

§ 273. In a subordinate clause a participle replaces a verb with a relative pronoun. If this verb is in the present tense, the present participle is used; if in the past, the past participle is used, e.g.

Я получи́л письмо́ от дру́га, **кото́рый живет** тепе́рь в Москве́,
Я получи́л письмо́ от дру́га, **живу́щего**, etc.
I received a letter from a friend who lives in Moscow.
А́втор, **кото́рый написа́л**....
А́втор, **написа́вший** э́ту кни́гу, давно́ уже́ у́мер.
The author of this book died a long time ago.

When a participle replaces a relative pronoun in this way, it agrees with the antecedent of this pronoun, as in the example above. **Живу́щего** is in the genitive because it qualifies дру́га. The same rule applies to passive participles.

§ 274. *Passive participles*, which may be used predicatively as well as attributively, are sometimes identical with adjectives.

Passive participles, like active, may be present or past.

§ 275. The *present passive participle* is formed from the 1st person plural of the present tense by adding -ый, -ая, -ое, -ые, e.g. чита́емый, -ая, etc.: "which is being read".

Many verbs, though transitive, have no present passive participle, e.g. пить, мыть, класть, etc. (see p. 213).

§ 276. The *past passive participle* is formed from the infinitive by taking off -ть, and adding -нный, -нная, -нное, -нные; or -тый, -тая, -тое, -тые, e.g. чита́ть: чи́танный, -нная, etc.: "which was being read". The predicative endings are: -н, -на, -но; -т, -та, -то.

The endings -тый, -тая, etc., are less frequently used—mostly in monosyllabic verbs (see Grammar, p. 213 (2)).

When a verb ends in -ить, the -и is changed into -e before -нный, e.g. встре́тить: встре́ченный. Observe the usual change of consonant (see p. 17). With regard to the accents see Grammar,

p. 214. If the stem ends in a consonant which undergoes permutation, the usual rules must be applied, as заплати́ть : запла́ченный; люби́ть : влюблённый, etc.

§ 277. Passive participles are used in subordinate clauses in the same way as active, i.e. they replace a verb with a relative pronoun, the latter being the object of the sentence, e.g.

Я дам вам кни́гу, кото́рую тепе́рь везде́ и всю́ду чита́ют.

Я дам вам кни́гу, чита́емую везде́ и всю́ду.

I shall give you the book which is being read everywhere at present.

Кни́ги, кото́рые все в до́ме прочита́ли, я обыкнове́нно посыла́ю в больни́цу.

Кни́ги, прочи́танные все́ми в до́ме, etc.

I usually send the books which everyone in the house has read to the hospital.

§ 278. In their abbreviated form, present and past passive participles serve in the conjugation of passive verbs; the present in the imperfective, and the past in the perfective aspect, e.g.

Я хвали́м, -а.	I am (being) praised.
Я был хвали́м, -а.	I was (being) praised.
Я был похва́лен, -а.	I have been praised.
Я бу́ду хвали́м, -а.	I shall be (being) praised.
Я бу́ду похва́лен, -а.	I shall have been praised.

The forms are here given only to show their existence, since they are sometimes met in reading. In practice they are hardly ever used, being replaced by the 3rd person plural of the verb, e.g.

Меня́ хва́лят.	I am praised.
Меня́ хвали́ли.	I was praised.
Меня́ похвали́ли.	I have been praised.
Меня́ бу́дут хвали́ть.	I shall be praised.
Меня́ похва́лят.	I shall have been praised.

For the full conjugation of the passive voice see Grammar, p. 231. The rendering of the passive by reflexive verbs has already been given (see Lesson XIa).

Note that perfective verbs have of course neither active nor passive present participles.

§ 279. While they are not used in the same way as in other languages, Russian participles are widely used as adjectives, and often, too, as nouns. It is important, therefore, to obtain a good

understanding of their formation. Words formed from participles
are given in this lesson.

§ 280. The words given in the Vocabulary of this lesson have
been specially chosen to show how participles have come to be
used, often in a modified form, as true adjectives, and also as nouns.

Thus **нищий** (beggar) is derived from **неимеющий** (who has not)
through **неимущий** (indigent, poor), the opposite of **имущий**
(propertied, rich). Other examples include: **рабочий, прохожий,
сумасшедший, раненый, учёный**.

Рабочий (workman, worker) is used only in the masculine. For
the feminine **работница** is used, but **работник** (worker *or* "hand")
does not imply membership of a social class, e.g.

Он очень хороший работник. He is a very good worker.

Рабочий is used as an adjective in **рабочий класс, рабочий
день**, etc.

Сумасшедший (madman) is derived from **сходить** (perfective
сойти) **с ума**, *lit.* "to go out of one's mind".

True adjectives such as **могучий, зрячий, висячий, горячий**
(hot), etc., are derived from the participles **могущий, зрящий** (who
sees), **висящий, горящий** (burning).

Необходимый (necessary, unavoidable) is derived from the verb
обходить (see Grammar, p. 226) or, rather, **обходиться**, which
means "to do without". **Необходимое**, used as a noun, means
"necessaries".

EXERCISES XXI

A. 1. Это учёный, которого все уважают *or* Это уважаемый
      всеми учёный.

   He is a learned man whom all respect.

2. Девочка, которая заснула... *or* Девочка, заснувшая у меня
   на коленях.

   The little girl who fell asleep on my knee(s).

3. Мальчику, который так хорошо играет на скрипке, только
   семь лет *or* Мальчику, играющему так хорошо....

   The boy who plays the violin so well is only seven years old.

4. Книги, которые вы купили, никому не нужны *or* Книги,
   купленные вами....

   The books which you bought are of no use to anyone.

5. Я говорю́ о ла́мпе, вися́щей (prepositional, agreeing with lamp) в ва́шей ко́мнате. I am speaking of the lamp hanging in your room.

6. Что вы ви́дели во сне?⎫
   Что вам сни́лось?   ⎬ About what did you dream?

7. Он всегда́ про́сит, что́бы его́ разбуди́ли по-ра́ньше. He always asks to be wakened as early as possible.

8. Како́го цве́та обо́и у вас? What colour is your wall paper?

9. Тепе́рь у вас есть всё необходи́мое. Now you have everything that is necessary.

10. Са́мое необходи́мое. First essentials.

11. Перепиши́те э́то на пи́шущей маши́нке (typewriter). Type this.

12. Приводи́ть приме́р. To give an example.

13. Гла́дко вы́бритый. Clean-shaven.

14. Дитя́ умы́т, причёсан, нако́рмлен. (Пу́шкин.) The child (boy) is washed, combed and fed.

15. Э́тот ваго́н—"для некуря́щих". This carriage is "Smoking Prohibited".

16. Благодарю́ вас за ока́занную мне услу́гу. I thank you for the service you have rendered me.

17. Ска́занного не верну́ть. What has been said cannot be unsaid (*lit.* returned).

18. У́треннее представле́ние "Гамле́та" дава́лось то́лько для уча́щихся. The matinée performance of *Hamlet* was given for school children (scholars) only.

19. Челове́к, кото́рый име́ет до́брое се́рдце, не мо́жет равноду́шно смотре́ть на чужо́е го́ре. A man who has a kind heart cannot look unmoved on another's sorrow.

20. "Униже́нные и Оскорблённые"—так называ́ется рома́н Достое́вского. "The Injured (*lit.* humbled) and Insulted" is the title of a novel by Dostoievsky.

21. "И́бо вся́кий, возвыша́ющий сам себя́, уни́жен бу́дет, а унижа́ющий себя́ возвы́сится." "For every one that exalteth himself shall be humbled, but he that humbleth himself shall be exalted." (Luke xviii. 14.)

22. От лику́ющих, пра́здно-болта́ющих,
    Омыва́ющих ру́ки в крови́
    Уведи́ меня́ в стан погиба́ющих
    За вели́кое де́ло любви́. (Некра́сов.)
    Lead me away from those who exult, who talk idly, whose

hands are washed in blood, to (the camp of) those who perish
in the great cause of Love.

23. Там на неве́домых доро́жках
Следы́ неви́данных звере́й. (Пу́шкин.)
There (in Fairyland), on unknown ways, are tracks of strange
beasts.

24. Я мечто́ю лови́л уходя́щие тени,
Уходя́щие те́ни погаса́вшего дня. (Ба́льмонт.)
In my dream I was chasing the fleeting shadows of the
dying day.

B. 1. На сле́дующий день я просну́лся ранёхонько;
со́лнце то́лько что вста́ло. (Турге́нев.) 2. Из-за шу́ма
воды́ послы́шалось гогота́нье ("gabbling") засыпа́ющих
гусе́й, а потом на дере́вне ста́ли переклика́ться ра́но
просну́вшиеся петухи́. (Толсто́й.) 3. Рождённый по́лзать
лета́ть не мо́жет. (Го́рький.) 4. Письмо́ по-ру́сски на-
чина́ют так: "уважа́емый господи́н N. (или това́рищ N.)",
а конча́ют: "уважа́ющий Вас или пре́данный Вам".
5. Письмо́ дру́гу начина́ют слова́ми: дорого́й или ми́лый,
а подписываются лю́бящий и́ли лю́бящая. 6. "Так бу́дут
после́дние пе́рвыми, а пе́рвые после́дними; и́бо мно́го
зва́нных, а ма́ло и́збранных." (Matt. xx. 16.) 7. Оте́ц
расска́зывал мне, что ви́дел лебеде́й, так высоко́ летѐвших,
что он едва́ мог разгляде́ть их. (Акса́ков.) 8. Спроси́л
слепо́й зря́чего: Како́го цве́та молоко́? (Folk-tale.) 9. Но
ско́лько приме́ров зря́чий ни приводи́л, слепо́й не мог
поня́ть, како́й быва́ет бе́лый цвет молока́. (do.)

10. Всю ты жизнь прожила́ нелюби́мая,
Всю ты жизнь прожила́ для други́х. (Некра́сов.)

11. Все игра́ющие ста́ли в круг. 12. Я вчера́ встре́тил
на́шего бы́вшего учи́теля. 13. Дед умира́л, окружённый
детьми́ и вну́ками. 14. Все зна́ют и уважа́ют э́того
заслужённого учёного. 15. В больни́цу ка́ждый день
привози́ли ра́неных. 16. "Остри́жен по после́дней мо́де,
как 'dandy' Ло́ндонский оде́т." (Пу́шкин.) 17. Го-

ворят, что стриженые во́лосы ско́ро вы́йдут из мо́ды.
18. На на́шей доро́ге всегда́ мно́го прое́зжих и прохо́жих.
19.   Мне сни́лось вече́рнее не́бо
             И кру́пные звёзды на нём.   (Надсо́н.)
20. Гляжу́—поднима́ется ме́дленно в го́ру лоша́дка,
везу́щая хво́росту воз (load of brushwood). (Некра́сов.)
21. Ни один (not a single) учени́к не мог рассказа́ть про-
чи́танного.   22. Никто́ не мог сказа́ть, настоя́щий ли э́то
ли́сий мех.   23. "Ско́лько про́жито—ско́лько ви́дано",
тихо́нько бормота́л дед.   24. Разбуди́те меня́ по-ра́ньше
за́втра: мне самому́ не просну́ться.   25. Мне необходи́мо
быть в конто́ре пре́жде всех

C. 1. Form present and past (imperfective and perfective) *active*
participles from: Стоя́ть, продава́ть, дава́ть, встава́ть, просы-
па́ться, засыпа́ть, ви́деть, быва́ть, переставать, оставля́ть,
пла́кать, смея́ться.

2. Form present and past (imperfective and perfective) *passive*
participles from: ви́деть, чита́ть, понима́ть, игра́ть, встреча́ть,
дава́ть, закрыва́ть, получа́ть, возвраща́ть.

(When doing this exercise consult the section on Permutation
of consonants.)

D. 1. Put the lamp on the table which stands beside my bed.
2. Don't sit on the chair which was brought yesterday.   3. I refer
to (speak about) the carpet lying in your father's room.   4. She
never wears the coat which she bought in Paris.   5. We were
speaking to the doctor (c + instr.) who had just come from Russia.
6. The mother was dressing her little daughter, who had awakened.
7. The father was carrying the child (use ребёнок) who had fallen
asleep (put the participle before "child").   8. He brought back
the book which he had finished.   9. This is the road leading to the
station.   10. All who came after eight o'clock could not get
tickets.   11. All who are playing must sit down in a circle.
12. Those who are standing at the door outside must not make
such a noise.   13. The gentleman who was here an hour ago is
going to Moscow.   14. I know the young ladies who are passing
(use идти́ ми́мо with gen.) our house.   15. Do you know this man
who is taking vegetables and fruit to the market? 16. The merchant
who sells such good butter is a foreigner.   17. He was talking to

the foreigner who bought my house. 18. Everybody was speaking about the boy who played at the concert yesterday. 19. Did you recognise the woman who was looking out of the train? 20. Nobody understood a single word spoken in Russian (use сказа́ть). 21. You must pack (уложи́ть) in this trunk everything you need first (пре́жде всего́). 22. She asked to be wakened early, because her train is (use идёт) at six o'clock. 23. I have bought (себе́) an alarm-clock for myself, because I cannot awake myself in time. 24. All the books lying on this shelf are necessary for my work. 25. What colour of dress have you chosen for your little sister?

LESSON XXII

гость (m.) guest, го́стья (f.)

ходи́ть, идти́ в го́сти to go visiting (acc.)

быть в гостя́х to be on a visit

гости́ть (гощу́, -сти́шь) to visit, be on a visit

гости́ница hotel

гости́нная drawing-room

приёмная reception-room

принима́ть, приня́ть to receive

принима́ться to set about, start

обнима́ть to embrace

поднима́ть to lift, raise

поднима́ться to rise

снима́ть to take off

занима́ть to occupy, interest

занима́ться (instr.) to study

за́нятый busy

я за́нят I am busy

вынима́ть, вы́нуть to take out

сле́довать, по- to follow

мне сле́дует I ought

как сле́дует properly

прия́тель (m.) friend

прия́тный pleasant

спеши́ть, по- to hurry

спе́ть, по- to mature, ripen

успева́ть, успе́ть to succeed, be in time

успе́х progress, success

де́лать успе́хи to make progress

спе́шный hurried, urgent

извиня́ть, -и́ть to excuse, pardon

извиня́ться, -и́ться to apologise

винова́тый guilty

же́ртва victim

же́ртвовать, по- to sacrifice

приготовля́ть, пригото́вить to prepare

гото́вый ready

просту́живаться, простуди́ться to catch cold

кошелёк purse

по кра́йней ме́ре at least

чтобы that, in order that

CONDITIONAL OR SUBJUNCTIVE.

§ 281. In Russian the *conditional* and the *subjunctive* mood happen to be the same in form, although they have different meanings. In other words, it may be said that the conditional is used to express the meaning of the subjunctive (see Use of tenses, § 348).

For both purposes there is only one tense, namely the past, formed by placing **бы** or **б** after the past indicative, e.g.

Imperfective: я читáл бы   I should read
Perfective: я прочитáл бы   I should have read

(See Grammar, p. 204.)

§ 282. When this form is used as the *conditional*, the conjunction *if* is **éсли бы** or **éсли б**, e.g.

Я читáл бы весь день, éсли бы у меня бы́ло врéмя.

I should read all day if I had the time.

Я прочитáл бы кни́гу, éсли бы вы мне не мешáли.

I should have finished the book if you had not disturbed me.

Éсли бы я был там, я уви́дел бы вас.

Had I been there, I should have seen you.

The particle **бы** usually follows the verb in the principal clause, but it may follow *any* word, for the purpose of emphasis on that word, e.g.

Я бы читáл весь день, éсли бы...
Я весь день бы читáл, éсли бы...etc.

§ 283. When the particle **бы** is used to express the meaning of the *subjunctive*, it *either*:

(*a*) follows a pronoun or an adverb, as, **что, кто, какóй, котóрый, когдá, где, кудá**, etc., the verb being preceded by **ни**, e.g.

Что бы вы **ни** дéлали, вы не помóжете.

Whatever you (may) do, you will be unable to help.

Где бы я **ни** гуля́л, я встречáл егó.

Wherever I happened to be walking, I met him.

or (*b*) is added to the conjunction **что**, which becomes **чтобы** or **чтоб**, and is followed by the past tense, e.g.

Я хочу́, чтобы вы бóльше читáли.

I want you to read more (that you may read more).

Я не хочу́, чтобы вы éхали за-грани́цу.

I do not want you to go abroad.

§ 284. The various English auxiliaries are rendered in Russian as follows:

I should write (if). Я писáл бы (éсли бы). See § 282.

I should have written (if). Я написáл бы (éсли бы).

I should be writing.   Я до́лжен бы писа́ть.

I should have been writing.   Я до́лжен бы́л бы писа́ть.

I should have written (but I did not).   Я до́лжен был бы написа́ть.

I ought to write.   Мне сле́дует писа́ть.[1]

I ought to be writing.   Мне сле́довало бы писа́ть.

I ought to have written.   Мне сле́довало бы написа́ть.

I must (have to) write.   Я до́лжен писа́ть.

I had to write.   Я до́лжен был писа́ть.

I must have written.   Я должно́ быть написа́л.

I must have been writing.   Я должно́ быть писа́л.

I may write.   Я мо́жет быть бу́ду писа́ть *or* напишу́.

but I may write (i.e. it is allowed).   Я могу́ *or* мне мо́жно писа́ть.

I may have written.   Я может быть написа́л.

I might have written.   Я мо́г бы написа́ть.

I might have been writing.   Я мог бы писа́ть.

Observe that wherever "have written" is used in English, the perfective **написа́ть** is used in Russian.

GERUNDS.

§ 285. The Russian gerund is a *verbal adverb*. As such, it differs from the same part of speech in other languages, but the term is here retained, since it is in common use. Gerunds, like adverbs, are not declined.

Gerunds may be present or past.

§ 286. The *present gerund* is formed from the 3rd person plural of the present tense, by taking off the ending -ют, -ут, or -ят, -ат, and adding -я, or -a if the consonant of the stem cannot be followed by -я (see p. 15), e.g. чита́-ют gives чита́я; плач-ут, пла́ча.

§ 287. The *past gerund* is formed from the infinitive by taking off -ть and adding -в or -вши, e.g. сказа́-ть: сказа́в or сказа́вши (having said).

Reflexive verbs have their past gerund ending in -вшись, e.g.

умы́ться—умы́вшись   having washed oneself

§ 288. Both present and past gerunds are used in subordinate adverbial clauses, replacing a finite verb and a conjunction, e.g.

Так как **он** жела́л скоре́е уе́хать, **он** не ко́нчил рабо́ту.

Жела́я скоре́е уе́хать, etc.

He did not finish his work, as he wanted to go away sooner.

[1] From сле́довать, to follow; *lit.* "it follows to me to read".

The verb in the subordinate clause is here in the past tense, and, strictly speaking, the past gerund желав should be used, but the present form is more common.

§ 289. Although the past gerund of imperfective verbs exists, it is rarely found, the perfective form being more commonly used, e.g.

As soon as he had finished his work he went home.

Как то́лько он ко́нчил рабо́ту....

or   Ко́нчив рабо́ту, он пошёл домо́й.

Such forms as говори́в, конча́в, etc., would mean "*whilst* speaking", "*whilst* finishing", in the past.

§ 290. The past gerund of verbs in -сть, -сти, and -чь usually ends in -ши and is formed from the past tense, by adding -ши to the stem of the past, e.g.

лечь	лёг	лёгши
нести	нёс	нёсши

But in вёдши (from вести) the д of the present is reinstated. Note also ше́дши, from шёл.

§ 291. The substitution of a phrase containing a gerund for a clause introduced by a conjunction is only possible when the subject of the subordinate clause is the *same* as that of the principal clause. See examples in §§ 288, 289.

§ 292. Gerunds are often used as adverbs, e.g. мо́лча (in silence), зря́ (at random), and even as conjunctions, e.g. хотя́ (although).

§ 293. The verbs принима́ть, занима́ть, обнима́ть, etc. (perfective приня́ть, заня́ть, обня́ть), form a homogeneous group, having in common the meaning "to take" (Group D in the Grammar, p. 220). The future tenses are займу́, займёшь; приму́, при́мешь..., etc.

The Church Slavonic form of приму is прие́млю, hence прие́мная. The perfective stem in Slavonic прият- (cf. приня́ть) may be seen in прия́тный (pleasant, *lit.* acceptable) and прия́тель. Cf. also необъя́тный (immense) and заня́тный (interesting).

Взима́ть (to exact), as the imperfective of взять, has been mentioned in § 252, cf. взя́тка (bribe), which is a derivative of взять, used in this sense.

§ 294. The verbs зреть, спеть (to ripen) have the perfectives созре́ть, поспе́ть. But успе́ть (imperfective успева́ть) means *to succeed,* or *be in time,* e.g.

Я не успе́л ко́нчить.   I had not time to finish.

Cf. успе́х, *success*; успе́хи (pl.), *progress.* Cf. успе́шный and спеши́ть (to hurry) (perfective по-).

Note the permutation of the consonants х and ш (see p. 18).

EXERCISES XXII

A. 1. Е́сли бы у него́ была́ скри́пка, он игра́л бы весь день.
If he had a violin, he *would play* the whole day.

2. Он до́лжен бы игра́ть лу́чше тепе́рь, он уже́ давно́ берёт уро́ки. He *should play* better now; he has been taking lessons for a long time.

3. Ему́ сле́дует игра́ть два часа́ в день. He *ought to play* two hours a day.

4. Не то́лько "сле́дует", он до́лжен и́грать, по кра́йней ме́ре, два часа́. He not only "ought to" but *must play* at least two hours.

5. Оди́н раз он до́лжен был игра́ть три часа́. At one time he *had to play* three hours.

6. Вы должно́ быть слы́шали, как он игра́ет. You *must have heard* him play.

7. Он, мо́жет быть, сыгра́ет вам сего́дня ве́чером. He *may play* to you to-night.

8. Вы могли́ бы дать ему́ сове́т. You *might have given* him some advice.

9. Он мог бы игра́ть бо́льше тепе́рь. He *might have been playing* more now.

10. Вам сле́довало бы поговори́ть с ним об э́том пре́жде. You *ought to have spoken* to him about it before.

11. Он мог бы сыгра́ть вам ещё что-нибу́дь. He *might have played you* something else.

12. Чем вы занима́етесь? What is your occupation?

13. Я о́чень спешу́. I am in a great hurry.

14. Спе́шно. Urgent.

15. У меня́ спе́шное де́ло. I have pressing business.

16. Извини́те, но я не успе́ю ко́нчить во́ время. I am sorry, but I shall not have it finished in time.

17. Я извиня́юсь (перед ва́ми), что не написа́л ра́ньше. I apologise (to you) for not having written sooner.

18. Виноват, виновата.   I beg your pardon.
19. Это не его вина.   It is not his fault.
20. Я хотел бы вас спросить.   I should like to ask you.
21. Мне хотелось бы пойти с вами.   I should have liked to go
    with you.
22. Если бы вы были готовы, мы могли бы пойти вместе.   Had
    you been ready, we could have gone together.
23. Магазин готового платья.   A shop selling ready-made clothes.
24. Будь готов! Всегда готов!   Be prepared! Always ready!
25. Вы могли бы простудиться.   You might have caught cold.
26. Я простужен.   I have caught cold.
27. Нельзя верить, чтобы такой язык не был дан великому
    народу. (Тургенев, о русском языке.)   It is impossible to
    believe that such a language has not been given to a great
    people.
28. Всё это было бы смешно,
    Когда бы не было так грустно. (Лермонтов.)
    All this would be laughable, were it not so sad.
29. Направо и налево чернели мрачные пропасти; и туманы,
    клубясь и извиваясь как змеи, сползали туда, будто
    чувствуя и пугаясь приближения дня. (Лермонтов.) To
    right and left the dark ravines showed black, and the mists,
    rolling and twisting like serpents, crawled down into them, as
    if aware and afraid of the approaching day.
30. Не убив медведя, шкуру не продают. (Пословица.) "First
    catch your hare" (lit. "Not having killed a bear, one cannot
    sell the skin").
31. Зреешь ты и спеешь,
    Колос наливая,
    О людских заботах
    Ничего не зная. (Жадовская.)
    You mature and ripen, filling the corn-ears, and knowing
    nothing of human cares.
32. И, шумно катясь, колебала река
    Отражённые в ней облака. (Лермонтов.)
    And, noisily rolling, the river rocked the clouds reflected in it.
33. И долго его поджидая,
    Стоит Император, один. (Лермонтов.)
    And for a long time the Emperor stands waiting for him, alone.

B. 1. Принимая гостей, он был одинаково мил и

любе́зен со все́ми. 2. Вы́нув кошелёк, он дал всем ни́щим по́ две сере́бряных моне́ты. 3. Собира́ясь ехать в го́сти, они всегда́ надева́ли лу́чшие пла́тья и одева́лись неспеша́, чтобы всё было как сле́дует. 4. Сняв шля́пу и перча́тки, и пове́сив пальто́ на ве́шалку, он ждал, когда́ его попро́сят в приёмную. 5. Подня́вшись наве́рх, о́бе сестры́ разде́лись и сно́ва сошли вниз. 6. Спусти́вшись по широкой, покры́той ковро́м, ле́стнице, они вошли́ в гости́нную. 7. Войдя́ в ко́мнату, они поздоро́вались с хозя́йкой и жда́ли, чтобы их предста́вили други́м гостя́м. 8. Верну́вшись из гостей, они расска́зывали до́ма как провели́ вре́мя. 9. Они оста́лись бы до́льше в гостя́х, е́сли бы до́ма не ждала́ их больна́я ба́бушка. 10. В гостя́х хорошо́, а до́ма лу́чше. 11. Сде́лайте это, пожа́луйста, как сле́дует. 12. Если вы поспеши́те, вы успе́ете ко́нчить во́ время. 13. Мы, мо́жет быть, оста́немся здесь ещё год. 14. Он, должно́ быть, заходи́л к нам вчера́; я ви́дела его ка́рточку на столе́ в пере́дней. 15. Вы мо́гли бы говори́ть по-ру́сски мно́го лучше, е́сли бы вы говори́ли до́ма. 16. Она могла́ бы сказа́ть вам ра́ньше, что ей не на́до бы́ло биле́тов. 17. За́втра я уе́ду, что бы ни случи́лось. 18. Просну́вшись поутру́ дово́льно по́здно, я уви́дел, что бу́ря ути́хла. (Пу́шкин.) 19. Два дня спустя́, всё семе́йство, от ма́ла до вели́ка, находи́лось в избе́. (Григоро́вич.)

20.
> Люблю́ грозу́ в нача́ле ма́я,
> Когда весе́нний пе́рвый гром,
> Как бы резвя́ся и игра́я,
> Грохо́чет в не́бе голубо́м.   (Тю́тчев.)

21. Вот поку́шайте, сказал он, возвраща́ясь к пре́жнему почти́тельному то́ну и развёртывая и подава́я Пьеру не́сколько печёных карто́шек. (Л. Толсто́й.) 22. Он ра́достно улыба́лся, слу́шая таки́е расска́зы, вставля́я слова́ и де́лая вопро́сы.... (Л. Толсто́й.)

C. 1. Taking out. 2. Whilst speaking. 3. Picking up.
4. Having picked up. 5. Hurrying. 6. Having hurried.
7. Following. 8. Having accepted. 9. I had to accept. 10. You
ought to take off. 11. He ought to have taken off. 12. I might
have succeeded. 13. I should study. 14. You might have been
studying. 15. I am in a hurry. 16. Take off your coat. 17. I beg
your pardon. 18. Excuse me. 19. I did not succeed. 20. Pick
up the book. 21. She has picked it up. 22. Whilst accepting.
23. Having prepared. 24. Embracing. 25. Having embraced.

D. 1. Having brought the book from the library, I at once
started to read it. 2. Having started reading, I could not stop,
because it was so interesting. 3. Having finished the book, I
shut it. 4. Only after I had closed the book, did I look at my
watch. 5. Looking at my watch, I could not believe that it was
past midnight. 6. Seeing that it was so late, I went to bed
without supper. 7. Having awakened in the morning, I felt very
hungry. 8. My father does everything very deliberately (without
hurrying); he says that in this way he can do more than if he
hurried. 9. Having taken out his note-book, he wrote down my
address. 10. She was reading the newspaper standing in front of
the fire. 11. I should speak Russian if somebody at home spoke
it too. 12. You should speak better, because you have lived in
Moscow. 13. Your mother is Russian; you ought to speak with
her. 14. You simply *must* speak Russian to her; it is your duty.
15. You ought to have spoken about your trip to my brother.
16. I must have spoken about it before. 17. I may speak about
it to-morrow. 18. You might have spoken to her last week.
19. She might have spoken to me, if she had come earlier.
20. Do you think you will manage to copy your translation before
Wednesday? 21. She apologised to me for having forgotten to
bring back my book. 22. You ought to take off your coat; it is
too hot here. 23. If you don't take off your coat you may catch
cold. 24. He must have caught cold last Tuesday when it was
snowing; he was very lightly dressed. 25. Had he studied more,
he would have known the language better. 26. Had you told me
that you were coming, supper would have been ready. 27. I want
you to write to me about yourself. 28. She always wants me to
prepare everything for her.

LESSON XXIII

надея́ться to hope, (на + acc.) to rely upon
наде́жда hope
наде́жный reliable
любова́ться, по- or за- (instr.) to admire
каса́ться, косну́ться (gen.) to touch, touch upon
серди́ть, рас- to make angry
серди́ться, рас- to become angry
се́рдце heart
скуча́ть, соску́читься to feel bored, lonely
ску́чный dull, tiresome
мне ску́чно I am lonely, bored
ску́ка boredom
стро́ить, по- to build
строе́ние building
настра́ивать, настро́ить to tune

настрое́ние mood, frame of mind
я расстро́ен I am out of sorts, distraught
дари́ть, по- to give a present
пода́рок present
дар gift
да́ром gratis, in vain
лицо́ face
ли́чный personal
ли́чно personally
прили́чный decent
отли́чный excellent, distinguished
отли́чно splendid
отлича́ть, отличи́ть to distinguish
кста́ти by the way
из-за́ (gen.) from behind
из-под (gen.) from under
по́дле (gen.) beside

PREPOSITIONS; THE USE OF CASES.

The meaning and use of various prepositions have been given as they occurred in previous lessons, in connection with nouns, and as prefixes of verbs. A systematic treatment of prepositions is given in the present lesson.

§ 295. Prepositions followed by the *genitive* are the most numerous; a full list will be found in the Grammar, p. 265. It should be noted that the prepositions до, из, от, с (off) are mostly used in conjunction with verbs containing the respective prepositions as prefixes, e.g.

дописа́ть до конца́   to finish (in writing)
исходи́ть из   to issue from
отказа́ться от рабо́ты   to refuse work
сня́ть со стола́   to take off the table

Из (ис) is also used after verbs with the prefix вы-, e.g.

выходи́ть из до́ма   to leave the house

§ 296. Adverbs used as prepositions usually require the genitive; such are **вокру́г** (round), **по́дле** (beside), etc.

§ 297. For the use of the genitive:

(*a*) In rendering the verb "to have" in the real sense of possession, see § 39.

(*b*) In the partitive sense, see § 57.

(*c*) After numerals, see § 259.

(*d*) After the comparative, see § 182.

(*e*) After negative, see § 41.

A list of verbs followed by the genitive will be found at the end of the Grammar, p. 269.

§ 298. The genitive is also used after certain adjectives in the predicative form, as **досто́ин** (worthy of), **по́лон** (full of), e.g.

Он досто́ин похвалы́. He is worthy of praise.

Она́ полна́ наде́жды. She is full of hope.

§ 299. Only three prepositions are followed by the *dative*, namely, **к** (to, towards), **по** (along, over), **вопреки́** (contrary to).

§ 300. Verbs compounded with the prefixes **при-**, **под-**, and sometimes **пред-** are followed by the preposition **к** with the dative, e.g.

призыва́ть к де́йствию   to call to action

подъе́хать к подъе́зду   to approach (driving) the entrance

предста́вить к награ́де   to recommend for a prize

§ 301. Verbs followed directly by the dative are very numerous; some of them require the preposition **к** as well (see Grammar, pp. 269, 270).

§ 302. Note also the use of the dative (*a*) in impersonal expressions, already treated in § 65, and (*b*) with the infinitive, as:

Что мне де́лать?   What am I to do? (see p. 48).

Э́тому не быва́ть.   This is not to be.

§ 303. The fact that the preposition **по** requires the dative can be easily remembered by bearing in mind the words **почему** and **потому что**, which are formed with this preposition: cf. also **по-моему**, **по-вашему**, etc. (see p. 262).

По is used in certain common idioms, as:

ударить по плечу	to slap on the shoulder
мáло-по-мáлу	little by little
по-тихóньку	géntly
по суббóтам	on Saturdays

Further idioms are given in Exercise A of this lesson.

§ 304. Certain prepositions are used with the *accusative*. For the use of в and на with the accusative, to indicate *motion*, see § 47.

§ 305. Под and за are similarly used with the accusative (instead of with the instrumental), to indicate *motion*, e.g.

Я положил книги под стол.	I put the books under the table.
Я сел за стол.	I sat down at the table.

§ 306. О (об, обо), *against*, is used with the accusative after only a very few verbs, notably облокотиться (see Grammar, p. 266), e.g.

Он облокотился о стéну. He leaned against the wall.

§ 307. The accusative is used after чéрез, *through* (place), *in* or *after* (time), e.g.

Идти через лес.	To go through the forest.
Приéду через недéлю.	I shall come in a week.

§ 308. Note the following idiomatic expressions, in which the prepositions acquire a slightly different meaning:

дýмать про себя	to think to oneself (*not* "about" oneself)
взять зá руку	to take by the hand
об э́ту пóру	about this time
вó сто раз лýчше	a hundred times better

§ 309. The use of the accusative (*a*) to express *distance* and *duration of time* has been given in § 164, and (*b*) to express "*per* day", "*per* week", etc., in § 37. Note also the following expressions of time and distance:

за недéлю до отъéзда	a week before departure
за пять миль от гóрода	within five miles from town

§ 310. The principal prepositions which take the *instrumental* case are с (see § 62) and пéред, за, под, над. The four latter indicate *position*, and have been treated in Lesson V*a*.

§ 311. The preposition мéжду, *between*, also requires the instrumental case, and should not be confused with **меж**, *among*, which takes the genitive. Note the expressions:

между тем	meanwhile
между нами	between you and me (confidentially); *also lit.* "among us"
между прочим	among other things

(See examples in Exercise A of this lesson.)

§ 312. For the use of the instrumental case in adverbial expressions (such as **днём, ночью,** etc.) see § 62, and the Grammar, p. 262. This use of the instrumental is of very common occurrence; further examples will be found in Exercise A.

§ 313. The instrumental case is used in the expression of the *dimensions*: **длиной, высотой, шириной, глубиной**; in length, in height, in breadth, in depth, e.g.

высотой в тысячу фут	one thousand feet in height
длиной в три мили	three miles long

§ 314. Verbs which require the instrumental case, and also verbs requiring a complement in the instrumental case, are given in the Grammar, pp. 270, 271. For examples of the complement in the instrumental case see Ex. XII A 25, 28. Cf. also § 179.

§ 315. *The prepositional* case is never used without a preposition, hence its name. **В** and **на** are used with this case to indicate *state of rest*; in this construction it is sometimes called the locative (see § 4).

§ 316. **По** is used with the prepositional in the meaning *immediately after* (cf. **понедельник,** the day after Sunday, formerly "неделя"), e.g.

по приезде	on arrival
по возвращении	on returning

also in idioms

скучать по родине	to be homesick
по чём?	at what price?

§ 317. **При,** "in the *presence of*", when used as a prefix, gives the meaning of *nearness*, as **приходить, придавать**. Note also:

при дворе	at the court (hence **придворный,** courtier)
при чём	in addition to which
при том	besides, in addition

§ 318. When a noun and a preposition are used together as an adverbial expression, though not written as one word, the accent is on the preposition, e.g.

во́ время	in time
за́ руку	by the hand
и́з дому	out of the house
за́ морем	overseas
по́ морю	by sea
о́т роду	from birth

Exercises XXIII

A. 1. Мне не до того́.   I have no time for that.

2. Из-за меня́.   Because of me.

3. Со вто́рника.   Since Tuesday.

4. С го́ря.   From grief.

5. Пла́кать от ра́дости.   To weep for joy.

6. С головы́ до ног.   From head to foot.

7. С утра́ до́ ночи.   From morning till night.

8. Изо дня́ в день.   From day to day.

9. Эта шля́па вам к лицу́. ⎫
   Эта шля́па вам идёт. ⎬ This hat suits you.

10. Лицо́м к лицу́.   Face to face.

11. Он подари́л нам всем по кни́ге.   (See § 263.)   He gave us all a book each.

12. По пра́вую ру́ку.   On the right.

13. Чем бога́ты, тем и ра́ды.   You are welcome to all we have.

14. Тем лу́чше.   So much the better.

15. Тем бо́лее.   All the more.

16. Это о́чень кста́ти.   This is very much to the point.

17. Вы пришли́ кста́ти.   You came just at the right moment.

18. Я наде́юсь на вас.   I rely (hope) upon you.

19. Как вам уго́дно; это ва́ше ли́чное де́ло.   Just as you please; it is your personal affair.

20. Бо́льшею ча́стью.   For the most part.

21. Одни́м сло́вом.   In a word.

22. Други́ми слова́ми.   In other words.

23. С како́й це́лью?   With what object (aim)?

24. По чём я́блоки?   How much are apples?

25. Сиде́ть на со́лнце.   To sit in the sun.

26. Это ему́ сто́ило жи́зни.   It cost him his life.

27. Ми́лости про́сим. You are welcome !
28. У вас хоро́ший вид (*or* вы хорошо́ вы́глядите) сего́дня. You look well to-day.
29. С него́ взя́ли сли́шком до́рого. They made him pay too much (dear).
30. Вме́сто двух часо́в дня, он прие́хал в по́лночь. Instead of two o'clock in the afternoon, he came at midnight.
31. Они́ живу́т про́тив це́ркви (gen.). They live opposite the church.
32. Жела́ю вам всего́ лу́чшего. I wish you the best of everything.
33. Что каса́ется ва́шего прие́зда.... As to your arrival....
34. Чита́ть вслух. To read aloud.
35. Учи́ть стихи́ наизу́сть. To learn poetry by heart.
36. Кто-то идет нам навстре́чу. Here is some one coming to meet us.
37. Сего́дня, родна́я, я сто́ю награ́ды (gen.). (Надсо́н.) To-day, dearest, I deserve a reward.
38. За гора́ми, за дола́ми,
    За широ́кими моря́ми,
    Про́тив не́ба на земле́
    Жил стари́к в одно́м селе́. (Ершо́в.)
    Beyond the mountains and the valleys, beyond the broad seas, on the earth and opposite the sky, lived an old man in a certain village.
39. Меж высо́ких хлебо́в затеря́лося
    Небога́тое на́ше село́. (Некра́сов.)
    Among the tall corn-fields our poor village was lost.
40. Ме́жду ме́сяцем и на́ми
    Кто-то хо́дит по земле́. (Пу́шкин.)
    Some one is walking over the earth between the moon and us.
41. Кто при звезда́х и при луне́
    Так по́здно е́дет на коне́? (Пу́шкин.)
    Who is this riding so late, in the moonlight and the starlight?
42. При всём том его́ почита́ли и слу́шали. (Григоро́вич.) In spite of all this he was esteemed and obeyed.
43. "Так ты Бирю́к", повтори́л я: "я, брат, слыха́л про тебя́...." (Турге́нев.) "So you are Biryuk", I repeated, "well, my friend, I have heard of you."
44. Во́зле де́вочки малю́тки
    Собрался́ кружо́к...
    И с трудо́м от сло́ва к сло́ву
    Па́льчиком водя́,

По печа́тному чита́ет
Мужичка́м дитя́. (Ма́йков.)

Around the little girl a circle has gathered... and laboriously
pointing with her little finger from word to word the child
reads the print to the men.

B. 1. Мы жда́ли вас с утра́. 2. Вы пришли́ очень
кста́ти, мы как раз сади́мся обе́дать. 3. Приса́живайтесь
за стол, всё перед ва́ми, ку́шайте на здоровье. 4. Что
каса́ется ва́шего де́ла, мы поговори́м о нём по́сле обе́да.
5. Меня посади́ли по пра́вую ру́ку хозя́йки. 6. Пообе́дав,
все вы́шли из-за стола́, поблагодари́ли хозя́йку за
вку́сный обед и усе́лись напро́тив ками́на. 7. За обе́дом
нам бы́ло не до разгово́ров, а у огня́ бесе́да оживи́лась.
8. Хозя́ин предложи́л нам всем по сига́ре. 9. Все
любова́лись ма́ленькой до́чкой хозя́йки, кото́рая, си́дя
на ковре́, игра́ла с котёнком. 10. Кла́няйтесь от меня́
ва́шей жене́. 11. Това́рищ напо́мнил мне, что за́втра на́до
ра́но встава́ть, и мы поспеши́ли прости́ться. 12. Проведя́
тако́й хоро́ший ве́чер, мы верну́лись домо́й в очень
хоро́шем настрое́нии. 13. За́втра между́ двумя́ и тремя́
я схожу́ (see p. 225) в теа́тр за биле́тами. 14. Вот уже
год, как мы с сестро́й занима́емся ру́сским языко́м.
15. Как вы мо́жете чита́ть при тако́м я́рком со́лнце?
16. Я по́мню, вы это при мне объясня́ли. 17. Все о́чень
дорожа́т (see p. 270) его мне́нием, он счита́ется самым
изве́стным учёным. 18. Его мать должна́ горди́ться им:
в тако́е коро́ткое вре́мя он сде́лал таки́е успе́хи. 19. Все
смея́лись над его весёлым расска́зом и проси́ли его,
чтобы он рассказа́л ещё что-нибудь. 20. Скуча́я по
ро́дине, он был не в настрое́нии ходи́ть в го́сти. 21. Таки́м
о́бразом, он не имел возмо́жности встреча́ть люде́й и
говори́ть по-англи́йски. 22. Мы бо́льшею ча́стью про-
во́дим вечера́ вме́сте. 23. У него́ сла́бое се́рдце; ему
нельзя́ играть в фу́тбол. 24. Не серди́тесь на неё; она
не хоте́ла вас оби́деть.

25.   И ненави́дим мы, и лю́бим мы случа́йно,
       Ниче́м (instr.) не же́ртвуя ни зло́бе, ни любви́.
                                              (Ле́рмонтов.)

26.   Я не в состоя́нии же́ртвовать необходи́мым в
       наде́жде приобрести́ изли́шнее.   (Пу́шкин.)

27.   Но, Бо́же мой, кака́я ску́ка
       С больны́м сиде́ть и день, и ночь,
       Не отходя́ ни шагу прочь.   (Пу́шкин.)

C. 1. This story is not finished, perhaps some one will write an
ending for it (use дописа́ть).   2. He did not go out of the house
for a week.   3. She feels very lonely without her friend who has
gone abroad.   4. She has been living in France since last February
(February of the last year).   5. We have read all these books
several times from beginning to end.   6. I have been waiting for
you since morning, so that we might go (in order to go) to buy
something for a present.   7. For whom do you need to buy a
present?   8. It is for my little sister, her birthday is in two days.
9. Give her (use подари́ть) a book of poems, she is very fond of
poetry.   10. By the way, I have to buy some things (кое-что)
also.   11. Splendid! Then I won't be thinking that I am taking
up (отнима́ть) your time.   12. As to time, I am quite free
the whole day till dinner.   13. I hope I have not disturbed your
work; I know that you are hurrying to finish it in time.   14. Because of his illness he missed several lessons.   15. He is in a very
bad mood and you cannot make him laugh[1].   16. Next year about
this time I shall not be with you.   17. He called on me a week
before his departure for Germany (в + acc.).   18. If you have no
book, come and sit between us.   19. Hang this picture between
the windows.   20. Do you like the house which is being built
opposite our school?   21. Yes, I was admiring it this morning.
22. How dull it is to see all these houses; they are all alike.
23. Everybody says that you are like your father, but I think
that you are like your mother.   24. His father is very angry
with him because he is going to Russia.   25. Personally, I do
not understand why he does not want him to go.

____

[1] Use заста́вить смея́ться or рассмеши́ть (perf. of смеши́ть, to make
laugh).

искать (pres. ищу́, и́щешь), по- to seek, look for

сыска́ть (see p. 12) (perf.) to seek out

проходи́ть, пройти́ to cover ground in study (trans.)

про́йденное (noun) what has been learned

посеща́ть, посети́ть (посещу́, посети́шь) to visit, attend

пропуска́ть, пропусти́ть to miss

слу́шаться, по- to obey

послу́шный obedient

жать (pres. жму, жмёшь), по- to press

жать (pres. жну, жнёшь), с- to reap

охо́титься, по- (cf. хоте́ть) to hunt

охо́та hunt, desire

охо́тник hunter

охо́тно willingly

дыша́ть (по-, 2nd conj.) to breathe

отдыха́ть, отдохну́ть to rest, take a rest

о́тдых rest

иметь в виду́ to have in prospect

наро́чно on purpose

внима́ть, внять (see p. 220) (rarely used) to listen to (attentively)

слу́шать внима́тельно to listen to (attentively)

внима́ние attention

внима́тельный attentive

обраща́ть (обрати́ть) внима́ние на (acc.) to pay attention to

Conjunctions.

§ 319. In Russian various parts of speech are used as conjunctions, and certain words which in English are considered other parts of speech are classed as conjunctions.

Although a detailed classification is not essential, the use of conjunctions and the part they play in various constructions are important, since a knowledge of these is necessary in order that sentences may be built up correctly. It is possible to give a simplified classification under the two heads of *co-ordinating* and *subordinating* conjunctions.

§ 320. *Co-ordinating conjunctions.* The difference between и, the *joining* "and", and а, the *separating* "and", was explained as early as in Lesson I.

Да can also be used as a conjunction with the meaning *and*, and sometimes *but* (see p. 267), e.g.

Пусть поживёт он, да поу́чится, да порабо́тает.
Let him live, and learn, and work.

На взгля́д-то он хоро́ш, да зе́лен. (Крыло́в.)
The grapes look good, but green.

(Note that виногра́д, "grapes", is a singular word.)

§ 321. То... то... (now... now...) is also considered a conjunction, e.g.

То хо́лодно, то о́чень жа́рко. (Крыло́в.)
Now cold, now very hot.

§ 322. же has two contrasting meanings, namely, *but* and *also* or *same*, e.g.

Мне всё послу́шно, я же ничему́. (Пу́шкин.)
Everything obeys me: *but* I (obey) nothing.
Все э́ти кни́ги ва́ши; а э́та?—Моя́ же.
All these books are yours: what about this one?—(It is) mine *too*.

же is also used in an emphatic sense, e.g.

Говори́ же!   Speak then!

§ 323. То́лько (just, only) is a conjunction in Russian, e.g.

Я зайду́ к вам, то́лько не надо́лго.
I shall come to visit you, only not for long.

§ 324. *Subordinating conjunctions*, which serve to introduce subordinate clauses, are best studied together with such clauses. In addition to the true conjunctions е́сли, ли, что́бы, потому́ что, чем, что, etc., any part of speech by which a subordinate clause is introduced is in Russian considered a "conjunctive" word or expression, e.g. ско́лько... сто́лько or сто́лько... что, as in

Меня́ все сто́лько огорча́ет, что да́же мне и пи́ща не вкусна́.
                                        (Крыло́в.)
Everything grieves me so much, that I cannot even enjoy food.
Пуска́й я слаб—мой меч силён. (Жуко́вский.)
What though I (*lit.* let me) be weak, my sword is strong.
Ско́лько ни говори́ли, одна́ко ни до чего́ не договори́лись.
However much they talked, they came to no conclusion.

§ 325. When a subordinate clause begins with a relative pronoun, an adverb, or a conjunction, as кото́рый, что, како́й, где, как, для чего́, что́бы, etc., the principal clause of the sentence often has a corresponding demonstrative pronoun, or adverb, or conjunction, though it is sometimes omitted. E.g.

Что посе́ял, **то** и жни. (Крыло́в.)
What you have sown, that also you must reap.

§ 326. In adjective clauses the pronouns **кото́рый** and **како́й** are often replaced by **кто, что, чей**, e.g.

Не всегда́ та соба́ка куса́ет, **что** гро́мко ла́ет.
It is not always the dog which barks loudest that bites.
Cf. "His bark is worse than his bite".)

Я ду́мал о том челове́ке, в чьих рука́х находи́лась моя́ судьба́.
(Пу́шкин.)
I was thinking about the man in whose hands my fate lay.

or by an adverb, such as **где, куда́, отку́да, когда́, как**, e.g.

Дере́вня, где скуча́л Оне́гин,
Была́ преле́стный уголо́к. (Пу́шкин.)
The village where Onegin languished was a pleasant spot.
Вон ви́дишь ли тот мост, **куда́** нам путь лежи́т? (Крыло́в.)
Do you see that bridge yonder, over which our way lies?

or by a conjunction, e.g.

Сыщи́ ей жениха́, **чтоб** был краси́в, умён. (Крылов.)
Seek out a husband for her, who shall be handsome and wise.

§ 327. Subordinate adverbial clauses of *place* are introduced by such words as **где, куда́, отку́да** with the corresponding adverbs **там, туда́, отту́да** (sometimes omitted) in the principal clause, e.g.

Отку́да ветер, **отту́да** счастье. (See p. 135.)
Там бу́ду и я, **отку́да** никто́ не прихо́дит.
I too shall be there, whence no one returns.

§ 328. Adverbial clauses of *time* are introduced by **когда́, пре́жде чем, пока́, в то вре́мя как** *or* **когда́, с тех пор как** (since), **до тех пор, пока́, едва́, лишь то́лько** (just as), **то́лько что**, etc., e.g

С тех пор как я себя́ по́мню, я не люблю́ ко́шек.
Since as far back as I can remember I have disliked cats.
Пре́жде чем мы начнём (fut.), я хочу́ сказа́ть....
Before we begin I want to say....
Ва́ше сло́во, **пока́** вы жи́вы, мно́го зна́чит. (Пу́шкин.)
As long as you live your word carries weight (means a great deal).
То́лько что мы вошли́ в дом, **как** начала́сь гроза́.
As soon as we had entered the house, the storm broke.

§ 329. **Как, (как) будто, словно (как)** introduce adverbial clauses of *manner*, *degree* or *comparison*, the corresponding adverb in the principal clause being **так** or **подобно тому**, e.g.

Этот слепой не **так** слеп, **как** кажется. (Лермонтов.)
This blind man is not so blind as he seems.
Он **так** усердно копал, как будто хотел клад найти.
He was digging as eagerly as if he wanted to find a treasure.
Лиса притихла и лежит, **словно** мёртвая.
The fox became quiet, and lay (lies) as if dead.

§ 330. Adverbial clauses of *purpose* are introduced by **чтобы** often with **для того, затем, с тем**, etc., in the principal clause, e.g.

Всё это я пишу **для того, чтобы** вам было легче.
I am writing all this to make it easier for you.
Затем-то я и лаю, **чтоб** ты накормлен был. (Крылов.)
I am barking in order that you may be fed.

§ 331. Adverbial clauses of *condition* are introduced by **если, то** often being used in the principal clause, e.g.

Если бы я только знала, **то** я бы не уехала.
Had I only known I should not have gone away.

§ 332. **Пусть**, introducing adverbial clauses of *concession*, is balanced by **зато**, e.g.

Пусть это трудно, **зато** интересно.
Although this is difficult, it is nevertheless interesting.

§ 333. Since a subordinate adjective clause qualifies a noun in the principal clause, it should agree with it, just as an adjective agrees with the noun it qualifies (see § 273). Similarly other subordinate clauses are often required in an oblique case. This also occurs when a clause is introduced by a preposition used as a conjunction. But since a clause as a whole cannot be inflected, the pronoun **то** is as a rule inserted, and is used in the required case, thus reinforcing, as it were, the connection between the subordinate clause and the word which introduces it, or to which it is related: This **то**, however, is not translated.

Thus, in the expression я **рад вам** (I am glad (to see) you), **рад** takes the dative, hence in "I am glad that you have come" the clause "that you have come" should be used in the dative. Accordingly, **тому** (dative of **то**) is used (though it may be omitted):

Я рад **тому**, что вы пришли.

Again, in "I shall give you the book after I have finished with it", после requires the genitive, hence того (genitive of то) is used:

Я дам вам книгу после того, как прочту (fut. perf.).

Он не может обойтись без того, чтобы не ходить каждый день в театр.

He cannot do without going to the theatre every day.

Note, however, that без того, чтобы may be replaced by не with the past gerund, e.g.

Он не мог уйти без того, чтобы не кончить работу,

or   Он не мог уйти, не кончив работы (gen.).

He could not go without finishing his work.

The same applies to other cases:

Я объясню вам урок перед тем (instr.), как переводить его.

I shall explain the lesson to you before translating it.

Я доволен тем, что имею. (Жуковский.)

I am satisfied with what I have.

Расскажите о том (prep.), как вы ездили в Россию.

Tell us about your trip to Russia.

("о том" may be omitted.)

Он настаивал на том, что сделает всё сам.

He insisted on doing everything himself.

Не обращайте внимания на то (acc.), что он говорит.

Pay no attention to what he is saying.

§ 334. The following idiomatic uses of particular conjunctions should be noted:

Пока... не... (*lit.* while... not...), followed by the future, is used to express *until*; by the past, to express *before*, e.g.

пока я не приду   *until* I come

пока он не пришёл   *before* he comes

Зато... means *on the other hand, nevertheless*, or simply *but*, e.g.

Хотя эти ягоды мелкие, зато вкусные.

Although these berries are small, they are nevertheless good (tasty).

Кто... кто... is used as *some... others...*, e.g.

Кто приехал поездом, кто трамваем, а кто пришёл пешком.

Some came by train, some by tram, and some on foot.

Ведь is an emphatic word meaning *you know* or *surely* (see Grammar, p. 263), e.g.

Ведь вы знали об этом раньше.

Surely you knew about this before.

Exercises XXIV

A. 1. И скучно, и грустно, и некому руку подать
В минуту душевной невзгоды. (Лермонтов.)
One feels lonely, and sad, and there is no one to give one a
hand in moments of misfortune of the soul.

2. Желанье? Что пользы напрасно и вечно желать?
А годы проходят—всё лучшие годы. (Лермонтов.)
Wishes? What use eternally wishing in vain, while the years,
the best years, are ever slipping by?

3. А жаль, что незнаком
Ты с нашим петухом. (Крылов.)
But it's a pity that you don't know our cock.

4. "Ведь это дереву вредит",
Ей с дуба ворон говорит. (Крылов: "Свинья под Дубом".)
"But it harms the tree", the crow replies from the oak.

5. Хоть ты и в новой коже,
Но сердце у тебя все то же. (Крылов.)
Although you have a new skin your heart is the same as ever.

6. Ты виноват уж тем, что хочется мне кушать. (Крылов.)
You are already guilty in that I am hungry.

7. Али (или) я тебя не хою,
Али ешь овса не вволю? (Пушкин.)
Am I not tending you, and do you not get your fill of oats?

8. Охотно верим мы тому,
Чему нам верится охотно. (Крылов.)
We willingly believe what we are willing to believe.

9. Расхвастался о том, где он бывал. He was bragging about
the places where he had been.

10. Няня усаживалась в холодке с тем, чтобы вязать чулок
(Гончаров.)
The nurse used to sit down in the shade to knit a stocking.

11. Лишь только месяц золотой
Из-за горы тихонько встанет
И на тебя украдкой взглянет,—
К тебе я стану прилетать. (Лермонтов: "Демон".)
As soon as the golden moon rises silently from behind the hills,
and secretly gazes upon you, I shall fly to meet you.

12. Словно как мать над сыновней могилой,
Стонет кулик над равниной унылой. (Некрасов.)
Like a mother at the grave of her son the wood-cock groans
above the dismal plain.

13. Брожу́ ли я вдоль у́лиц шу́мных,
Вхожу́ ль во многолю́дный храм,
Сижу́ ль меж ю́ношей безу́мных,—
Я предаю́сь мои́м мечта́м. (Пу́шкин.)
Whether I wander along noisy streets, or enter a crowded temple, or sit among foolish youths I give myself up to my dreams.

14. Он стоя́л, бу́дто ка́менный.   He stood as if turned to stone.

15. Я бу́ду ждать до тех пор, пока́ вы не придёте.   I shall wait until you come (see § 334).

16. Пре́жде чем мы начнём, *or* пре́жде чем нача́ть.   Before we start.

17. Э́то был не кто ино́й, как наш ста́рый прия́тель.   It was none other than our old friend.

18. Весь го́род был не что ино́е, как собра́ние ма́леньких хат.   The whole town was nothing more than a collection of small huts.

19. Коне́чно это сукно́ до́рого, зато́ бу́дет носи́ться хорошо́.   This cloth is of course expensive, but (on the other hand) it will wear well.

20. Тот, кто мно́го чита́ет, мно́го зна́ет.   He who reads much, knows much.

21. Э́то тот господи́н, кото́рого мы вчера́ встре́тили.   This is the gentleman whom we met yesterday.

22. К чему́ вы всё э́то говори́те?—К тому́, чтобы вы зна́ли.   Why are you saying all this?—So that you may know.

23. Мне не охо́та сего́дня рабо́тать.   I don't feel like working to-day.

24. Ему́ не́ было охо́ты ни с кем говори́ть.   He had no desire to speak to anyone.

25. Мы прошли́ о́чень мно́го за э́тот год.   We have got through a great deal (i.e. studying) during this year.

26. Он име́ет в виду́ хоро́шую рабо́ту.   He has the prospect of a good "job".

27. Жму Вам[1] ру́ку.   I press your hand (often used at the close of a letter).

28. Позво́льте пожа́ть вам ру́ку.   Allow me to shake hands with you.

29. Обрати́те на э́то внима́ние.   Turn your attention to this.

---

[1] In letters Вы, Вас, Вам, Ваш are regularly spelled with capitals.

B. 1. Меня поймёт только тот, кто сам это пережил. (Лермонтов.) 2. Они приехали сюда не для того, чтобы только веселиться, но для того, чтобы изучить язык. 3. Он говорил это к тому, чтобы вы слишком на него не надеялись. 4. Я имел ввиду именно то, о чём мы говорили вчера. 5. Володя (boy's name) гордился тем, что приехал на охотничьей лошади. (Толстой.) 6. Я дам вам эту книгу, но только с тем, чтобы вы ее вернули мне завтра. 7. С какой целью вы занимаетесь русским языком? 8. С тем, чтобы читать русских писателей, а ещё с тем, чтобы поехать в Россию. 9. Напишите мне о том, что вам больше всего понравилось за-границей. 10. С тех пор, как я вас знаю, я не помню, чтобы вы так хорошо выглядели. 11. Прежде чем продолжать, давайте повторим пройденное. 12. Все это устроено для того, чтобы жить было легко и удобно. 13. Он лёг спать поздно, зато кончил работу. 14. Мой брат хочет быть или доктором, или учителем.[1] 15. Дело кончилось тем, что все рассмеялись. 16. Он стал таким, каким я всегда желал его видеть. 17. Несмотря на то, что вы живёте здесь всего второй год, вы уже хорошо говорите по-английски. 18. Он сначала посетил Германию, потом Швейцарию, затем Францию и, наконец, Англию. 19. Мне очень жаль, что я вошёл после того, как вы уже дали честное слово. (Лермонтов.) 20. Кто спешил (в город) поторговать, кто шёл погулять, а кто и оба дела зараз сделать. (Печерский.)

21. Зима. Что делать нам в деревне? Я встречаю
Слугу, несущего мне утром чашку чаю,
Вопросами: тепло ль? утихла ли метель? (Пушкин.)

22. Когда б надежду я имела,
Хоть редко, хоть в неделю раз,
В деревне нашей видеть вас.   (Пушкин.)

[1] Note the complement in the instr. case after быть; the same occurs after стать.

23. Мы побежа́ли наве́рх одева́ться, так чтобы как мо́жно бо́лее походи́ть на охо́тников. (Л. Толсто́й.)

24. За мое́ю теле́жкою четвёрка быко́в тащи́ла другу́ю, как ни в чём не быва́ло, несмотря́ на то, что она была́ до́ верху накла́дена. (Ле́рмонтов.)

25.   Я в э́тот мир пришёл, чтоб ви́деть Со́лнце,
    А е́сли день пога́с,
    Я бу́ду петь…. Я бу́ду петь о Со́лнце.
(Ба́льмонт.)

26.   Я тот, кото́рому внима́ла
    Ты в полуно́чной тишине́…
    Чей о́браз ви́дела во сне;
    Я тот, чей взор наде́жду гу́бит…
    Я тот, кого́ никто́ не лю́бит….
(Ле́рмонтов: "Де́мон".)

27. Ты все тако́в же, каки́м на э́том ме́сте со мной встре́тился впервы́е. (Жуко́вский.)

28.   …Вновь я посети́л
    Тот уголо́к земли́, где я провёл
    Отше́льником два го́да незаме́тных. (Пу́шкин.)

C. 1. The school where I teach was built three years ago. 2. He who finishes (fut.) first can go home. 3. The boy whose voice I hear always talks too much. 4. I was thinking of my friends, in whose house I had spent such a pleasant week. 5. This is the school to which I want to send (отда́ть) my son. 6. Do you see that tree under which a group of boys is sitting? 7. Don't you recognise him? He is the boy who was given first prize. 8. Do not go to London without letting me know. 9. After I have explained the grammar, we shall read the words. 10. Don't believe everything he tells you. 11. Write me a post-card before you come. 12. Before I visit France, I should like to go to Germany. 13. After they had visited France, they went to Switzerland. 14. He always comes when we are not at home, as if on purpose. 15. You should wait until he writes to you what to do. 16. He did not want to go away without saying "good-bye". 17. The whole evening she was telling us about the places she used to live in. 18. He insists (на + prepos.) that his mother should rest after dinner. 19. Tell

him about your success as soon as he comes home.   20. The field
to which we are going is beyond that wood.   21. They have not
written to us since they left England.   22. Please explain this to
us whilst you are here.   23. Don't decide anything until I write
to you.   24. Don't start writing until I tell you.   25. She is not
as tired as she seems, although she is very pale.   26. I have
written all this on the board so that you can copy it (use списа́ть).
27. I paid no attention to what he said in his lecture.   28. I thought
that you were always very attentive.   29. In spite of ill (плохо́й)
health, he has not missed a single lesson.

LESSON XXV

The use of tenses and moods

§ 335. *The present tense.* There is only one present tense in
Russian, which therefore means both *I do* and *I am doing*. Its use
instead of the near future, as in English, has already been pointed
out (see § 85), as has the use of the present, instead of the English
perfect, if the action is still going on, e.g.

Я живу́ здесь три го́да.   I have lived here for three years.

The present tense is often used in narration to impart vividness
to the events described, especially after the verbs ви́деть and
слы́шать, e.g. Пришёл я и ви́жу, followed by narration in the
present tense.

§ 336. In a subordinate clause the present tense is used when
the time referred to is really the present, e.g.

Он спроси́л меня́, ча́сто ли я хожу́ в теа́тр.

He asked me whether I went to the theatre often.

but   ча́сто ли я ходи́л в теа́тр пре́жде.

. . . whether I used to go to the theatre often before.

This difference between the Russian and English constructions is
due to the absence of sequence of tenses in Russian (see § 134).

After е́сли (if) and когда́ (when) the future is used when future
time is referred to (see Lesson XI), e.g.

Когда́ я приду́ домо́й, я бу́ду обе́дать.

When I come home I shall have dinner.

§ 337. Быва́ло, the past tense of быва́ть can be idiomatically
used with all tenses (see below). In combination with the present

tense it is frequently used in reminiscences, e.g. by Tolstoi, in *Childhood*:

Чу́вствуешь, быва́ло, впросо́нках, что чья́-то не́жная рука́ тро́гает тебя́.

You would feel, through sleep, that some one's tender hand was touching you.

Another passage from *Childhood* (Де́тство) is given in Exercise B of this lesson.

§ 338. *The past tense.* As has been frequently pointed out, there are only two past tenses in Russian: the imperfect, denoting *duration*, and the perfect, denoting *completion* of an action.

In certain cases in which it may seem that the perfective is required, the imperfective may be used if the action is considered in its duration, e.g.

Я писа́л вам об э́том.   I wrote to you about it.

Писа́л here shows that the *action* rather than the *fact* is referred to, cf.

Он говори́л мне, что уезжа́ет за́втра.

He told me he was going away to-morrow.

Вчера́ приходи́л до́ктор.

The doctor came (i.e. was here) yesterday.

It has also been mentioned that the perfective past is not always a translation of the English perfect, and *vice versa*. Examples are given in § 132.

§ 339. **Быва́ло** used along with the imperfect past imparts the idea of frequency of an action, e.g.

Пре́жде он, быва́ло, приходи́л по вечера́м.

Formerly he used to come in the evenings.

Бы́ло used with the perfect past means that the action was *about to be completed* (unfulfilled intention, cf. English "on the point of "), e.g.

Я бы́ло сказа́л вам, но вы ушли́.

I was on the point of telling you, but you went away.

Он на́чал бы́ло объясня́ть, но уро́к ко́нчился.

He was about to explain, but the lesson ended.

§ 340. **Чуть не** with the perfect past has a positive meaning (almost), e.g.

Она́ чуть не запла́кала.   She nearly burst into tears.

Cf. use of **пока́ не**, Lesson XXIV.

§ 341. The past tense of **пойти** and **поехать** is sometimes used instead of the imperative, e.g.

Пошёл!	Start! Go!
Пошли!	Go away!
Поехал!	Be off now! (Go! Start!)

§ 342. *The future tense.* The use of the imperfect future requires no special comment, except that the verb **стать** is sometimes used as the auxiliary instead of **быть** (see § 210). For the use of future after "when", etc., see §§ 133, 328; after **пока не**, see § 334.

§ 343. The perfect future may be used instead of the present to express habitual events, e.g.

Он встанет, оденется и выйдет в сад погулять, походит по дорожкам и вернётся домой. (Гончаров.)

He gets up, dresses, and goes out into the garden for a walk; walks along the paths a little way, and comes home.

§ 344. In combination with **бывало** the perfect future expresses the idea of an action which used to happen regularly, e.g.

Придёт он, бывало, ко мне и скажет.

He used to come to me and say (cf. English "would come").

For the future used instead of the past see Exercise A 16, 17.

§ 345. The future may be used instead of the imperative, e.g.

Не сдадимся! Let us not give in! (We shall not give in.)

§ 346. The use of the future (instead of the English *would* and *should*) in subordinate clauses, after a past in the principal clause, has been explained in § 134.

§ 347. The future is also sometimes used instead of **не могу** followed by the perfect infinitive, e.g.

Не могу ничего найти.⎱
Не найду ничего.   ⎰ I cannot find anything.

§ 348. *The conditional and subjunctive.* The use of the conditional in general has been explained in Lesson XXII.

As a subjunctive, it is used in particular after verbs or expressions of fear, doubt, desire, etc., as in English, e.g.

Боюсь, не упали бы вы. I am afraid you may fall.

Сомневаюсь, чтобы он написал. I doubt whether he will write.

Note that after verbs of *fearing* the verb is used in the *negative* although the meaning is positive.

§ 349. This construction may also be used to express a wish, a command, or advice, e.g.

Пошёл бы я теперь погуля́ть. I would like to go for a walk now.
Чтобы никто́ не вы́шел отсю́да ! No one is to leave the room !
Поговори́ли бы вы с ним. You should have a talk with him.

§ 350. *The imperative.* The difference between the imperfective and perfective imperative has been explained in Lesson XII, § 146.

The use of the imperfective imperative instead of the perfective, to express a more polite request or invitation, has been mentioned in § 163. The imperative is sometimes used instead of the indicative. See Ex. A 13, 14.

§ 351. The idiomatic use of the imperative instead of the conditional must be noted; in this construction the 2nd person singular is generally used, and can be applied to any person, e.g.

Приди́ он ра́ньше, он заста́л бы меня́.

Had he come earlier, he would have found me in.

Не откро́й вы мне дверь, я не смогла́ бы войти́.

Had you not opened the door for me, I should not have been able to get in.

Note that in spite of the negative in this construction, the perfect imperative is here used (cf. § 147).

Note also an imperative construction similar to the English:

Ребёнка обучи́, дашь ми́ру челове́ка.

Educate a child, and you will give a man to the world.

§ 352. *The infinitive.* The difference between the imperfective and perfective infinitive has been explained in Lesson XI, § 131.

Some idiomatic uses of the infinitive should be noted:

(*a*) Instead of the future, e.g.

Что нам де́лать ? What are we to do ?
Как быть ? What is to be done ?
Как вам сказа́ть ? How shall I explain to you ?

(*b*) Instead of the conditional, e.g.

Отчего́ бы и нам не пойти́ ? Why should we not go too ?

(*c*) As an imperative, see § 151.

(*d*) With чтобы, to express purpose, see Ex. XXIV, B 2.

Exercises XXV

A. 1. Сел орёл на скалу́, в тень под е́лями,
И гляди́т: из рассе́лины
Выполза́ет зме́я, извива́ется. (Поло́нский.)
An eagle sat on a rock in the shade under the fir trees, and
watched: out of a crevice a snake crawled and uncoiled itself.

2. Прибежа́ли в избу́ де́ти,
Второпя́х зову́т отца́. (Пу́шкин.)
The children ran into the hut and hurriedly called their father.

3. . . . Из шатра́
Выхо́дит Пётр. Его́ глаза́
Сия́ют. Лик его́ ужа́сен.
Движе́нья бы́стры. Он прекра́сен. . .
Идёт. Ему́ коня́ подво́дят. (Пу́шкин.)
Out of the tent stepped Peter. His eyes flashed; his counten-
ance was terrible; his movements quick; he was splendid. . . .
He came, and they led his horse forward.

4. Вдруг получи́л он в са́мом де́ле
От управи́теля докла́д,
Что дя́дя при́ смерти в посте́ли. (Пу́шкин.)
Suddenly he did indeed receive (lit. "in very fact") from his
steward the information that his uncle was lying at the point
of death.

5. Нельзя́ бы́ло в душе́ не согласи́ться, что Воло́дя поступа́ет
благоразу́мно. (Л. Толсто́й.) It was impossible not to agree
in one's innermost heart that Volodya acted wisely.

6. Со всех сторо́н соба́к сбежа́лося с полсо́тни,
Оди́н было́ уже́ прохо́жий ка́мень взял. (Крыло́в.)
Half a hundred dogs rushed up from all sides. One of the
travellers was just about to pick up a stone.

7. На ель воро́на взгромозди́сь,
Позавтракать было совсем уж собрала́сь,
Да призаду́малась, а сыр во рту́ держа́ла. (Крылов.)
The crow, having perched high up on a fir tree, was just about
to have lunch, but fell a-thinking, and kept holding the cheese
in her beak.

8. Зимо́й быва́ло в ночь глуху́ю
Зало́жим тро́йку удалу́ю,
Поём и свищем—и стрело́й
Лети́м над сне́жной глубино́й. (Пу́шкин.)

On a dark winter's night we would harness a swift troika; we would sing and whistle, and fly like an arrow over the deep snow.

9. Сидел бы ты дома. (Пушкин.) Would that you stayed at home.

10. Хоть бы пришёл кто-нибудь. I wish some one would come.

11. О если б мог от взоров недостойных
    Я скрыть подвал. (Пушкин.)
    If only I could hide my cellar (of gold) from unworthy eyes.

12. Чтоб ни одна душа не перешла за эту грань (=границу). (Пушкин.) Not a soul must pass the frontier.

13. Ему бы в сторону броситься, а он возьми да прямо и побеги. (Тургенев.) He should have rushed aside, but without a word he ran straight forward.

14. Ей бы помолчать, а она возьми да скажи всё прямо. She should have been silent, but she "went and said" everything straight out.

15. Мысль, что Мария Ивановна не успеет выехать, ужасала меня. (Пушкин.) The thought that Maria Ivanovna would not get away in time terrified me.

16. А он как выскочит, да как побежит. (Colloquial.) And then he leaped out and ran off.

17. Чурбан она то понесёт,
    То так, то сяк его обхватит,
    То поволочет, то покатит.... (Крылов.)
    Now she (a monkey) would carry the log; now she hugged it this way or that, now dragged it, and now rolled it....

18. Вору дай хоть миллион, он воровать не перестанет. (Крылов.) Give a thief a million; he won't stop stealing.

19. По синим волнам океана
    Лишь звёзды блеснут в небесах,
    Корабль одинокий несётся.... (Лермонтов.)
    As soon as the stars shine in the sky over the blue waves of the ocean, a lonely ship passes by....

20. Пусть я посватаюсь, вы что бы мне сказали? (Грибоедов.) If I were to woo you, what would you say?

21. Шестой уж год я царствую спокойно. (Пушкин.) For the sixth year now I am reigning in peace.

22. По одёжке встречают, по уму провожают. (Поговорка.) When you are met, you are judged by your clothes, and when you are seen off, by your ability (mind).

B. 1. Набе́гавшись до́сыта, сиди́шь, быва́ло, за ча́йным столо́м, на своём высо́ком кре́слице; уже́ по́здно, давно́ вы́пил свою́ ча́шку молока́ с са́харом, сон смыка́ет глаза́, но не тро́гаешься с ме́ста, сиди́шь и слу́шаешь. И как не слу́шать. Ма́ма говори́т с кем-нибу́дь, и зву́ки го́лоса её так сла́дки, так приве́тливы. (Л. Толсто́й: "Де́тство".)

2.   Пото́м уви́дел я́сно он,
        Что и в дере́вне ску́ка та́ же,
        Хоть нет ни у́лиц, ни дворцо́в,
        Ни карт, ни ба́лов, ни стихо́в.   (Пу́шкин.)

3.   Она́ опо́мнилась, но сно́ва
        Закры́ла о́чи—и ни сло́ва
        Не говори́т. Оте́ц и мать
        Ей се́рдце и́щут успоко́ить...
            Напра́сно. Це́лые два дня́
            Мари́я не пила́, не е́ла....   (Пу́шкин.)

4.   Что но́вого пока́жет мне Москва́?
        Сего́дня бал, а за́втра бу́дет два. (Грибое́дов.)

5. Ко́нчив моли́тву, ба́бушка мо́лча разде́нется, аккура́тно сло́жит оде́жду на сунду́к (box) в углу́ и подойдёт к посте́ли, а я притворя́юсь, что кре́пко усну́л. (М. Го́рький.)

6. Но в э́ту мину́ту он был оди́н...Свист ве́тра навева́л на него́ каку́ю-то дрёму. И перед глаза́ми молодо́го солда́та несу́тся родны́е карти́ны. Он то́же ви́дит дере́вню, и тот же бежи́т над не́ю ве́тер, и це́рковь гори́т огня́ми....

По времена́м он как бу́дто очнётся и тогда́ в его́ се́рых глаза́х отража́ется недоуме́ние: что э́то?—по́ле, ружьё и стена́.... (Короле́нко.)

7.   Не пуга́й меня́ злы́ми угро́зами,
        Нет. Возьми́ меня́ в ко́гти желе́зные,
        Познако́мь меня́ с тёмными гро́зами
        Иль умчи́ (carry away...) меня́ в сфе́ры надзвёздные.
                (Поло́нский: "Орёл и змея́".)

"Не спи́тся, ня́ня: здесь так ду́шно.
Откро́й окно́, да сядь ко мне."
—Что, Та́ня, что с тобо́й? "Мне ску́чно;
Поговори́м о старине́."
—О чём же, Таня? Я, быва́ло,
Храни́ла в па́мяти нема́ло
Стари́нных бы́лей....   (Пу́шкин.)

9.   Есть же́нщины в ру́сских селе́ньях
      С споко́йною ва́жностью лиц,
      С краси́вою си́лой в движе́ньях,
      С похо́дкой со взгля́дом цари́ц,—
      Их ра́зве слепо́й не заме́тит,
      А зря́чий о них говори́т:
      "Пройдёт—сло́вно со́лнце осве́тит.
      Посмо́трит—рублём подари́т".   (Некра́сов.)

10. Будь у меня́ де́ньги, я бы сам дал ему́, но у меня́
ничего́ нет, ни пятачка́. (Че́хов: "Ча́йка".)

11. Когда́ я сего́дня проснула́сь, вста́ла и умы́лась, то
мне вдруг ста́ло каза́ться, что для меня́ всё ясно на
э́том све́те, и я зна́ю, как на́до жить....

   Бо́же мой, не то что челове́ком, лу́чше быть воло́м,
лу́чше быть просто́ю ло́шадью, то́лько бы рабо́тать, чем
молодо́й же́нщиной, кото́рая встаёт в двена́дцать часо́в
дня, пото́м пьёт в посте́ли ко́фе, пото́м два часа́ одева́ется...
о какой ужас! (Че́хов: "Три сестры́".)

12. *А́ня.* Приезжа́ем в Пари́ж, там хо́лодно, снег. По-
францу́зски говорю́ я ужа́сно. Ма́ма живёт в пя́том
этаже́, прихожу́ к ней, у неё какие-то францу́зы, да́мы,
и наку́рено, неую́тно. Мне вдруг ста́ло жаль ма́мы, так
жаль, я обняла́ её го́лову, сжа́ла рука́ми и не могу́
вы́пустить....

   Ва́ря (сквозь слёзы). Не говори́, не говори́....

   Аня. Да́чу свою́ она́ уже́ продала́, у неё ничего́ не
оста́лось, ничего́. У меня́ тоже не оста́лось ни копе́йки,

едва́ дое́хали. И ма́ма не понима́ет. Ся́дем на вокза́ле обе́дать, и она́ тре́бует са́мое дорого́е, и на чай даёт по рублю́.

Ва́ря. В а́вгусте бу́дут продава́ть име́ние....

Аня (обнима́ет Ва́рю, ти́хо). Ва́ря, он сде́лал предложе́ние? (Ва́ря отрица́тельно кача́ет голово́й.) Ведь он же тебя́ лю́бит....Отчего́ вы не объясни́тесь, чего́ вы ждёте?

Ва́ря. Я так ду́маю, ничего́ у нас не вы́йдет, у него́ де́ла мно́го, ему́ не до меня́...и внима́ния не обраща́ет.

Аня. Пти́цы пою́т в саду́. Кото́рый тепе́рь час?

Ва́ря. Должно́, тре́тий. Тебе́ пора́ спать, ду́шечка. (Че́хов: "Вишнёвый Сад".)

13. Я́ркое со́лнце льёт косы́е лучи́ в на́шу кла́ссную ко́мнату, а у меня́ в мое́й ма́ленькой ко́мнатке в пансио́не сиди́т го́стья. Я то́тчас узна́л э́ту го́стью, как то́лько она́ вошла́: это была́ ма́ма. Мы сиде́ли вдвоём, и я стра́нно к ней пригля́дывался. Пото́м, уже́ мно́го лет спустя́, я узна́л, что она́ тогда́ прибыла́ в Москву́ на свои́ жа́лкие сре́дства еди́нственно, чтоб со мной повида́ться. С ней был узело́к, и она́ развяза́ла его́: в нём оказа́лось шесть апельси́нов, не́сколько пря́ников[1] и два обыкнове́нных францу́зских хле́ба. Но к гости́нцам[2] я да́же не притро́нулся. И́скоса то́лько я огля́дывал её тёмненькое ста́ренькое пла́тьеце, дово́льно гру́бые, почти́ рабо́чие ру́ки, совсе́м уже́ гру́бые её башмаки́ и си́льно похуде́вшее лицо́. (Достое́вский.)

14. Бы́стро несётся вниз по тече́нию краси́вый и си́льный парохо́д, и ме́дленно дви́жутся навстре́чу ему́ берега́ могу́чей краса́вицы-Во́лги...Всю́ду блеск воды́, всю́ду просто́р и свобо́да; ве́село-зе́лены луга́, и ла́сково-я́сно голубо́е не́бо; в споко́йном движе́нии воды́ чу́ется сде́ржанная си́ла, в не́бе над не́ю сия́ет ще́дрое со́лнце ма́я;

---

[1] пря́ник—a kind of ginger-bread (sweetmeat).
[2] гости́нец, гости́нцы—gifts, of eatables or otherwise.

воздух напоён сладким запахом хвойных деревьев[1] и свежей листвы. А берега всё идут навстречу, лаская глаза и душу своей красотой, и всё новые картины открываются на них.... (М. Горький.)

15. Образованным человеком называется тот, кто приобрёл много знаний и, кроме того, привык быстро и верно соображать, что хорошо и что дурно, что справедливо и что несправедливо, или, как выражаются одним словом, привык "мыслить", и, наконец, у кого понятия и чувства получили благородное и возвышенное направление, то-есть приобрели сильную любовь ко всему доброму и прекрасному. Все эти три качества — обширные знания, привычка мыслить и благородство чувств — необходимы для того, чтобы человек был образованным в полном смысле слова. У кого мало познаний, тот невежда; у кого ум не привык мыслить, тот груб и тупоумен; у кого нет благородных чувств, тот человек дурной.

В детстве, в первую пору молодости, человек учится в школах: уроки наставников имеют ту цель, чтобы сделать юношу образованным человеком. Но когда он выходит из школы, перестаёт учиться, его образование поддерживается чтением, то-есть вместо прежних наставников, которых слушал мальчик и юноша, взрослый человек имеет одну наставницу — литературу.

(Чернышевский.)

---

[1] хвойные деревья—coniferous trees.

PART II
GRAMMAR

THE VERB

Aspects

The most characteristic feature of the Russian verb is its *aspects*, or **ви́ды**, as they are called in Russian. The word **вид** means "view, appearance". A verb changes its form (appearance) according to the aspect or point of view from which the action is described.

The perfect infinitive of any verb is represented in Russian by a verb slightly different in appearance, without an auxiliary verb, e.g. **стоя́ть** (to stand), **постоя́ть** (to have stood). This perfect infinitive is the perfective aspect of the verb **стоя́ть**, and the perfect tenses are formed from it in the same way as the tenses of the imperfect infinitive, and have the same endings.

There are two aspects in Russian: the *imperfective* and the *perfective*. The name "perfective" suggests a similarity between the tenses of the verb in this aspect and the perfect tenses in any other language.

The *imperfective* aspect expresses the idea of *duration*, and the action is described as *lasting* in present, past or future time. The *perfective* aspect expresses the idea of *completion*, the action being described as completed, with its beginning and its end in either past or future time. In the perfective aspect stress is laid on the *result* of the action; in the imperfective on the *action itself*.

Thanks to its aspects, the Russian verb, in spite of having only three tenses and very few endings, is a very delicate instrument for the expression of every shade of meaning.

Though forms of *one and the same* verb, the infinitives of the imperfective and perfective aspects are treated as separate verbs, and are often called imperfective and perfective verbs, instead of the "imperfective aspect" and "perfective aspect" of the same verb.

The subject of the aspects and their use is fully discussed in Part I (Lessons XI–XIII). The formation of the aspects, however, is dealt with later in Part II (pp. 215–223), as well as in the Lessons. But one must first become acquainted with the conjugation of a verb in both aspects.

Imperfective Aspect	Perfective Aspect

I. Infinitive

Present	*Past*
чита́ть, to read	прочита́ть, to have read

Imperfective Aspect	Perfective Aspect

II. INDICATIVE
Present tense

I read *or* I am reading	None
я читá-ю	
ты читá-ешь	
он читá-ет	
онá читá-ет	
онó читá-ет	
мы читá-ем	
вы читá-ете	
они́ читá-ют	

Past tense

I read, was reading	I have *or* had read
я читá-л	я прочитá-л
ты читá-л	ты прочитá-л
он читá-л	он прочитá-л
онá читá-ла	она прочитá-ла
онó читá-ло	оно прочитá-ло
мы читá-ли	мы прочитá-ли
вы читá-ли	вы прочитá-ли
они́ читá-ли	они прочитá-ли

Future tense

I shall read	I shall have read
я бу́ду читать	я прочитáю
ты бу́дешь читать	ты прочитáешь
он, онá бу́дет читать	он, онá прочитáет
мы бу́дем читать	мы прочитáем
вы бу́дете читать	вы прочитáете
опи бу́дут читать	они прочитáют

III. CONDITIONAL OR SUBJUNCTIVE

I should read	I should have read
я читáл бы	я прочитáл бы
ты читáл бы	ты прочитáл бы
он читáл бы	он прочитáл бы
онá читáла бы	онá прочитáла бы
онó читáло бы	онó прочитáло бы
мы читáли бы	мы прочитáли бы
вы читáли бы	вы прочитáли бы
они́ читáли бы	они́ прочитáли бы

Imperfective Aspect	Perfective Aspect

IV. IMPERATIVE

читá-й ! Read !	прочитá-й ! Have [it] read ![1]
пусть он, онá читáет, Let him, her read	пусть он прочитáет, Let him have [it] read
читá-йте ! Read ! (pl.)	прочитá-йте ! Have [it] read ! (pl.)
пусть они читáют, Let them read	пусть они прочитáют, Let them have [it] read

V. PARTICIPLES

Active—Present

читáю-щий, -щая, -щее, -щие, [one] who is reading	None

Past

читá-вший, -ая, -ее, -ие, [one] who was reading	прочитá-вший, -ая, -ее, -ие, [one] who has or had read

Passive—Present

читáем-ый, -ая, -ое, -ые, or -м, -ма, -мо, -мы, which is being read	None

Past

чи́та-нный, -н	прочи́та-нный, -н
чи́та-нная, -на	прочи́та-нная, -на
чи́та-нное, -но	прочи́та-нное, -но
чи́та-нные, -ны	прочи́та-нные, -ны
which was read	which has or had been read

VI. GERUNDS

Present

читá-я, whilst reading	None

Past

читá-в, -вши, whilst [he, etc., was] reading	прочитá-в, -вши, having read

Studying the conjugation table of the verb in both aspects we learn that the Russian verb has four moods: infinitive, indicative, conditional or subjunctive, and imperative.

---

[1] [it] is here inserted to represent the object of прочитáй, which means "read *through*, i.e. *completely*".

I. The infinitive mood

The *infinitive* mood may be present or past: читáть (to read), прочитáть (to have read); стоя́ть (to stand), постоя́ть (to have stood). The infinitive usually ends in -ть, but sometimes in -ти (always accented), e.g. идти́, нести́, and in -чь, e.g. мочь (to be able), течь (to flow).

II. The indicative mood

The *indicative* mood has three tenses in the imperfective aspect—present, past and future; but in the perfective aspect only past and future, i.e. the past perfect and the future perfect.

The present is the only tense which has independent personal endings. The past tense changes its endings only by gender and number, and the future perfect has the same endings as a present. (The only passive forms are participles.)

The present tense. There are two sets of endings for the present tense, according to the two conjugations. The difference between the two conjugations applies only to the present tense and the forms derived from it (see p. 212). These endings are as follows:

	I.				II.
(a) я	читá-ю	(b)	ид-ý (ю́)[1]	я	говор-ю́ (у)[2]
ты	читá-ешь		ид-ёшь	ты	говор-и́шь
он	читá-ет		ид-ёт	он	говор-и́т
мы	читá-ем		ид-ём	мы	говор-и́м
вы	читá-ете		ид-ёте	вы	говор-и́те
они́	читá-ют		ид-ýт (ю́т)	они́	говор-я́т (ат)

It is difficult to formulate rules for foreigners as to which verbs belong to each conjugation. In general, however, to *the 1st conjugation* belong:

(1) Verbs in -ать and -ять, e.g. дéлать (to do), гуля́ть (to take a walk); *except* стоя́ть (to stand), боя́ться[3] (to fear). Exceptions in -ать will be found under the 2nd conjugation. Verbs in -ать with the stem of the infinitive ending in с, з, к, х, and sometimes т,

---

[1] Set (b) of the 1st conjugation shows the variations which occur in the case of accented endings.

[2] For endings given here in brackets see p. 15.

[3] Боя́ться is a reflexive verb (see p. 229).

have the stem of the present tense ending in a consonant, changing
с, з, к, х, т into ш, ж, ч, щ, e.g.

Present tense of писать (*to write*)

я пиш-у́	мы пи́ш-ем
ты пи́ш-ешь	вы пи́ш-ете
он пи́ш-ет	они пи́ш-ут

ре́зать (to cut): ре́жу, ре́жешь, etc.
пла́кать (to weep): пла́чу, пла́чешь, etc.
пря́тать (to hide): пря́чу, пря́чешь, etc.
маха́ть (to wave): машу́, ма́шешь, etc.

Соса́ть (to suck) is an exception: сосу́, сосёшь, etc.; also куса́ть
(to bite): куса́ю, куса́ешь, etc.

Notice that the changed stem is retained *throughout* the tense.

The rule governing these changes in the stem is given in the
chapter on Permutation of consonants, p. 17.

N.B. *Accent.* In most such verbs the accent, which in the
1st person singular is on the ending, is shifted in the other persons
to the stem; *except* in the verbs ре́зать, пла́кать, пря́тать, i.e.
verbs with the accent on the stem.

(2) Verbs in -еть formed from adjectives, e.g. старе́ть, старе́ю
(to grow old), from ста́рый (old); красне́ть (to blush), from
кра́сный (red).

(3) Monosyllabic verbs, *except* спать (to sleep) (see § 99), гнать
(to chase; pres. гоню́, го́нишь), and зреть (Slav. for to see; зрю,
зришь).

Five monosyllabic verbs: пить (to drink), бить (to beat), вить
(to twist), лить (to pour), and шить (to sew) have the stem of
the present tense пь-, бь-, etc., instead of пи-, би-, etc., e.g.

Present tense of пить

я пь-ю́	мы пь-ём
ты пь-ёшь	вы пь-ёте
он пь-ёт	они пь-ю́т

but жить (to live): живу́, живёшь, etc.

Monosyllabic verbs in -ыть, as мыть (to wash), and also петь
(to sing), have present tense:

мо́ю, мо́ешь, мо́ет, etc.
пою́, поёшь, поёт, etc.

N.B. *Accent.* Note the accent in the case of мыть, which is the
same in all verbs in -ыть.

(4) Verbs in -сть and -сти; -зть and -зти. These verbs usually have a present tense of the (*b*) type, as идти; they may lose the -с-, and insert -д- or -т- in the present tense, e.g.

красть (to steal): краду́, крадёшь
мести́ (to sweep): мету́, метёшь
but   нести́ (to carry): несу́, несёшь

The ending -сти is identical with -сть, the и being used for euphony. Thus verbs in -сти may be regarded as monosyllabic verbs.

N.B. *Accent.* The ending -сти́ is always accented.

Some monosyllabic verbs insert -н- before the endings, e.g.

жать (to reap): жну, жнёшь
(*but* жать (to press) gives жму, жмёшь)
мять (to crush): мну, мнёшь
клясть (to curse): кляну́, клянёшь

Some insert -б- or -в-, e.g.

грести́ (to row): гребу́, гребёшь
жить (to live): живу́, живёшь
плыть (to swim): плыву́, плывёшь

(5) Verbs in -уть, e.g.

тону́ть (to sink): тону́, то́нешь

These verbs have -у in the 1st person singular, but the endings are not accented (е instead of ё).

(6) Verbs in -оть (very few in all), e.g.

коло́ть (to pierce): колю́, ко́лешь

(7) Verbs in -чь, e.g. мочь (to be able), печь (to bake), etc. These verbs have the stem of the 1st person singular and the 3rd person plural ending in г or к, but in other persons г changes into ж and к into ч, e.g.

я	мог-у́	пек-у́
ты	мо́ж-ешь	печ-ёшь
он	мо́ж-ет	печ-ёт
мы	мо́ж-ем	печ-ём
вы	мо́ж-ете	печ-ёте
они	мо́г-ут	пек-у́т

Other common verbs of the 1st conjugation with changes in the stem of the present tense are given in the lessons.

To *the 2nd conjugation* belong:

(1) Verbs in -ать which form exceptions to the 1st conjugation, i.e. disyllabic verbs with the stem in ж, ч, ш, щ, as

лежа́ть (to lie): лежу́, лежи́шь
молча́ть (to be silent): молчу́, молчи́шь
слы́шать (to hear): слы́шу, слы́шишь
пища́ть (to squeak): пищу́, пищи́шь

Except a very few, notably слу́шать (to listen to), конча́ть (to finish), which belong to the 1st conjugation, type (*a*).

(2) All verbs in -ить, *except* monosyllabic verbs, and the perfective verb ушиби́ть (to bruise): ушибу́, ушибёшь (which is of course a future tense).

(3) Verbs in -еть, *except* уме́ть (to be able), име́ть (to have), боле́ть (to ail), реве́ть (to roar), робе́ть (to be timid), жале́ть (to pity), and verbs formed from adjectives (see above).

Verbs in -ить and -еть with the stem ending in д, з, с, т, ст, change these consonants into ж, ш, ч, щ (see p. 17) in the 1st person singular *only*, and the ending -ю becomes -у, e.g.

Present tense of ходи́ть (*to go*)

я хож-у́	мы хо́д-им
ты хо́д-ишь	вы хо́д-ите
он хо́д-ит	они хо́д-ят

возить (to convey): вожу́, во́зишь
проси́ть (to beg): прошу́, про́сишь
плати́ть (to pay): плачу́, пла́тишь
блесте́ть (to shine): блещу́, блести́шь

Verbs in -ить and -еть with the stem ending in б, п, в, ф, м, insert -л- before the ending of the 1st person singular only (see p. 18), e.g.

Present tense of люби́ть (*to love*)

я люб-л-ю́	мы люб-им
ты лю́б-ишь	вы лю́б-ите
он лю́б-ит	они лю́б-ят

In the case of 1st conjugation verbs, i.e. those ending in -ать, preceded by the same consonants, the inserted -л- is retained *throughout* the tense, e.g.

дрема́ть (to slumber): дрем-л-ю́, дрём-л-ешь, дрём-л-ет, etc.

The past tense. The past tense changes its endings not by person, but by gender and number. These endings are: -л, -ла, -ло, -ли. This peculiarity of the past tense is explained by the fact that in Old Slavonic this form in -л, -ла, etc., was a participle, used with an auxiliary verb. This form, however, has long been obsolete and can only be traced in such a verb as **я устáл** (I am tired), which is the past perfect of **устáть**; but **устáл** is at the same time the predicative form of the adjective **устáлый**, which must previously have been one of these participles.

The only irregularity in the past tense occurs in:

(1) The verb **идти́**: шёл, шла, шло, шли.

(2) Verbs ending in -сть, -сти, -зть, and -зти.

If the stem of the present tense of these verbs ends in д or т, the last consonant of the stem is left out, e.g.

> класть (to put): я кладý; past: клал, -лá, -ли
> мести́ (to sweep): я метý; past: мёл, мелá, -ли́

But if the stem of the present tense ends in **б, з, с**, the **л** is omitted only in the masculine, e.g.

> грести́ (to row): я гребý; past: грёб, греблá
> везти́ (to convey): я везý; past: вёз, везлá
> нести́ (to carry): я несý; past: нёс, неслá

The same happens in the case of verbs in **-чь**, in which the stem of the present tense ends in **г, к**, e.g.

> мочь: могý; past: мог, моглá
> печь: пекý; past: пёк, пеклá

and in the perfective past of the verbs **умерéть** (to die), **заперéть** (to shut), **вы́тереть** (to wipe out):

> у́мер, умерлá
> зáпер, заперлá
> вы́тер, вы́терла

and the same verbs with other prefixes.

(3) Some perfective verbs in **-нуть**, which form the past tense with the stem in a consonant, losing the whole ending **-нуть**, and in this way having no ending at all for the masculine, e.g.

вы́сохнуть (to dry up): вы́сох, вы́сохла
достúгнуть (to attain): достúг, достúгла
привы́кнуть (to get accustomed): привы́к, привы́кла, etc.

The future tense. The imperfect future is the only tense in Russian which is formed with an auxiliary verb, as **я бýду читáть** (I shall read). **Бýду** is the future of the verb **быть** (to be) (see p. 230).

The verb **стать** is sometimes used as an auxiliary instead of **быть** and with the same meaning as **быть**, e.g.

> Стáну скáзывать я скáзки. (Лермонтов.)
> I shall tell you fairy tales.

The perfect future is never compound and has the form of a present perfect which serves as a future. It is formed from the perfect infinitive in the same way as the present tense from the imperfect infinitive; e.g. сказа́ть, which is a perfective verb, has the future я скажу́, ты ска́жешь, etc., like the present of писа́ть (see p. 207).

All that has been said about differences in the present tense in respect of the two conjugations applies also to the future perfect.

III. The conditional or subjunctive mood

The *conditional* or *subjunctive* mood has only one tense, the past, in both imperfect and perfect forms. This tense is the same as the past indicative with the addition of the particle бы, e.g.

> На ва́шем ме́сте я писал бы ча́ще.
>
> In your place I should write oftener.
>
> Я написа́л бы вчера́, но у меня́ не́ было вре́мени.
>
> I should have written yesterday but I had no time.

As there is no separate subjunctive mood in Russian, the same form serves as both conditional and subjunctive. (See the use of these tenses, p. 192.)

IV. The imperative mood

The *imperative* mood is formed from the 2nd person singular of the present indicative by taking off -ешь and -ишь and adding -й, -йте, or -и, -ите, e.g.

> ты чита́-ешь: чита́-й, чита́-йте
>
> ты говор-и́шь: говор-и́, говор-и́те

Notice that й is used when the stem ends in a vowel, and the ordinary и when it ends in a consonant; but if the stem ends in a consonant and is *accented*, the endings are: -ь, -ьте, e.g.

> гла́дить (to smooth): гла́д-ь, гла́д-ьте

For the imperative of verbs in -чь, see § 167.

The 3rd person singular and plural, i.e. "let him *or* them speak", is formed by adding пусть to the present tense, e.g. пусть он говори́т; пусть они́ говоря́т.

Пусть itself is a shorter form of пусти́, the imperative of пусти́ть (to (have) let).

The imperative in Russian may be perfect as well as imperfect, as is clear from the table (p. 205). The perfect imperative is formed from the perfect future. For the use of the imperative see p. 193.

V. Participles

Russian participles are *verbal adjectives*. They qualify a noun with regard to its action or state; they have the same endings as adjectives, and are therefore declined. Only passive participles, however, have the abbreviated or predicative form. In a subordinate adjectival clause the participle takes the place of a verb with a relative pronoun.[1]

There are present and past participles, both active and passive.

Active participles. The *present* active participle is formed from the 3rd person plural of the present tense by taking off the ending -т and adding -щий, -щая, -щее, -щие, e.g.

они чита́ю-т: чита́ю-щий, -щая, -щие (who is reading)

Thus, чита́ющий учени́к *or* учени́к, кото́рый чита́ет

говоря́щая же́нщина *or* же́нщина, кото́рая говори́т

пи́шущее перо́ *or* перо́, кото́рое пи́шет

The *past* active participle is formed from the infinitive or the past tense by taking off the ending -ть or -л and adding -вший, -вшая, -вшее, -вшие, e.g.

чита́-ть: чита́-вший (one who was reading)

прочита́-ть: прочита́-вший (one who has *or* had read)

Sometimes the past participle ends in -ший, -шая, -шее, -шие, e.g.

нес-ти́: нёс-ший; вез-ти́: вёз-ший; спас-ти́ (to have saved): спа́с-ший

and sometimes in -дший, -дшая, -дшее, -дшие, e.g.

шё-л (he was going): ше́дший; вё-л (he was leading): ве́дший; па-л (he fell): па́дший

N.B. *Accent.* Active participles never have the accent on the ending; it is usually on the same vowel as in the present tense.

Passive participles. The *present* passive participle is formed from the 1st person plural of the present tense by adding -ый, -ая, -ое, -ые, e.g.

мы чита́ем: чита́ем-ый, -ая, -ое, -ые

---

[1] Note that in Russian it is considered that a participle, used in this way, introduces a *clause*, in the same way as a relative pronoun or an adverb. This also explains the occurrence, contrary to English usage, of commas before and after any phrase containing a participle. The same applies to gerunds.

Всёми читáемая книга *or* книга, котóрую все читáют.
The book which is being read by everybody.

There is another way of expressing the passive voice, namely, by means of a reflexive form, e.g.

Эта книга читáется всёми.
This book is read by everybody.

(See Exercises XXI.)

The *present* passive participle is seldom used in Russian; there are many verbs of which it is never used, as: берём (we take), мóем (we wash), поём (we sing), бьём (we beat), льём (we pour), шьём (we sew), кладём (we put), пóртим (we spoil).

The *past* passive participle is formed from the infinitive in two ways:

(1) By taking off -ть and adding -нный, -нная, -нное, -нные, e.g. чита-ть: чи́танный, -нная.

Всеми чи́танная книга *or* книга, котóрую все читáли.
The book which was read by everybody.

If a verb ends in -ить, и is changed into е, making the ending -енный, e.g. получи́ть: полу́ченный.

As to the changes of consonants before -енный or -анный in the formation of participles, the general rules of permutation of consonants should be observed (see p. 17).

(2) By taking off -ть and adding -тый, -тая, -тое, -тые, e.g.

поня́-ть: пóнятый, -ая, -ое, -ые
мы-ть: мы́тый, -ая, -ое, -ые

This form is the less common of the two. The following verbs form their past participle in this way: бить, and other monosyllabic verbs in -ить and -ыть (see p. 207): петь (to sing), начáть (to have begun), одéть (to have put on), жать (to reap), греть (to warm), мять (to crumble); all verbs in -уть and -оть (see p. 208), терéть (to rub) and запере́ть (to lock).

The passive past participle of these last two verbs is formed from the past tense—тёр, тёртый; зáпер, зáпертый.

Passive participles in -нный, used predicatively, i.e. in the abbreviated form, have one н in the ending. The ending -тый gives -т, e.g.

чи́тан, чи́тана, чи́тано, чи́таны
пóнят, пóнята, пóнято, пóняты

The perfective aspect, having no present tense, has of course no present participles, either active or passive.

N.B. *Accent.* Passive past participles have the accent on the stem; *except* in the case of verbs in -сти.

VI. GERUNDS

This form of the verb is in Russian not a noun but an *adverbial participle* or a *verbal adverb*; it is therefore not declined.

The *present gerund* is formed from the 3rd person plural of the present tense by taking off -ют, -ут, or -ят, -ат, and adding -я or, after certain consonants, -а (see p. 15).

> читá-ют: читáя (whilst reading)
> сид-я́т: си́дя (in a sitting position)
> молч-áт: мóлча (in silence)

E.g.   Он говори́л стóя.   He spoke (whilst) standing.

The *past gerund* is formed from the infinitive by taking off -ть and adding either -в or -вши: сказá-ть: сказáв *or* сказáвши (having said), e.g.

Сказáв э́то, он ушёл.

Having said this (*or* When he had said this), he went away.

Сказáв is thus used instead of an adverbial clause. It must be noticed that the past gerund is mostly used in the perfective aspect. Although forms such as **читáв, говори́в**, etc., exist, they are usually replaced by the present forms, as: **читáя, говоря́**, e.g. читáя кни́гу, онá заснýла (whilst reading a book, she fell asleep) is better than читáв кни́гу, онá заснýла, which is the equivalent of когдá онá читáла (while she *was* reading).

In some perfective verbs it is preferable to use what looks like a present gerund instead of the past, especially in compounds of the verb идти́ (see p. 225), e.g. войди́ (having entered), instead of вошéд, which is, strictly speaking, more correct, but clumsy. Войди́, вы́йдя, принеси́, etc., are present gerunds only by form, since perfective verbs cannot have present gerunds any more than other present forms.

Уви́дя and **возврати́сь** may be considered as exceptions, especially as the forms уви́дев and возврати́вшись are used just as frequently. Other perfective "present" gerunds in -я and -а are used in certain common phrases instead of a past form in -в, e.g.

два дня спустя́	two days later
слома́ го́лову	at breakneck speed
сложа́ ру́ки	with folded arms
положа́ ру́ку на се́рдце	with hand on heart
отступя́ на шаг	stepping back
разиня́ рот	gaping

Although the endings -в and -вши are interchangeable, it must be noted that reflexive verbs have the past gerund only in -вшись, e.g. вы́мывшись (having washed oneself), оде́вшись (having dressed).

Some verbs have no present gerunds at all. Such are the five verbs пить, бить, etc., mentioned on p. 207, most other monosyllabic verbs, e.g. гнуть, ждать, ткать, лгать, петь, etc., and the verbs писа́ть, вяза́ть.

FORMATION OF THE PERFECTIVE ASPECT

As has already been mentioned, the perfective aspect (or the perfect infinitive) is mostly formed by prefixes. For this purpose the prefix по- is used much more than any other prefix. It may even be assumed that this prefix was originally the only one for expressing the perfective meaning of an action. Only with the development of the language has the use of other prefixes with this function been introduced. Even now in some parts of the country there is a tendency to use this prefix for certain verbs which have different forms in literary language; e.g. for класть (to put), the perfective покла́сть is used instead of положи́ть, and побра́ть instead of взять (to have taken).

Another evidence that по- was originally the only prefix used for the perfective is that practically every verb *may* be used with по-. But such a form may now be insufficient, e.g. почита́ть is a perfective form of чита́ть, as is поде́лать of де́лать, but they mean "to have done some reading" and "to have done some doing" and not "to have read (or done) something from beginning to end", which is the meaning of a "perfect" action.

For English-speaking people the verbs with the prefix по- may be compared with such forms as "to have a talk" (поговори́ть), "to have a look" (посмотре́ть), etc. Thus it can be said that the prefix по- indicates a certain amount of action, performed within a certain time, but not necessarily including the result.

Verbs forming their perfective with по-

держа́ть	to hold	сиде́ть	to sit
жела́ть	to wish	слу́шать	to listen to
ку́шать	to eat	смотре́ть	to look
люби́ть	to love	спать	to sleep
лежа́ть	to lie	стоя́ть	to stand, etc. (see also pp. 78, 79)

Other prefixes are used in the formation of the perfective aspect according to their meaning. It is not very difficult to see why a certain prefix, which is usually a preposition, has been used to form a perfective infinitive, e.g. "to have written" is написа́ть; it is obvious that all writing must be *on* something. The same applies in нарисова́ть (to have drawn (a picture)). One must know the meaning of the prefixes, which can be learnt along with the groups of verbs given later (see pp. 225, 226).

Almost all prepositions may be used as prefixes, *except* к and для, but there are some prefixes which are not prepositions, as вы-, воз-, низ-, раз-.

In addition to forming a perfective aspect, various prefixes also change the meaning of the verb. Thus написа́ть means only "to have written", and is therefore *the* perfect infinitive of писать, but подписа́ть means something different, and must be a perfect infinitive of some other verb. From the meaning of the preposition под (under), we see that it means "to have written under" or "to have signed". The verb подписа́ть (to sign) has its own imperfective infinitive. In such cases the *imperfective* infinitive is formed from a perfective verb by inserting -ива- or -ыва- between the stem of the verb and the ending, as подпи́с-ыва-ть. These suffixes -ыва-, -ива- are *suffixes of the imperfective aspect in general*.

Here is a group of verbs, compounds of писа́ть.

Imperfective aspect		*Perfective aspect*
подпи́сывать	to sign	подписа́ть
запи́сывать	to jot, write down	записа́ть
перепи́сывать	to copy	переписа́ть
выпи́сывать	to write out[1]	вы́писать
впи́сывать	to write in, enter	вписа́ть
надпи́сывать	to address (an envelope)	надписа́ть
допи́сывать	to finish writing	дописа́ть
припи́сывать	to ascribe *or* add in writing	приписа́ть

[1] Or "take in" a paper: выпи́сывать газе́ту или журна́л.

списывать	to copy, "crib"	списа́ть
предпи́сывать	to instruct	предписа́ть
пропи́сывать	to prescribe	прописа́ть
опи́сывать	to describe	описа́ть
испи́сывать	to fill with writing	исписа́ть
распи́сывать	to assign, indicate, paint	расписа́ть
распи́сываться	to receipt	расписа́ться

Compound verbs in **-ивать, -ывать** are found very frequently, and are easily recognisable as imperfective verbs with prefixes.

A number of imperfective verbs are formed by inserting **-ва-** between the stem and the infinitive ending, e.g.

Imperfective aspect		*Perfective aspect*
бить	to hit	поби́ть
убива́ть	to kill	уби́ть
разбива́ть	to break	разби́ть (and many others)
петь	to sing	спеть
запева́ть	to lead a song	запе́ть (and others)
лить	to pour	поли́ть
налива́ть	to fill	нали́ть
пролива́ть	to spill	проли́ть (and others)
крыть	to cover	покры́ть
открыва́ть	to open	откры́ть
закрыва́ть	to shut	закры́ть (and others)
мыть	to wash	помы́ть
умыва́ть	to wash the face	умы́ть (and others)

There are a few verbs in **-чь**, including compounds of **мочь** (to be able) which form their imperfective infinitive from the stem of the 1st person singular, as **помога́ть** (to help), **помо́чь** (from помогу́); **привлека́ть** (to attract), **привле́чь** (from привлеку́).

Compound imperfectives are similarly formed by inserting -ы- or -и- between the two consonants in the stem of a perfective verb, e.g.

пос-ы-ла́ть	to send	посла́ть
подж-и-да́ть	to wait	подожда́ть
заж-и-га́ть	to light	зажечь

In the last example the -и- is inserted between the consonants of the 1st person singular of **жечь, -жгу** (see p. 208).

The compound imperfectives of the verb **брать** (to take) with prefixes must also be mentioned, as these verbs are of very common occurrence:

уб-и-ра́ть	to clear away	убра́ть
выбира́ть	to choose	вы́брать
отбира́ть	to select	отобра́ть
собира́ть	to gather	собра́ть
собира́ться	to get ready	собра́ться
прибира́ть	to tidy	прибра́ть
подбира́ть	to pick, to match	подобра́ть
забира́ть	to take all	забра́ть
разбира́ть	to take to pieces, to examine	разобра́ть
набира́ть	to compose, print	набра́ть
перебира́ть	to examine, turn over	перебра́ть
обира́ть	to pluck	обобра́ть

But there are other imperfective verbs with prefixes, which do not have the suffixes -ыва-, -ива-, etc.; these verbs for the most part are verbs little used in the earlier formation of the language. Some of them even have по- as a prefix and must originally have been perfective verbs, e.g. получа́ть (to receive), понима́ть (to understand), покупа́ть (to buy).

Verbs which already have prefixes in the imperfective form their perfective infinitives by a difference in conjugation or by other changes in suffixes, and may be grouped in the following way:

Group A. Verbs of the 1st conjugation which in the perfective change into the 2nd conjugation:[1]

Imperfective aspect		*Perfective aspect*
броса́ть	to throw	бро́сить
изуча́ть	to study	изучи́ть
конча́ть	to finish	ко́нчить
лиша́ть	to deprive	лиши́ть
обнажа́ть	to strip	обнажи́ть
отлича́ть	to distinguish	отличи́ть
объясни́ть	to explain	объясни́ть
ошиба́ться	to be mistaken	ошиби́ться[2]
повторя́ть	to repeat	повтори́ть
позволя́ть	to allow	позво́лить
перемени́ть	to change	перемени́ть
получа́ть	to receive	получи́ть

---

[1] Some verbs in this group have no prefixes, but cannot have a perfective in по- which, from its meaning, would be inapplicable.

[2] 1st conjugation: ошибу́сь, ошибёшься. Past: оши́бся, оши́блась.

покупа́ть	to buy	купи́ть
поступа́ть	to act	поступи́ть
поселя́ть	to settle (trans.)	посели́ть
продолжа́ть	to prolong, continue	продо́лжить
реша́ть	to decide	реши́ть
ударя́ть	to strike	уда́рить
хвата́ть	to seize	(с)хвати́ть

All these verbs form their future perfect from the infinitive in the same way as the present tense. Whenever a consonant has to be changed in the 1st person singular, it is changed in the usual way according to the demands of euphony (see p. 17).

Group B. Verbs changing from the 1st conjugation to the 2nd, but with a change of consonant in the stem (see p. 17):

возража́ть	to retort, reply	возрази́ть
встреча́ть	to meet	встре́тить
замеча́ть	to notice	заме́тить
огражда́ть	to protect	огради́ть
освобожда́ть	to set free	освободи́ть
отвеча́ть	to answer	отве́тить
посвяща́ть	to dedicate	посвяти́ть
посеща́ть	to visit	посети́ть
приглаша́ть	to invite	пригласи́ть
проща́ть	to forgive	прости́ть
снабжа́ть	to provide	снабди́ть
угоща́ть	to stand treat	угости́ть
украша́ть	to decorate	укра́сить
укроща́ть	to tame	укроти́ть

There are other similar verbs, and the student will be able to form their perfectives, as this change of consonant is always in accordance with the general rule of permutation of consonants (see p. 17).

Group C. Verbs changing -**блять** into -**бить**, -**влять** into -**вить**, -**млять** into -**мить**, -**плять** into -**пить** (see p. 209):

забавля́ть	to amuse	(по)заба́вить
поправля́ть	to correct	попра́вить
приготовля́ть	to prepare	пригото́вить
употребля́ть	to use	употреби́ть
уведомля́ть	to inform	уве́домить
укрепля́ть	to fasten, fortify	укрепи́ть
явля́ть	to manifest	яви́ть

(and others from the same stem)

Group D. Verbs in -**имáть** having the perfective in -**ять**:

взимáть	to exact	взять
внимáть	to listen attentively	внять
вынимáть	to take out	вы́нуть[1]
донимáть	to plague, vex	доня́ть
занимáть	to occupy	заня́ть
нанимáть	to hire	наня́ть
обнимáть	to embrace	обня́ть
перенимáть	to imitate, catch	переня́ть
поднимáть	to lift	подня́ть
понимáть	to understand	поня́ть
принимáть	to accept	приня́ть
пронимáть	to bore (a hole)	проня́ть
разнимáть	to separate (trans.)	разня́ть
снимáть	to take off	снять
унимáть	to appease	уня́ть

The verb **имáть**, with its meaning "to take", is seldom used in its imperfective aspect (mostly in the North), but in the perfective aspect, as **поймáть**, it means "to have caught" or "to catch". All compound verbs of **имать** have retained the meaning "to take", though sometimes not directly. They all have their perfective in -**ять**, as can be seen from the list above, and their future is in -**иму**, e.g.

Future of **снять**

я сним-у́	мы сним-ем
ты сним-ешь	вы сним-ете
он сним-ет	они сним-ут

заня́ть: займу́, займёшь, займёт, etc.

Notice that after a vowel -**й**- is used.

Взять is now used as the perfective of **брать**; future: возьму́, возьмёшь, etc.

Group E. Verbs forming the perfective by deleting -**ва**- and -**ин**-:

вставáть	to get up	встать
давáть	to give	дать
девáть[2]	to put	деть
одевáть	to dress (trans.)	одéть
начинáть	to begin	начáть

[1] An older form was вы́нять, like the others; future, выму, вымешь, etc.
[2] Present: девáю, девáешь, etc.

The perfect future of these verbs:

    встать: встáну, встáнешь, etc.

    дать: дам, дашь, даст, дадúм, дадúте, дадýт

    одевáть: одéну, одéнешь, etc.

    начáть: начнý, начнёшь, etc.

Group F. Verbs with the perfective in -перéть, -мерéть, -терéть:

запирáть	to lock	заперéть
отпирáть	to unlock	отперéть
умирáть	to die	умерéть
вытирáть	to wipe	вытереть

These verbs are also found with other prefixes.

The past perfect tense of these verbs is: вытер, вытерла, -ло, -ли, etc. Future perfect: вытру, вытрешь, etc.; умрý, умрёшь, etc.; отопрý, отопрёшь, etc.

Group G. Verbs having a special perfective in -уть, with the particular meaning of a single action, known as the "aspect of unity":

глядéть	to look	глúнуть
двúгать	to move	двúнуть
дышáть	to breathe	дохнýть
избегáть	to avoid	избéгнуть
исчезáть	to disappear	исчéзнуть
касáться	to touch upon	коснýться
кидáть	to throw	кúнуть
кричáть	to cry out	крúкнуть
махáть	to wave	махнýть
моргáть	to wink	моргнýть
обмáнывать	to deceive	обманýть
плевáть	to spit	плюнуть
привыкáть	to get accustomed	привыкнуть[1]
совáть	to thrust, shove	сунуть
стучáть	to knock	стýкнуть
толкáть	to push	толкнýть
трóгать	to touch	трóнуть
тыкать	to poke	ткнуть
чихáть	to sneeze	чихнýть
шептáть	to whisper	шепнýть

[1] Past tense: привык, привыкла, etc. (see p. 210).

The "aspect of unity" should not be considered as a separate aspect. It is simply a variation of the perfective aspect to denote a single action. These verbs usually end in -уть and belong to the 1st conjugation, but they should not be confused with the imperfective verbs in -уть, which also belong to the 1st conjugation, e.g. тянуть (to pull), тонуть (to sink), etc. These form their perfective in the usual way, by adding prefixes: потянуть, потонуть.

The perfective verbs in -уть have compound forms with prefixes, as:

взглянуть	to look up
высунуть	to push out
вскрикнуть	to scream
дотронуться	to touch (come into contact)

The imperfective of these compound verbs is the simple imperfective, lengthened by the suffixes -ыва-, -ива- as has already been shown, e.g. взглядывать, высовывать, вскрикивать, дотрагиваться. (Note that the о in трогать becomes а.) These imperfective verbs are sometimes described as forming the "iterative aspect", denoting an action frequently repeated, but generally they are treated as imperfective verbs with this particular meaning.

Group H. Verbs which have *no* perfective aspect:

выглядеть	to look, appear
зависеть	to depend
значить	to mean
иметь	to have
нуждаться	to be in need of
обожать	to adore
отрицать	to deny
принадлежать	to belong
повиноваться	to obey
подлежать	to be subject to, liable
подражать	to imitate
предчувствовать	to have a presentiment
приветствовать	to greet
покровительствовать	to protect
походить	to resemble
предвидеть	to foresee
преследовать	to persecute

разгова́ривать	to converse
разуме́ть	to reason
содержа́ть	to contain
сожале́ть	to regret
состоя́ть	to consist
сочу́вствовать	to sympathise
сто́ить	to cost
угрожа́ть	to threaten (and others)

It will be noticed that most of these verbs have prefixes. Such verbs have their origin in the Church Slavonic, where they were used as perfective verbs. This confirms the statement that originally all verbs with prefixes were perfective.

Group I. Verbs with *only* a perfective aspect:

очути́ться	to find oneself suddenly
очну́ться	to come back to one's senses
состоя́ться	to take place

Group J. Verbs which can be used in both aspects, i.e. their present tense is sometimes a future:

веле́ть	to order
жени́ться	to marry (of a man only)
ра́нить	to wound
дарова́ть	to grant
казни́ть	to execute
насле́довать	to inherit (may have perf. у-)
образова́ть	to form, mould
организова́ть	to organise
обеща́ть	to promise
телеграфи́ровать	to telegraph

The perfective aspect of other particular groups of verbs is treated together with those verbs (see pp. 225–228).

VERBS "TO GO"

Russian verbs have no progressive form, i.e. "I read" *or* "I am reading" is я чита́ю; "I was reading" *or* "I read", я чита́л, etc.

But in order to indicate the action of *going* (any mode of going, such as walking, running, swimming, etc.), there are always two verbs: one to give the meaning "to go", and the other "to be going", or an action *with a definite purpose* (see Lesson VII).

Verbs with the meaning "to go"

ходи́ть	to go	(pres.: хожу́, хо́дишь, etc.)
идти́	to be going	(past: шёл, шла, шло, шли)
е́здить	to go (not on foot)	(pres.: е́зжу, е́здишь, etc.)
е́хать	to be going (not on foot)	(pres.: е́ду, е́дешь, etc.)
носи́ть	to carry	(pres.: ношу́, но́сишь, etc.)
нести́	to be carrying	(pres.: несу́, несёшь; past: нёс, несла́-, -ли́)
вози́ть[1]	to convey	(pres.: вожу́, во́зишь, etc.)
везти́	to be conveying	(pres.: везу́, везёшь; past: вёз, везла́, -ли́)
води́ть	to lead	(pres.: вожу́, во́дишь, etc.)
вести́	to be leading	(pres.: веду́, ведёшь; past: вёл, вела́, -ли́)
бе́гать	to run	
бежа́ть	to be running	(pres.: бегу́, бежи́шь, -и́т, -и́м, -и́те, бегу́т)
броди́ть	to roam, wander	(pres.: брожу́, бро́дишь, etc.)
брести́	to be roaming	(pres.: бреду́, бредёшь; past: брёл, -ла́, -ли́)
лета́ть	to fly	
лете́ть	to be flying	(pres.: лечу́, лети́шь, etc.)
пла́вать	to swim	
плыть	to be swimming	(pres.: плыву́, плывёшь, etc.)
по́лзать	to crawl	
ползти́	to be crawling	(past: полз, ползла́, -ло́, -ли́)
ла́зить	to climb	(pres.: ла́жу, ла́зишь, etc.)[2]
лезть	to be climbing	(pres.: ле́зу, ле́зешь; past: лез, -ла, -ли)
гоня́ть	to chase	
гнать	to be chasing	(pres.: гоню́, го́нишь, etc.)
таска́ть	to drag	
тащи́ть	to be dragging	(pres.: тащу́, та́щишь)
ката́ть(ся)	to push (for the use of ката́ться see § 175)	
кати́ть(ся)	to be pushing	(pres.: качу́(сь), ка́тишь(ся), etc.)

[1] Cf. воз, cart.
[2] Another form is ла́зать (ла́заю, ла́заешь, etc.), but it is seldom used.

валя́ть(ся)	to throw down, roll
вали́ть(ся)	to be throwing down
блужда́ть	to wander
блуди́ть	to be wandering, err (pres.: блужу́, блуди́шь, etc.)[1]

It must be particularly noted that although all these verbs have their perfective aspect formed with по-, the perfective verbs meaning "to go", i.e. походи́ть, пое́здить, повози́ть, etc., are very seldom used, and only with a limited meaning (see' Lesson XIII). The usual perfective forms are пойти́, пое́хать, повезти́, i.e. the verbs meaning "to be going" with the addition of по-. These are the only forms for "to have gone".

All verbs "to go" with other prefixes remain imperfective and have for their perfective the form "to be going" with the same prefix, e.g.

> приходи́ть (to come), perf. прийти́
> уходи́ть (to go away), perf. уйти́

(See Lesson XIII.)

The verb ходи́ть *with prefixes.* The verb ходи́ть when studied with its prefixes gives an opportunity of learning the meanings of these prefixes (cf. § 159). Note the perfective aspect.

Imperfective	Perfective	Meaning	Preposition and case
приходи́ть	прийти́	to come	в (acc.) *or* к (dat.)
уходить	уйти	to go away	из (gen.)
выходить	вы́йти[2]	to go out	из (gen.)
входить	войти	to go in	в (acc.)
подходить	подойти	to approach	к (dat.)
отходить	отойти	to depart	от (gen.)
сходить[3]	сойти	to descend	с (gen.)
сходиться	сойтись	to gather, meet	
„	„	to become intimate	с (instr.)
восходить	взойти	to ascend	на (acc.)
заходить	зайти	to call on	к (dat.)

[1] Блиста́ть, блестѣ́ть (present: блещу́, блести́шь; also: блещу́, бле́щешь), to shine, to be shining, is another pair of verbs belonging to this group, although the meaning *to go* or *cause to go* is here less obvious.

[2] N.B. *Accent.* The prefix вы- in the perfective infinitive and its derivatives is always accented. In perfectives, formed with other prefixes, the accent remains as in the imperfective infinitives, and is therefore not marked in the text.

[3] Сходи́ть (за + instr.), to fetch, is a perfective verb.

заходить	зайти	to call for	за (instr.)
,,	,,	to set (of the sun) (cf. восходить)	за (acc.), motion; (instr.), rest
проходить	пройти	to pass	мимо (gen.), через (acc.)
переходить	перейти	to cross	через (acc.)
обходить	обойти	to avoid	trans.
обходиться	обойтись	to do without	без (gen.)
находить	найти	to find	trans.
,,	,,	to overcome	на (acc.)
расходиться	разойтись	to disperse	
доходить	дойти	to reach	до (gen.)
происходить	произойти	to proceed	
превосходить	превзойти	to surpass	
снисходить	снизойти	to condescend	до (gen.), к (dat.)

The verb **ездить** *with prefixes.* The verb **ездить** (to go *not on foot*) becomes **езжать** when used with prefixes. **Езжать** without a prefix means "to go frequently", and is seldom used.

| приезжать | приехать | to arrive | в (acc.) and (dat.) |
| уезжать | уехать | to go away | из (gen.), от (gen.) |

Езжать is used in this way with the same prefixes as **ходить**, except that there is no verb "to ascend", nor any corresponding to the last three in the list above. The verb **наезжать, наехать** means "to raid". **Объезжать** means "to train a horse", as well as "to avoid", but in the former meaning it has no perfective form[1].

Verbs with the meaning "to put"

Imperfective aspect	*Perfective aspect*	
класть	положить	to put *lying* (to lay)
ложиться	лечь	to lie down
ставить	поставить	to put *standing*
становиться	стать	to stand up
сажать ⎫ садить ⎬	посадить	to put *sitting* to plant
садиться	сесть	to sit down

| класть | Pres.: кладу, кладёшь |
| | Past: клал, -ла, -ли |

[1] The verbs бегать, плавать, ползать, лазить, таскать, катать, валять, with prefixes become: -бегать, -плывать, -ползать, -лезать, -таскивать, -катывать, -валивать.

лечь	Past: лёг, легла́, -ли́
	Fut.: ля́гу, ля́жешь, ля́гут
	Imper.: ляг, ля́гте (see § 209)
ста́вить	Pres.: ста́влю, ста́вишь
станови́ться	Pres.: становлю́сь, стано́вишься
стать	Fut.: ста́ну, ста́нешь
сади́ть	Pres.: сажу́, са́дишь
сесть	Fut.: ся́ду, ся́дешь
	Past: сел, се́ла, -ли

Verbs "to put" with prefixes. The verb **класть** with prefixes becomes in the imperfective **кла́дывать**, which is not used alone.

Imperfective	Perfective	Meaning	Preposition and case
вкла́дывать	вложи́ть	to put in	в (acc.)
укла́дывать	уложи́ть	to pack	в (acc.)
откла́дывать	отложи́ть	to postpone	на (acc.)
скла́дывать	сложи́ть	to put together	в (acc.) *or* none
закла́дывать	заложи́ть	to pawn	за (acc.) *or* none
„	„	to harness	
накла́дывать	наложи́ть	to fill up	на (acc.) *or* none
раскла́дывать	разложи́ть	to unpack, spread	
докла́дывать	доложи́ть	to report, announce	(dat.)
перекла́дывать	переложи́ть	to change the places of	с (gen.), на (acc.)
прикла́дывать	приложи́ть	to apply, join	к (dat.)
подкла́дывать	подложи́ть	to lay under, line	под (instr.)
выкла́дывать	вы́ложить	to lay out	из (gen.)
обкла́дывать	обложи́ть	to lay round	

In figurative senses the verb **лага́ть** is mostly used instead of **кла́дывать**, having for its perfective aspect **ложи́ть** with the same prefix, e.g.

налага́ть	наложи́ть	to impose
излага́ть	изложи́ть	to expostulate
прилага́ть	приложи́ть	to enclose
слага́ть	сложи́ть	to compose
разлага́ть	разложи́ть	to analyse
влага́ть	вложи́ть	to put in
облага́ть	обложи́ть	to tax
низлага́ть	низложи́ть	to depose, dismiss
предлага́ть	предложи́ть	to offer
перелага́ть	переложи́ть	to transpose (music)
возлага́ть	возложи́ть	to confer, bestow

The verb "to put" (standing), with prefixes, i.e. **-ставить**, becomes **-ставля́ть**, e.g.

Imperfective	*Perfective*	
вставля́ть	вста́вить	to put in
выставля́ть	вы́ставить	to exhibit
отставля́ть	отста́вить	to put aside
заставля́ть	заста́вить	to compel
доставля́ть	доста́вить	to deliver
представля́ть	предста́вить	to produce, introduce

Other verbs have the same meaning as the verbs formed with **кла́дывать**.

The verb "to put" (sitting), i.e. **сажа́ть**, with prefixes, becomes **са́живать** (see p. 226), e.g.

уса́живать	усади́ть	to make a person sit down
переса́живать	пересади́ть	to transplant
выса́живать	вы́садить	to set ashore, *or* down from a carriage

The verb **стать** can also be used with prefixes, changing the meaning, e.g.

отста́ть	to lag behind
устать	to get tired
приста́ть	to stick to, molest
переста́ть	to cease
доста́ть	to reach, procure
заста́ть	to find at
раста́ться	to part

The corresponding imperfectives are **отста-ва́-ть, уста-ва́-ть**, etc. Cf. verbs listed on p. 138.

The verbs **сесть** and **лечь** are less frequently used with prefixes. The following, however, are found:

подсе́сть к (imperf. подса́живаться)	to sit down beside
присе́сть (imperf. приса́живаться)	to sit down for a moment
присе́сть (imperf. приседа́ть)	to curtsey
(засе́сть) imperf. заседа́ть	to sit (of a committee)
залечь (imperf. залега́ть)	to lie down behind, to hide; to lie in ambush (perf.)
прилечь (imperf. прикла́дываться)	to lie down for a moment

but **прилега́ть** (to be adjacent) has no perfective.

REFLEXIVE VERBS

Reflexive verbs in Russian are formed by adding to the infinitive of active verbs the reflexive pronoun **себя**, shortened into **-ся**, or, after a vowel, into **-сь**.

The verb **мы́ться** (to wash oneself) is formed from **мыть + себя**, added for all persons as **-ся** or **-сь**.

Present Indicative		Past Indicative
я	мо́юсь	мы́лся
ты	мо́ешься	мы́лся
он, она, оно	мо́ется	мы́лась
мы	мо́емся	мы́лись
вы	мо́етесь	
они	мо́ются	

The other tenses are formed in the same way. The infinitive perfect is **помы́ться** (to have a wash), or **вы́мыться** (to have washed oneself). In the perfective aspect the verb is conjugated similarly, according to the form of the perfect infinitive.

Imperfective aspect	Perfective aspect
Imperative	
мо́йся, мо́йтесь	вы́мойся, вы́мойтесь
Participles	
Pres. мо́ющийся	None
Past мы́вшийся	вы́мывшийся
Gerunds	
Pres. мо́ясь	None
Past (мы́вшись)	вы́мывшись

Notice that reflexive verbs always form their past gerund with the ending **-вши**, *not* **-в**.

Not all verbs in **-ся** are reflexive verbs. Apart from real reflexive verbs, in which **-ся** means **себя**, there are three groups of verbs in **-ся**.

I. Verbs in **-ся** with a passive meaning, e.g.

чита́ться	to be read
стро́иться	to be built

II. Reciprocal verbs, i.e. those which imply two or several agents, e.g.

дра́ться (деру́сь, -ёшься)	to fight
встреча́ться	to meet one another

III. Verbs in which -ся has no special meaning, and which are never found without it, e.g.

смеяться	to laugh
надеяться	to hope
бояться	to be afraid

But all verbs in -ся are conjugated in the same way, so that it makes no difference to which group a verb actually belongs.

THE VERB быть (TO BE)

Infinitive: быть. Of the *present indicative* only the 3rd person singular and plural are used: есть (is) and суть (are) (see Lesson III *a*).

Past tense		*Future tense*	
я	был	я	буду
ты	был	ты	будешь
он	был	он	будет
она	была	она	будет
оно	было	оно	будет
мы	были	мы	будем
вы	были	вы	будете
они	были	они	будут

Conditional or subjunctive

я был бы, она была бы, оно было бы; мы, вы, они были бы.

Imperative

| будь | будьте |
| пусть он будет | пусть они будут |

Participles		*Gerunds*	
Pres.	сущий[1]	Pres.	будучи
Past	бывший	Past	быв, бывши
Fut.	будущий[2]	Fut.	None

N.B. The verb бывать means "to be usually" (see Lesson XVIII *a*).

PASSIVE VERBS

The table below shows the conjugation of a passive verb, but this form is seldom used. For the use of passive forms see Lesson XXI.

[1] Used only as an adjective, in the sense of "mere".
[2] Used as an adjective: "future". This is the only future participle found in Russian.

Imperfective aspect	Perfective aspect

Infinitive

быть обучаем-ым, -ой (instr.)	быть обученн-ым
[быть обучаем-у, -ой (dat.)]	[быть обучён-у, -ой)]
to be instructed	to have been instructed

Indicative—Present

я обучаем, -а	None
I am being instructed	

Past

я был обучаем, -а	я был обучён, -а
I was being instructed	I have or had been instructed

Future

я буду обучаем	я буду обучён

Conditional or subjunctive

я был бы обучаем	я был бы обучён

Imperative

будь обучаем	будь обучён
пусть он будет обучаем	пусть он будет обучён
будьте обучаемы	будьте обучёны
пусть они будут обучаемы	пусть они будут обучёны

Participles—Present

обучаемый, -ая, -ое	None

Past

None	обучённый, -ая, -ое

Gerunds—Present

будучи обучаем	None

Past

быв(ши) обучаем	быв(ши) обучён

IMPERSONAL VERBS AND EXPRESSIONS

Although impersonal expressions are very numerous in Russian, and very frequently used, impersonal verbs are comparatively few, and, in some ways, are different from impersonal verbs in other languages as, for example, in French and German.

These verbs are never used with the personal pronoun "it"; nor is "it" used in impersonal expressions (see p. 121), e.g. морозит, it is freezing; светает, it dawns. The common impersonal verbs, as "it rains", дождит, "it snows", снежит, are seldom used, but instead the verb идти; as дождь идёт, снег шёл, etc.

Impersonal verbs may also be reflexive in form. In such cases they are often used with the dative, e.g.

смеркáется	it is growing dusk
мне вéрится	I am ready to believe
мне хóчется	I "feel like"
мне не спи́тся	I cannot sleep
мне нездорóвится	I feel "off colour"
разумéется	certainly, that is understood

Verbs used in impersonal expressions, i.e. in expressions with the 3rd person neuter, are not, strictly speaking, impersonal verbs, since they can also be used in other persons, though sometimes with a different meaning. Such are:

темнéет	it is growing dark
светлéет	it is growing light
пáхнет	it smells
бýдет	that will do!
хвáтит	enough!
не хватáет	it is wanting
должнó быть	probably, it must be
стáло быть	therefore
мне слéдует	I ought to
мне предстои́т	I have before me

Even in such expressions as **мне нрáвится** (I like), **мне кáжется** (it seems to me), **мне прихóдится** (I have to), the verbs **нрáвиться, казáться, приходи́ться** are ordinary verbs which can be used in all persons.

Certain impersonal expressions contain no verb, since the 3rd person singular of "to be" is understood. Such are:

ничегó	it does not matter
не нáдо	Don't!
нýжно	it is necessary
нельзя́	it is not allowed
мóжно	it is allowed, it is possible

THE NOUN

GENDER ENDINGS

Masculine: (ъ) ь, й: стол(ъ), вождь (leader), слýчай.
Feminine: а, я, ь: кóмната, ня́ня, кость (bone).
Neuter: о, е, ё: лицó, мóре, питьё (drink).

A few masculine nouns end in -а, -я, -е, as: дéдушка (grand-father), дя́дя (uncle), подмастéрье (foreman), but their gender is generally obvious from the meaning. Such nouns, however, are declined according to their ending.

Nouns in -ь may be masculine or feminine, and should be learned with their gender, though help may be given. Thus, masculine are:

(*a*) Names of months in -ь, as январь.

(*b*) Names of male animate beings, as гусь (gander), медвéдь (bear), *except* лóшадь (horse), мышь (mouse).

(*c*) Names of towns, as Севастóполь, *except* Казáнь, Астраханъ, Тверь, Керчь.

Feminine are:

(*a*) Abstract nouns, as любóвь (love), нéнависть (hatred), *except* день (day), вопль (cry), вихрь (whirlwind).

(*b*) Names of rivers and countries: Обь, Сибúрь.

There are only two names of animate beings which are neuter: дитя́ (child), чудóвище (monster).

There are also ten nouns in -мя which are neuter, and are declined in a special way, like úмя (see table, p. 237). These are:

брéмя	burden	плáмя	flame
врéмя	time	плéмя	tribe
вы́мя	udder	сéмя	seed (gen. pl. семя́н)
знáмя	flag	стрéмя	stirrup
úмя	name	тéмя	crown (of the head)

Some nouns in -а and -я, names of animate beings, are of common gender. The commonest of these are:

бродя́га	vagabond	плáкса	cry-baby, sniveller
вы́скочка	upstart	пья́ница	drunkard
гуля́ка	idler, rake	самоýчка	self-taught
зáйка	stutterer	сиротá	orphan
лáкомка	sweet-tooth	тёзка	namesake
левшá	left-handed person	убúйца	murderer
невéжда	ignorant person	ýмница	clever person
обжóра	glutton	ханжá	hypocrite

PRINCIPAL SUFFIXES OF NOUNS

1. To form *augmentative* nouns: -ище, -ина, for *masculine*, e.g. домúще (a huge house), дурачúна (a great blockhead), холодúна (excessive cold); -ища for *feminine*, e.g. ручúща (a great big hand), дурúща (a great fool), жарúща (great heat).

2. To form *diminutive* nouns, to express sometimes tenderness, sometimes contempt: **-ик, -ок, -ец** for *masculine*, e.g. до́мик (little house), сыно́к (little son), заво́дец (little factory), бра́тец (little brother); **-ышко, -ко, -це** for *neuter*, e.g. со́лнышко (dear sun), де́ревце (little tree); **-ка, -ица** for *feminine*, e.g. ру́чка (little hand), вещи́ца (little thing), сестри́ца (little sister).

If a noun ends in -я, as ня́ня, **-ь-** is inserted after the soft consonant before the **-ка**, e.g. ня́нька, земе́лька (from земля́, land).

Also, for all genders, **-ушка, -юшка, -енька** (to express tenderness), e.g. ба́тюшка, ма́мушка, до́ченька; **-ишко, -ишка, -ёнка** (to express contempt), e.g. доми́шко (a miserable little house), мальчи́шка (a mere boy), девчёнка (a mere girl), лошадёнка (a miserable little horse).

3. To form nouns denoting *agents*, from the infinitive of verbs, the suffix **-тель** (m.), **-тельница** (f.) is used, e.g.

учи́ть	учи́тель	teacher
жить	жи́тель	inhabitant
писать	писа́тель	writer
дви́гать	дви́гатель	motor
мно́жить	мно́житель	multiplier

4. Nouns denoting various occupations are also formed with **-ник, -чик, -щик**, and in the feminine, **-ница, -чица, -щица**, e.g.

помо́щник	помо́щница	assistant, helper
учени́к	учени́ца	pupil
попу́тчик	попу́тчица	fellow-traveller
носи́льщик	носи́льщица	porter
прика́зчик	прика́зчица	shop assistant

5. Abstract feminine nouns are formed from adjectives with the suffixes **-ость, -ота, -изна**:

хра́брый	хра́брость	bravery
бе́дный	бе́дность	poverty
кра́сный	краснота́	redness
бе́лый	белизна́	whiteness

6. Verbal nouns are neuter, and are formed with **-ание, -ение, -анье, -енье**:

чита́ть	чте́ние	reading
внима́ть	внима́ние	attention
купа́ться	купа́нье	bathing

7. Neuter nouns in -ство are formed from different parts of speech:

Госуда́рство	the State	(госуда́рь, sovereign)
бога́тство	riches	(бога́тый, rich)
произво́дство	production	(производи́ть, to produce)

8. Nouns which have different suffixes in the feminine:

Господи́н	master, Mr	Госпожа́	mistress, Mrs
граждани́н	citizen	гражда́нка	
тесть	father-in-law	тёща	
дура́к	fool	ду́ра	
гость	guest	го́стья	
лгун	liar	лгу́нья	
сосе́д	neighbour	сосе́дка	
слуга́	servant	служа́нка	
крестья́нин	peasant	крестья́нка	
пасту́х	shepherd	пасту́шка	
стари́к	old man	стару́ха	
саме́ц	male	са́мка	
хозя́ин	host, "boss"	хозя́йка	
по́вар	chef, cook	повари́ха	
купе́ц	merchant	купчи́ха	
мона́х	monk	мона́хиня	nun
князь	prince	княги́ня, княжна́	
царь	tsar	цари́ца	
госуда́рь	sovereign	госуда́рыня	
геро́й	hero	геро́йня	
бог	god	боги́ня	
граф	count	графи́ня	
коро́ль	king	короле́ва	
баро́н	baron	бароне́сса	

TABLES OF DECLENSIONS OF NOUNS

Masculine and *neuter* nouns are declined practically alike.[1] In all genders there are hard and soft declensions according to the endings of the nominative, i.e. according to the hard or soft vowel in the ending.

[1] This is true also of adjectives and pronouns; except that neuter nouns take -a and -я in the plural. The genitive plural must be studied separately. With the exception of this case, *all* genders are declined alike in the plural.

Singular

Masculine and neuter[1]

		Hard		Soft			
Nom.	стол-	лиц-о́	слу́ча-й	вожд-ь	мо́р-е	зна́ни-е
Gen.	,, а́	,, а́	,, я	,, я́	,, я	,, я
Dat.	,, у́	,, у́	,, ю	,, ю́	,, ю	,, ю
Acc.	,, —	,, о́	,, й	,, я́[3]	,, е	,, е
Instr.	,, о́м	,, о́м	,, ем	,, ём	,, ем	,, ем
Prep. o	,, е́	,, е́	,, е	,, е́	,, е	,, и

Feminine

	Hard		Soft		
Nom.	ко́мнат-а	ня́н-я	кост-ь	ли́ни-я
Gen.	,, ы	,, и	,, и	,, и
Dat.	,, е	,, е	,, и	,, и[2]
Acc.	,, у	,, ю	,, ь	,, ю
Instr.	,, ой, ою	,, ей, ею	,, ью	,, ей, ею
Prep. o	,, е	,, е	,, и	,, и

Plural

Masculine and neuter

		Hard		Soft			
Nom.	стол-ы́	ли́ц-а	слу́ча-и	вожд-и́	мор-я́	зна́ни-я
Gen.	,, о́в	,, —	,, ев	,, е́й	,, е́й	,, й
Dat.	,, а́м	,, ам	,, ям	,, я́м	,, я́м	,, ям
Acc.	,, ы́	,, а	,, и	,, е́й[3]	,, я́	,, я
Instr.	,, а́ми	,, ами	,, ями	,, я́ми	,, я́ми	,, ями
Prep. o	,, а́х	,, ах	,, ях	,, я́х	,, я́х	,, ях

Feminine

	Hard		Soft		
Nom.	ко́мнат-ы	ня́н-и	ко́ст-и	ли́ни-и
Gen.	,, —	,, ь	,, е́й	,, й
Dat.	,, ам	,, ям	,, я́м	,, ям
Acc.	,, ы	,, ь	,, и	,, и
Instr.	,, ами	,, ями	,, я́ми, ьми́	,, ями
Prep. o	,, ах	,, ях	,, я́х	,, ях

[1] Neuter nouns in -ё (e.g. питьё) are declined like мо́ре, but with the endings accented (ё instead of e). Neuters in -ье (e.g. сча́стье) may take either -е or -и in the prepositional.   [2] Note и in the dative of fem. nouns in -ия.

[3] See § 29 and p. 108 (footnote).

N.B. *Genitive plural endings.*

(1) -ов, -ев: masculine nouns in -(ъ)[1] and -й.

(2) -ей: masculine and feminine in -ь, masculine with the stem ending in ж, ч, ш, щ, neuter nouns in -е.

(3) -(ъ),[1] -ь: feminine nouns in -а and -я, and neuter in -о.

(4) -й: feminine nouns in -ия, and neuter in -ие.

Declension of feminine and neuter nouns with insertion of suffixes -ер-, -ен-, -ят-; and of the masculine noun путь (way).

Singular

Nom.	мать	дитя́ (child, n.)	и́мя	путь
Gen.	ма́тери	дитя́ти	и́мени	пути́
Dat.	ма́тери	дитя́ти	и́мени	пути́
Acc.	мать	дитя́	и́мя	путь
Instr.	ма́терью	дитя́тею, ей	и́менем	путём
Prep.	о ма́тери	о дитя́ти	об и́мени	о пути́

Plural

Nom.	ма́тери	де́ти	имена́	пути́
Gen.	матере́й	дете́й	имён	путе́й
Dat.	матеря́м	де́тим	имена́м	путя́м
Acc.	матере́й	дете́й	имена́	пути́
Instr.	матерьми́	детьми́	имена́ми	путя́ми
Prep.	о матеря́х	о де́тях	об имена́х	о путя́х

Like мать is declined дочь (daughter).

Like имя all other nouns in -мя.

Це́рковь (f., church) is declined in the singular like кость, deleting the -о-: це́ркви, etc. The plural is: це́ркви, -ве́й, -ва́м, -ва́ми, -ва́х.

Notes on accent. Not many words like стол have the accent shifted from the stem to the ending, but when this occurs, the accent usually remains on the ending in the plural as well.

Feminine nouns in -ость and some in -есть have the accent on the first syllable, e.g. мо́лодость (youth), го́ресть (sorrow), ра́дость (joy). The ending -ов is usually accented *except* sometimes in the case of words with prefixes and compound words in which the accent is on the same syllable throughout.

Peculiarities in the declensions of nouns.

1. Some masculine nouns, signifying divisible matter, have -у

[1] See § 9.

and -ю in the genitive singular instead of -а and -я, after an expression of quantity (a partitive genitive), or after a negative, e.g.

	стака́н ча́ю	a glass of tea
	кусо́к са́хару	a lump of sugar
	ку́ча песку́	a heap of sand
but cf.	сла́ще са́хара	sweeter than sugar (normal gen. after comparative)
	за́пах ча́я	the aroma of tea

Such nouns include: пе́рец (pepper), сыр (cheese), виногра́д (grapes), таба́к (tobacco), мел (chalk), шёлк (silk), снег (snow), песо́к (sand).

2. Some masculine nouns take -у́ (accented) in the prepositional case after the prepositions в and на; nouns in -й take -ю, e.g. в саду́ (in the garden), на полу́ (on the floor), на берегу́ (on the shore), в лесу́ (in the wood), на лугу́ (in the meadow), на мосту́ (on the bridge), в пруду́ (in the pond), на краю́ (on the edge), во рту́ (in the mouth), в углу́ (in the corner), в году́ (in a year), etc.

3. Some masculine nouns in -ок, -ец, -ень, -оть, -ер, and some monosyllabic nouns, delete -о- or -е- in declension, e.g. кусо́к, piece, куска́, куску́, куско́м, о куске́:

ка́мень, stone, ка́мня	осёл, donkey, осла́
день, day, дня	оте́ц, father, отца́
ковёр, carpet, ковра́	рот, mouth, рта
лоб, forehead, лба	сон, sleep, сна
ломо́ть, slice, ломтя́	у́гол, corner, угла́
орёл, eagle, орла́	у́голь, coal, угля́

After the consonants л and н such nouns change е into ь, e.g.

конёк, steed, конька́	лёд, ice, льда
лев, lion, льва	лён, flax, льна

After a vowel, е or я is changed into й, e.g.

за́яц, hare, за́йца	бое́ц, fighter, бойца́

4. Nouns in -ей in declension change е of the nominative into ь, e.g. воробе́й, sparrow, воробья́, воробью́, etc.:

мураве́й, ant, муравья́	солове́й, nightingale, соловья́
руче́й, brook, ручья́	у́лей, beehive, у́лья

5. In nouns in -а, -о, -я, preceded by two consonants, or by

one consonant and **й** or **ь**, -e- or -o- is inserted in the genitive plural between these two consonants, e.g.

ло́жка, spoon, ло́жек   ви́шня, cherry, ви́шень *or* ви́шен

сестра́, sister, сестёр   ча́шка, cup, ча́шек

ша́пка, cap, ша́пок   ска́зка, tale, ска́зок

овца́, sheep, ове́ц   у́тка, duck, у́ток

копе́йка, copeck, копе́ек (-a preceded by й and a consonant)

окно́, window, око́н   доска́, plank, досо́к

зерно́, grain, зёрен   пятно́, spot, пя́тен

письмо́, letter, пи́сем (e inserted in place of ь)

число́, date, чи́сел   се́рдце, heart, серде́ц

кольцо́, ring, коле́ц   полоте́нце, towel, полоте́нец

земля́, earth, земе́ль   ту́фля, slipper, ту́фель

дере́вня, village, дереве́нь   петля́, loop, пе́тель

ку́хня, kitchen, ку́хонь   кро́вля, roof, кро́вель

The -o- or -e-, however, is inserted only for the sake of easier pronunciation, for if the two or even three consonants can be articulated without difficulty, the insertion does not take place, as in:

про́сьба, request, просьб   же́ртва, victim, жертв

тайна, secret, тайн   война́, war, войн

Nouns in -здо, -ско, -ство, -сто form their genitive without inserting -e:

ме́сто, place, мест   гнездо́, nest, гнёзд

во́йско, army, войск   чу́вство, feeling, чу́вств

6. Some nouns which formerly ended in -ъ, i.e. some of those ending now in a hard consonant, have the genitive plural like the nominative singular, as:

раз, time   сапо́г, boot

солда́т, soldier   глаз, eye

чуло́к, stocking   рука́в, sleeve

во́лос, hair (gen. pl. воло́с)   цыга́н, gipsy

7. Feminine nouns in -ья end in the genitive plural in -ей if the accent is on the last syllable, e.g.

скамья́, bench, скаме́й   статья́, article, стате́й

свинья́, pig, свине́й   семья́, family, семе́й

but лгу́нья, liar, лгу́ний

8. Some masculine nouns have their plural in -a or -я, as глаз, eye, глазá (the ending is always accented). Such are:

бéрег	shore	луг	meadow
бóк	side	мех	fur
вéк	century	óстров	island
вéчер	evening	óрден	order (decoration)
год	year (also гóды)	пáрус	sail
гóлос	voice	пáспорт	passport
гóрод	town	пóвар	cook, chef
дом	house	пóезд	train
дóктор	doctor, and other	рог	horn
	foreign words	рукáв	sleeve
кóлокол	bell	пóяс	belt
край	edge	счёт	account
лéкарь	physician	стóрож	watchman
лес	forest	учítель	teacher

The following nouns have a double plural, in -ы and in -a, with different meanings:

óбраз	óбразы	forms	*but* образá	images
хлеб	хлéбы	loaves		хлебá	corn (in pl.)
цвет	цветú	flowers		цветá	colours
лист	листú	sheets		лíстья	leaves

9. Some masculine and neuter nouns end in the plural in -ья:

брат	brother, -тья, -тьев, -тьям
стул	chair, -лья, -льев, -льям
лист	leaf, -тья, -тьев, -тьям
зять	son *or* brother-in-law, -тьá, -тьёв
сват	kinsman, -тьá
кол	stake, -лья
клин	wedge, -нья
прут	twig, -тья
перó	pen, пéрья
дéрево	tree, дерéвья
крылó	wing, крúлья
полéно	log, полéнья
друг	friend, друзьá, -зéй, -зьáм
муж	husband, -жьá, -жéй, -жьáм
князь	prince, -зьá, -зéй
сын	son, сыновьá, -вéй
кум	godfather, кумовьá

друг, муж, сын, and князь end in the genitive plural in -ей without ь, but in the dative, etc., retain the ь. The genitive of the others ends in -ьев.

10. Nouns in -анин, -янин end in the nominative plural in -ане, -яне, and in the genitive plural in -ан, -ян, e.g.

граждани́н	citizen	гра́ждане, граждан
крестья́нин	peasant	крестья́не
дворяни́н	nobleman	дворя́не
христиани́н	Christian	христиа́не
англича́нин	Englishman	англича́не

11. The names of the young of animals usually end in -ёнок, and in the nominative plural in -я́та, -а́та; genitive plural: -я́т, -а́т. Such are:

ягнёнок, ягня́та, ягня́т lamb

жеребёнок	foal	медвежёнок	bear cub
телёнок	calf	львёнок	lion's whelp, львёнки
котёнок	kitten	мышёнок	young mouse
поросёнок	piglet	цыплёнок	chicken
ослёнок	young ass	галчёнок	young jackdaw
козлёнок	kid	гусёнок	gosling
волчёнок	wolf cub	ребёнок	child

12. The following masculine nouns form their plural in various ways:

господи́н	master, Mr	господа́, госпо́д (gen.)
сосе́д	neighbour	сосе́ди, сосе́дей
чёрт	devil	чёрти, чертёй
челове́к	man	лю́ди, люде́й people (declined like ко́сти, see p. 236)

13. Neuter nouns in -ще end in the plural in -ща (see p. 15), e.g.

учи́лище   school   учи́лища

But masculine nouns in -ще (augmentative) take -щи, e.g.

доми́ще   huge house   доми́щи

Three words insert -ec- in the plural:

небо, sky, небеса́   чу́до, wonder, чудеса́
дре́во (old form of де́рево), древеса́

Neuter nouns in **-ко**, including diminutives, end in the plural in **-ки**, as

	я́блоко	apple	я́блоки
	око́шко	little window	око́шки
except	о́блако	cloud	облака́
	во́йско	army	войска́

Плечо́ (shoulder), **коле́но** (knee) also have the plural in **-и**: **пле́чи, коле́ни**. **О́ко** (eye, poetic) and **у́хо** (ear) have in the plural **о́чи, у́ши** (gen. **оче́й, уше́й**). (Note change in consonants, see p. 17.)

14. Some nouns are used only in the plural, as:

щипцы́	tongs	щипцо́в (gen.)
но́жницы	scissors	но́жниц
обо́и	wall-paper	обо́ев *or* обо́й
дрова́	firewood	дров
воро́та	gateway, gates	воро́т
око́вы	chains, fetters	око́в
носи́лки	stretchers	носи́лок
са́ни	sledge	сане́й
сли́вки	cream	сли́вок
ни́тки	thread	ни́ток
слю́ни	spittle	слюне́й
де́ньги	money	де́нег

ADJECTIVE AND PRONOUNS

ADJECTIVAL ENDINGS: ALL GENDERS.

The adjective in Russian agrees in gender, number and case with the noun which it qualifies; it therefore has different endings for gender, number and case.

The adjective used attributively always ends in two vowels, which are of the same kind as the gender endings of nouns, i.e. two of the "*i*" kind for the masculine, of the "*a*" kind for the feminine, and of the "*o*" kind for the neuter (see Vowel Table). The second of these vowels is always soft. If the first vowel is hard, the ending and the whole declension of the word is considered *hard*, e.g.

но́в-**ый** (m.), new
но́в-**ая** (f.) } но́в-**ые** (pl.)
но́в-**ое** (n.)

If an adjective has the ending accented, and not the stem, the ending for the masculine is -ой instead of -ый, but for feminine and neuter the same as the unaccented hard endings, i.e. -ая and -ое, e.g. молодóй (young), молодáя, молодóе, молодые.

If both the vowels in the ending are soft, the declension is considered soft, e.g.

> син-ий (m.), blue
> син-яя (f.)   } син-ие (pl.)
> син-ее (n.)

N.B. *Accent.* Since adjectives have a special ending -ой when the ending is accented, the endings -ый and -ий are never accented, either as such, or when changed in declension.

Pronouns

The pronoun in Russian is a word which stands not only instead of a noun, but also instead of an adjective or a numeral, the latter being considered a separate part of speech. In accordance with this definition, pronouns which take the place of adjectives are declined like adjectives, and are in this way distinguished from pronouns proper, which are declined partly like adjectives and partly like nouns. For a foreign student, however, this distinction is not essential. Having in view the English-speaking student, adjectives and pronouns are arranged together in the declension tables for the reason that many Russian pronouns, such as *possessive, relative, demonstrative,* and *indefinite* do the work of adjectives; some, indeed, are in English considered adjectives. Such an arrangement will also help in remembering the endings.

The classification of pronouns is also slightly different in Russian. The classes of pronouns are:

Personal pronouns: я (I), ты (thou), он (he), онá (she), онó (it), мы (we), вы (you), они (they). For the declension of the 1st and 2nd persons see below; the 3rd person is declined along with adjectives.

The reflexive pronoun: себя (self). This is the same for both singular and plural; the declension is similar to that of the 1st and 2nd person singular.

Possessive pronouns: мой (my), твой (thy), наш (our), ваш (your), свой (one's own). Свой corresponds to the reflexive pronoun себя. For the 3rd person the genitive of the personal pronoun is used, and is invariable.

Interrogative pronouns: кто? (who), что? (which), кото́рый? (which), како́й? как

о́в? (what, of what kind), чей? (whose). These are declined like adjectives, and are grouped along with adjectives. Чей is declined like and grouped with "relative" adjectives.

Relative pronouns: the same as interrogative pronouns, but with a different function, and used without the (?), as in English.

Demonstrative pronouns: э́тот (this), тот (that), тако́й (such), тако́в (of that kind), etc.

Indefinite pronouns: не́кто (some one), не́что (something), не́кий, не́который (a certain), кто-то (some one), что-то (something), что-нибу́дь (anything), не́сколько (several), etc.

Negative pronouns: никто́ (no one), ничто́ (nothing), не́кого (no one), не́чего (nothing), никако́й (of no kind), ниче́й (no one's), etc.

The pronoun сам, сама́, само́ may be compared with the English *emphatic*. In Russian it has a different name (*definite*), and to the same class belong весь (all, whole), са́мый (the same), вся́кий (each), ка́ждый (every), ино́й (other).

Declension of personal pronouns (1st and 2nd person) and the reflexive pronoun себя́

	Singular		Plural		(all persons)
Nom.	я	ты	мы	вы	None
Gen.	меня́	тебя́	нас	вас	себя́
Dat.	мне	тебе́	нам	вам	себе́
Acc.	меня́	тебя́	нас	вас	себя́
Instr.	мно́й, о́ю	тобо́й, о́ю	на́ми	ва́ми	собо́й, о́ю
Prep.	обо мне	о тебе	о нас	о вас	о себе́

DECLENSION OF ADJECTIVES AND PRONOUNS

Singular

Masculine and neuter

	Adjectives		Pronouns			
	Hard	Soft				
Nom.	но́в-ый, -ое	си́н-ий, -ее	он, оно́	сам, само́	кто	что
Gen.	но́в-ого	си́н-его	его́	сам-ого́	кого́	чего́
Dat.	но́в-ому	си́н-ему	ему́	сам-ому́	кому́	чему́
Acc.	Like nom. or gen.[1]		его́	сам-ого́	кого́	что
Instr.	но́в-ым	си́н-им	им	сам-и́м	кем	чем
Prep.	о но́в-ом	си́н-ем	нём	сам-о́м	ком	чём

[1] See § 90.

Молодо́й, како́й are declined like но́вый, but the endings are accented.

Note that the instrumental case of како́й ends in -им (after к-, see p. 14).

-им also occurs in the instrumental of сам (pron.); ct. -ым in са́мый (adj.) (see p. 256).

The instrumental case of кто and что is кем and чем.

Pronouns

Nom.	э́тот, это	тот, то	весь, всё	мо-й, моё
Gen.	э́того	того́	всего́	мо-его́
Dat.	э́тому	тому́	всему́	мо-ему́
Acc.		Like nom. or gen.		
Instr.	э́тим	тем	всем	мо-и́м
Prep.	об э́том	о том	о всём	о мо-ём

Оди́н (одно́) is declined like э́тот (gen. одного́, etc.).

Наш (на́ше), ваш (ва́ше), твой (твоё), свой (своё) are declined like мой.

Note that the instrumental case of э́тот is э́тим, and that of тот is тем.

Feminine Adjectives

	Hard	Soft
Nom.	но́в-ая	си́н-яя
Gen.	но́в-ой	си́н-ей
Dat.	но́в-ой	си́н-ей
Acc.	но́в-ую	си́н-юю
Instr.	но́в-ой, ою	си́н-ей, ею
Prep.	о но́в-ой	о си́н-ей

Feminine Pronouns

Nom.	она	сам-а́	э́т-а	мо-я́
Gen.	её	сам-о́й	э́т-ой	мо-е́й
Dat.	ей	сам-о́й	э́т-ой	мо-е́й
Acc.	её	сам-оё	э́т-у	мо-ю́
Instr.	е́ю, ей	сам-о́й, ою	э́т-ой, ою	мо-е́й, е́ю
Prep.	о ней	о сам-о́й	об э́т-ой	о мо-е́й

Одна́, та are declined like э́та; на́ша, ва́ша, своя́, вся like моя́; the accusative, however, has -у in на́шу, ва́шу.

Plural for all three genders

Adjectives

	Hard	Soft
Nom.	нóв-ые	сúн-ие
Gen.	нóв-ых	сúн-их
Dat.	нóв-ым	сúн-им
Acc.	Like nom. or gen.	
Instr.	нóв-ыми	сúн-ими
Prep.	о нóв-ых	о сúн-их

Pronouns

Nom.	они	сáм-и	э́т-и	те	все
Gen.	их	сам-úх	э́т-их	тех	всех
Dat.	им	сам-úм	э́т-им	тем	всем
Acc.	их	сам-úх	Like nom. or gen.		
Instr.	úми	сам-úми	э́т-ими	тéми	всéми
Prep.	ó них	сам-úх	об э́т-их	тех	всех

Мой, твой, нáши, вáши, свой are declined like эти.

Скóлько (how many) and **нéсколько** (several) are declined like **сáми** (скóльк-о, скóльк-их, скóльк-им, etc.).

Adjectives with the stem ending in a *guttural*, г, к, х, as **рýсский, рýсская, рýсское,** belong to the hard declension, with the exception of the nominative and instrumental masculine where -ы becomes -и (see p. 15). In the plural all the endings are soft. Adjectives with the stem ending in a *sibilant*, ж, ч, ш, щ, as **горячий, горячая, горячее,** belong to the soft declension, except the nominative and accusative feminine where -я becomes -а and -ю becomes -у. In the plural all the endings are also soft. Adjectives ending in -ой after a sibilant as **большóй** are declined like **нóвый,** but have -úм in the instrumental case; in the plural all the endings are soft.

"*Relative*" *adjectives.* Russian "relative" adjectives should not be confused with English relative pronouns. These adjectives show the *relation* of the noun qualified *to some other person or thing,* thus answering the question asked by "**чей?**" (whose?), which is itself a relative pronoun. The declension of чей is similar to that of **лисий,** i.e. that of a relative adjective in -ий, -ья, -ье. This fact brings out the connection between Russian relative adjectives and relative pronouns.

Declension of the relative pronoun чей, *and of relative adjectives*

	Singular		Plural
	Masculine and neuter	*Feminine*	
Nom.	чей, чьё	чья	чьи
Gen.	чьего	чьей	чьих
Dat.	чьему	чьей	чьим
Acc.	Like nom. or gen.	чью	Like nom. or gen.
Instr.	чьим	чьей	чьими
Prep.	о чьём	о чьей	о чьих
Nom.	лис-ий, -ье	лис-ья	лис-ьи
Gen.	лис-ь-его	лис-ь-ей	лис-ь-их
Dat.	лис-ь-ему	лис-ь-ей	лис-ь-им
Acc.	Like nom. or gen.	лис-ь-ю	Like nom. or gen.
Instr.	лис-ь-им	лис-ь-ей, -ею	лис-ь-ими
Prep.	о лис-ь-ем	о лис-ь-ей	о лис-ь-их

Like **лисий** are declined other adjectives in -ний, -бий, -жий, -чий, -сий, -ший, -вий, formed from the names of animals, as **медвежий** (bear's), **собачий** (dog's), **рыбий** (fish's), etc. (*but* **рыбный** means "made of fish").

Relative adjectives which indicate possession are sometimes called *possessive* adjectives. They are formed from the names of individuals, as **материн** (mother's),[1] **отцов** (father's),[1] **сестрин** (sister's), **Семёнов** (Simeon's), **Иванов** (John's), etc. They end in -ов, -ев, -ин, -ын; feminine and neuter: -ова, -ово; -ева, -ево; -ина, -ино; and plural: -овы, -евы, etc. These endings are added to the stem of the nouns, e.g. сестр-а: сестр-ин; in some words -н- is inserted between the stem and the ending, e.g. брат: брат-н-ин (brother's). In declension, this class of relative adjectives has some cases like nouns, others like adjectives. Relative adjectives are used only attributively.

---

[1] Other forms are материнский, отцовский (and отчий), which are used when the idea of *possession* is absent, e.g.

материнская любовь	mother-love
отчий дом	parental home

Declension of "possessive" adjectives

	Singular		Plural
	Masculine and neuter	Feminine	
Nom.	сéстрин, -о	сéстрин-а	сéстрин-ы
Gen.	сéстрин-а	сéстрин-ой	сéстрин-ых
Dat.	сéстрин-у	сéстрин-ой	сéстрин-ым
Acc.	Like nom. or gen.	сéстрин-у	Like nom. or gen.
Instr.	сéстрин-ым	сéстрин-ой, -ою	сéстрин-ыми
Prep.	о сéстрин-ом	о сéстрин-ой	о сéстрин-ых

N.B. *Accent.* Possessive adjectives in -ин have the accent on the stem in all cases.

Like **сéстрин** are declined **Иванóв, Петрóв**, and other adjectives formed from proper names. But when these adjectives are used as surnames the prepositional case in the masculine has the noun ending, e.g. о господúне Иванóве. Patronymics in -вич and -вна, e.g. Ивáнович, Ивáновна, are declined like nouns.

Adjectives of nationality and of material, as well as adjectives signifying time or place, also have only the attributive form. Such are: **рýсский, золотóй** (golden), **стальнóй** (steel), **здéшний** (local), **вчерáшний** (yesterday's), etc. Adjectives of nationality are written with a small letter.

THE ABBREVIATED FORM OF ADJECTIVES

The endings of the attributive form are also called *full* endings to distinguish from the *abbreviated* endings of the predicative form, which are the same as noun endings, e.g.

Hard: нов- (m.) Soft: син-ь (m.)
нов-á (f.) син-я́ (f.)
нóв-о (n.) сúн-е (n.)
нóв-ы (pl.) сúн-и (pl.)

When the stem of the adjective ends in two consonants difficult to pronounce together, -о- or -е- is inserted between the consonants in the abbreviated form of the masculine, e.g.

ýмный (clever): умён, умнá, умнó, умны́.
любéзный (kind): любéзен, любéзна, любéзно, любéзны.
лёгкий (easy): лёгок, легкá, легкó, лёгки.

This is done merely to satisfy euphony, and comes naturally, because if these consonants are easily articulated, insertion does not take place, as in

мёртвый (dẹad): мёртв   чёрствый (stale): чёрств

The process is the same as in the case of the genitive plural of nouns (see p. 239).

Only adjectives of quality, and of these only those which have degrees of comparison, can have the abbreviated form. This form, otherwise called the *predicative*, is not very much used, and being used only as a part of a predicate, is usually found only in the nominative case, i.e. it is not declined. The other cases exist, but are used only in poetry, especially in folk-poetry.

Some adjectives have only the full form, as **большой**. To express "big" predicatively **велик** is used, which is the predicative form of **великий** (great). **Маленький** is also used only attributively. "Small" used predicatively is **мал**, the abbreviated form of **малый**, which itself is very seldom used.

Some adjectives, as **рад** (glad) and **горазд** (skilled), are used only in the abbreviated or predicative form, e.g.

Я рад вас видеть.   I am glad to see you (see § 177).

THE COMPARISON OF ADJECTIVES

The *comparative* degree is formed by cutting off -ый (or -ой) of the adjective, and adding -ee (or -ей) to the stem, e.g. умный (clever): умнее.

This comparative form of the adjective is not declined, and can only be used predicatively, e.g.

Он умнее брата.   He is cleverer than his brother.

When the object of comparison is mentioned, as above, the comparative form is followed *either* by the genitive, e.g.

Наш дом красивее вашего.   Our house is prettier than yours.

or by **чем** (or **нежели**) with the nominative, e.g. наш дом красивее, чем ваш.

But the comparative may also stand alone, e.g. этот дом красивее.

If the comparative is followed by его, её, их, used as possessive adjectives, the conjunctions **чем** or **нежели** *must* be used, e.g. наш дом красивее, чем их.

Красивее их would mean "prettier than they are".

Another way of forming the comparative is by adding **более** (more) or **менее** (less) to the positive, e.g. более красивый, менее о́пытный. This form is used when the comparative is used attributively, e.g.

Ему́ ну́жен бо́лее тёплый кли́мат.
He needs a warmer climate.

especially if an oblique case is required, e.g.

Я люблю́ писа́ть бо́лее о́стрым карандашо́м.
I like to write with a sharper pencil.

A few adjectives can be used attributively in the comparative degree, ending in -ший, sometimes assuming, however, the meaning of a superlative. Such are:

высо́кий	tall, high	вы́сший	
ни́зкий	low	ни́зший	
ста́рый	old	ста́рший	senior, elder
молодо́й	young	мла́дший	junior, younger
худо́й	bad	ху́дший	
хоро́ший	good	лу́чший	
большо́й	big	бо́льший	
ма́лый	small	ме́ньший .	

These adjectives also have another form ending in -e, which will be found in the list of adjectives with the comparative in -e. This form of the comparative is usually considered irregular, but it is really formed in accordance with the same demand for euphony which causes the usual permutation of consonants (see pp. 17, 18).

Adjectives with the comparative in -e

бога́тый	rich	бога́че
большо́й	big	бо́льше
бли́зкий	near	бли́же*
ве́тхий	ancient	ве́тше
высо́кий	high	вы́ше
го́рький	bitter	го́рче
глубо́кий	deep	глу́бже
га́дкий	filthy	га́же
гла́дкий	smooth	гла́же
гро́мкий	loud	гро́мче
густо́й	thick	гу́ще
далёкий	far	да́льше*
дешёвый	cheap	деше́вле
дорого́й	dear	доро́же
до́лгий	long (of time)	до́льше*

жа́лкий	pitiful	жа́льче
жа́ркий	hot	жа́рче
жи́дкий	thin (of a liquid)	жи́же
зво́нкий	sonorous	звонче
зо́ркий	keen-sighted	зо́рче
кра́сный	handsome	кра́ше
круто́й	steep	кру́че
кре́пкий	fast	кре́пче
коро́ткий	short	коро́че
лёгкий	easy, light	ле́гче
молодо́й	young	моло́же, мла́дше
ма́лый (ма́ленький)	little	ме́ньше
ме́лкий	small (fine), shallow	ме́льче
ни́зкий	low	ни́же
плохо́й	bad	пло́ше
просто́й	simple	про́ще
по́здний	late	по́зже*
ра́нний	early	ра́ньше*
ре́дкий	rare	ре́же
сла́бый	weak	сла́бже
сла́дкий	sweet	сла́ще
ста́рый	old	ста́рше[1]
стро́гий	strict	стро́же
сухо́й	dry	су́ше
то́лстый	thick, fat	то́лще
то́нкий	thin	то́ньше
тяжёлый	heavy	тяже́ле
туго́й	stiff	ту́же
ти́хий	quiet	ти́ше
твёрдый	firm	тве́рже
у́зкий	narrow	у́же
хоро́ший	good	лу́чше
худо́й	bad	ху́же[2]
ча́стый	frequent	ча́ще
чи́стый	clean	чи́ще
широ́кий	wide	ши́ре

Comparatives marked (*) are mostly used as adverbs. For comparatives with по- see Lesson XV.

[1] Also старе́е, used chiefly of *things*.
[2] худо́й, thin, lean, has the comparative худе́е.

The superlative degree. The superlative can be formed in several ways:

(1) By adding **са́мый** to the positive, and sometimes to the comparative, e.g.

са́мый краси́вый	the most beautiful
са́мый у́мный	the cleverest
са́мый лу́чший	the very best

The superlative can be used only attributively.

(2) By adding to the stem the endings **-е́йший, -е́йшая, -е́йшее, -е́йшие,** e.g. **миле́йший, миле́йшая, миле́йшее** (the dearest), **нове́йший,** etc. (the newest).

The endings **-а́йший, -а́йшая, -а́йшее** are added when the stem ends in a guttural, which in the superlative is changed into a sibilant, e.g.

широ́кий	broad	широча́йший
глубо́кий	deep	глубоча́йший
дорого́й	dear	дража́йший

This form is commonly used as an absolute superlative, indicating a *very high degree* of a quality, e.g.

Он носи́л широча́йшее пальто́.   He wore a very wide coat.

In addition to these two forms, there are others which are very seldom used and must be known only in order to be recognised. These are:

(1) With prefixes **наи-** and **пре-**, e.g.

наилу́чший	the very best
предо́брый	the kindest

(2) A predicative form of the superlative which is really the same as the comparative, followed by **всего́** and **всех**, e.g.

ле́гче всего́	the easiest (i.e. easier than all)
бо́льше всех	most of all

N.B. *Accent.* For rules concerning accents in the comparative and superlative degrees see Part I, pp. 115, 116.

PRINCIPAL ADJECTIVAL SUFFIXES

(1) The commonest suffix forming an adjective from a noun is **-н-** added to the stem of a noun, e.g.

ры́ба	fish	ры́бный
хлеб	bread	хле́бный
труд	labour	тру́дный
зима́	winter	зи́мний

If a noun already has -н- in the stem, the н is doubled, e.g.

о́сень	autumn	осе́нний
весна́	spring	весе́нний (obs. inserted -e-)

If the stem ends in к, г, ж, х the usual permutation of consonants occurs (see p. 17), e.g.

рука́	hand	ручно́й
нога́	foot	ножно́й
век	century	ве́чный

The suffix -н- is often preceded by -тель- when the adjective is formed from a verb through a noun in -тель, though this noun itself may not exist, e.g. очарова́тельный, charming; отврати́тельный, repulsive.

(2) The suffixes -ин, -ов, -ев, -ын are used in forming adjectives from the names of individuals, as has already been mentioned, e.g.

дя́дя	uncle	дя́дин
купе́ц	merchant	купцо́в

(3) The suffix -к- is used to form adjectives from nouns or adverbs, e.g.

низ	bottom	ни́зкий	low
близ	near	бли́зкий	near

(4) -ен- and -ан- are used in adjectives formed from verbs; these are really variations of past participles used as adjectives, e.g.

варёный	cooked
точёный	carved
пу́ганый	frightened

Obs. One н here instead of the two in participles.

(5) With the suffixes -ск-, -цк- are formed adjectives of nationality, and also adjectives from the names of towns, institutions, and some occupations, e.g.

Русь	Russia	ру́сский
Францу́з	Frenchman	францу́зский
Москва́	Moscow	моско́вский
Сове́т	Council	сове́тский
Каза́к	Cossack	каза́цкий

(6) With -ов-, -ев- are formed adjectives mostly from the names of trees and some fruits, e.g.

дуб	oak	дубо́вый
гру́ша	pear	гру́шевый

(7) With -ян- (after sibilants, -ан-) are formed adjectives from the names of materials, e.g.

кость	bone	костяно́й
ко́жа	leather	ко́жаный

The letter н is doubled in only three words: деревя́нный (wooden), оловя́нный (leaden), стекля́нный (glass).

(8) Adjectives in -чий are formed from the present participle, changing щ into ч, e.g.

горя́чий (hot) from горя́щий (burning)
могу́чий (powerful) from могу́щий (one who can)

The meaning of adjectives is sometimes partially modified by suffixes which assume a magnifying (augmentative), diminutive, or endearing sense.

(9) The suffixes -аст-, -ущ-, -ющ- are augmentative, e.g.

глаз-а́ст-ый big-eyed
больш-у́щ-ий huge
зл-ю́щ-ий ill-natured

(10) -еньк-, -оньк- imply endearment, or have a diminutive force, e.g.

ма́ленький small сла́вненький nice

(11) -ова́т-, -ева́т-, -ист-, -ова́тист-, -ева́тист- help to express various degrees of a certain quality, e.g.

красн-ова́т-ый reddish
горьк-ова́т-ый slightly bitter
син-ева́т-ый bluish

These adjectives are very frequent in chemistry and indicate differences in formulae, e.g. азотн-ова́т-ый, азо́т-ист-ый, азотн-ова́тист-ый (nitrogen compounds).

(12) The less common suffixes -лив-, -чив-, -ес- are found in certain important words, as follows: -лив-, in such adjectives as

счаст-ли́в-ый (happy) from сча́стье (happiness)
со́вест-лив-ый (scrupulous) from со́весть (conscience)
приве́т-лив-ый (affable) from приве́т (greeting)

But *note* the forms несча́стный (unhappy), бессо́вестный (unscrupulous). In these words the -т- is scarcely pronounced, though it must not be omitted in writing.

-чив-, in

нахо́дчивый (ready-witted) from находи́ть (see § 160)
усй́дчивый (persevering) from усиде́ть (to keep one's seat)

-ес-, in the words чуде́сный (wonderful), небе́сный (heavenly), древе́сный (wood, adj.), is identical with -ес- in the plural of не́бо, небеса́, etc. (see p. 241).

ADJECTIVES USED AS SURNAMES

The suffixes -ов-, -ев-, -ск, -овск serve in the formation of Russian surnames, e.g.

Иван-о́в, Иван-о́ва
Я́ков-л-ев, Я́ков-л-ева

Observe the -л- in **Яковлев**, inserted before the suffix (see p. 18).

Names in -ов and -ев are declined as relative adjectives (see tables) and those in -ский as adjectives in -ий (like **русский**).

COMPOUND ADJECTIVES

In compound adjectives the joining letter is either -о- or -е-.

If the first part is an adjective with a hard ending the joining letter is -о-, e.g.

| све́тлый | светл-о-зелёный | light green |
| тёмный | тёмн-о-се́рый | dark grey |

But if the first part is an adjective with a soft ending, the joining letter is -е-, e.g.

| дре́вний | древн-е-ру́сский | Old Russian |
| синий | син-е-гла́зый | blue-eyed |

ADJECTIVES USED AS NOUNS

Some adjectives, with both hard and soft endings, are used as nouns, e.g.

портно́й	tailor
живо́тное	animal
больно́й	patient
столо́вая	dining-room
ни́щий	beggar

They are declined as adjectives and the gender is clearly seen from the endings.

SOME REMARKS ON PRONOUNS

Many Russian pronouns, such as **са́мый, кото́рый, не́который, не́кий, како́й, тако́й**, are in English often treated as adjectives. In Russian, these pronouns, according to their function, i.e. being used instead of adjectives, are declined like adjectives, so that it is immaterial what they are called.

One feature in their declension should, however, be noticed, namely, that the instrumental case of **како́й, тако́й, не́кий**, as well as of **этот** and **сам**, ends in **-им**, although the two latter belong to the hard declension. The ending **-им**, however, is characteristic of pronouns in general, and in this way **самим** (from **сам**, himself) is distinguished from **самым** (from **самый**, the same, very). The first is a pronoun proper and the second a pronoun used as an adjective.

Notice also, in particular, the difference between the accusative of **сама** and that of **самая**. The accusative of **сама** is **самоё** (cf. **её**) while that of **самая** is **самую** (like the accusative of adjectives).

Another ending peculiar to pronouns is **-ем** in the instrumental: **кем, чем, всем**.

Some particular points about pronouns proper should be noticed:

(1) The personal pronouns **он, она, оно, они** after prepositions prefix the letter **н-**, e.g. **у него** (he has), **от неё** (from· her), **с ним** (with him), **к ней** (to her), **от них** (from them), etc. But if these pronouns correspond to English possessive adjectives, the letter **н-** is not added, e.g.

у его брата	his brother has
с их сестрой	with their sister

(2) The pronouns **никто** (nobody), **ничто** (nothing) are declined like **кто** and **что**, but when used with a preposition, the latter is inserted between **ни** and **кто** or **что** and is written separately, e.g.

мы ни о ком не говорили	we spoke of nobody
ни с кем	with nobody
ни с чём	with nothing

(3) The indefinite pronouns **некто** and **нечто**, when used with a positive meaning, are used only in the nominative:

некто	a certain person
нечто	something

For expressions with the oblique cases of these pronouns see Lesson XIX, p. 144. In these expressions the pronouns **некто** and **нечто** assume a negative meaning.

(4) The pronoun **сей, сия, сие, сии**, is the old variant of **этот**. It is now used mostly in compound words or expressions, e.g.

сейчас	directly, immediately (*lit.* this hour)
сию минуту	in a minute
до сих пор	up till now (till this time)

(5) Compound pronouns with the particles **-то, -либо, -нибудь**, are joined by a hyphen, e.g. **кто-нибудь** (anybody), **что-то** (some-

thing). The particle **-то** gives the pronoun a meaning of "definiteness", e.g.

> Кто́-то пришёл. Somebody has come.

-либо and **-нибудь** indicate *any* person or *any* thing, e.g.

> Скажи́те мне что́-нибудь.
> Tell me something (i.e. anything you like).

(See Lesson XIX, p. 144.)

NUMERALS

CARDINAL AND ORDINAL NUMERALS

Numerals may be *cardinal* or *ordinal*, but there are also *collective* and *fractional* numerals.

The cardinal numerals are in form like nouns, *except* **оди́н, два, три, четы́ре, о́ба** (both), and are declined mostly as nouns.

The ordinal numerals are formed from the cardinal, with the exception of **пе́рвый** and **второ́й**; in form they are like adjectives, and agree with their nouns in gender, number and case.

	Cardinal numerals	*Ordinal numerals*	
1	оди́н, одна́ (f.), одно́ (n.)	пе́рвый, -ая, -ое	first
2	два, две	второ́й, -а́я, -о́е	second
3	три	тре́тий, -ья, -ье	third
4	четы́ре	четвёртый, -ая, -ое	fourth
5	пять	пя́тый	
6	шесть	шесто́й	
7	семь	седьмо́й	
8	во́семь	восьмо́й	
9	де́вять	девя́тый	
10	де́сять	деся́тый	
11	оди́ннадцать	оди́ннадцатый	
12	двена́дцать	двена́дцатый	
13	трина́дцать	трина́дцатый	
14	четы́рнадцать	четы́рнадцатый	
15	пятна́дцать	пятна́дцатый	
16	шестна́дцать	шестна́дцатый	
17	семна́дцать	семна́дцатый	
18	восемна́дцать	восемна́дцатый	
19	девятна́дцать	девятна́дцатый	
20	два́дцать	двадца́тый	
21	два́дцать оди́н	два́дцать пе́рвый	

22	двадцать два́	двадцать второ́й
30	три́дцать	тридца́тый
40	со́рок	сороково́й
50	пятьдеся́т	пятидеся́тый
60	шестьдеся́т	шестидеся́тый
70	се́мьдесят	семидеся́тый
80	во́семьдесят	восьмидеся́тый
90	девяно́сто	девяно́стый
100	сто	со́тый
200	две́сти	двухсо́тый
300	три́ста	трёхсо́тый
400	четы́реста	четырёхсо́тый
500	пятьсо́т	пятисо́тый
600	шестьсо́т	шестисо́тый
700	семьсо́т	семисо́тый
800	восемьсо́т	восьмисо́тый
900	девятьсо́т	девятисо́тый
1,000	ты́сяча	ты́сячный
2,000	две ты́сячи	двухты́сячный
5,000	пять ты́сяч	пятиты́сячный
10,000	де́сять ты́сяч	десятиты́сячный
100,000	сто ты́сяч	стоты́сячный
1,000,000	миллио́н	миллио́нный

COLLECTIVE NUMERALS

The collective numerals are formed from the cardinal as far as
де́сять. They are:

дво́е	two of
тро́е	three of, etc.
че́тверо	
пя́теро	
ше́стеро	
се́меро	
во́сьмеро ⎫	
де́вятеро ⎬ (rarely found)	
де́сятеро ⎭	

The words пято́к (five), деся́ток (ten), дю́жина (dozen), со́тня
(a hundred) may also be considered collective numerals.

FRACTIONAL NUMERALS

The fractional numerals are:

полови́на	a half
тре́ть	a third
че́тверть	a quarter
восьма́я (*or* восьму́шка)	an eighth
полтора́	one and a half, etc.

Other fractional numerals are formed in the same way as in English, e.g.

⅖, две пя́тых, i.e. two fifth (parts), **пя́тых** being the genitive plural of the ordinal **пятая**, which is declined like an adjective.

⅔, две тре́ти, ¾, три че́тверти, **тре́ти** and **че́тверти** being the genitive singular of **тре́ть** and **че́тверть**, which, according to their endings, are declined like feminine nouns in -ь.

DECLENSION OF NUMERALS

Оди́н (одна́, одно́, одни́) is declined like э́тот (see p. 245).

Nom.	два, две	дво́е	три	четы́ре	че́тверо
Gen.	двух	двои́х	трёх	четырёх	четверы́х
Dat.	двум	двои́м	трём	четырём	четверы́м
Acc.		Like nominative or genitive			
Instr.	двумя́	двои́ми	тремя́	четырьмя́	четверы́ми
Prep.	о двух	о двои́х	о трёх	о четырёх	о четверы́х

	Masc. and neut.	*Feminine*	*Masc. and neut.*	*Feminine*
Nom.	о́ба	о́бе	полтора́	полторы́
Gen.	обо́их	обе́их	полу́тора	полу́тора
Dat.	обо́им	обе́им	полу́тора	полу́тора
Acc.	Like nom. or gen.		полтора́	полторы́
Instr	обо́ими	обе́ими	полу́тора	полу́тора
Prep.	об обо́их	об обе́их	о полу́тора	о полу́тора

Nom.	со́рок	пятьдеся́т	две́сти
Gen.	сорока́	пяти́десяти	двух со́т
Dat.	сорока́	пяти́десяти	двум ста́м
Acc.	со́рок	пятьдеся́т	две́сти
Instr.	сорока́	пятью́десятью	двумя́ ста́ми
Prep.	о сорока́	о пяти́десяти	о двух ста́х

CASES USED WITH NUMERALS

After **один** in the compound numerals, such as **двáдцать одúн, стó одúн**, etc., the noun is always put in the singular, e.g.

Стó одúн день.   One hundred and one days.

After **два, три, четы́ре, полторá, óба**, and also **двáдцать два, тридцать четы́ре**, etc., nouns are used in the genitive *singular*, and after all other numerals in the genitive *plural*, but only when the numeral is in the nominative or accusative, e.g.

Я купúл три столá (gen. sing.).   I have bought three tables.
Пять книг (gen. plur.).   Five books.
Двáдцать шесть слов (gen. plur.).   Twenty-six words.

But when the numeral is used in an oblique case, the noun takes the same case as the numeral, e.g.

Я купúл стол с четырьмя́ я́щиками (instr. pl.).
I bought a table with four drawers.

All numerals ending in **-ь**, as **пять, шесть, одúннадцать, двáдцать**, etc., are declined like feminine nouns in **-ь** (see p. 236).
Трóе is declined like **двóе**, but **пя́теро**, etc., like **чéтверо**.
Шестьдеся́т, сéмьдесят, вóсемьдесят are declined like **пятьдеся́т**.
Девянóсто and **стó** are declined like **сóрок**.
Трúста and **четы́реста** are declined like **двéсти**. In oblique cases these words may be written as one word or as two.
Пятьсóт and other hundreds are also declined in both parts, i.e. like **пять** and the second part of **двéсти**.
Половúна, треть, чéтверть, ты́сяча, миллиóн are declined like nouns according to their endings; **треть** and **чéтверть** like feminine nouns in **-ь**.
Пол, meaning "half", is an old form of **половúна**, and is now used only in compound words, as:

полчасá	half an hour	полгóда	half a year
полбуты́лки	half a bottle	полфýнта	half a pound

COMPOUNDS OF NUMERALS

Numerals are often found in compound nouns and adjectives such as:

единица	digit (from един, Slavonic for один)
пятилетка	five-year plan
двухъэтажный	two-storied
двойка	figure 2
вдвоём (adv.)	tête-à-tête
трилистник	trefoil
пятница	Friday
пятак	five-copeck coin
четвертак	25 copecks (quarter of a rouble)
столетие	century

Further examples may be found in the Lessons (see p. 154).

THE ADVERB

Classes of adverbs

According to their meaning, adverbs are divided into different classes:

(1) Adverbs of *quality* or *manner*, e.g.

| хорошо | well | плохо | badly |
| скоро | quickly | вместе | together |

(2) Adverbs of *time*, e.g.

| сегодня | to-day | теперь | now |
| прежде | before | сначала | at first |

(3) Adverbs of *place*, e.g.

здесь	here	там	there
сюда	hither	туда	thither
всюду	everywhere	отсюда	hence

(4) Adverbs of *reason* or *cause*, e.g.

поэтому	therefore
почему	for which reason *or* why
сгоряча	in a passion
по-глупости	for a foolish reason

(5) *Implicit* adverbs, which express confirmation, negation, supposition, limitation, doubt, wish, e.g.

да	yes	нет	no
не	not	ни...ни	neither...nor
так	so	конечно	of course
лишь, только	only	едва-ли	hardly
неужели, разве	surely		

FORMATION AND DERIVATION OF ADVERBS

Russian adverbs are mostly derived from other parts of speech.
Adverbs of quality or manner are formed from adjectives by
changing the endings -ый or -ой into -o, and sometimes -ий into
-e, e.g.

холо́дный	хо́лодно	coldly
горя́чий	горячо́	warmly
лёгкий	легко́	easily

In the last two examples -ий is changed into -o because of the
ч and к in the stem (see p. 16).

| ве́чный | ве́чно | for ever |
| кра́йний | кра́йне | extremely |

This form is identical with the neuter of the abbreviated form
of adjectives, but should not be confused with it. If the word is
a predicate in the sentence, it is an adjective, e.g. мне хо́лодно
здесь (хо́лодно is here an adjective). But if the word modifies
a verb, it is an adverb, e.g. они́ встре́тили нас хо́лодно (they met
us coldly) (хо́лодно is here an adverb).

Adverbs formed from "relative" adjectives in -ский end in -ски,
e.g. дру́жеский: дру́жески (in a friendly way).

The form with the prefix по- means "in the manner of", e.g.
по-ру́сски, по-де́тски (see p. 134).

The same prefix по- is added to the dative singular of adjectives
or pronouns, e.g.

| по-но́вому | in the modern way | по-ста́рому | in the old way |
| по-мо́ему | in my opinion | по-ва́шему | as you wish |

Some adverbs formed from *nouns*, as:

ве́чером	in the evening	у́тром	in the morning
весно́й	in spring	ша́гом	at a foot pace
да́ром	for nothing	ря́дом	close by

etc., are really the instrumental case of these nouns. Some nouns
from which such adverbs are derived are no longer used as nouns,
e.g.

| пешко́м | on foot | босико́м | barefoot, etc. |

Other adverbs formed from nouns, as:

| вверх, вверху́ | upstairs | вниз, внизу́ | downstairs |
| вме́сте | together | вслух | aloud |

are formed from oblique cases with prepositions (see Lesson
XVIII).

As has already been mentioned, adverbs end in -o or -e when formed from adjectives; they also end in -o when derived from the accusative case of neuter forms, as:

напра́во   to the right   набело́   as a fair copy

Adverbs from the genitive of neuter nouns with the prepositions с, из, до end in -a, e.g.

снача́ла   at first, from the beginning
сперва́   at first   спра́ва   on the right
сле́ва   on the left   и́зредка seldom
до́бела   white-hot, etc.   и́здавна long since

Adverbs formed from the genitive, dative, and prepositional cases end in -и, e.g.

и́сстари (gen.)   from olden times
кста́ти (dat.)   by the way
назади́ (prep.)   behind

Adverbs formed from *verbs* occur in either (a) the form of gerunds (see § 219):

мо́лча   in silence   шутя́   in jest
несмотря́ in spite of   спустя́ later

or (b) an imperative form, e.g.

ведь (from ве́дать, Slavonic for "to know")   you know
почти́ (поче́сть, to consider as)   almost

Adverbs derived from *numerals* are formed either by adding -жды, or with prefixes, e.g.

одна́жды   once   заодно́   at once, at the same time
вчетверо́м four together   во-пе́рвых firstly

Some adverbs are formed from *pronouns*, e.g.

совсе́м   altogether   во́все   at all

From *prepositions* and *prefixes*, adverbs are formed by the suffixes -ве and -ле, e.g.

ра́зве   surely not   во́зле, по́дле   beside

Lastly, there are some compound adverbs, i.e. adverbs consisting of several other words joined, as: исподтишка́: из-под-тишка (from the root тих, see p. 18), on the sly; ма́ло-по-ма́лу, little by little; наизу́сть: на-из-уст (Slavonic for "lips"), by heart, without book.

Comparison of adverbs

Adverbs formed from adjectives of quality have *degrees of comparison*, and may also be used with a diminutive or an augmentative meaning, e.g.

скоро, скорее *and* скоренько ("quick-quick")
мало, меньше *and* маленько (a little bit)
немного, немножко (not much)
прескверно (superlative) (in a most hideous way)

Orthography of adverbs

Some adverbs are similar in pronunciation to other parts of speech, but are written differently, e.g.

Так же, when written as two words, is an adverb, and means "in the same way" or "just as", e.g.

Он говорит по-английски так же хорошо, как по-русски.

He speaks English just as well as Russian.

Также, one word, is in Russian considered a conjunction, e.g.

Я также говорю по-русски.   I also speak Russian.

Cf. **по этому** (two words) when это is a pronoun, e.g.

Он пошёл по этому пути.   He adopted this course.

По этому is here used in its literal meaning: "he went *by this* course".

But **поэтому** (therefore) is an adverb, and is written as one word.

The *rule* is that adverbs proper, formed with prepositions, are always written as one word, as: **покуда** (whilst), **донынe** (up till now), **навсегда** (for ever), etc. Adverbs composed of other parts of speech with prepositions may be written either as one word or as two, according to the sense, as:

встороне aside   в стороне   at the side

Some adverbs end in -**ь**, e.g. **наизусть** (by heart), **въявь** (in reality); and almost all adverbs ending in a sibilant, as: **лишь** (only), **сплошь** (completely, without interruption), **вскачь** (at a gallop), *except* **меж** (among), **уж** (already).

The adverbs не and ни

The adverb **не** is written together with a noun when this noun has no meaning without it, as in **негодование** (indignation), **невеста** (bride), etc., or when the resulting word has a positive meaning, e.g. неволя (captivity), неприятель (enemy), незнание (ignorance).

The same rule applies to adjectives, e.g. неуклюжий (clumsy), небрежный (careless), недорогой (cheap), некрасивый (ugly).

Не and ни in the indefinite pronouns are written in one word with the pronoun, e.g. некто (somebody), нечто (something), некого, нечего (gen.), некоторый (certain), никто, ничего. But when these pronouns are used with prepositions, the preposition is placed between the не and the pronoun, and is written separately, e.g. не у кого, ни с кем, ни о ком, etc. The use of these pronouns and their proper construction in sentences are treated in Lesson XIX.

Не and ни with other adverbs are always written in one word, e.g. негде, нигде, некуда, никогда, некогда, etc.

The whole subject of adverbs cannot be exhaustively treated here. Complete lists of the various classes have not been given, but, with the help of the rules concerning their formation, the student will be able to recognise adverbs in reading.

PREPOSITIONS

A list of prepositions, with the cases they govern, follows:

Prepositions governing the *genitive*:

без (безо) without	меж among
близ near	мимо by, past
вдоль along	около beside
вместо instead of	от (ото) from (a person) *or* further from
вне without (outside)	
внутри inside, within	подле beside
возле beside	позади behind
вокруг round	после after
впереди in front of	посреди in the middle
для for (the sake of)	против opposite, against
до up to, till	ради for the sake of
из (изо) out, from (a place)	сверх above
из-за from behind	с (со) off
из-под from underneath	среди amongst
кроме besides	у at (as a prefix means "away")
кругом round	

Governing the *dative*:

вопреки contrary	по along (according to)
к (ко) to (towards)	

Governing the *accusative*:

в (во) in, into (to denote motion)
за behind (motion); for (in exchange for)
на on, on to
о (об, обо) against
по up to, till

под under (motion)
про about, concerning
с about (approximately)
сквозь through
чéрез in (after the lapse of),
  through

Governing the *instrumental*:

за for (after), behind, at (to
  indicate state of rest)
мéжду between
над (надо) above, over

пéред in front of (state of rest)
под (подо) under (state of rest)
с (со) with (along with)

Governing the *prepositional* or *locative*:

в in (state of rest)
на on (state of rest)
о (об, обо) about (concerning)

по about, on account of
при in the presence of

PREPOSITIONS AS PREFIXES

As has already been mentioned (see p. 216) prepositions as prefixes give to verbs a definite change of meaning, and in general are very important in the vocabulary. Compound words are extremely numerous in Russian, but when the student knows the meaning of these prefixes, the actual memorising is not difficult.

Some prefixes, though originally prepositions, are no longer used as such. These are: воз (взо, вз), вы, низ (низо), пере, пре, раз (разо), роз, су, пра, па. The three last are very seldom found, the commonest words formed with them being: супрýг (spouse), прáдед (forefather), пáсынок (stepson), пáдчерица (stepdaughter).

The meaning of воз is "up" (cf. воз, loaded cart). Before a vowel воз becomes взо- or вз-, e.g.

    взойти́   to ascend   взыскáть   to exact
вы (out), e.g.
    выходи́ть   to go out   выставля́ть   to put out
низ (down) (cf. низ, bottom), e.g.
    нисходи́ть   to descend   низвергáть   to overthrow
пере (over, across, afresh), e.g.
    переводи́ть   to translate   перемéна   change
пре (round, over, across), e.g.
    преступáть   to transgress   прервáть   to interrupt

The prefix **пре-** should not be confused with the prefix **при-** which is used also as a preposition. **При-** indicates *nearness, joining*, whereas **пре-** indicates *motion over* (Latin "*trans*") implying some obstacle or difficulty, e.g.

приступа́ть, to start (come near to); преступа́ть, to transgress, hence преступле́ние (crime), престу́пник, criminal, *but* при́ступ, assault (of a fortress).

раз (asunder; English dis- *or* un-), e.g.

разби́ть   to smash   разда́ть   to distribute
разде́тый   undressed

раз- or **рас-** becomes **ро́з-** or **ро́с-** when accented, e.g. ро́здали, ро́спись; *but* разда́ть, расписа́ть.

The prefixes **раз-, роз-, воз-, вз-, из-, низ-, без-, чрез-** change **з-** into **с-** before the unvoiced consonants: к, п, т, с, х, ц, ч, ш, щ, ф, e.g. расска́з, восхо́д, беспоко́йный, etc.

They keep **з**, however, before voiced consonants and before vowels, e.g.

извини́те   excuse me   разу́мный   sensible

For the meaning imparted to verbs by the prepositions proper as prefixes see Lesson XIII.

THE CONJUNCTION

In Russian various parts of speech may be used as conjunctions. Conjunctions are of many different types according to their function in a sentence, but it is sufficient to divide them into (*a*) *co-ordinating conjunctions*, which join similar clauses or words, and (*b*) *subordinating conjunctions*, which introduce a subordinate clause.

(*a*) The co-ordinating conjunctions are:

а and (separating)	**лишь** only
впро́чем however	**наконе́ц** at last
да and	**не то́лько...но и** not only...
да́же even	but also
ещё besides	**ни...ни** neither...nor
же (ж) also, but (see p. 70)	**но** but
зато́ on the other hand	**одна́ко** however
и and (joining)	**та́кже, то́же** also
и́ли or	**то** then
ка́к-то such as	**то...то** now...now
ли́бо either	**то́лько** merely

(b) The subordinating conjunctions are:

бу́дто as if	потому́ что because
е́сли, е́жели if	пусть, пуска́й let it
и́бо because	ско́лько ни however much
ита́к therefore	сле́довательно consequently, therefore
как as	
ка́к-ни however much	ста́ло-быть therefore
когда́ when	хотя́ although
ли, ль whether	чем than
не́жели than	что that
положим suppose	чтобы in order that
посему́ thereby	

The use of conjunctions in connection with subordinate clauses is described in Lesson XXIV.

THE INTERJECTION

The principal interjections are:

To express:

Surprise	а! ах! ай! да! ого́!
Joy	ура́!
Pain	ой-ой! ох!
Fear	ух! ой!
Assurance	ей-ей! да-да!
Calling	эй! гей! ау!
Indignation	тьфу!
Aversion	фу! фи!
Encouragement	ну! ну-же! ну-те!
Threat	ага́! ужо́!
Regret	увы́! а́хти!
Pointing	вот, вон (see § 5)
Laughter	ха-ха! хи-хи! хо-хо!
Handing over	на! на-те!
Silence!	тс! цыц! (to dogs)

There are some verbs formed from interjections, as:

о́хать	to groan	хихи́кать	to titter
понука́ть	to urge	мяу́кать	to mew, etc.

A LIST OF VERBS USED WITH VARIOUS CASES

I. *Verbs followed by the genitive*

боя́ться, по-	to be afraid of
пуга́ться, испуга́ться	to fear
держа́ться	to hold to, abide by
добива́ться, доби́ться	to pursue, strive for
жа́ждать	to thirst for
ждать, подожда́ть	to wait
жела́ть, по-	to wish
хоте́ть, за-	to want
избега́ть, избе́гнуть	to avoid
иска́ть, по-	to seek
каса́ться, косну́ться	to touch
лиша́ть, лиши́ть	to deprive
набира́ть, набра́ть	to collect
напива́ться, напи́ться	to drink one's fill
проси́ть, по-	to beg
слу́шаться, по-	to obey
сто́ить (no perf.)	to deserve
тре́бовать	to demand

II. *Verbs followed by the dative*

ве́рить, по-	to believe
внуша́ть, внуши́ть	to suggest, instil
грози́ть, по-	to threaten
гото́виться, при- (к)	to get ready for
дава́ть, дать	to give
дари́ть, по-	to give a present
досажда́ть, -сади́ть	to spite, annoy
зави́довать, по-	to envy
запреща́ть, запрети́ть	to forbid
изменя́ть, измени́ть	to be unfaithful, betray
кла́няться, поклони́ться	to bow, greet
меша́ть, по-	to hinder
моли́ться, по-	to pray
мсти́ть, ото-	to take vengeance on
надоеда́ть, -е́сть	to bore
напомина́ть, напо́мнить	to remind
насле́довать (no perf.)	to succeed (inherit)
обраща́ться, обрати́ться (к)	to address, apply

отвечáть, отвéтить	to answer (a person)
откáзывать, -казать	to refuse
относи́ться, отнести́сь (к)	to regard, concern
повиновáться (no perf.)	to obey
подлежáть (no perf.)	to be liable, subject to
подражáть (no perf.)	to imitate
позволя́ть, позвóлить	to allow
помогáть, помóчь	to help
предлагáть, предложи́ть	to offer
предоставля́ть, предостáвить	to leave to
принадлежáть (no perf.)	to belong
равня́ться, с-	to be equal to
рáдоваться, по-, об-	to rejoice
служи́ть, по-	to serve
смея́ться, за-[1]	to laugh at a thing
совéтовать, по-	to advise
содéйствовать, по-	to co-operate
сопротивля́ться (no perf.)	to oppose, resist
стреми́ться (к), устреми́ться	to rush, yearn
удивля́ться, удиви́ться	to be surprised at
уступáть, уступи́ть	to give in, yield
учи́ться, вы́учиться	to learn

III. *Verbs with the accusative after prepositions*

выдавáть, вы́дать за	to pass as
надеяться нá	to rely upon
обжигáться о (*or* на + prepos.), обжéчься	to burn oneself
отвечáть, -тить на	to reply to
отклáдывать, отложи́ть на	to postpone (also with по + gen.)
полагáться, положи́ться на	to count upon, rely
походи́ть на (no perf.)	to resemble
ручаться за	to vouch for
серди́ться, рас- (на)	to become angry with
ушибáться (о), ушиби́ться	to hurt oneself

[1] To laugh at a person: смея́ться над with the instrumental.

IV. *Verbs followed by the instrumental*

владе́ть, о-	to possess, own
вооружа́ться, вооружи́ться	to arm
восхища́ться	to be enraptured
горди́ться, воз-	to take pride in
грози́ть, по-	to threaten with
дорожи́ть	to value
дыша́ть, по-	to breathe
же́ртвовать, по-	to sacrifice
занима́ться, заня́ться	to occupy oneself in
интересова́ться, за-	to take interest in
кома́ндовать	to command
любова́ться, по-, за-	to admire
наслажда́ться, наслади́ться	to enjoy
наполня́ть, напо́лнить	to fill with
одева́ться, оде́ться	to be dressed as
отзыва́ться	to taste of
отлича́ться, отличи́ться	to distinguish oneself
па́хнуть, за-	to smell of
по́льзоваться, вос-	to make use of
пра́вить	to drive (horses), ply (a boat)
рискова́ть, -кнуть	to risk
руководи́ть	to direct
управля́ть	to govern
хва́стать (ся), по-	to boast

Verbs *requiring* a complement *in the instrumental case*

быть	to be (as)
вы́глядеть (no perf.)	to appear (as)
де́латься, с-	to become
каза́ться, по-	to seem
называ́ться, назва́ться	to be called
признава́ть, -зна́ть	to recognise
притворя́ться, притвори́ться	to pretend
рожда́ться, роди́ться	to be born
служи́ть, по-	to serve as
слыть, про-	to be reputed
станови́ться, стать	to become
счита́ться	to be considered, reputed
умира́ть, умере́ть	to die (a natural death)
явля́ться, яви́ться	to appear

RUSSIAN-ENGLISH VOCABULARY

Words given as examples in Part II, and a few uncommon words, appearing only in "A" exercises and there translated, are not given in the Vocabulary. On the other hand, certain common words and phrases not actually used in the Lessons are given in both the Russian-English and the English-Russian sections.

Verbs are given in both aspects; if only one form is given, it is to be understood that the perfective (or imperfective, as the case may be) is rarely, if ever, used. Verbs forming their perfective simply by the addition of a prefix are given thus: слушать, по-. In the English-Russian Vocabulary noteworthy forms in the present, future perfect, etc., are given along with the infinitives, or references are given to the Lessons or the Grammar. The same is done when the genitive or plural of nouns presents any irregularity or variation in accent.

A, and (separating), but
áвгуст, August
автомоби́ль (m.), motor-car
áвтор, author
áдрес, address
аккура́тный, accurate; аккура́тно, punctually
акце́нт, accent (pronunciation)
англи́йский, English; по-англи́йски (adv.), in English
англича́нин, Englishman; англича́нка, Englishwoman
А́нглия, England
апельси́н, orange
аппети́т, appetite.
апре́ль (m.), April
апте́ка, chemist's shop, pharmacy
аэропла́н, aeroplane

Ба́бушка, grandmother
база́р, bazaar
бал, ball (dance)
банк, bank
башма́к, shoe
беда́, trouble

бе́дный, poor; бе́дность (f.), poverty
без (gen.), without
безрабо́тный, unemployed
безу́мный, mad, foolish
беле́ть, по-, to appear white
бе́лый, white
бе́рег, bank, shore
бесе́да, chat; бесе́довать, по-, to chat, converse
беспоря́док, disorder, confusion
библиоте́ка, library
биле́т, ticket
благодари́ть, по-, to thank; благода́рный, grateful
благоро́дный, noble
благоро́дство, nobility
бледне́ть, to turn pale; бле́дный, pale
блеск, shine, glitter
блесте́ть, блесну́ть, to shine
блестя́щий, brilliant
бли́зкий, near; бли́зко (followed by от) (adv.), near; бли́же (comp.), nearer

богáтый, rich; богáче (comp.), richer

бок, side; нáбоку, sideways; сбóку, at the side

болéзнь (f.), illness

болéть, за-, to be ill, ache (see § 119)

болтáть, по-, to chatter

боль (f.), pain

больни́ца, hospital

больнóй, ill, patient (noun); бóльно, it is painful

бóльше (comp.), bigger, more

большóй, large, big

бормотáть, про-, to mutter

бородá, beard

боя́ться (gen.), to fear

брат, brother; брáтский, fraternal

брать, взять, to take

брести́, за-, to be wandering

бри́тый, shaven

бри́ться, по-, to shave (oneself)

броди́ть, по-, to wander

бросáть, брóсить, to throw; -ся, to rush

буди́льник, alarum-clock

буди́ть, раз-, to awaken, rouse

бýдто, as if

бýдущее, the future

бýдущий, future

бýква, letter (of alphabet)

бумáга, paper, cotton; бумáжный (adj.)

бýря, storm

бывáлый, experienced

бывáть, to be (usually), to exist, visit

бы́вший (past part.), former, who was

бык, ox, bull

быть, to be

бы́стрый, swift

В (acc.), in, into, to (*motion*); (prep.) in (*rest*)

вагóн, carriage (railway)

вáжный, important, serious; вáжность (noun)

вáнна, bath; вáнная (noun), bath-room

ваш, -а, -е, your, yours

вверх, up (*motion*); вверхý, up, above (*rest*)

вдвóе (adv.), double; вдвоём (adv.), two together

вдоль (adv.), along

вдруг (adv.), suddenly

ведь (adv.), you know, surely

вездé, everywhere

везти́, по-, to convey (see вози́ть)

век, century, lifetime; вéчный, eternal

вели́кий, great

вéрить, по- (dat.), to believe; вéра, belief

вернýть (see возвращáть), to cause to return, call back; -ся, to return (intr.)

вéрный, true, faithful; -но, it is true, correct, -ly

вероя́тный, probable; -но, probably

весёлый, merry; вéсело, merrily

весели́ться, по-, to be merry, enjoy oneself

веснá, spring (season)

вести́, по-, to be leading, take (a person) (see води́ть)

весь, вся, всё, все, whole, all

вéтер, breeze, wind

вéчер, evening; дóбрый вéчер, good evening

вéчный, eternal

вéшалка, peg (hanging)

вéшать, повéсить, to hang, hang up (tr.)

вещь (f.), thing

взгляд, glance, look

взглянýть (imperf. взгля́дывать), to glance

вздор, nonsense, rubbish

взор, look, glance

взрóслый, grown up

взять (see p. 220), to take

вид, appearance, aspect (of verb), view; имéть в видý, to have in prospect, view видáть, по-, to see (often); -ся, to visit one another

вúдеть, у-, to see; вúдеться, повидáться, to see each other

вúлка, fork

винá, guilt, fault; виновáтый, guilty; виновáт, -а, I beg your pardon

винó, wine

виногрáд, grapes

висéть, по-, to hang (intr.)

висячий, hanging (adj.)

вúшня, cherry

вклáдывать, вложúть, to put in (lying)

вкýсный, tasty, good; вкус, taste

власть (f.), power

вмéсте (adv.), together

вмéсто (gen.), instead of

вниз, down, downstairs (motion)

внимáние, attention

внимáтельный, attentive

внимáть, внять, to listen attentively

внук, grandson; внýчка, granddaughter

внутрú (adv.), inside

водá, water

водúть, по-, to lead (see § 82)

воз, cart, cart-load; возóк, coach

возвращáться, возвратúться, to return; возвращéние, return

возвы́шенный, high, lofty

возúть, по-, to convey (see § 82)

вóзле (gen.), beside

возмóжность (f.), possibility, opportunity

войнá, war; воéнный, military

вокзáл, station (building)

вол, bull, ox

волк, wolf; вóлчий, wolf's, wolfish

волнá, wave

вóлос, вóлосы (pl.), hair

волочúть, по-, to drag

вóля, freedom, liberty, will

вон, there is (pointing), yonder

воображáть, -зúть, to imagine; воображéние, imagination

вообщé, in general

вопрóс, question; задавáть, -дáть вопрóс, to ask a question

вор, thief

воровáть, украсть, to steal

вóсемь, eight; восьмóй, eighth

воскресéнье, Sunday

воспрещáть, воспретúть, to forbid

востóк, east; востóчный (adj.)

восходúть, взойтú, to ascend, rise; восхóд сóлнца, sunrise

вот, here is

впервы́е (adv.), for the first time

вперёд, forward, in future

вполнé, in full, fully

впослéдствии, afterwards, in course of time

вредúть, по-, to injure, harm; врéдный, harmful

врéмя (n.), time

вряд-ли, hardly

всáдник, rider, horseman

все, everyone; всё (pron.), everything; (adv.), continually

всегдá, always

всётаки, all the same, in any case, nevertheless

вслéдствие, in consequence of, consequently

вставáть, встать, to get up, rise

вставлять, встáвить, to insert, put in

всторонé, aside

встречáть, встрéтить, to meet (tr.); -ся, to meet (intr.)

всякий, every, any

втóрник, Tuesday

вторóй, second

второпях (adv.), in a hurry

втроём, three together

вход, entrance, entry

входúть, войтú, to enter, come in

въезд, entrance (into a country, town, etc.); carriage entrance

вы, you

выбира́ть, вы́брать, to choose; вы́бор, choice

вы́бритый, clean-shaven

выгля́дывать, вы́глянуть, to look out; вы́глядеть (no perf.), to look, appear

вы́говор, reprimand, pronunciation (accent)

выкла́дывать, вы́ложить, to empty, put out

вынима́ть, вы́нуть, to take out

выпи́сывать, -писа́ть, to subscribe to a paper, order goods

выпуска́ть, -пусти́ть, to let out

выража́ться, to express oneself

выса́живать, -сади́ть, to set down (passengers)

высо́кий, tall, high

высота́, height

выставля́ть, вы́ставить, to exhibit; вы́ставка, exhibition

выть (во́ю), за-, to howl, wail

вы́ход, exit; выходи́ть, вы́йти, to go, come out

вчера́, yesterday

вяза́ть, по-, с-, to knit; за-, to tie

Газе́та, newspaper

где, where

Герма́ния, Germany; герма́нский, German (see неме́цкий)

гла́дкий, smooth; -ко, smoothly

глаз, eye

Гла́зго, Glasgow

глубина́, depth; глубо́кий, deep

глу́пый, stupid

глухо́й, deaf, dull, desolate (of a place)

гляде́ть, по-, to look, gaze

гнездо́, гнёздышко (dim.), nest

говори́ть, по-, to speak, talk, be saying

год, year

годи́ться, при-, to be useful

годовщи́на, anniversary

голова́, head; глава́, chapter; гла́вный, principal

го́лос, глас (old word), voice

голубо́й, blue, sky-blue

гора́, mountain

горди́ться, воз-, to be proud

го́ре, grief

горе́ть, с-, to burn (intr.)

го́род, град, town

городово́й (noun), policeman

го́рький, bitter

горя́чий, hot

господи́н, master, Mr, gentleman; госпожа́, mistress, Mrs

гости́ть, to be on a visit

гость, го́стья (f.), visitor, guest; гости́ная, drawing-room

госуда́рство, state

гото́вый, ready; гото́вить, при-, to prepare

грамма́тика, grammar

грани́ца, грань (f.), frontier

греме́ть, за-, to rumble, rattle

гроза́, thunderstorm

гром, thunder; гро́мкий, loud; -ко, loudly

грохота́ть, за-, to rumble

гру́бый, rough, coarse

гру́да, heap

грудь (f.), breast, chest

гру́ппа, group

гру́стный, sad; грусти́ть, за-, to be sad; грусть (f.), sadness

губи́ть, по-, to ruin

гуверна́нтка, governess

гуля́ть, по-, to take a walk

гусь (m.), goose

Да, yes, and, but

дава́ть, дать, to give (see § 64)

давно́, давны́м-давно́, long ago

далёкий (adj.), далеко́ (adv.), far

да́льний, distant

да́ма, lady

дар, gift; да́ром, gratis, in vain

дари́ть, по-, to present, to give

да́ча, country house

два, две (f.), two; двойка, two (of cards)

дверь (f.), door

двигаться, (по)двинуться, to move (intr.)

движение, movement

двор, yard, court; дворец, palace

девица, maiden; девочка, girl, little girl; девушка, young girl

девяносто, ninety

девять, девятый, nine, ninth

дед, дедушка, grandfather

действие, action, act (theat.)

декабрь (m.), December

делать, to do, make; дело, affair, matter, business, work

день (m.), day

деньги (pl.), money

деревня, village

дерево, tree, wood; деревянный, wooden

держать, по-, to hold, keep

десять, ten; десяток, ten (collective); десятый, tenth

детский, children's; детская, nursery (room)

детство, childhood

дешёвый, cheap; дёшево (adv.)

диван, couch, sofa

дикий, wild

дитя, child, (pl.) дети

длинный, long

для (gen.), for (the sake of)

Днепр, Dnieper

до (gen.), till, until

доброта, kindness; добрый, kind

довольный, pleased; довольно (cf. воля), enough, rather; довольство, plenty

дождь, rain

доклад, report; докладывать (verb), -ложить, to announce

доктор, doctor

долг, duty, debt

долго (adv.), long; долгий (adj.)

должен, must, obliged (cf. долг)

доля, lot, share

дом, house; дома, at home; домой, homewards

домашний, domestic, home-made

дописывать, -писать, to finish writing, write to the end

дорога, road, way

дорогой, dear, expensive

дорожить (instr.), to value, prize

до-свидания, good-bye (au revoir)

доска, board, blackboard

доставать, -стать, to procure, reach

доставлять, -вить (доставлю, -вишь), to deliver

достигать, -гнуть (gen.), to attain, reach

достойный, достоен (pred.), (gen.), worthy

досыта, till satisfied

доходить, дойти, to reach (place)

дочь, дочка, daughter

дражайший, dearest (superlative of дорогой)

дремать, за-, to slumber; дрема, дремота (noun)

друг (pl. друзья, -зей), friend; друг друга, one another, each other

другой, other

дуб, oak

думать, по-, to think

дурной, bad

дуть, по-, to blow

дух, spirit

душа, soul; душевный (adj.)

душечка, darling

душный, stifling, sultry

дышать (2nd conj.), to breathe

дюжина, dozen

дядя, uncle

Европа, Europe; европейский, European

его, him, his, it, its

едва, scarcely

единственный, unique, sole; -нно (adv.)

её, her, hers

éздить, по-, поéхать, to go (not on foot), ride, drive

éле-éле, hardly

ель (f.), fir

éсли, if

есть, is, there is

есть, по-, съ-, to eat (see § 68)

éхать, по-, to be going (not on foot) (see § 82)

ещё, still, more, yet; ещё не, not yet

Жалéть, по-, to pity, regret

жáлкий, pitiful, piteous; жáлко, жаль, it is a pity; мне жаль, I regret

жáркий, -ко, hot (intangible); жáрить, за-, to roast

жать, по-, с-(pres. жму), to press

жать, с- (pres. жну), to reap

ждать, подо- (жду, ждёшь), to wait for (see § 161)

-же (-ж), also, but

желáние, wish, desire; желáть, to wish, desire

желéзный, iron (adj.); желéзо (noun)

женá, wife

женúться (на + prepos.), to marry (of a man)

женúх, bridegroom, fiancé

жéнщина, woman; жéнский, feminine

жéртвовать, по- (instr.), to sacrifice (жéртва, victim)

живóтное (noun), animal

жизнь (f.), life

жить, про-, по-, to live (see § 136); жил-был, "once upon a time..."; живóй, living; житьё, life (mode of life)

журнáл, magazine

За, (acc.) for, (instr.) benind

забóта, care, worry

забывáть, забыть, to forget

завóд, factory

зáвтра, to-morrow

зáвтрак, breakfast, lunch; зáвтракать, по-, to breakfast, lunch

за-граниицей, abroad (to live); за-граниицу (to go)

зáдний, hind, back (adj.)

закáз, order; закáзывать, заказáть (y + gen.), to order (from)

заклáдывать, заложúть, to pawn, harness

заключáть, заключúть, to conclude; (in imperf.), contain

закрывáть, закрыть, to close, shut; закрытый, closed

закýривать, закурúть, to light (a cigarette)

зал, зáла, hall, salon

зáмужем (adv.), married (of a woman); выходúть зáмуж, to get married

занимáть, -нять, to take up, occupy; зáнятый, occupied, busy; -ся, to study, be occupied in, etc.

зáпад, west; зáпадный (adj.)

зáпах, smell, odour

запúска, -ки, note, memoirs; записнáя книжка, note-book; запúсывать, записáть, to note

зарáз, at once, at the same time

заседáние, sitting, session, meeting; заседáть, to sit (of a committee)

заслужённый, worthy, deserving; заслýживать, -жúть, to deserve

заставáть, застáть, to find in or at

заставлять, застáвить, to compel, cause to do

засыпáть, заснýть, to fall asleep

затéм, then, for that reason

затó, on the other hand

зачéм? why?

звать, по- (зовý, -ёшь), to call

звездá, star

зверь (m.), wild beast

звонúть, по-, to ring; звонóк, bell

звук, sound; звучáть (verb)

здесь, here

здорóваться, по-, to greet

здорóвый, healthy, well; здорóвье, health

здрáвствуй(те), how-do-you-do

зелёный, green

земля́, land, earth; земнóй, earthly (adj.)

зимá, winter; зи́мний (adj.)

злóба, malice; злой, wicked

змея́, snake

знакóмить, по-, to introduce, make acquainted; -ся, to get acquainted

знакóмый, (noun) acquaintance, (adj.) familiar

знáмя, flag, banner

знать, y-, to know; узнавáть, -знáть, to recognise, to learn (news); знáние, knowledge

знáчить, to mean; знак, sign

зóлото, gold; золотóй, golden

зóнтик, umbrella

зрéние, sight, (from зреть (Old Slav.), to see)

зреть, co-, to ripen, mature

зрáчий, seeing (opp. blind)

зуб, tooth; зубнóй врач, dentist

И, and (joining), also; и...и, both...and

и́бо (conj.) (Slav.), for, because

игрáть, по-, to play

идти́, пойти́, to be going, be coming; suit (see § 85)

из (gen.), from, out of

избá, hut

и́збранный, chosen; избрáть, to have chosen

извéстный, well-known, famous; вéсти, извéстия (pl.), news

извиня́ть, -и́ть, to pardon; -ся, to apologise (cf. винá)

и́здали, from a distance; даль (f.), distance

из-зá (gen.), from behind

изли́шний, superfluous

изобретéние, invention

из-пóд (gen.), from under

изучáть, -чи́ть, to study (tr.)

и́ли, or

имéть, to have, имéние, estate

и́менно, precisely

и́мя (n.), name

инáче, otherwise

иногдá, sometimes

инóй, other

инострáнец, -нка (f.), foreigner; инострáнный, foreign

интерéсный, interesting

интересовáть, за-, to interest; -ся (+ instr.), to be interested in

искáть, по- (ищý, и́щешь), to seek

исполня́ть, -нить, to fulfil, execute; -ся, to be fulfilled

их, them, their

ию́ль (m.), July

ию́нь (m.), June

К (dat.), to, towards

Кавкáз, Caucasus

кáждый, each, every

казáк, Cossack

казáться, по-, to appear, seem; кáжется, it seems

как, how, as; как рáз, just as; как слéдует, properly

какóй, of what kind, what; каки́м óбразом? how?

калóши, goloshes

кáмень (m., gen. кáмня), stone; кáменный (adj.)

ками́н, fire-place

карандáш, pencil

карéта, carriage

кармáн, pocket

кáрта, card, map

карти́на, picture

картóфель (m.), картóшка, potato

касáться (gen.), to touch, touch upon; что касáется, as to

катáть, по-, to roll; катáться, to go (for pleasure) (see § 175) ка́чество, quality

ка́ша, porridge

кварти́ра, quarters, lodgings, flat

кино́, cinema

кла́няться, поклони́ться, to bow, greet; кла́няйтесь ей, remember me to her

класс, class, class-room

класть, положи́ть (see § 206), to put (lying), lay

кли́мат, climate

клуб, club

ключ, key

кни́га,. book; кни́жный (adj.)

ковёр (gen. -вра́), carpet

когда́, when

ко́готь (m.), claw, (pl.) -гти

кое-что́, something

ко́жа, skin, hide, leather; ко́жаный (adj.)

козёл (gen. козла́), goat; коза́ (f.)

кой-кто́, some one

колеба́ть, to shake, rock; -ся, to hesitate

коле́но (pl. коле́ни), knee

ко́ли (colloq.), if

ко́лос (pl. коло́сья), ear of corn

ко́мната, room

конве́рт, envelope

коне́ц, end

коне́чно, of course, certainly

конто́ра, office

конце́рт, concert

конча́ть, ко́нчить, to end, finish; ко́нчен, finished

конь (m.), steed, horse

коньки́, skates

копа́ть, вы́-, to dig

копе́йка, copeck

кора́бль (m.), ship

корми́ть, на-, to feed

коро́ва, cow

коро́ткий, short; кра́ткий, brief

косо́й, slanting, oblique, squint

костю́м, costume

кото́рый, which; кото́рый час, what time is it?

ко́фе, coffee

кофе́йня, café

кошелёк (gen. -лька́), purse

ко́шка, кот, cat; котёнок (gen. -нка, pl. котя́та), kitten

край, edge, part (of country); кра́йний, extreme; по кра́йней ме́ре, at least

краса́вица, beauty (belle); краси́вый, beautiful; -во (adv.)

красне́ть, по-, to blush

кра́сный, red, beautiful

кратча́йший, shortest (see коро́ткий)

кре́пкий, fast, strong

кре́сло, arm-chair

крова́ть (f.), bed (bedstead)

кровь (f.), blood

кро́ме (gen.), except, besides

круг, circle; кру́глый (adj.), round; круго́м (adv.), round, around

кру́пный, large, coarse

круто́й, steep; круто́е яйцо́, hard-boiled egg

кста́ти, by the way

кто, who; кто-нибу́дь, anybody; кто́-то, somebody

куда́, whither, where

купе́ц (gen. купца́), merchant

купи́ть (perf.), to buy (see покупа́ть)

кури́ть, по-, за-, to smoke

ку́рица, hen

куса́ть, укуси́ть, to bite

кусо́к (gen. куска́), piece, bite

ку́шать, по-, с-, to eat

Ла́вка, bench, small shop

ла́мпа, lamp

ласка́ть, при-, to caress; ла́сковый, caressing, affectionate

ла́ять, за-, to bark

ле́бедь (m.), swan

ле́вый, left (hand)

лёгкий, easy, light (weight); легко́ (adv.)

лежа́ть, по-, to lie

ле́кция, lecture

Ленингра́д, Leningrad

лени́ться, to be lazy; лень (f.), laziness; лени́вый, lazy

лес, forest, wood

ле́стница, stair, ladder

лета́ть, по-, to fly; лете́ть, по-, to be flying

ле́то, summer; ле́тний (adj.)

лечь (perf.), ля́гу, ля́жешь, to lie down (see ложи́ться)

ли́ния, line

лиса́, лиси́ца, fox

лист (pl. ли́стья), leaf; (pl. листы́), sheet (of paper)

литерату́ра, literature

лицо́, face, person; ли́чный, personal

лиша́ть, лиши́ть, to deprive; лиша́ться, to lose

ли́шний, superfluous (cf. сли́шком)

лишь (то́лько), only

лови́ть, пойма́ть, to catch

ло́дка, boat

ложи́ться, лечь, to lie down

ло́жка, spoon

ложь (f.), lie (falsehood)

ло́шадь (f.), horse

луг, meadow

луна́, moon

лу́чше (comp.), better; лу́чший (superl.), best

любе́зный, kind, amiable

люби́мый, favourite

люби́ть, по- to love; любо́вь (f.), love; любо́й, any

любова́ться, за-, по-, to admire

лю́ди (pl.), people

ля́гу (fut. of лечь) (see p. 227)

Магази́н, shop

май, May

ма́ленький, small, little

ма́ло (adv.), little; ма́ло-пома́лу, little by little

ма́льчик, boy

малю́тка, baby, infant

ма́рка, postage stamp

март, March

ма́сло, butter, oil

мате́рия, cloth, stuff, material

мать, ма́ма, mother

маши́на, -нка, machine

ме́бель (f.), furniture

медве́дь (m.), bear

ме́дленный, slow; -нно, slowly

меж (gen.), among; ме́жду (instr.), between

ме́лкий, fine, small; ме́лочь, small change

ме́нее, ме́ньше, less

меня́ть, перемени́ть, to exchange, change

ме́сто, place, room

ме́сяц, month, moon (poet.)

мете́ль (f.), snow-storm

метр, metre

мех, fur

мечта́, dream

миллио́н, million

ми́лость (f.), favour

ми́лый, dear, sweet, "nice"

ми́ля, mile

ми́мо (gen.), by, past

мину́та, -ка, minute

мир, peace, world

мла́дший, younger, junior; младе́нец, baby (cf. молодо́й)

мне́ние, opinion

мно́го, much, many; мно́гие (adj.), many; мно́гое, much, many things

моги́ла, grave

могу́чий, powerful, mighty (cf. мочь)

мо́да, fashion, mode

мо́жет быть, perhaps

мо́жно, possible, allowed

мой, -я, -ё, my, mine

мо́лвить, utter

моли́тва, prayer

молодо́й, young

мо́лодость (f.), youth

молоко́, milk

молча́ть, за-, to be silent; мо́лча (adv.), silently, in silence

моне́та, coin

мо́ре, sea

моро́з, frost

Москва́, Moscow

мочь, с-, to be able (see § 167)

мра́чный, sombre, gloomy

муж, húsband

мужи́к, peasant, man

мужчи́на, man, male; **мужско́й**, masculine

му́зыка, music; **музыка́нт**, musician

мы, we

мы́ло, soap

мысль (f.), thought; **мы́слить**, to think (reflect)

мыть, по-, вы́- (мо́ю, -ешь), to wash (tr.), -ся (intr.)

мя́со, meat

мяч, ball

На (acc.), on, on to, to (*motion*); (prep.), on (*rest*); (acc.), for

навева́ть, to blow

наве́рно, for certain, surely

наве́рх, **наверху́**, up, upstairs (cf. вверх)

навсегда́, for ever

навстре́чу, идти́ —, to go to meet

награ́да, reward

над (instr.), over, above

надева́ть, **наде́ть**, to put on

наде́жда, hope, expectation, trust; **надёжный**, reliable

наде́яться, to hope

на-дня́х, one of these days, the other day

на́до, **на́добно**, one must, it is necessary

надо́лго, for a long time (future)

наза́д, back; **тому́ наза́д**, ago

назва́ние, name, appellation

называ́ть, **назва́ть**, to name, call; **-ся**, to be named

наизу́сть, by heart, without book

наказа́ние, punishment; **нака́зывать**, **-за́ть**, to punish (see § 143)

накану́не, on the eve, the day before

накла́дывать, **наложи́ть**, to lay (put) on, apply

наконе́ц, at last

накрыва́ть, **накры́ть** (накро́ю), to cover, lay (a table)

наку́рено, filled with smoke (накури́ть)

нале́во, on the left

палива́ть, **-ли́ть**, to fill, pour out (tea)

нам (dat.), to us

напе́в, melody, tune

напои́ть (perf.), to give to drink; **напоённый** (past p. p.)

напомина́ть, **напо́мнить**, to remind

направле́ние, tendency

напра́во, on the right

напра́сно, in vain

наприме́р, for example

напро́тив, on the contrary, on the other hand, opposite

наро́д, people, nation; **наро́дный** (adj.)

наро́чно, on purpose

нару́жу, outside (*motion*)

нас, us

населе́ние, population

наста́вник, **-ница**, tutor

настоя́щий, real, present (time)

настра́ивать, **настро́ить**, to tune (cf. стро́ить); **настрое́ние**, frame of mind, mood

находи́ть, **найти́**, to find; **находи́ться**, to be situated

нача́ло, beginning; **начина́ть**, **нача́ть** (начну́), to begin

наш, **-а**, **-е**, our, ours

не́бо, sky, heaven

небыва́лый, unprecedented

неве́жда, ignoramus

неве́ста, bride, fiancée

невида́нный, not seen before

него́дный, worthless

недалеко́, not far

неде́ля, week

недорого́й, inexpensive

недостава́ть, **недоста́ть**, to lack; **мне недостаёт**, I want (lack); **недоста́ток** (gen. -тка), fault, defect, want, scarcity

недосто́йный, unworthy

недоуме́ние, perplexity
не́жели, than
не́жный, tender; не́жность (f.), tenderness
незаме́тный, imperceptible
нездоро́вый, unhealthy
незнако́мец, stranger; незнако́мый, unfamiliar
не́кий, не́который, some, a certain
не́когда, at one time
не́кого (gen.), no one
не́кто, some one
нельзя́, impossible, one must not
неме́цкий, German; по-неме́цки, in German
немно́го, a little; немно́гие, few
ненави́деть, воз-, to hate
необходи́мое (noun), essential(s)
необходи́мый, necessary, inevitable
непра́вда, untruth
непреме́нно, without fail
не́сколько, some, several
несмотря́ на (acc.), in spite of
несовсе́м, not entirely
нести́, по-, to be carrying (see § 82); нести́сь, to be borne, lay (eggs); pass quickly
нет, no
неуже́ли, surely not?
неую́тный, uncomfortable
не́чего, nothing
не́что, something
ни...ни, neither...nor
нигде́, nowhere
ни́зкий, low
никако́й, of no kind
никогда́, never
никто́, no one
никуда́, nowhere (whither)
ниче́й, no one's
ничто́, ничего́, nothing
ни́щий, beggar; ни́щая (f.)
но, but
нови́нка, new thing
но́вый, new; но́вости, news
нога́, leg, foot
нож, knife
но́жницы, scissors

нос, nose
носи́льщик, porter
носи́ть, to carry, wear
ночь (f.), night; ночно́й (adj.)
ноя́брь (m.), November
нра́виться, по-, to please (мне нра́вится, I like) (see § 118); нрав, temper, humour
нужда́, need, necessity
ну́жный, necessary; ну́жно, one must (cf. на́до)
ны́не, ны́нче, now, at present
ня́ня, nurse

О, об, о́бо (prep.), about, concerning; (acc.) against
о́ба, о́бе (f.), both
обе́д, dinner; обе́дать, по-, to dine
обижа́ть, оби́деть, to offend
о́блако, cloud
обнима́ть, -ня́ть, to embrace
обо́и (pl.), wall-paper
о́браз, image, form, way
образова́ние, education, culture
образо́ванный, educated
обраща́ть внима́ние, обрати́ть, to pay attention
обуча́ть, обучи́ть, to educate
обхва́тывать, -хвати́ть, to envelop, embrace
обходи́ть, обойти́, to avoid; -ся, to do without
обши́рный, extensive, vast
о́бщий, common, general
объясня́ть, -ни́ть, to explain
обыкнове́нный, usual; -нно (adv.); обы́чай, custom
о́вощи, vegetables
огля́дывать, -гляде́ть, to eye, examine
огля́дываться, огляну́ться, to look back
ого́нь (m.) (gen. огня́), fire
огорча́ть, -чи́ть, to grieve, vex
одева́ть, оде́ть, to dress; -ся, to dress oneself
оде́жда, оде́жка (dim.), clothing, dress

оди́н, одна́, одно́, one, alone
одина́ковый, same, like, identical
одна́жды, once
одна́ко, however
оживля́ться, ожива́ться, to become animated
ока́занный, shown, expressed; ока́зывать, оказа́ть, to show
океа́н, ocean
окно́, window
окружённый, surrounded
октя́брь, October
он, he; она́, she; оно́, it; они́, they
опо́мниться, to recover, come to oneself
опя́ть, again
орёл (gen. орла́), eagle
орга́н, organ
оригина́л, original
освеща́ть, освети́ть, to light, illumine
освобожда́ть, освободи́ть, to free; -ся, to be free
о́сень (f.), autumn; осе́нний (adj.)
оскорбля́ть, -би́ть, to insult
осо́ба, person; осо́бенный, particular; осо́бенно, especially
остава́ться, оста́ться, to remain
оставля́ть, оста́вить, to leave
остана́вливать, останови́ть, to stop (tr.); -ся, to stop (intr.)
осторо́жный, careful
о́стров, island
от (gen.), from, away from
отве́т, answer
отвеча́ть, отве́тить, to answer
о́тдых, rest
отдыха́ть, отдохну́ть, to rest
оте́ц (gen. отца́), father
отка́зывать, -каза́ть, to refuse; -ся (от + gen.), to give up
откла́дывать, -ложи́ть, to postpone, put away
открыва́ть, откры́ть, to open; откры́тый, open
откры́тка, post-card

отку́да, whence
отлича́ть, отличи́ть, to distinguish, discriminate; отли́чный, excellent; отли́чно! splendid!
отража́ться, отрази́ться, to be reflected
отреза́ть, отре́зать, to cut off
отрица́тельно, negatively
отстава́ть, отста́ть, to lag behind, slacken
отставля́ть, отста́вить, to discharge, dismiss; отста́вка, retirement
отсю́да, hence
оттого́ что, for that reason, because
отчего́, why? for what reason?
отхо́д, отъе́зд, departure
отходи́ть, отойти́, to depart
отше́льник, hermit
охо́титься, to hunt, chase; охо́тник, hunter
охо́тно, willingly
о́чень, very
о́чи (poet., sing. о́ко), eyes
очки́, glasses, spectacles
очну́ться, to awake, recover one's senses

Па́дать, упа́сть, to fall
па́лец (gen. па́льца), па́льчик (dim.), finger
па́лка, stick
пальто́ (indecl.), coat
па́мять (f.), memory
пансио́н, boarding-house
папиро́са, cigarette
па́ра, pair
Пари́ж, Paris
парк, park
парохо́д, steamer
па́рус, sail
пе́рвый, first, former
перево́д, translation; переводи́ть, -вести́, to translate
пе́ред (instr.), in front of, before; пере́дняя (noun), hall, entrance-hall

передумывать, -думать, to change one's mind

переезжать, -ехать, to remove (intrans.)

перекликаться, -кликнуться, to call to one another

перемирие, armistice, truce

переодеваться, -одеться, to change one's clothes

переписывать, -писать, to copy, transcribe; -ся, to correspond (exchange letters)

пересадка, change (railway journey)

пересаживать, -садить, to transplant, change the position of

переставать, -стать, to cease, stop (intr.)

переходить, перейти, to cross

перо, pen, feather

перчатки (sing. -ка), gloves

песня, song

петух, петушок, cock

петь, за-, to sing; пение, singing (noun)

печальный, sad; печаль (f.), sadness

печатать, на-, to print; печать (noun), seal; печатный, printed

печь (f.), stove

печь, с- (пеку, печёшь), to bake

пешком (adv.), on foot

писатель, -ница (f.), author, writer

писать, на-, to write

письмо, letter, writing

пить, вы-, to drink

питьё, drink

пища, food

плакать, за-, to weep, cry

план, plan

платить, за-, to pay

платок, handkerchief

платье, платьеце, dress, clothes

племя (n.), tribe, race

плечо (pl. плечи), shoulder

плохой, bad; плохо, badly, ill

площадь (f.), square, area; плоский, flat

по (dat.), according to, by, along

повторять, повторить, to repeat

погасать, погаснуть, to be extinguished

погибать, погибнуть, to perish

поговорка, saying (popular)

погода, weather

под (acc. or instr.), under, beneath

подарок, gift, present

подвал, cellar

подводить, -вести, to lead up to

поддерживать, to keep up

подле (gen.), beside, near

поднимать, -нять, to lift; -ся, to rise, ascend

подписчик, subscriber

подписывать, -писать, to sign; -ся, to sign one's name; -ся на + acc., subscribe to a paper

подпись (f.), signature

подруга, friend (f.), chum

подходить, подойти (к + dat.), to approach

подъезд, entrance

поезд, train; поездка, trip

пожалуйста, please

поживать, to "be", get on, fare

познания (pl.), information

позади, behind

позволять, позволить, to allow

поздний, late; поздно (adv.)

пока, while; пока не, till, until

поклон, bow, greeting

покрытый, covered

покупать, купить, to buy; покупатель, customer; покупка, purchase

пол, floor

полгода, half a year

полдень (m.), noon; по-полудни, p.m.

поле, field

ползать, to crawl; полати, p. 224

по́лка, shelf

по́лночь (f.), midnight; по-полу́ночи, a.m.

по́лный, full

полови́на, half

положи́ть (perf. of класть), to put down

полтора́, one and a half

получа́ть, получи́ть, to receive, obtain

по́льза, use, utility

по́мнить, за-, to remember

помога́ть, помо́чь, to help; по́мощь (f.), help; помо́щник (f. -ница), helper, assistant

по-мо́ему, in my opinion (cf. по-тво́ему, etc.)

понеде́льник, Monday

понима́ть, поня́ть, to understand; поня́тие, idea

по-но́вому, in the (modern) new way

поправля́ть, попра́вить, to correct, set right

пора́, time, season, fit time

портно́й (noun), tailor

поря́док, order, orderliness

поря́дочный, honest, respectable, considerable

посади́ть (imperf. сажа́ть), to put (sitting), plant

посеща́ть, посети́ть, to visit

по́сле (gen.), after; после-за́втра, the day after tomorrow

после́дний, last

посло́вица, proverb

послу́шный, obedient

посте́ль (f.), bed, bedding

постоя́нный, constant, continual; -но (adv.)

поступа́ть, поступи́ть, to act, behave

посыла́ть, посла́ть, to send, send away

потоло́к (gen. потолка́), ceiling

пото́м, then, thereupon, next

потому́ что, because

поутру́, in the morning

похвала́, хвала́, praise

походи́ть на (+acc.) (no perf.), to be like, resemble

похо́дка, gait

похуде́вший, grown thin

почему́, why

по́черк, handwriting

по́чта, post, post-office

почтальо́н, postman

почти́, almost, nearly

почти́тельный, respectful

поэ́т, poet

поэ́тому, therefore

пра́вда, truth

пра́вильный, correct, right, regular; -но (adv.)

пра́вый, right (hand)

пра́здник, holiday; пра́здничный (adj.); пра́здновать, to celebrate

предава́ть, преда́ть, to betray, give up

пре́данный, devoted

предлага́ть, предложи́ть, to offer, propose

представле́ние, performance, "show"

представля́ть, предста́вить, to present, introduce; представля́ться, to present oneself

пре́жде, (gen.) before, (adv.) formerly; пре́жний, former

прекра́сный (superl.), very beautiful

прибыва́ть, -бы́ть, to arrive

приве́тливый, welcoming, courteous; приве́т, greeting, welcome

приводи́ть, -вести́, to bring, lead

привози́ть, -везти́, to bring (in a vehicle)

привя́зывать, -вяза́ть, to tie to

привыка́ть, to get accustomed

привы́чка, habit

приглаша́ть, -гласи́ть, to invite (cf. го́лос, глас)

пригля́дываться, -де́ться, to look closely

приготовля́ть, -гото́вить, to prepare

придава́ть, прида́ть, to add, augment

придво́рный, courtier

приезжа́ть, -е́хать, to come, arrive (not on foot)

приёмная (noun), reception-room, drawing-room

призаду́мываться, -ду́маться, to become thoughtful

призыва́ть, -зва́ть, to call, summon

прика́з, order, ordinance

прика́зчик, assistant, steward

прика́зывать, -каза́ть, to order, summon

прикла́дываться, -ложи́ться, to lie down for a little

прили́чный, decent

приме́р, example

принадлежа́ть, to belong

принима́ть, приня́ть, to receive, accept; -ся, to start

приноси́ть, принести́, to bring

приобрета́ть, -брести́, to acquire (past, приобрёл)

приса́живаться, -се́сть, to sit down (for a short time)

при́смерти, at the point of death, dying

присыла́ть, присла́ть, to send (hither)

притворя́ться, -и́ться, to pretend

притра́гиваться, притро́нуться, to touch

прихо́д, прие́зд, arrival

приходи́ть, прийти́, to come, arrive

причёсывать, -чеса́ть, to comb, do one's hair

прия́тель, прия́тельница (f.), friend

прия́тный, pleasant; -но (adv.) (cf. принима́ть, p. 220)

про́ (acc.), about; про себя́, to oneself

провожа́ть, -води́ть, to escort, accompany, see off; проводи́ть вре́мя, провести́, to spend time

продава́ть, -да́ть, to sell

продаве́ц, -вщи́ца, salesman, saleswoman

продолжа́ть, -до́лжить, to prolong, continue

прое́зжий, passer-by (not on foot)

про́йденное, what has been gone through, learned

произноси́ть, -нести́, to pronounce

произноше́ние, pronunciation

пролива́ть, -ли́ть, to spill

пропуска́ть, -пусти́ть, to miss

проси́ть, по-, to ask, beg; про́сьба, request

просто́й, simple, common

просто́р, space, expanse

просту́живаться, -студи́ться, to catch cold

просыпа́ться, -сну́ться, to wake, awake (intrans.)

про́тив (gen.), opposite

проходи́ть, пройти́, to pass; проходи́ть ми́мо (gen.), to pass by

прохо́жий, passer-by (cf. прое́зжий)

проце́ссия, procession

прочёсть (perf.), alt. form of прочита́ть, to read

прочь (adv.), away, gone, begone!

проше́дший (adj.), past, bygone

про́шлое (noun), the past; про́шлый, past, last

проща́ть, прости́ть, to forgive; -ся, to take leave, say goodbye

проясни́ться (perf.), to clear up, brighten (intr.)

пря́мо (adv.), straight, direct

пря́тать, с-, to hide (tr.); -ся (intr.)

пти́ца, пти́чка (dim.), bird

пуга́ть, ис-, to frighten; -ся (gen.) (intr.), to get frightened

пуска́й, пусть, let (imper.)

пуска́ть, пусти́ть, to let (go); also вы-

путеше́ствие, journey; путеше́ствовать, по-, to travel

путь (m.), way, road

пье́са, play (theatrical)

пята́к, -чо́к, five-copeck coin

пя́тница, Friday

пять, five; пя́тый, fifth; пятиле́тка, five-year plan

Рабо́та, work

рабо́тать, по-, to work

рабо́тник, worker; рабо́чий, worker (member of working class); рабо́тница (f.)

ра́венство, equality; ра́вный, equal

равни́на, plain

равноду́шно, with equanimity; равноду́шный, indifferent

рад, -а, -ы (dat.), glad; ра́доваться (dat.), to be glad, rejoice

ра́дость (f.), joy; ра́достный, joyful

раз, time (occasion), once

разбива́ть, разби́ть, to break, smash

ра́зве, surely not?

развёртывать, разверну́ть, to unwrap

развя́зывать, -вяза́ть, to untie

разгля́дывать, разгляде́ть, to view, examine

разгова́ривать, to converse, hold a conversation

разгово́р, conversation

разгоня́ть, разогна́ть, to dispense (tr.)

раздева́ть, разде́ть, to take off, undress; -ся, to undress (intr.), take off one's things

разлу́ка, separation

разлуча́ть, -чи́ть, to separate, part (tr.); -ся (с + intr.)

ра́нить, to wound; ра́неный (adj. as noun), wounded (person)

ра́но, early

расска́з, story, narration; расска́зывать, -сказа́ть, to tell, narrate

расстава́ться, -ста́ться, to part (intr.)

расстро́енный, distraught; расстро́ить, put out of tune

расти́, вы́-, to grow; расте́ние, plant

расходи́ться, разойти́сь, to disperse; (с + intr.), part

расхо́ды, expenses

ребёнок (pl. реба́та, де́ти), child (see p. 241)

револю́ция, revolution

ре́дкий, rare, thin, sparse

ре́дко, seldom; ре́же (comp.), less often

ре́зать, по-, to cut (от-, "off")

резви́ться, to frolic, play

река́, river

рекомендова́ть, to recommend

респу́блика, republic

рестора́н, restaurant

реша́ть, реши́ть, to decide

ро́вный, even; ро́вно, just, exactly

род, kind, species, generation; роди́тели, parents

ро́дина, native country, land

родно́й, own, dear

рожда́ться, роди́ться, to be born

рожде́нье, birth; день рожде́нья, birthday

ро́за, rose; ро́зовый, pink

рома́н, novel

Росси́я, Russia

рост, stature, height (cf. расти́)

рот, mouth (gen. рта)

роя́ль (m.), piano (grand)

рубль (m.), rouble

ружьё, rifle

рука́, hand, arm; ру́чка (dim.), also handle

ру́сский, Russian; по-ру́сски (adv.), in Russian

рыба, рыбка, fish
рынок, market
ряд, row; рядом, side by side, next door

С (instr.), with; (gen.), off, out of
сад, garden; в саду, in the garden
садиться, сесть, to sit down
сажать, садить, посадить, to plant, put sitting
салфетка, serviette
сам, сама, сами (pl.), self
самовар, samovar
самый, same, very; в самом деле, indeed
сани (pl.), sledge
сахар, sugar
свежий, fresh
свет, light, world; светает, it dawns
светлеть, по-, to brighten, clear up (intr.); светлый, light (opp. dark)
свинья, pig
свист, whistle
свистеть, за-, свистнуть, to whistle
свобода, freedom, liberty; свободный, free
свой, -я, -ё, one's own
сгоряча, in a passion, in haste
сдаваться, сдаться, to give in, yield; сдача, change (money)
сдержанный, reserved, reticent
себя, self (reflexive), oneself
север, north; северный (adj.)
сегодня, to-day
седьмой, seventh
сейчас, presently; сей, сия, сие (old word), this
село, селенье, village
семейство, семья, family
семь, seven; семёрка, seven (cards)
сентябрь, September

сердиться, рас-, to be angry, become angry; сердитый, angry; сердце, heart
серебро, silver; серебрянный (adj.)
серый, grey
сестра, сестрица, sister
сесть (perf. of садиться), to sit down
сеять, по-, to sow
сзади, behind, from behind
сигара, cigar
сидеть, по-, to sit
сила, strength; сильный, strong; strongly, very
синий, blue
сирота, orphan (com. gen.)
сияние, radiance, gleam
сиять, to shine, gleam
сказать (perf.), to say; говорить (imperf.), to be saying; сказывать, to tell
сказка, tale, fairy-tale
скала, rock
скандал, scandal
скатерть (f.), table-cloth
сквозь (acc.), through
склонять, -нить, to incline, bend
сколько, how much, how many
скоро, soon, quickly; скорей (comp.), quickly; скорость, speed, quickness; скорый, quick
скрипка, violin
скучать, соскучиться, to be bored, lonely; скука, boredom, weariness; скучный, bored, lonely
слабый, weak
слава, glory; славный, glorious, renowned, charming, "nice"
сладкий, sweet
след, trace, track
следовать, по-, to follow; следующий, following, next
слеза, слёзы (pl.), tear
слепой, blind
слишком, too (much) (cf. лишний)

словарь (m.), dictionary
словно, as if, just as
слово, word
слуга (m.), servant; служанка, maid-servant
служба, service
служить, по-, to serve; служитель, servitor
случай, chance, occasion, opportunity; случайно, by chance
елучаться, случиться, to happen
слушать, по-, to listen to; слушатель, listener, student; -ли (pl.), audience; слух, hearing
слушаться, по-, to obey (cf. послушный)
слышать, у-, to hear
смелый, bold; -ло (adv.)
смеркается, it grows dark; dusk falls
смерть (f.), death
смешной, funny, laughable; смех, laughter
смеяться, за- or по-, to laugh
смотреть, по-, to look
смыкать, сомкнуть, to shut (one's eyes)
смысл, sense
снаружи, outside
сначала, at first, from the beginning
снег, snow; снежный (adj.)
снимать, снять, to take off
сниться, мне снится, снилось, to appear in a dream, I dream, dreamed
снова, again, anew
собирать, собрать, to collect, gather (tr.); -ся, to get ready, to gather; собрание, gathering, meeting, collection
Совет, advice, council, Soviet; советский (adj.), Soviet; советовать, по-, to advise
совсем, altogether, quite
солдат, soldier
солнце, солнышко, sun

соль (f.), salt
сомневаться, to doubt
сон, dream, sleep; видеть во сне, to dream
соображать, to ponder, consider
сорок, forty
сосна, pine-tree
составлять, -вить, to compose, constitute
состояние, state, condition
социализм, socialism; социалистический, socialist (adj.)
сочинение, composition, essay, works (writings)
союз, union
спасать, спасти, to save; (past perf. спас, -ла, see p. 210)
спасибо, thank you
спать, по-, to sleep; спальная. bedroom
сперва, at first
спереди (adv.), in front
спеть, по-, to mature, ripen
спешить, по-, to hurry; спешный, urgent
спички (sing. -ка), matches
спокойный, calm, quiet, restful; -но (adv.); покой, repose, quietude
справедливый, just
спрашивать, спросить, to ask, enquire
спускаться, спуститься, to descend, come down
спустя (adv.), later, afterwards, after the lapse; два дня спустя, two days later
сразу, at once
среда, Wednesday; средний, ·middle
среди (gen.), among
средство, means
ставить, по-, to put standing
стакан, glass, tumbler
становиться, стать, to stand up, become
станция, station
стареть, по-, to grow old; старый, old; старший, elder

старик, old man; старуха, old woman

старина, old times, antiquity; старинный, antique

стать, see становиться; стану used as auxiliary = буду

стена, wall

стихи (sing. стих), verse; стихотворение, poem

сто, hundred

стоить, to cost

стол, table

столетие, century

столовая (noun), dining-room

столько, so much; столь, so

стонать, за- or по-, to groan

сторона, side; страна, country

стоять, по-, to stand

страница, page

странный, strange

стрела, arrow

стриженный, short (hair); стричь, о-, to shear, cut (hair)

строгий, strict, severe

строить, по-, to build

студёный, cold

стул, chair

суббота, Saturday

судьба, fate

сукно, cloth

сума, сумка, bag

сумасшедший, mad, insane

суп, soup

сутки (pl.), twenty-four hours

сухой, dry

сходить, сойти, to come down; сходить (as perf.), to fetch

сфера, sphere

сцена, stage, scene

счесть (perf.), alternative form of сосчитать

счёт, account

считать, сосчитать, to count; -ся (instr.), to be considered

сын, son; сыновний (adj.)

сыр, cheese

сыскать (perf.), to seek out

сюда, here, hither

Табак, tobacco

так, thus, so; так как, as, since; так себе, "so-so"

также, also, in the same way

такой, such

там, there

тарелка, plate

таскать, to drag; тащить, по-, to be dragging

твой, -я, -ё, thy, thine

театр, theatre

телега, cart

телефон, telephone

тёмный, dark; темнеть, to grow dark

теннис, tennis

тень (f.), shadow

теперь, now

тёплый, warm

тетрадь (f.), copy-book, exercise-book

тётя, тётка, aunt

течение, current

тихий, quiet; тихонько, quietly; тишина, quietness, quiet, calm

то, that (pron., see тот); (conj.), then; то...то, now...now

товарищ, companion, comrade

тогда, then

тоже, also

толпа, crowd

толстый, thick, fat

только, only, just; только что, just, newly

тон, tone

тонкий, thin, fine

торговать, to trade; -ся, to bargain

тот, та, то, that; тем не менее, nevertheless

тотчас, immediately, at once

трамвай, tram, tramway

тратить, ис-, to spend

требовать, по-, to demand, ask

третий, third; третьего дня, the day before yesterday; три, three; тройка, troika тро́гать, тро́нуть, to touch, stir; -ся, to move; тро́гательный, touching

труба́, chimney, trumpet; тру́бный (adj.); тру́бка, pipe, tube

труд, labour, toil; тру́дный, difficult; труди́ться, to work, take-pains

туда́, there, thither

туз, ace

тума́н, mist

тупо́й, blunt

туноу́мный, dull

тут, here

ту́ча, thunder-cloud

тюрьма́, prison

тяжёлый, difficult, heavy

У (gen.), with, at

убира́ть, убра́ть, to take away, tidy

уважа́ть, to esteem, respect; уважа́емый, esteemed, respected

угожда́ть, угоди́ть, to please

у́гол (gen. угла́), corner, angle; уголо́к (dim.)

угро́за, threat

удало́й, daring, cold

ударе́ние, accent, stress

ударя́ть, -ить, to strike; уда́рник, "shock-brigader"

удо́бный, comfortable

удово́льствие, pleasure

уезжа́ть, уе́хать, to leave, go away

у́жас, terror; ужа́сный, terrible; ужаса́ть, ужасну́ть, to terrify

уже́, уж, already

у́жин, supper; у́жинать, по-, to sup, have supper

узёл (gen. узла́), узело́к, bundle, knot

узнава́ть, узна́ть, to recognise

ука́з, decree, "ukase"; ука́зывать, указа́ть, to point

укла́дывать(ся), уложи́ть(ся), to put away, pack

укра́дкой (adv.), stealthily; укра́сть (perf.), to steal

у́лица, street

улыба́ться, улыбну́ться, to smile; улы́бка, smile

ум, mind

уме́ть, суме́ть, to be able, know how

у́мный, clever, "good"; у́мница, clever person

умира́ть, умере́ть, to die

умыва́ться, умы́ться, to wash oneself

унижа́ть, уни́зить, to humiliate

уноси́ть, унести́, to take away

уны́лый, dejected

управи́тель, manager

упражне́ние, exercise

уро́к, lesson

уса́живаться, усе́сться, to take one's place

усе́рдный, zealous, ardent

услу́га, service, good turn

успева́ть, успе́ть, to succeed, be in time; успе́х, success; успе́шный, successful

успоко́ить, to calm, pacify

устава́ть, уста́ть, to get tired; уста́лый, tired

устра́ивать, устро́ить, to arrange, organise

утиха́ть, ути́хнуть, to quieten down

у́тро, morning; у́тренний (adj.)

у́хо (pl. у́ши), ear

уходи́ть, уйти́, to go away

уча́щийся, scholar, student

уче́бник, text-book

учени́к, -и́ца, pupil

учёный, sage, scientist

учи́тель, учи́тельница, teacher

учи́ть, вы́-, to learn; учи́ть, на-, to teach

учи́ться, вы́- or на-, to study

Фа́брика, factory

фами́лия, surname

февра́ль (m.), February

фи́рма, firm (noun)

Фра́нция, France; францу́зский, French

фру́кт, фру́кты, fruit

фунт, pound
фут, foot (measure)
футбол, football

Хата, hut, cottage
хвалить, по-, to praise
хитрый, cunning, sly
хлеб, bread, corn
ходить, по-, to go, walk
хозяин, host, master; хозяйка,
    hostess, mistress
холодный, cold
хороший, good; хорошо, well, all
    right; хорошенький, pretty
хотеть, за-, to wish, want; мне
    хочется, "I feel like", desire
хотя, хоть, although
храм, temple
хранить, со-, to keep, preserve

Царить, царствовать, to reign,
    rule; царь (m.), tsar; царица
    (f.); царство, realm, kingdom,
    reign
цвести, за-, to bloom, flower
цвет (pl. цвета), colour; цветок
    (pl. цветы), flower
целый (adj.), whole
цель, (f.), end, aim
цена, price; ценить, to value;
    ценный, costly, valuable
церковь (f.) (gen. -кви), church
цифра, цыфра, figure, cipher

Чай, tea; чайный (adj.); чай-
    ник, tea-pot, kettle; на чай,
    tip
чайка, sea-gull
час, hour; часы, clock, watch
часто, often; частый, frequent
часть (f.), part, fraction
чашка (gen. pl. чашек), cup
человек (pl. люди), man, person
чем, than
чемодан, trunk
через (acc.), over, across, in,
    after
чёрный, black; чернеть, по-, to
    appear black; чернила, ink

честный, honest; честное слово,
    indeed, truly (word of honour)
честь (f.), honour
четверг, Thursday
четвёртый, fourth; четверть
    (f.), quarter; четыре, four
число, date, number
чистый, clean, pure; чистить,
    по-, вы-, to clean
читать, про-, по-, to read;
    читатель, -ница (f.), reader
чтение (noun), reading
что, what, that
чтобы, that, in order that
что-нибудь, anything; что-то,
    something
чувство, feeling; чувствовать,
    по-, to feel
чужой, alien, strange, foreign,
    others
чулок (pl. чулки), stocking
чуткий, sensitive, understand-
    ing (of sense, tact)
чутьё, fine feeling, scent (dog's)
чуть (не), almost; чуть-чуть, a
    very little
чуять, по-, to scent, to hear;
    (fig.) to understand

Шаг, pace, step; езда шагом!
    drive slowly!
шапка, cap
шар, sphere, ball, globe
Швейцария, Switzerland
шествие, procession; шество-
    вать, to go (cf. путешество-
    вать)
шесть, six; шестой, sixth
шея, neck
шиллинг, shilling
ширина, breadth, width; широ-
    кий, broad, wide; шире
    (comp.)
шить, с-, to sew
шкап, шкаф, cupboard
школа, school; школьный (adj.);
    школьник, -ца, scholar
шкура, skin, hide
шляпа, hat

Шотла́ндия, Scotland; шотла́ндский (adj.)
шу́ба, fur coat
шум, noise; шу́мный, noisy; шуме́ть, за-, to make a noise

Ще́дрый, generous
щека́ ·(gen. щеки́, pl. щёки), cheek
щи (pl.), cabbage soup

Эдинбу́рг, Edinburgh
экипа́ж, carriage
экску́рсия, excursion
эта́ж, storey, flat
э́тот, э́та, э́то. this

Юг, south; ю́жный (adj.)
ю́ноша, youth; ю́ность (f.), youth
ю́ный, youthful

Я, I
я́блоко (pl. -ки), apple
я́года, berry
язы́к, language, tongue
яйцо́ (pl. я́йца), egg
ямщи́к, driver, coachman
янва́рь (m.), January
я́ркий, bright
я́сный, clear; я́сно (adv.)
я́щик, box; почто́вый я́щик, letter box

ENGLISH-RUSSIAN VOCABULARY

Able, to be, мочь, с- (§ 167); (to
know how), уме́ть, суме́ть
(1st conj.)

about, о, об, о́бо (prep.); про
(acc.); о́коло (gen.)

above, над (instr.)

abroad, (жить) за-грани́цей,
(е́хать) за-грани́цу (§ 203)

accent (pronunciation), акце́нт;
(stress), ударе́ние

accept, принима́ть, -ня́ть (§293)

accompany, провожа́ть, -во-
ди́ть (§ 43)

according to, по (dat.)

account, счёт

accurately, аккура́тно

ace, туз

ache, боле́ть

acquaintance, знако́мый

acquire, приобрета́ть, -обрести́
(-брету́, -тёшь)

across, че́рез (acc.)

act (behave), поступа́ть, -пи́ть
(-плю́, -пишь)

action, де́йствие

active, де́ятельный

address, а́дрес

admire, любова́ться, по-, за-
(instr.) (§ 176)

advice, сове́т; **to advise,** сове́-
товать, по- (§ 176)

aeroplane, аэропла́н, самолёт

affair, де́ло

after, по́сле (gen.), че́рез (acc.);
a week after, спустя́ неде́лю;
afterwards, впосле́дствии

again, опя́ть; (anew), сно́ва

ago, тому́ наза́д; **long ago,** давно́

agree, соглаша́ться, -си́ться
(cf. го́лос)

aim, цель (f.)

alarum-clock, буди́льник

alien, чужо́й

alike, одина́ковый

all, весь, вся, всё, все (pl.)

allow, позволя́ть, -во́лить

almost, почти́, чуть не (§ 254)

alone, оди́н, одна́, -но, -ни

along, по (dat.), вдоль (gen.)

already, уже́

also, -же, то́же, та́кже; и (§ 21)

although, хотя́, хоть

altogether, совсе́м

always, всегда́

amiable, любе́зный

among, меж (gen.), среди́ (gen.)

amusement, развлече́ние

and, и, а, да

anew, сно́ва

angry, to be, серди́ться, рас-
(§§ 43, 119)

animal, живо́тное; (wild), зверь
(m.)

anniversary, годовщи́на

answer, отве́т; **to answer,** отве-
ча́ть, -ве́тить (§ 60), — a
question, — на вопро́с

any, вся́кий, любо́й

anybody, anyone, кто-нибудь;
anything, что-нибудь; **in any
case,** всётаки

apologise, извиня́ться, -ни́ться

appear, каза́ться, по- (p. 232);
appearance, вид

appetite, аппети́т

apple, я́блоко (pl. -и)

approach, подходи́ть, подойти́
(к + dat.)

April, апре́ль (m.)

ardent, усе́рдный

area, пло́щадь (f.)

arm, рука́; **arm-chair,** кре́сло,
кре́слице

arrange, устра́ивать, устро́ить

arrive, приходи́ть, приезжа́ть
(§ 157); прибыва́ть, -бы́ть;
arrival, прихо́д, прие́зд, при-
бы́тие (of a train)

arrow, стрела

as, как, так как; **as if,** будто, словно

ascend, восходить, взойти

aside, встороне

ask (enquire), спрашивать, спросить (§ 152); (request), просить, по-

aspect (of verb), вид

assistant, помощник, -ница (f.); (shop-), приказчик, -ца

at, у (gen.), в (prep.), на (prep.)

attain, достигать, достигнуть (past: достиг, -гла) (gen.)

attention, внимание; **to pay attention,** обращатьвнимание (на+acc.), обратить

attentive, внимательный (adv. -но)

audience, слушатели

August, август

aunt, тётя, тётка

author, автор, писатель

autumn, осень (f.), осенний (adj.)

avoid, обходить, обойти

awake (intr.), просыпаться, проснуться

away, begone! прочь

Baby, малютка, младенец

back (adj.), задний; (adv.), назад; **at the back,** назади

bad, плохой; **-ly,** плохо

bag, сума, сумка

bake, печь, с- (§ 167)

ball, мяч; (dance), бал

bank (shore), берег (p. 240); (money), банк

bark, лаять, за- (лает)

bath, ванна; **bathroom,** ванная

bazaar, базар

be, быть; (usually), бывать, по-

bear, медведь (m.)

beard, борода

beast, зверь (m.)

beautiful, красивый, прекрасный; **beauty** (belle), красавица

because, потому что

become, становиться, стать (§ 208)

bed, постель (f.); **bedstead,** кровать (f.); **bedroom,** спальня

before (in front of), перед (instr.); (formerly), прежде (gen.)

beg, просить, по-; **for alms,** просить милостыню

beggar, нищий

begin, начинать, начать (начну, -ёшь); **beginning,** начало; **from the beginning,** сначала

behave, поступать, -ступить (p. 18); вести себя (§ 82)

behind (prep.), за (instr.), позади (gen.); **from behind** (prep.), из-за (gen.); (adv.), сзади

believe, верить, по- (dat.); **I cannot believe,** мне не верится (§ 200); **belief,** вера

bell, звонок

belong, принадлежать (2nd conj.)

bench, лавка

beneath (prep.), под (acc. and instr.); **from beneath,** из-под (gen.)

berry, ягода

beside, возле, подле (gen.)

besides, кроме (gen.)

better, лучше

between, между (instr.)

big, большой; **bigger,** больше

bird, птица, птичка (dim.)

birth, рожденье; **birthday,** день (m.) рожденья

bite, кусать, укусить, от-; (noun), кусок (gen. куска)

bitter, горький

black, чёрный; **to appear black,** чернеть (§ 119)

blind, слепой

blood, кровь (f.)

bloom, цвести, за- (цветёт)

blow (verb), дуть, по-

blue, синий; (sky-blue), голубой

blush, краснéть, по- (§ 119)

board, доскá

boarding-house, пансиóн

boat, лóдка

bold, смéлый

book, кнúга; кнúжный (adj.)

bored, скýчный; to be bored, скучáть; boredom, скýка; I am bored, мне скýчно

born, to be, рождáться, родúться (§ 114)

both, óба; both...and, и...и

bow, greet, клáняться, поклонúться; (noun), поклóн

box, ящик

boy, мáльчик

bread, хлеб

breadth, ширинá

break, ломáть, с-, разбивáть, -бúть (разобью)

breakfast, зáвтрак; to have breakfast, зáвтракать, по-

breast, грудь (f.)

breathe, дышáть

breeze, вéтер

bride, невéста; bridegroom, женúх

bright, яркий, свéтлый

brighten, свéтлеть, по-

brilliant, блестящий

bring, приносúть, -нести; (convey), привозúть, -везтú; (lead), приводúть, -вестú (§ 162)

broad, ширóкий

brother, брат (pl. брáтья)

build, стрóить, по-; building (noun), здáние, пострóйка

bull, бык, вол

bundle, ýзел (gen. узлá)

burn, горéть (intr.), с- (2nd conj.); жечь (tr., cf. kindle)

business, дéло

busy, зáнятый, я зáнят, -á

but, но, -же, а; крóме (gen.)

butter, мáсло

buy, покупáть, купúть (p. 18)

by (past), мúмо (gen.); by-gone, прошéдший, прóшлый

Café, кофéйня

call, звать (зовý, -ёшь), по-; (name), называть, -звать; (summon), призывáть; call back, вернýть

calm, спокóйный

cap, шáпка

card, кáрта; visiting card, кáрточка

care (worry), забóта; to take care, забóтиться, по- (забóчусь, -тишься)

careful, осторóжный

caress, ласкáть, при-; caressing (adj.), лáсковый

carpet, ковёр (gen. коврá)

carriage, карéта, экипáж; (railway), вагóн

carry, носúть, нестú; (convey), возúть, везтú (§ 82)

cart, воз (p. 224), телéга

cat, кóшка, кот; kitten, котёнок (gen. -нка; pl. котята)

catch, ловúть, perf. поймáть

Caucasus, Кавкáз

cease, переставáть, -стать (стáну)

ceiling, потолóк

celebrate, прáздновать (-ную, -нуешь)

cellar, подвáл

century, век, столéтие

certainly, конéчно; for certain, навéрно; a certain, нéкий, нéкоторый, одúн

chair, стул; arm-chair, крéсло

chance, слýчай; by chance, случáйно

change, exchange, менять (perf. переменúть); change one's clothes, переодевáться (§ 138); change one's mind, передýмывать, -дýмать; change on a railway journey, пересáдка (noun); change (money), сдáча; (small), мéлочь (f.)

chat, бесéдовать, по- (-дую, -дуешь); (noun) бесéда

chatter, болтáть, по-cheap, дешёвый; (adv.) дёшево

cheek, щека (gen. -и; pl. щёки)

cheese, сыр

chemist's (shop), аптека

chest (breast), грудь (f.)

child, дитя, ребёнок; children's, детский; childhood, детство

chimney, труба

chin, подбородок, -дка.

choose, выбирать, выбрать (p. 143); choice, выбор; chosen, избранный

church, церковь (f.), церкви

cigar, сигара

cigarette, папироса

cinema, кино, синематограф

circle, круг

class, класс

claw, коготь (m.), когтя (pl. когти)

clean, чистый; (verb) чистить (чищу, -стишь); вы-; clean-shaven, выбритый

clear, ясный; to clear up, проясниться, светлеть (1st conj.)

clever, умный; clever person, умница

climate, климат

clock, часы (pl.); alarum-clock, будильник

close, закрывать, -крыть (§ 138); closed, закрытый

cloth, сукно, материя; table-cloth, скатерть (f.)

clothes, clothing, одежда, платье

cloud, облако; thunder-cloud, туча

club, клуб

coarse (large), крупный (§ 194); (rough), грубый

coat, пальто; fur —, шуба

cock, петух

coffee. кофе

coin, монета

cold, холодный (студёный); to catch cold, простудиться (§ 43)

collect, собирать(ся), -брать(ся) (§ 252); collection, собрание; collected works, сочинения

colour, цвет, (pl. цвета)

come, приходить, приезжать; be coming, идти; come in, входить (§ 159)

comfortable, удобный, уютный

common, general, общий; generally, вообще; community (society), общество

companion, comrade, товарищ

compel, cause to do, заставлять, -ставить (-влю, -вишь)

concert, концерт

condition, состояние, условие (terms)

consequently, вследствие этого, следовательно (cf. следовать)

considerably, порядочно

considered, to be, считаться (instr.)

constitute, compose, составлять

content, довольный (-лен, -льна)

continually, постоянно; всё (§ 229)

continue, продолжать, продолжить

contrary, on the, напротив

converse, разговаривать, беседовать (-дую); conversation, разговор, беседа (talk)

convey, возить, везти (§ 82)

copeck, копейка

copy, переписывать, -писать

copy-book, тетрадь (f.)

corn, хлеб; corn-ear, колос (pl. колосья)

corner, угол (gen. угла) (p. 238)

correct, поправлять, -вить (p. 18); (adj.) правильный (cf. правило, rule)

correspond, переписываться

Cossack, казак

cost, стоить; costly, ценный

costume, костюм

couch, диван, софа

council, совéт

count, считáть, со-; счесть (§ 153); account, счёт

country, странá; (native land), рóдина

course, of—, конéчно

court, двор; courtier, придвóрный

cover, покрывáть, -крыть (§ 138); covered, покрытый

cow, корóва

crawl, пóлзать, ползти (p. 224)

cross, переходить, перейти

crowd, толпá

cry (weep), плáкать (плáчу, -ешь), по-, за- (burst out crying)

cunning, хитрый

cup, чáшка (gen. pl. чáшек)

cupboard, шкаф (loc. в—ý)

current, течéние

customer, покупáтель, -ница

cut, рéзать, по-; cut off, отрезáть, отрéзать (p. 207); cut the hair, стричь вóлосы, о- (§167)

Dark, тёмный; it grows dark, темнéет

darling, дýшечка, дýшенька

date, числó

daughter, дочь, дóчка (dim.)

dawns, it, светáет

day, день (m.); one of these days, the other day, на-днях; daily, (adj.) ежеднéвный, (adv.) -о

deaf, глухóй

dear, дорогóй, милый (sweet), роднóй (own)

death, смерть (f.); at the point of death, присмерти

debt, долг (§ 107)

December, декáбрь (m.)

decent, приличный, порядочный

decide, решáть, -шить

deep, глубóкий

deliver, доставлять, -вить (p. 18)

depart, отходить, отъезжáть; departure, отхóд, отъéзд (§ 158)

deprive, лишáть, лишить

depth, глубинá

descend, сходить, сойти (с +gen.), спускáться, -ститься (-пущýсь, -пýстишься)

desire, желáть, по-; (feel like), мне хóчется (§ 200) (impers.); (noun) желáние

devoted, прéданный

dictionary, словáрь (m.)

die, умирáть, умерéть (p. 221)

difficult, трýдный (cf. труд)

dig, копáть, вы-

dine, обéдать, по-; dinner, обéд; dining-room, столóвая

direct, прямо (adv.)

disappear, исчезáть, исчéзнуть

disorder, беспорядок

disperse (tr.), разгонять, разогнáть (p. 224); (intr.), расходиться (§ 157)

distant, дáльний; distance, даль (f.), расстояние; from a distance, издали

distinguish, отличáть, -чить

Dnieper, Днепр

do, дéлать, с-; do without, обходиться, обойтись (§ 157)

doctor, дóктор

domestic, домáшний (also home-made)

door, дверь (f.)

double, вдвóе

doubt, сомневáться (§ 176)

down, downstairs, вниз, внизý (§ 214)

dozen, дюжина

drag, таскáть, потащить; волочить, поволóчь (§ 167)

drawing-room, гостиная, приёмная

dream, сон, мечтá; to dream, видеть во сне; сниться, при-; I dreamed, мне снилось (§ 200)

dress, плáтье; to dress, одевáть(ся), -дéть(ся) (§ 138)

drink, пить, вы- (§ 64); (noun) питьё; to give to drink, напоить (perf.)

drive, éздить, etc. (§ 79)

dry, сухо́й

dull, ску́чный; I feel dull, мне ску́чно

dusk falls, смерка́ется (past perf.: сме́рклось) (§ 200)

duty, долг; it is my duty, я до́лжен, -жна́

Each, ка́ждый; each other, друг дру́га (§ 235)

eagle, орёл (gen. орла́)

ear, у́хо (pl. у́ши)

early, ра́но, ра́нний (adj.)

earn, зарабо́тать (imperf. зараба́тывать)

earth, земля́

east, восто́к, восто́чный (adj.)

easy, лёгкий, легко́ (adv.)

eat, ку́шать, есть (§ 68)

edge, край

Edinburgh, Эдинбу́рг

educate, обуча́ть, -чи́ть; education, образова́ние; educated, образо́ванный

egg, яйцо́; soft-boiled egg, яйцо́ всмя́тку; hard-boiled egg, круто́е яйцо́

eight, во́семь; eighth, восьмо́й

embrace, обнима́ть (§ 293)

empty (to), выкла́дывать (§ 220)

end, коне́ц (gen. конца́); (aim), цель (f.); to end, конча́ть(ся), ко́нчить(ся)

England, А́нглия; English, англи́йский; in English, по-англи́йски; Englishman, англича́нин; Englishwoman, англича́нка

enough, дово́льно, бу́дет

enter, входи́ть, войти́; entrance, entry, вход, въезд, подъе́зд (§ 159)

envelope, конве́рт

equal, ра́вный; equality, ра́венство

essay, сочине́ние

essential(s) (noun), необходи́мое

esteem, уважа́ть; esteemed, уважа́емый

eternal, ве́чный (cf. век)

Europe, Евро́па; European, европе́йскай

even, ро́вный

evening, ве́чер; good evening, до́брый ве́чер; on the eve, накану́не (pl. вечера́)

ever, когда́-нибудь; for ever, навсегда́

every, ка́ждый, вся́кий; everyone, все; everything, всё; everywhere, везде́

exactly, ро́вно

examine, огля́дывать, разгля́дывать, -гляде́ть (§ 43), рассма́тривать, -смотре́ть (2nd conj.)

example, приме́р; for example, наприме́р

excellent, отли́чный, -о (adv.)

exchange, меня́ть, перемени́ть (-меню́, -ме́нишь)

excursion, экску́рсия

excuse, извиня́ть, -ни́ть

execute, исполня́ть, -по́лнить

exercise, упражне́ние

exhibit, выставля́ть, вы́ставить (p. 18); exhibition, вы́ставка

exit, вы́ход

expense, расхо́д; expensive, дорого́й

experienced, о́пытный, быва́лый; experience, о́пыт

explain, объясня́ть, -ни́ть

extra, ли́шний

extreme, кра́йний

eye, глаз, -а́ (pl.); eye-brows, бро́ви (sing. -ь, f.)

Face, лицо́, лично́й (adj.)

factory, фа́брика, фабри́чный (adj.)

fail, without —, непреме́нно

fall, па́дать, упа́сть (-паду́, -ёшь)

familiar, знако́мый

family, семья́, семе́йство

famous, изве́стный

far, далёкий (adj.), далеко (adv.); **not far**, недалеко
fashion, мода
fast (strong), крепкий
fate, судьба
father, отец (gen. отца)
fault (guilt), вина; (shortcoming), недостаток
favour, милость (f.)
favourite, любимый
fear, бояться (gen.), боюсь, бойшься
February, февраль (m.)
feed, кормить, на-, питать, на- (cf. пища)
feel, чувствовать, по- (-вую); **I feel like**, мне хочется; **feeling** (noun), чувство
fetch, сходить, съездить (за +instr.) (perf.)
few, мало (+gen. pl.) немногие; **a few**, несколько
field, поле
fill, наполнять, -полнить (instr.), наливать, -лить (p. 207) (liquid); накладывать, -ложить
find, находить, найти; **find at home, in, at, etc.**, заставать, -стать (стану)
fine (small), мелкий (§ 194); (thin), тонкий; (weather), хороший
finger, палец (gen. пальца), пальчик (dim.)
finish, кончать, кончить; **finished**, конченный
fir, ель (f.)
fire, огонь (gen. огня)
firm (noun), фирма; (adj.), крепкий, твёрдый
first, первый; **at first**, сперва; **for the first time**, впервые
fish, рыба
five, пять; **fifth**, пятый; **five-year plan**, пятилетка
flag, знамя (§ 197)
flat (quarters), квартира; (storey), этаж

floor, пол; **on the floor**, на полу
flower, цветок (pl. цветы)
fly, летать; **to be flying**, лететь (§ 89)
follow, следовать, по- (-дую); **following** (next), следующий
food, пища
fool, дурак (f. дура); **foolish**, глупый
foot (leg), нога; **on foot**, пешком; **football**, футбол; **foot** (measure), фут
for (sake of), для (gen.); (in exchange for), за (acc.); (after), за (instr.); (because), потому что; (time, etc.), на (acc.)
forbid, воспрещать, -претить (-прещу, -тишь)
force, cause to do, заставлять, -вить (-влю, -вишь)
foreign, иностранный, чужой; **foreigner**, иностранец (f. -нка)
forest, лес; лесной (adj.)
forget, забывать, -быть (забуду)
forgive, прощать, -стить (p. 18)
fork, вилка
former, бывший, прежний, первый (opp. of "latter"); **formerly**, прежде
forty, сорок
forward (adv.), вперёд
four, четыре, четверо (§ 266); **fourth**, четвёртый
fox, лиса, лисица
France, Франция; **French**, французский
free (verb), освобождать, -бодить; **to be free**, -ся; **свободный** (adj.); **freedom**, свобода, воля
fresh, свежий
Friday, пятница
friend, друг (pl. друзья, друзей); приятель, -ница; подруга (f., "chum")
frighten, пугать, ис-; **be frightened**, -ся (gen.)

from (a person), от (gen.); (out of), из (gen.)

front, in (adv.), впереди, спе́реди; in front of, пе́ред (instr.)

frontier, грани́ца

frost, моро́з, моро́зный (adj.)

fruit, фру́кт(ы) (pl.)

full, по́лный; full of, по́лон, полна́ (gen.); in full, fully, вполне́

funny, смешно́й

fur, мех; fur coat, шу́ба

furniture, ме́бель (f.)

future (adj.), бу́дущий; (noun), бу́дущее

Garden, сад; in the garden, в саду́

gather, собира́ть (tr.), -бра́ть (p. 143); собира́ться (intr.); gathering (meeting), собра́ние

generous, ще́дрый

gentleman, господи́н (pl. госпо́да)

Germany, Герма́ния; German (adj.), герма́нский, неме́цкий; in German, по-неме́цки; a German, не́мец (f. не́мка)

get ready, собира́ться (§ 252); get up, встава́ть, -ста́ть (вста́ну); get on (fare), пожива́ть (§ 136)

girl, де́вушка, деви́ца; little girl, де́вочка

give, дава́ть (perf. дать) (§ 138); give in (yield), сдава́ться; give up (betray), предава́ть; gift, дар, пода́рок

glad, рад, -а, -ы; to be glad, ра́доваться (dat.)

glance, взгля́дывать, взгляну́ть; (noun) взгляд, взор

Glasgow, Гла́зго

glass, стекло́; (drinking), стака́н; glasses (spectacles), очки́

gloomy, мра́чный

gloves, перча́тки (sing. -ка)

go, ходи́ть; be going, идти́; (not on foot), е́здить, е́хать; (for pleasure), ката́ться (§ 175); go away, уходи́ть, уезжа́ть; go out, выходи́ть (§§ 157, 158)

goat, козёл (gen. козла́; f. коза́)

gold, зо́лото; golden, золото́й

goloshes, кало́ши

good, хоро́ший; good-bye, проща́й, -те; до-свида́ния; to say good-bye, проща́ться (§ 116)

goose, гусь (m.)

governess, гуверна́нтка

grammar, грамма́тика

granddaughter, вну́чка; grandfather, дед, де́душка; grandmother, ба́бушка; grandson, внук

grapes, виногра́д

gratis, да́ром (see дар)

grave, моги́ла

great, вели́кий (super. -ча́йший)

green, зелёный

greet, здоро́ваться, по-; кла́няться, поклони́ться; greeting, покло́н

grey, се́рый

grief, го́ре; grieve, огорча́ть, -чи́ть

groan, стона́ть, за-

group, гру́ппа

grow, расти́ (расту́); (past: рос, росла́) вы́-

guest, гость (m.), го́стья (f.)

guilt, вина́; guilty, винова́тый

Hair, во́лос(ы) (p. 239); to do one's hair, причёсываться, причеса́ться (p. 207); short-haired, стри́женный

half, полови́на; one and a half, полтора́; half a year, полго́да; half a pound, полфу́нта

hall, зал (public), пере́дняя (entrance)

hand, рука́; handle, ру́чка

handkerchief, плато́к (gen. -тка́)

handwriting, по́черк

hang, ве́шать, пове́сить (tr.);
висе́ть (2nd conj.) (intr.);
hanging, вися́чий

happen, случа́ться, случи́ться
(cf. слу́чай)

hardly, е́ле-е́ле, вря́д ли

harm, вреди́ть, по- (§ 43);
harmful, вре́дный

hasten, спеши́ть, по-

hat, шля́па

hate, ненави́деть, воз-

have, име́ть; I have, у меня́ (есть)

he, он

head, голова́, глава́ (old word);
гла́вный (cf. principal)

health, здоро́вье; healthy, здо-
ро́вый

hear, слы́шать, у- (2nd conj.);
hearing, слух

heart, се́рдце; by heart, наи-
зу́сть

heavy, тяжёлый

height, высота́; (stature), рост

help (verb), помога́ть, помо́чь
(§ 167); (noun), по́мощь (f.);
helper, помо́щник (f. -ца)

hen, ку́рица

hence, отсю́да

her, hers, её

here, здесь, тут; here is, вот

hesitate, колеба́ться, по-

hide, пря́тать(ся), с- (пря́чу,
-ешь)

high, высо́кий

him, his, его́

hind (adj.), за́дний

hither, сюда́

hold, держа́ть, по- (2nd conj.)

holiday, пра́здник, пра́здничный (adj.)

home, дом; at home, до́ма;
homewards, домо́й

honour, честь; honest, че́стный,
поря́дочный

hope (verb), наде́яться (-де́юсь,
-де́ешься); (noun), наде́жда

horse, ло́шадь (f.); конь (m.);
horseman, вса́дник; on horseback, верхо́м

hospital, больни́ца

host, хозя́ин; hostess, хозя́йка

hot, горя́чий, жа́ркий (intangible)

hour, час; 24 hours, су́тки (pl.)

house, дом (pl. дома́)

how, как; how many, much,
ско́лько; how-do-you-do?
здра́вствуйте; how are you?
как пожива́ете?

howl, выть, за- (во́ю, -ешь)

humiliate, унижа́ть, уни́зить

humour, нрав, настрое́ние

hundred, сто

hunt, охо́титься (p. 17); hunter,
охо́тник

hurry, спеши́ть, по-; I am in a
hurry, я спешу́

husband, муж

hut, изба́, ха́та

I, я

if, е́сли, ко́ли (colloq.)

ill (adj.), больно́й; illness, бо-
ле́знь (f.); to be ill, боле́ть,
за- (1st conj.)

image, о́браз; imagine, воображать, -брази́ть (p. 17);
imagination, воображе́ние

immediately, сейча́с-же, то́тчас-
же

important, ва́жный

impossible, it is, нельзя́

in, в (acc. and prep.); (after,
time), че́рез (acc.)

indeed, в са́мом де́ле

indifferent, равноду́шный

inexpensive, недорого́й

injure, вреди́ть, по- (§ 43)

ink, черни́ла (pl.)

insert, вставля́ть, -вить (p. 18)

inside (adv.), внутри́

instead of, вме́сто (gen.)

insult, оскорбля́ть, -би́ть (p. 18);
(noun) оскорбле́ние

interest (verb), интересова́ть,
за- (-сую); be interested, -ся;
interesting, интере́сный

into, в (acc.)

introduce (people), знакóмить,
по-; представля́ть, -вить (p.
18)

invention, изобретéние

invite, приглаша́ть, -гласи́ть
(cf. гóлос, глас (old word))

iron, желéзо, желéзный (adj.)

is, there is, есть (§ 38)

island, óстров

it, онó (он, она́)

January, янва́рь (m.)

journey, путешéствие

joy, ра́дость (f.); joyful, ра́дост-
ный

judge (verb), суди́ть, рас-;
judgment (mind), рассу́док;
judge (n.), судья́ (m.); суд
(cf. trial, court)

July, ию́ль (m.)

June, ию́нь (m.)

junior, мла́дший

just (only), тóлько; (newly),
тóлько что; (exactly), как
ра́з; (adj.), справедли́вый

Keep (hold), держа́ть, по- (2nd
conj.); (protect), храни́ть,
со-

key, ключ

Kharkov, Ха́рьков

kill, убива́ть, уби́ть (p. 207)

kind, дóбрый, любéзный; kindness, доброта́

kind (species), род; kinsman,
рóдственник (f. -ница)

kindle, зажига́ть, -жéчь, -жгу́,
-жжёшь

kitten, котёнок (see cat)

knee, колéно (pl. колéни)

knife, нож

knit, tie, вяза́ть, по-, за- (p. 207)

knock, стуча́ть, по- (2nd conj.)

knot, у́зел (узла́)

know, знать, у-; know how,
умéть, с- (1st conj.); well-
known, извéстный; you know,
ведь (adv.) (p. 263); knowledge, зна́ние

Labour, труд

lack, недостава́ть; I lack, мне
недостаёт (gen.)

ladder, лéстница

lady, да́ма

lag behind, отстава́ть, -ста́ть
(-ста́ну)

lamp, ла́мпа

land, земля́

language, язы́к

large, большóй; (coarse, of large
size), кру́пный

last, послéдний; (past), прóшлый; at last, наконéц; to last,
продолжа́ться (see prolong)

late (adj.), пóздний; (adv.),
пóздно; an hour later, час
спустя́

laugh, смея́ться, за- (§ 120);
laughter, смех; laughable,
смешнóй

lay, класть (perf. положи́ть)
(§ 206); to lay on, накла́ды-
вать (§ 220); to lay eggs,
нести́ яйца or нести́сь

lazy, лени́вый; laziness, лень
(f.); to be lazy, лени́ться

lead, води́ть; be leading, вéсти;
(bring a person), приводи́ть,
привести́ (§ 82)

leaf, лист (pl. ли́стья, -тьев)

learn, учи́ть, вы́-; изуча́ть,
-чить (tr.); learn by heart,
учи́ть наизу́сть; (to get to
know), узна́ть

least, at, по крайней мере

leave, оставля́ть, -та́вить; (go
away), уходи́ть, уезжа́ть
(§ 157); to take leave, про-
ща́ться, -сти́ться (p. 18)

lecture, лéкция

left, лéвый; on the left, налéво

leg, нога́

Leningrad, Ленингра́д

less, мéнее, мéньше

lesson, урóк

let go, пуска́ть, -сти́ть (p. 18);
(imp.) пусть; to let out,
выпуска́ть, -пустить

letter (alphabet), бу́ква; epistle, письмо́

liberty, во́ля, свобо́да

library, библио́тека

lie, лежа́ть, по- (2nd conj.); lie down, ложи́ться (perf. лечь) (§ 209); — for a little, приле́чь (p. 227)

lie (falsehood), ложь (f.); (verb) лгать, лгу, лжёшь

life, жизнь (f.); mode of life, житьё; lifetime, век

lift, поднима́ть, -ня́ть (§ 293)

light (noun), свет; (adj., bright), све́тлый; to give light, све́тить, по-; (weight), лёгкий; (verb, tr.), зажига́ть, -же́чь (-жгу́, -жжёшь)

light (a cigarette), заку́ривать, -кури́ть

like, love, люби́ть, по-; I like, мне нра́вится (§ 117); to be like, походи́ть (на + асc.)

like (same), одина́ковый

line, ли́ния

listen (to), слу́шать, по-

little, (adj.) ма́ленький; (adv.), ма́ло; a little, немно́го; a very little, чуть-чуть; little by little, ма́ло-по-ма́лу

live, жить (§ 64); living, живо́й; alive, жив-а́

lodgings, кварти́ра (sing.)

London, Ло́ндон

lonely, одино́кий; to be lonely, скуча́ть

long, дли́нный, до́лгий; (adv. time), до́лго; for long, надо́лго

look, смотре́ть, по- (2nd conj.), гляде́ть, по- (2nd conj.); (appear), вы́глядеть; look back, round, огля́дываться, огляну́ться; look out, выгля́дывать, вы́глянуть; look closely, разгля́дывать, -де́ть; look (noun), взор

lose, теря́ть, по-, лиша́ться, -ши́ться (gen.); to be lost, потеря́ться

loud, гро́мкий

love (verb), люби́ть, по-; (noun), любо́вь (f.)

low, ни́зкий

lunch, за́втрак; to have lunch, за́втракать, по-

Machine, маши́на, маши́нка

mad, сумасше́дший, безу́мный

magazine, журна́л

maid (servant), служа́нка; maiden, деви́ца, де́вушка

make, де́лать, с-

man (person), челове́к; (male), мужчи́на

manager, управи́тель

many, мно́го; мно́гие (adj.) (§ 250); how many, ско́лько

March, март

market, ры́нок

marry, (of a man) жени́ться; (of a woman) выходи́ть за́муж, вы́йти —; to be married, быть за́мужем

master, хозя́ин, господи́н (pl. -да́)

matches, спи́чки (sing. спи́чка)

matter, де́ло; what is the matter? в чём де́ло?

mature, ripen, зреть, со-, спеть, по-

May, май

me, меня́; to me, мне

meadow, луг (pl. -а́)

mean, зна́чить; what does it mean, что зна́чит

means, сре́дство

meat, мя́со

meet, встреча́ть(ся) (§ 137); to go to meet, идти́ навстре́чу; meeting, собра́ние, заседа́ние

memory, па́мять (f.)

merchant, купе́ц (gen. купца́)

merry, весёлый; to be merry, весели́ться

metre, метр

middle (adj.), сре́дний; in the middle, в середи́не, среди́ (gen.)

midnight, по́лночь (f.)

mile, ми́ля

milk, молоко́

mill, заво́д; заво́дский (adj.) (cf. фа́брика)

million, миллио́н

mind, ум; **frame of mind**, настрое́ние

minute, мину́та, мину́тка; **in a minute**, сию́ мину́ту

miss, пропуска́ть, -пусти́ть (p. 18); **I miss**, мне недостаёт (gen.) (see недостава́ть)

mist, тума́н

mistress, хозя́йка, госпожа́

modern, совреме́нный; **in the modern way**, по-но́вому

Monday, понеде́льник

money, де́ньги (pl.); gen. де́нег

month, ме́сяц; **monthly**, ежеме́сячный

moon, луна́, ме́сяц (poet.)

more, бо́льше, ещё; **no more**, бо́льше не + verb

morning, у́тро; у́тренний (adj.); **in the morning**, у́тром, поутру́

Moscow, Москва́

mother, мать (p. 237), ма́ма

motor-car, автомоби́ль (m.)

mountain, гора́

mouth, рот (gen. рта)

move (intr.), дви́гаться, подви́нуться, тро́гаться, тро́нуться; **movement**, движе́ние

Mr, господи́н, Г-н; **Mrs**, госпожа́, Г-жа

much, мно́го; мно́гое (adj.) (§ 250); **how much**, ско́лько; **so much**, сто́лько

music, му́зыка; **musician**, музыка́нт

must, **I must**, я до́лжен; **she must**, она́ должна́; **we must**, мы должны́; **must be**, должно́ быть

my, mine, мой, моя́, моё, мой

Name, и́мя (n.) (p. 237); назва́ние; **surname**, фами́лия; **to name**, называ́ть, -зва́ть (§ 197)

narrate, расска́зывать, -сказа́ть (§ 142); **narration, story**, расска́з

near (adj.), бли́зкий; (adv.), бли́зко + от (gen.); (prep.), по́дле (gen.); **-ly**, почти́

necessary, ну́жный, необходи́мый; **it is necessary**, ну́жно, на́до, на́добно; **necessity, need**, нужда́; **I need**, мне на́до, ну́жно (§ 106)

neck, ше́я

neither...nor, ни...ни

nest, гнездо́ (dim. гнёздышко)

Neva, Нева́

never, никогда́

nevertheless, тем не ме́нее, всё-таки

new, но́вый; **newly**, то́лько что

news, но́вости, изве́стия

newspaper, газе́та

next (adj.), сле́дующий; (adv.), пото́м; **next door**, ря́дом (с + instr.)

"nice", ми́лый

night, ночь (f.)

nine, де́вять; **ninth**, девя́тый

ninety, девяно́сто

no, нет

noise, шум; **noisy**, шу́мный; **to make a noise**, шуме́ть, за- (p. 18)

nonsense, вздор

noon, по́лдень (m.)

no one, никто́, не́кого (§ 237); **no one's**, ниче́й

north, се́вер; се́верный (adj.)

nose, нос

not, не; **not far**, недалеко́; **not quite**, несовсе́м

note (verb), запи́сывать, -писа́ть; (noun), запи́ска; **notebook**, записна́я кни́жка

nothing, ничто́, ничего́; не́чего (§ 237)

notice, замечáть, -мéтить

novel, ромáн

November, ноя́брь (m.)

now, тепéрь, ны́не, ны́нче; now...now, то...то

nowhere, нигдé; no whither, никудá

nurse, ня́ня

Oak, дуб

obey, слу́шаться, по-; obedient, послу́шный

obliged, дóлжен, -жнá, -жны́ (see must)

obtain, получáть, -чи́ть (-гу́, -лу́чишь)

occasion (chance), слу́чай; (time), раз (p. 239)

occupy, занимáть, -ня́ть (§ 293); occupied, busy, зáнятый

ocean, океáн

October, октя́брь (m.)

odour, зáпах

of (gen., § 55); (out of), из (gen.)

off (prep.), с (gen.)

offend, обижáть, оби́деть

offer, предлагáть, -ложи́ть

office, контóра

often, чáсто; less often, рéже; not so often, порéже

oil, мáсло

old, стáрый; to grow old, старéть, по- (§ 119); old man, стари́к; old woman, старýха; old times, старинá; old-time, (adj.) стари́нный

on, на (acc. and prep.)

once, раз, однáжды; at once (immediately), тóтчас, -же, сейчáс; (at the same time), зарáз, срáзу, заоднó; once upon a time, use жил-был

one, оди́н, однá, однó; oneself (refl.), себя́; one's own, свой; one another, друг дру́га (§ 235)

only, тóлько, лишь

open (verb), открывáть, -кры́ть (§ 138); (adj.), откры́тый

opinion, мнéние; in my opinion, по-мóему, etc. (§ 218)

opportunity, слу́чай, возмóжность (f.)

opposite, прóтив (gen.)

or, и́ли

orange, апельси́н

order (from), зака́зывать (у + gen.); (noun), зáказ; give an order, прикáзывать (§ 143); ordinance, прикáз; (orderliness), поря́док; in order that, чтóбы (+ infin.)

organ, оргáн

original (noun), оригинáл

orphan, сиротá (m. or f.)

other, другóй, инóй, чужóй; each other, друг дру́га (§ 235); otherwise, инáче; on the other hand, затó, напрóтив

ought, I, мне слéдует; мне нáдо бы (§ 284)

our, наш, -а, -е, -и

out of, из (gen.); outside, снару́жи, нару́жу; to go out, выходи́ть

over, над (instr.); over there, там

own, свой (§ 199); (by birth), роднóй

ox, бык, вол

Pace, step, шаг

pack, уклáдывать(ся), -ложи́ться (§ 220)

page, страни́ца

pain, боль (f.); it is painful, бóльно; I feel pain, мне бóльно

pains, to take, труди́ться, по-

pair, пáра

palace, дворéц (gen. дворцá)

pale, блéдный; to turn pale, бледнéть, по- (§ 119)

paper, бумáга; newspaper, газéта

pardon, прощáть, -сти́ть (p. 18); I beg your pardon, виновáт

Paris, Пари́ж

park, парк

part (fraction), часть (f.)

part (verb), разлучáть(ся), -лучи́ть(ся); расставáться, -стáться (-стáнусь с + instr.); parting, разлýка

particular, осóбенный; in particular, осóбенно

pass (by), проходи́ть (ми́мо) (§ 157); passer-by, прохóжий (on foot), проéзжий (not on foot)

passion, in a, сгорячá

past (last), прóшлый; by-gone, прошéдший; the past, прóшлое

pay, плати́ть, за- (§ 145); payment, плáта

peace, мир; peaceful, ми́рный

peasant, крестья́нин (f. -нка, pl. -я́не); (= man), мужи́к

peg, вéшалка

pen, перó (pl. пéрья, -ьев)

pencil, карандáш

people, лю́ди; (nation), нарóд

perhaps, мóжет быть

perish, погибáть, погибнуть

person, осóба, человéк, лицó; personal, ли́чный

piano (grand), роя́ль (m.)

picture, карти́на

piece, кусóк (gen. кускá)

pig, свинья́

pine-tree, соснá

pipe, трýбка

pity (verb), жалéть, по- (1st conj.); it is a pity, жаль; piteous, pitiful, жáлкий

place, мéсто; to take one's place, занимáть мéсто (§ 293), усáживаться

plan, план

plant (verb), сажáть, сади́ть, посади́ть (§ 206); (noun), растéние (cf. расти́)

plate, тарéлка

play, игрáть (instrument, на + prepos., game, в + acc.), по-, с-; (theatre) (noun), пьéса

pleasant, прия́тный

please, пожáлуйста

please (verb), нрáвиться, угождáть, -ди́ть (§ 43); pleased, довóльный (instr.)

pleasure, удовóльствие

plenty (wealth), довóльство

pocket, кармáн

poem, стихотворéние

poet, поэ́т

point (verb), укáзывать, -казáть (§ 143)

policeman, городовóй

poor, бéдный; poverty, бéдность (f.)

population, населéние

porridge, кáша

porter, носи́льщик

possible, it is, мóжно; possibility, возмóжность (f.)

post, post-office, пóчта; postcard, откры́тка; postman, почтальóн; by post, по-пóчте

postpone, отклáдывать, -ложи́ть (§ 220)

potato, картóфель (m.), картóшка

pound, фунт

pour, лить, по- (p. 207)

pour out, наливáть, -ли́ть (p. 207)

power, власть (f.); powerful, могýчий

praise, хвали́ть, по-; (noun), хвалá, похвалá

prayer, моли́тва

prepare, приготовля́ть; готóвить, при- (p. 18)

present (introduce), представля́ть, -вить (p. 18); presentation (of a play), представлéние

present (noun), подáрок; (to give) (verb), дари́ть, по-

presently, сейчáс

press (verb), жать, по- (я жму)

pretend, притворя́ться, -твори́ться

pretty, хорóшенький

price, ценá; priceless, бесцéнный

print (verb), печа́тать, на-;
 printed, печа́тный
prison, тюрьма́
probably, вероя́тно
procession, проце́ссия, ше́ствие
procure, доставать, -ста́ть (-ста́-
 ну)
prolong, продолжа́ть, -до́лжить
pronounce, произноси́ть, -нести́
 (§ 82); pronunciation, произ-
 ноше́ние, вы́говор
properly, как сле́дует
propose, предлага́ть, -ложи́ть
protect, охраня́ть, -ни́ть
proud, го́рдый; to be proud,
 горди́ться, воз- (p. 270);
 pride, го́рдость (f.)
proverb, посло́вица
punish, нака́зывать (§ 143);
 punishment, наказа́ние
pupil, учени́к, учени́ца
purchase, поку́пка
purpose, on, наро́чно
purse, кошелёк, -лька́
put (lying), класть, положи́ть;
 (sitting), сажа́ть, посади́ть;
 (standing), ста́вить, по-; put
 aside, откла́дывать, -ложи́ть;
 put in, вкла́дывать, встав-
 ля́ть; put on, накла́дывать;
 — clothes, надева́ть, -де́ть;
 put out, выставля́ть (§ 220)

Quarter, че́тверть (f.); quarters
 (lodgings), кварти́ра (sing.)
question, вопро́с; to ask question, задава́ть, -да́ть (§ 138)
 вопро́с
quickly, ско́ро, скоре́й, бы́стро
quiet, споко́йный, ти́хий; quietly, тихо́нько; quiet (noun),
 тишина́; to quieten (intr.),
 утиха́ть, ути́хнуть
quite, совсе́м; not quite, не-
 совсе́м

Rain, дождь (m.); it is raining,
 дождь идёт
rare, ре́дкий

rather, дово́льно, поря́дочно
reach (a place), доходи́ть, -йти́
 (§157); (stretch to), достава́ть,
 -ста́ть (-ста́ну)
read, чита́ть, проче́сть (perf.)
 (§ 153); reader, чита́тель;
 reading (noun), чте́ние
ready, гото́вый; to get ready,
 собира́ться (§ 252), приго-
 товля́ть (tr.), -вить
real, настоя́щий
reap, жать (я жну)
reason, for that, зате́м, чтобы;
 оттого́ что
receive, получа́ть, -чи́ть, при-
 нима́ть, -ня́ть (§ 293); reception-room, приёмная; re-
 ceipt, распи́ска
recognise, узнава́ть, -зна́ть
recommend, рекомендова́ть (ре-
 комендую, -у́ешь)
red, кра́сный
reflected, to be, отража́ться
refuse, отка́зываться, -каза́ться
 (§ 143)
regret, жале́ть, по- (p. 209);
 I regret, мне жаль
reign, ца́рствовать (-вую)
rejoice, ра́доваться (dat.)
 (-уюсь)
reliable, надёжный
remain, остава́ться, -ста́ться
 (-ста́нусь)
remember, по́мнить, за-; remember! не забу́дь, -те!
 (§ 147)
remind, напомина́ть, -по́м-
 нить
remove (intr.), переезжа́ть (p.
 226)
repeat, повторя́ть, -ри́ть
report, докла́д
reprimand, reproof, вы́говор
republic, респу́блика
request, про́сьба
reserved, reticent, сде́ржанный
respect (verb), уважа́ть; respected, уважа́емый; respectful, почти́тельный

rest (verb), отдыха́ть, -дохну́ть; (noun), о́тдых

restaurant, рестора́н

retirement, отста́вка; **to retire**, выходи́ть (вы́йти) в отста́вку

return, возвраща́ться, (intr.) -врати́ться, (tr.) верну́ть; (noun) возвраще́ние; **on returning**, по возвраще́нии

revolution, револю́ция; револю́цио́нный (adj.)

reward, награ́да, (verb) награжда́ть, -гради́ть (§ 43)

rich, бога́тый; **rich man**, бога́ч

ride, е́здить, ката́ться (§ 175); **on horseback**, — верхо́м (see p. 262); **rider**, вса́дник

rifle, ружьё

right, пра́вый; **on the right**, напра́во; **to set right, correct**, поправля́ть, -пра́вить (p. 18)

ring, звони́ть, по-

ripen, зреть, со-; спеть, по-

rise, поднима́ться, -ня́ться (§ 293), встава́ть, -стать (-ста́ну)

river, река́

road, доро́га

roast, жа́рить, за-

rock, скала́

roll, ката́ть (tr.) (§ 175)

room, ко́мната; (space), ме́сто

rose, ро́за

rouble, рубль (m.)

rough, гру́бый

round (adj.), кру́глый; (adv.), вокру́г, круго́м (gen.)

row, ряд

ruin, губи́ть, по- (гублю́, гу́бишь)

rumble, грохота́ть, за- (грохо́чет); греме́ть, за-

rush, броса́ться, -ситься (p. 17)

Russia, Росси́я; **Russian**, ру́сский; **in Russian**, по-ру́сски

Sacrifice (instr.), же́ртвовать, по- (-вую)

sad, печа́льный, гру́стный; **sadness**, печа́ль (f.), грусть (f.)

sage (learned man), учёный, мудре́ц; му́дрый (adj.)

sail (noun), па́рус

salesman, продаве́ц (gen. -вца́); **saleswoman**, продавщи́ца

salt, соль (f.), солёный (adj.)

same, са́мый, одина́ковый; **at the same time**, зара́з; **in the same way**, та́кже

samovar, самова́р

Saturday, суббо́та

save, спаса́ть, спасти́ (§ 83)

say, сказа́ть (§ 142); **saying**, погово́рка

scarce, недоста́точный, ре́дкий; **scarcity**, недоста́ток; **scarcely**, едва́

school, шко́ла; шко́льный (adj.); **scholar**, шко́льник, уча́щийся (partic. as noun)

scientist, учёный; **science**, нау́ка

scissors, но́жницы

Scotland, Шотла́ндия; **Scottish**, шотла́ндский

sea, мо́ре; морско́й (adj.)

second, второ́й

see, ви́деть, вида́ть; **see each other**, вида́ться, ви́деться (§ 115); **see off**, провожа́ть (§ 204); **not seen before**, неви́данный

seek, иска́ть (ищу́, и́щешь); **seek out**, сыска́ть

seem, каза́ться, по- (§ 143); **it seems**, ка́жется

seldom, ре́дко

self (emphatic), сам, -а́, -о́; (reflexive), себя́ (§ 112)

sell, продава́ть, -да́ть (§ 138)

send, посыла́ть, -сла́ть, присыла́ть, -слать (hither) (p. 17)

sensitive, чу́ткий; **to sense**, чу́ять, по-

separate, разлуча́ть(ся), -чи́ть(ся); **separation**, разлу́ка

September, сентя́брь (m.)

servant, слугá (m.); **maid-servant**, служáнка

serve, служи́ть, по-; **service**, слу́жба; (good turn), услу́га; **servitor**, служи́тель

serviette, салфéтка

set down (passengers), выса́живать, вы́садить (§ 222)

seven, семь; **seventh**, седьмóй

several, нéсколько (gen.)

severe, стрóгий

sew, шить, с- (p. 207)

shadow, тень (f.)

share, дóля

shave, бри́ться, по- (брéюсь, -ешься); **shaven**, (вы́)бри́тый

she, онá

shelf, пóлка (cf. пол)

shilling, ши́ллинг

shine (verb), блестéть, за- (p. 225), сия́ть

ship, корáбль (m.)

shoe(s), башмáк(и́)

shop, магази́н; **small shop**, лáвка

shore, бéрег (p. 240)

short, корóткий, крáткий (brief); (of hair), стри́женный

shoulder, плечó (pl. плéчи)

show, покáзывать, окáзывать, -казáть (§ 143)

shut, закрывáть, -кры́ть (§ 138)

side, сторонá; **side by side**, ря́дом; **sideways**, нáбоку

sign (verb), подпи́сывать (§ 165); **signature**, пóдпись (f.); **sign** (noun), знáк (see знáчить)

silent, to be, молчáть, за-; **silently**, мóлча; **silence**, молчáние

silver (noun), серебрó; (adj.), серéбряный

simple, простóй

since (as), так как; (time), с тех пор, как

sing, петь, с- (§ 75); **singing**, пéние

sister, сестрá

sit, сидéть, по-; **sit down**, сади́ться, сесть (§ 206); — **for a little**, приса́живаться (p. 228); **sit** (of a committee), заседáть; **sitting**, заседáние

situated, to be, находи́ться (§ 160)

six, шесть; **sixth**, шестóй

skates, коньки́; **to skate**, катáться на конькáх (§ 175)

skin, кóжа, шку́ра

sky, нéбо, небéсный (adj.)

slacken, отставáть, -стáть (-стáну)

slanting, косóй

sledge, сáни (pl.); **to sledge**, катáться на саня́х (§ 175)

sleep, спать, по-; **fall asleep**, засыпáть, -сну́ть; **sleep** (noun), сон (gen. сна)

slow, мéдленный; **slowly**, мéдленно

slumber, дремáть, за- (дремлю́, дрéмлешь)

sly, хи́трый

small, мáленький; (fine), мéлкий; **small change**, мéлочь (f.)

smash, разби́ть (perf.) (p. 217)

smell, зáпах

smile, улыбáться, -бну́ться

smoke, кури́ть, по-; (noun) дым

smooth, глáдкий

snake, змея́

snow, снег; снéжный (adj.); **it is snowing**, снег идёт; **snowstorm**, метéль

so, так, столь; **so much**, стóлько; "**so-so**", так себé

soap, мы́ло

socialism, социáлизм; **socialist**, социалисти́ческий (adj.)

soldier, солдáт

some, нéкоторый, нéкий; (number), нéсколько

somebody, some one, ктó-то, кой-ктó, нéкто (p. 256)

something, чтó-то, кое-чтó, нéчто

sometimes, иногдá

son, сын (pl. сыновья́, сыновéй) (see p. 240)

song, пéсня

soon, скóро

soul, душá; душéвный (adj.)

sound, звук; (verb), звучáть, про- (2nd conj.)

soup, суп; **cabbage soup,** щи (pl.)

south, юг; ю́жный (adj.)

Soviet (noun), Совéт; совéтский (adj.)

sow, сéять, по- (сéю)

space (expanse), простóр; (room), мéсто

speak, говори́ть, по-; **speech,** речь (f.)

spectacles, очки́ (gen. -кóв)

spend, трáтить; ис-, трáчу; **spend time,** проводи́ть, -вести́ врéмя (§ 82)

sphere, сфéра, шар

spill, пролива́ть, -ли́ть (p. 207)

spirit, дух, духóвный (adj.)

spite of, in, несмотря́ на (acc.)

spoon, лóжка

spring (season), веснá; весéнний (adj.)

square, плóщадь (f.)

stage (theatre), сцéна

stamp (postage), мáрка (почтóвая)

stand, стоя́ть, по- (2nd conj.); **stand up,** станови́ться, стать (§ 206)

star, звездá

state (condition), состоя́ние; **State** (country), госудáрство

station, стáнция; (building), вокзáл

stature, рост

steal, укрáсть (perf. of красть: краду́, -дёшь), воровáть (§ 176); **stealthily,** украдкой (adv.)

steamer, парохóд

steed, конь (m.)

steep, крутóй

step, шаг

stick, пáлка

stifling, ду́шный

still (yet), ещё; (quiet), ти́хий (adj.)

stocking, чулóк (pl. чулки́)

stone, кáмень (m.) (gen. кáмня); кáменный (adj.)

stop, переставáть, -стáть (-стáну) (intr.), остана́вливать(ся), -нови́ть(ся) (§ 227)

storey, этáж

storm, бу́ря; **snow-storm,** метéль (f.)

story, расскáз

stove, печь (f.)

straight, прямóй

strange, стрáнный, чужóй; **stranger,** незнакóмец (f. -мка)

street, у́лица; у́личный (adj.)

strength, си́ла

strict, стрóгий

strike, ударя́ть, удáрить; (noun), стáчка

strong, си́льный, крéпкий

student, учáщийся, студéнт (f. -ка)

study, учи́ться, вы́-; изучáть, -учи́ть (tr.); занимáться, -ня́ться (§ 293)

stuff, матéрия

stupid, глу́пый; **stupidity,** глу́пость (f.)

subscribe (to a paper), выпи́сывать, подпи́сываться (§ 165); **subscriber,** подпи́счик

succeed, успевáть, -спéть; **success,** успéх; **make progress,** дéлать успéхи

such, такóй

suddenly, вдруг

sugar, сáхар

suit (verb), идти́ (§ 85)

sultry, ду́шный

summer, лéто; лéтний (adj.)

summon, призывáть, -звáть (зову́, -ёшь)

sun, со́лнце; со́лнечный (adj.)

Sunday, воскресе́нье

superfluous, ли́шний, изли́шний

supper, у́жин; to sup, have supper, у́жинать, по-

surely (you know), ведь; surely not, ра́зве, неуже́ли

surname, фами́лия

swan, ле́бедь (m.)

sweet, сла́дкий

swift, бы́стрый

Switzerland, Швейца́рия

Table, стол; table-cloth, ска́терть (f.)

tailor, портно́й

take, брать, взять (p. 143); take away, убира́ть (p. 218), уноси́ть, -нести́ (§ 82); take off, снима́ть, снять; (undress), раздева́ться; take out, вынима́ть (p. 220)

tale, ска́зка

talk, говори́ть, по-

tall, высо́кий

tasty, вку́сный; taste, вкус

tea, чай; ча́йный (adj.); tea-pot, ча́йник

teach, учи́ть, на-; teacher, учи́тель, учи́тельница

tear, слеза́ (pl. слёзы); shed tears, пролива́ть слёзы

telephone, телефо́н; (verb) говори́ть по телефо́ну

tell (relate), расска́зывать, -сказа́ть (§ 142)

ten, де́сять; (collective), деся́ток; tenth, деся́тый

tender (loving), не́жный

tennis, те́ннис

terror, у́жас; terrible, ужа́сный; terrify, ужаса́ть, ужасну́ть

text-book, уче́бник

than, чем, не́жели

thank, благодари́ть, по-; thank you, спаси́бо

that, тот, та, то; что (conj.); in order that, что́бы (+infin.)

theatre, теа́тр

their, them, их

then, тогда́, то; (next), пото́м

thence, отту́да

there, там; there is (exists), есть; (pointing), вон

therefore, поэ́тому, оттого́

they, они́

thief, вор

thin, то́нкий; (of a person), худо́й; grown thin, похуде́вший; (sparse), ре́дкий

thing, вещь (f.)

think, ду́мать, по-, мы́слить

third, тре́тий; (fraction), треть (f.)

this, э́тот, э́та, э́то; сей (see p. 139)

thither, туда́

thou, ты

thought, мысль (f.); become thoughtful, призаду́маться

threat, угро́за

three, три; three together, втроём

through, че́рез, сквозь (acc.)

thunder, гром; thunderstorm, гроза́; thunder-cloud, ту́ча

Thursday, четве́рг

thy, твой, -я́, -ё, -и́

ticket, биле́т

tidy (verb), убира́ть (p. 218)

tie, вяза́ть, привяза́ть (p. 207)

till (conj.), пока́ не; (prep.), до (gen.)

time, вре́мя (see p. 233); fitting time, пора́; (occasion), раз; at the same time, зара́з; to spend time, проводи́ть вре́мя, -вести́ (§ 82); to be in time, успева́ть, -спеть

tired, уста́лый; be tired, устава́ть, -ста́ть (-ста́ну)

to, к (dat.), в, на (acc.)

tobacco, таба́к

to-day, сего́дня

together, вме́сте

to-morrow, за́втра; day after to-morrow, по́сле-за́втра

tone, тон

tongue, язы́к

too (much), слишком; (also),
тóже
tooth, зуб; зубнóй (adj.); dentist, зубнóй врач
touch, трóгать, притрáги-
ваться (perf. трóнуть, при-
трóнуться); touch upon, касáться, коснýться; touching,
трóгательный
towards, к (dat.)
town, гóрод; городскóй (adj.)
trade, торговáть, по- (-гýю);
-ся (to bargain)
train, пóезд; by train, пóездом
tram, tramway, трамвáй
translate, переводить, -вести
(§ 82); translation, перевóд
transplant, пересáживать, -са-
дить (§ 222)
travel, путешéствовать (-ствую,
-ствуешь) (cf. путешéствие)
tree, дéрево
trip, поéздка
troika, трóйка
trouble, бедá
true, вéрный; truly, вéрно
trunk, чемодáн
truth, прáвда; truthful, прав-
дивый
try, судить, присудить (§ 43) (to
condemn)
Tuesday, втóрник
tumbler, стакáн
tune (verb), настрáивать,
-стрóить; (noun), напéв
two, два, две (f.); two together,
вдвоём

Umbrella, зóнтик
uncle, дядя
uncomfortable, неуютный (of a
house or room)
under, под (instr.); from under,
из-под (gen.)
understand, понимáть, -нять
(§ 137); understanding, чýт-
кий (adj.)
unemployed, безрабóтный
unfamiliar, незнакóмый

unhealthy, нездорóвый
union, союз
unique, единственный
untie, развязывать, -вязáть
untruth, непрáвда
unworthy, недостóйный
unwrap, развёртывать, -вер-
нýть
up, upstairs, навéрх(ý), вверх(ý)
(§ 214)
urgent, спéшный
us, нас
use (noun), пóльза; (verb), упо-
треблять (р. 219); be of use,
годиться, при- (§ 43)
usually, обыкновéнно
utter (verb), мóлвить, про-
(р. 18)

Vain, in, напрáсно, дáром
value (verb), ценить, о-; дорожить (no perf.); (noun),
ценá; valuable, цéнный
vegetables, óвощи (sing. óвощь
(m.))
verses, стихи
very, óчень, (in superl.) самый
view (noun), вид; (verb), раз-
глядывать, -глядéть (§ 43)
village, дерéвня, селó
violin, скрипка
visit, посещáть, -тить (р. 18),
видáться, по-; to be on a
visit, гостить (р. 18); visitor,
гость (m.), гóстья (f.)
voice, гóлос
Volga, Вóлга

Wait for, ждать, подо- (§ 161)
wake, просыпáться, проснýть-
ся (intr.); будить (tr.), раз-
(§ 43)
walk (take a walk), гулять,
по-; (go), ходить, по-
wall, стенá; wall-paper, обóи
(pl.)
wander, бродить; be wandering,
брести (see р. 224)
want (wish), хотéть, за- (§ 69);

I want (lack), мне недостаёт;
(noun: lack), недостаток

war, война; war-like, военный

warm, тёплый

wash, мыть(ся), умываться,
умыться (p. 229)

watch, часы (pl.)

water, вода

wave, волна

way, путь (see p. 237), дорога;
in the same way, также; by
the way, кстати

we, мы

weak, слабый

wear, носить (§ 84), по-, из-

weariness, скука

weather, погода

Wednesday, среда

week, неделя

weep, плакать, за- (§ 145)

well (adv.), хорошо; (healthy),
здоровый (adj.); well-known,
известный

west, запад; западный (adj.)

what, что; of what kind, какой

when, когда

whence, откуда

where, где; whither, куда

which, который, какой

while, пока

whistle (noun), свист; (verb),
свистать, свистеть, за-
(свищу, -ешь or -стишь)

white, белый; appear white,
белеть (§ 119)

whither, куда

who, кто; whose, чей, чья, чьё

whole, целый, весь, вся, всё

why, почему, зачем, отчего

wicked, злой

wide, широкий; width, ширина

wife, жена

wild, дикий

will, воля; good-will, добрая
воля

willingly, охотно

wind, ветер, ветреный (adj.)

window, окно

wine, вино

winter, зима; зимний (adj.)

wish, хотеть, за- (§ 69), желать,
по-; (noun) желание

with, с (instr.); у (gen.)

without, без (gen.); without fail,
непременно

wolf, волк; волчий (adj.) (p. 247)

woman, женщина; (peasant),
баба

wood (forest), лес; (material),
дерево; wooden, деревянный

word, слово

work, работать, по-, трудиться,
по- (§ 43); работа, труд
(noun); worker, работник,
-ница; (member of working
class), рабочий

world, мир, мировой (adj.); свет

worry, забота; беспокоиться
(verb), за-

worthy, достойный, заслужённый; worthless, негодный

wound, ранить; wounded, раненый

write, писать, на-; writer, писатель, -ница (f.); writing
(noun), письмо; finish writing,
дописывать, -писать

Yard, двор

year, год; half a year, полгода;
yearly, ежегодный

yes, да

yesterday, вчера; day before
yesterday, третьего дня

yet, ещё, всётаки

you, вы; your, yours, ваш, -а,
-е

young, молодой

youth (pers.), юноша; youthful,
юный; youth (abstr.), юность
(f.)

Zealous, усердный

zero, нуль (m.); above zero,
выше нуля; below zero, ниже
нуля

INDEX

Numerals in ordinary type refer to *paragraphs*; those in
italic type to *pages*.

Russian Index

чуть не, 254, 340
-чь, 167, *206, 208, 210, 217*

Шёл, 83, *210, 212*

-ыва-, 143, 166, *216–17, 222*

ъ, 9, 24, *12*

ь, 9, 24–6, *12*

Этот, эта, это, эти, 32, 108, *244–6*

Я, (letter) 23, *9*; (pronoun) 34, 112, *243*

Subject Index

Abbreviated form, (adj.) 100, 105–6, 144, *248–9*; (partic.) 278, *213*
abstract nouns, *233–4*
accent (stress), 35, 72, 91, 135, 171, 188–9, 237, 318, *89, 207–8, 212, 214, 225* (f.n.), *237–8, 240, 243*
accusative case, (m. and n.) 15, 29; (f.) 28, 52, 94; (pl.) 169; 47, 55, 161, 164, 263, 305–9, *266, 270*
active participles, 271–2, *212*
adjectival endings, 31, 51, 78 (dim.), 90–3 (decl.); 100–1 (pred.); *242–3, 246*
adjectival suffixes, 74, *252–4*
adjectives, (abbr.) *248–9*; (compound) *255*; (decl.) *244–6*; (from verbs) 280; (as nouns) 154, *255*; (possessive) *247–8*; (relative) 205, *246–7*; (in surnames) *255*
adverbial clauses, 327–32
adverbs, 53, 102, 318; (classes of a.) 213, *261*; (comparison) *264*; (compound) 243–9; (dim.) 232; (formation) 214–19, *262–3*; (as prepos.) 296; (verbal a.) 285; (не and ни) *265*
any, 240
article, 2
aspects, 19, 124–5, *203*; (formation) *215, 223, 225–8*
augmentative nouns, *233–4*; adjs. *254*
auxiliary verbs, 3, 210

Be, to, 3, 34–5, 40–1, 122, 179, *230*
bring, to, 162

"Cannot help", 201
cardinal numerals, 36, 97, 256–9, *257–8*
carry, to, 80
"carrying" (hyphenation), *12*
cases, 55–61; (use after numerals) *260*
collective numerals, 266, *258*
common gender, 155, *233*
comparative degree, 180–4, 188, 191–2, *249–50*; (in -ший) 185, *250*; (in -e) *250–1*; (of adv.) 187, *264*
complement, 179, 210, *271*
compound adjectives, *255*; adverbs, 243–7; numerals, 262, *260*; pronouns, 236–42
compounds of verbs, 220–2, *216–18, 222*
conditional, 281–2, 348–9, *204, 211, 230–1*
conjugations, *203–6*
conjunctions, 320–4, 334, *267–8*
consonants, *10* (f.n.), *12, 13* (double c.); (insertion of c.) *18*; (permutation of c.) *17–18*

Date, 261
dative, 55, 60, 65, 76, 117, 177, 299–303, *44* (f.n.); (after verbs) *269*
days of the week, *62*